Thomas Hobbes and the Natural Law

THOMAS HOBBES
and
THE NATURAL LAW

KODY W. COOPER

University of Notre Dame Press

Notre Dame, Indiana

University of Notre Dame Press
Notre Dame, Indiana 46556
www.undpress.nd.edu

Copyright © 2018 by the University of Notre Dame

Paperback edition published in 2022

All Rights Reserved

Published in the United States of America

Library of Congress Cataloging-in-Publication Data

Names: Cooper, Kody W., author.
Title: Thomas Hobbes and the natural law / Kody W. Cooper.
Description: Notre Dame : University of Notre Dame, [2018] | Includes bibliographical references and index. |
Identifiers: LCCN 2017055611 (print) | LCCN 2018003935 (ebook) |
 ISBN 9780268103033 (pdf) | ISBN 9780268103040 (epub) |
 ISBN 9780268103019 (hardcover : alk. paper) | ISBN 0268103011
 (hardcover : alk. paper) | ISBN 9780268103026 (paperback : alk. paper)
Subjects: LCSH: Hobbes, Thomas, 1588-1679. | Natural law. | Common good.
Classification: LCC JC153.H66 (ebook) | LCC JC153.H66 C62 2018 (print) |
 DDC 320.1—dc23
LC record available at https://lccn.loc.gov/2017055611

For My Children

Hitherto I have set forth the nature of Man, whose Pride and other Passions have compelled him to submit himselfe to Government; together with the great power of his Governour, whom I compared to *Leviathan*, taking that comparison out of the two last verses of the one and fortieth of *Job*; where God having set forth the great power of *Leviathan*, calleth him King of the Proud. *There is nothing*, saith he, *on earth to be compared with him. He is made so as not to be afraid. Hee seeth every high thing below him; and is King of all the children of pride*. But because he is mortall, and subject to decay, as all other Earthly creatures are; and because there is that in heaven, (though not on earth) that he should stand in fear of, and whose Lawes he ought to obey; I shall in the next following Chapters speak of his Diseases and the causes of his Mortality, and of what Lawes of Nature he is bound to obey.

—Thomas Hobbes, *Leviathan*

CONTENTS

	Acknowledgments	ix
	Introduction	1
1	The Foundations of Hobbes's Natural Law Philosophy	19
2	Hobbesian Moral and Civil Science: Rereading the Doctrine of Severability	53
3	Hobbes and the Good of Life	95
4	The Legal Character of the Laws of Nature	133
5	The Essence of Leviathan: The Person of the Commonwealth and the Common Good	181
6	Hobbes's Natural Law Account of Civil Law	231
	Conclusion	257
	Notes	267
	Index	321

ACKNOWLEDGMENTS

In the course of writing this book over several years, I have accumulated many debts of gratitude. I first thank my parents, Kevin and Karen. Without their love, sacrifice, and support through the years, I would not be where I am today.

I am lucky to have received broad and varied academic mentoring support over the years. My dissertation co-advisors, J. Budziszewski and Al Martinich, stand out. They were excellent teachers—but their excellence went well beyond the classroom. J. and his wife, Sandra, opened their home to my family and me for many a fine meal and conversation. Al and I chatted Hobbes and all things politics over many cups of coffee. These advisors did not always agree with my take on Hobbes, but their criticism and advice were always patient, incisive, and charitable. They were the best mentors a young graduate student could hope for.

I must thank Tom D'Andrea for his mentorship and also my fellow cohort of visiting scholars at Wolfson College, Cambridge University: Kevin Stuart, Brandon Wall, Brandon Dahm, Peter Swanson, Paul Rogers, and Mike Breidenbach. I will always treasure our friendship and the year we spent together.

I am grateful to a number of my other professors who have taught me much over the years while patiently entertaining my ideas and challenging me in various ways to sharpen my arguments: Laurie Johnson, Rob Koons, Devin Stauffer, John Hittinger, Gary Jacobsohn, and Tom and Lorraine Pangle. And thanks to Rob Moser, whose support for a poor graduate student with children will not be forgotten.

Thanks are also due to Robby George, Brad Wilson, and all the people at the James Madison Program at Princeton University, where I was fortunate to spend a year as a postdoctoral fellow. It not only was an ideal environment for a young scholar to engage in research but also provided a forum for serious intellectual engagement. I especially thank all of the fellows of the 2014–15 academic year for their conversations as well as their feedback on and criticism of my work on Hobbes. Also, a special thanks to Duanyi Wang, who helped me track down a number of obscure books and articles.

I further thank Justin Dyer, Jeff Pasley, and all the faculty and staff at the Kinder Institute on Constitutional Democracy at the University of Missouri, which provided me continued support for my research. I was fortunate to be a Kinder Fellow and part of yet another ideal environment for research and intellectual engagement.

A number of outlets have entertained my ideas about Hobbes over the years. I thank *Hobbes Studies* and the *British Journal of American Legal Studies* for their permission to publish parts of articles here. I have also had occasion to present my work on Hobbes in a number of forums. In particular, I thank the Manchester Workshops in Political Theory: Hobbes Section; Rosamond Rhodes and the International Hobbes Association; and Paul Kerry and the Rothermere American Institute (RAI) at Oxford for the opportunity to present my work to groups of serious scholars. My thanks to Theresa Bejan as well for her comments at the RAI roundtable, and to the librarians at the Bodleian for their help in accessing John Aubrey's papers.

A number of other friends with whom I have talked all things political philosophy and who have commented on my work over the years deserve my gratitude for everything they have taught me: Douglas Minson, Matt O'Brien, Matthew Wright, Bill McCormick, Pete Mohanty, Paul DeHart, Patrick Gardner, Gladden Pappin, James Patterson, Nicholas Drummond, Sara Henary, and Michael Krom. I am also grateful to the two anonymous reviewers for the University of Notre Dame Press and copyeditor Marilyn Martin, who provided helpful feedback and suggestions for improvement of the manuscript.

I thank my department head, Michelle Deardorff, and the rest of my colleagues in the Department of Political Science and Public Service at the University of Tennessee at Chattanooga for their ongoing support of my scholarship and for providing a wonderful environment for teaching and research.

Finally, I am most grateful to my wife, Deirdre, whose support on this journey has been absolutely essential. The debt is incalculable. I am thankful that love does not keep a ledger.

Introduction

"Doceo," Thomas Hobbes famously wrote, "sed frustra" (I teach, but in vain). It has been nearly 350 years since Hobbes died, and if there is one thing that political philosophers and historians of political thought agree on, it is this: that Hobbes failed to persuade his contemporaries to adopt his moral and political doctrines. The Glorious Revolution of 1688 set England on the path toward a stable constitutional monarchy that was animated by a notion of limited sovereignty. Over the next couple of centuries, the path of Anglophonic political theory would bear the marks of such liberal and progressive thinkers as John Locke, Jeremy Bentham, and John Stuart Mill more than those of Hobbes, whose "radicalism" was considered to have been put in the service of reaction. Hobbes's teachings were arguably in vain from the late nineteenth century to the early twentieth, which, as Edwin Curley recounts, saw a drought in Hobbes scholarship.[1] Yet the latter half of the twentieth century saw a renaissance in Hobbes scholarship. Gregory Kavka captured the general feeling: "Though he has been more than three hundred years in the grave, Thomas Hobbes still has much to teach us."[2] This judgment was apparent when the preeminent Anglo-American political theorist of the twentieth century paid homage to Thomas Hobbes's *Leviathan* as "surely the greatest work of political philosophy in English."[3] John Rawls thus solidified a judgment that many have arrived at in the era of the Hobbes renaissance. Indeed, the Hobbes literature has become so mountainous that one wonders what, if anything, can be contributed to our understanding of the political philosophy of Thomas Hobbes of Malmesbury. Indeed, it would not be an intellectual foul to be initially skeptical that another book on Hobbes is necessary or fitting.

Yet what if the most celebrated and influential scholarly interpretations of Hobbes's natural law theory have often been misleading and even fundamentally incorrect? If so, not only might it be the case that Hobbes's teaching is still in vain over three hundred years after his death, but also a new scholarly contribution might be in order.

Thomas Hobbes famously referred to his doctrine of the laws of nature as "the true and only moral philosophy."[4] Most readers of Hobbes agree that he intended these laws to be understood as the firmest basis on which to secure peace. Moreover, they agree that they are at the heart of Hobbes's moral and political theory. And yet, beyond these points of agreement, Hobbes's natural law doctrine has been the most controversial and debated feature of his thought. It is well known that Hobbes's writings generated considerable controversy when they were published.[5] Shortly after the publication of *Leviathan* in 1651, one of Thomas Hobbes's most intelligent critics, Bishop John Bramhall, published a scathing critique. Bramhall contended that Hobbes's natural law theory, including his list of twenty laws of nature in *Leviathan*, was incoherent and just one of many instances in which Hobbes was "inconsistent and irreconcilable" with himself. In Bramhall's view, Hobbes had scorched the whole scholastic tradition. In particular, Hobbes was taken to jettison the characteristic doctrines of classical natural law that had reached their highest expression in the thought of Thomas Aquinas. For the nearly four centuries since the publication of *Leviathan*, most readers of Hobbes have followed Bramhall in their assessment of Hobbes's moral and political doctrines vis-à-vis the classical natural law tradition. Yet few of the standard accounts of Hobbes's political philosophy give much, if any, detailed attention to Hobbes's doctrine in light of classical natural law. While Hobbes does break from the older tradition in several ways, I contend that scholars have largely misunderstood how Hobbes breaks from the tradition, and I argue that he maintains key features of classical natural law. Against orthodox interpretations, I contend that Hobbes's novelty flows not from supposedly secular foundations, nor from a rejection of the legal character of natural law, nor from a rejection of the objectivity of the human good rooted in a notion of human nature as fixed, nor from the ability of practical reason to tame the passions in line with its own goals. Rather, Hobbes's novelty flows chiefly from his thin theory of the human good. According to my interpretation, Hobbes retains an understanding of the role of God and practical reason in morality that has more in common with the Aristotelian-Thomistic tradition than has been recognized. This book develops and defends a reading of Hobbes as a natural law theorist in his account of morality, commonwealth, church-state relations, and positive law.

Hobbes's theory counts as a natural law theory because he retains two key notions that classical natural law theory considered requirements for a properly *natural law theory*. First, the human good, which is grounded in a notion of human nature as fixed, provides basic reason(s) for action. Second, the norms or precepts that correspond to the human good have a legal character. I argue that Hobbes's various breaks from the apex of the classical natural law tradition—including his natural law account of morality, his common good account of commonwealth, and his natural law account of civil law—flow chiefly from his thin theory of the good. We can get an initial grasp of the outlines of the argument if we first consider classical natural law theory's thick theory of the good and the legal character of natural law precepts.[6]

The core notion of classical natural law theory lies in those standards—principles, rules, or norms that give or purport to give direction in deliberation about what to do—of right judgment in matters of practice (conduct or action). We can speak of these standards as *natural* inasmuch as they are not the products of individual or collective choice and not subject to repeal—"however much they may be violated, defied, or ignored"—because mere individual or collective choice cannot change the kind of thing man is.[7] And we can speak of these standards as *lawful* inasmuch as they bind or ought to bind in one's deliberations about what to do. These rules, norms, or laws are rooted in the first principles of practical reason, which are fittingly described as those most basic reasons for action that direct us to the range of human goods. I shall discuss the classical natural law tradition in more detail in chapter 1.

For the moment, let us briefly consider Thomas Aquinas's thick theory of the good in his presentation of classical natural law theory.

As John Finnis correctly points out, Aquinas's presentation of the thick theory of the human good proceeds according to a "metaphysical stratification" of human nature: (1) what we have in common with all substances, (2) what, more specifically, we have in common with other animals, and (3) what is peculiar to us as human beings.[8] Hence, in Aquinas's formulation, the human goods include preservation of one's substantial being, marriage and childrearing, friendship with others in society, and knowledge of the truth, including the truth about God.

Notably, Finnis himself has been at the forefront of the twentieth-century revival of a classical natural law approach to ethics, law, and political philosophy. In collaboration with the theologian Germain Grisez and the philosopher Joseph Boyle, Finnis has formulated a thick theory of the good that is presented as broadly within the spirit of Aquinas. According to their "new natural law" theory, the basic goods include bodily life and health, friendship, marriage, knowledge, skillful performance in work and play, harmony between one's inner and outer life, and harmony with the ultimate source of reality. There is a dispute between the new natural lawyers and their critics about how true to Aquinas this theory is.[9] I would emphasize with Christopher Wolfe that new natural law theory and traditional natural law have this essential element in common: acting according to reason means acting according to certain human goods that are naturally known.[10] Thinkers in both of these camps can agree about this core claim of natural law theory. Moreover, I believe that the terminology of "basic goods" and "reasons for action" is helpful to elucidate natural law theory. But it must be pointed out that, in using this terminology, I do not commit myself to new natural law theory's particular theses, such as its action theory (its theory of intention) and its axiology (its version of the incommensurability thesis).[11] As will become apparent, I incline to the more traditional views of these matters *qua* interpreter of Aquinas. But, as far as the argument of this book is concerned, it is conceivable that a genuine natural law theory could come down on different sides of these questions. I note this simply to point out that my account of natural law, and my argument that Hobbes has a (peculiar) place in that tradition, can be affirmed by natural law theorists in both of these camps.[12]

Returning to Aquinas, the range of goods corresponding to the metaphysical stratification makes up the objective content of happiness because they are required by human nature and are objectively knowable by all rightly reasoning persons. Corresponding to these goods is the order of precepts of the natural law, that is, the norms regarding preservation of human life, sex and the education of children, shunning ignorance, and living peaceably with one's fellows. This is, in very short outline, classical natural law's thick theory of the good, which makes up the objective content of authentic human well-being, fulfillment, or happiness, and is how Thomistic teaching meets the first requirement for something to count as a natural law theory.

It is also a sketch of classical natural law theory's grounds for judging the moral validity of human positive law, since the flourishing of individuals and communities in their pursuits of basic forms of the human good is the standard guiding those who are charged with care of the whole community when they deliberate about what to enact, decide, require, promote, and so on. Since that which authorities have care over is a *communitas communitatum*, a community of communities, the authority's charge will be twofold. First, it must foster and protect the unity and well-being of the range of communities that enjoy noninstrumental common goods, including the *communiones* of friendships, families, and religious believers. Second, it must foster and protect the unity and well-being of the community at large. In other words, classical natural law theory held that legislators are, or ought to be, guided by the common good.

Regarding the second requirement of something qualifying as a natural law theory, Finnis is correct that, for Aquinas, the ultimate source of reality enhances "both the content and the normativity" of the first principles.[13] Another way to put the point is to say that, for Aquinas, the norms of natural law have a legal character. How is that?

For Aquinas, the basic norms of natural law have the character of law because they meet the four necessary conditions for something to be law: each is (a) an ordinance of reason (b) for the common good (c) made by a proper authority and (d) promulgated.[14] Aquinas believes natural law is law because he holds a vision of the universe—all of "nature," including human nature—as created and ordered by a providential and loving God (doctrines that Aquinas believed were demonstrable by unaided reason in the science that we would today call philosophical theology). Human beings in particular are ordered toward a form of flourishing available only to rational creatures. The flourishing available to man by his unaided powers is an end that specifies good and bad action. Good acts are those ordered to happiness and bad acts are those not ordered to happiness or flourishing. As we have seen, those goods that are basic or the basic reasons for action specify precepts that, while not sufficient to secure one's full-fledged flourishing, keep one from falling off the cliff in one's moral life. For Aquinas, the precepts take on the character of law prior to human positive law, inasmuch as God—the being who has care of the common good of the whole universe—promulgates them or makes them known in the very act of creating and ordering man with reason and will. Moreover, since Aquinas holds that law is properly the imperium or command of an authority, the natural law is commanded in God's act of creating nature.[15]

Suppose we take Aquinas's theory to be the apex of classical natural law theory. On this understanding, modern moral theory breaks from classical natural law theory in at least two ways: in its treatment of practical reasoning as essentially in the service of subrational passions and in its secular foundations. Hume stated the modern view most sharply when he claimed that reason is and only can be a slave of the passions and in his skepticism of natural theology.[16] But on Finnis's reading—which is one of the most influential narratives of the history of ethical, legal, and political thought written from a perspective sympathetic to classical natural law—the modern understanding of practical reason as enslaved to the passions is traceable to Thomas Hobbes.[17] I call this understanding of practical reason the impotent thesis, because it claims that practical reason does not have the power to set its own goals or to tame the passions in accord with objects determined by reason. In other words, practical reason is incapable of apprehending noninstrumental reasons for action. Indeed, the impotent thesis is the orthodox interpretation of Hobbes's theory of practical reason among Hobbes scholars. Hence, standard interpretations of Hobbes's natural law theory tend to posit a universal desire to which reason is instrumental. The universal desire typically posited is the desire for self-preservation, given its strong textual basis in Hobbes's corpus. This desire is supposed to secure the normativity of the laws of nature.

Moreover, the standard interpretation of Hobbes's natural law theory includes what we can broadly call the secularist thesis, the claim that God plays no substantive role in Hobbes's moral and political thought. This claim is defended on the basis of three subtheses: the historical thesis, the concealment thesis, and the practical severability thesis. God plays no substantive role either because Hobbes is an atheist, as attested to by the reactions of his contemporaries (the historical thesis)[18] and by the ironic hints hidden in his texts suggesting that his religious and theistic statements are so many genuflections to the religious authorities of his day (the concealment thesis),[19] or because, even supposing Hobbes is a theist, he renders God irrelevant to his political philosophy (the practical severability thesis).[20] On the secularist view, Hobbes's laws of nature are mere "qualities" or "theorems" and do not attain the status of law until the erection of an absolute sovereign. While these features of the standard interpretation—the pure instrumentality of practical reason and secularism—have not gone unchallenged, they probably remain the conventional wisdom.

But these two features of the standard interpretation of Hobbes's natural law theory—the impotent thesis and the secularist thesis—do not fit well with two principles Hobbes holds: first, on the diverse psychology of persons, and second, on the eternal, immutable, and universal bindingness of the laws of nature, *in foro interno*.[21] Call these the psychological diversity principle and the bindingness principle. Regarding the first, Hobbes observes a number of cases in which persons fail to desire self-preservation. He believed that people may be and often are willing to lay down their lives for the sake of personal honor, or what Sharon Lloyd has called "transcendent interests." Recognizing the force of this point, one might water down the putatively necessary desire for self-preservation to a predominant desire in order to make it more psychologically fitting. But this option is ruled out if we take seriously Hobbes's second principle regarding the eternal, immutable, and universal bindingness of the laws of nature, because then the laws of nature would bind only usually or for the most part. They would not bind universally, since not everyone actually has the putatively universal desire. In short, as Lloyd has insightfully put it, "If [the laws of nature] are always to bind everyone *in foro interno*, their claim on us must either depend on no desires, or on a desire that no human can fail at any time to have."[22]

Now this may be another example of instances in which Hobbes is simply irreconcilable with himself, as Bramhall alleged was evident in a whole range of Hobbes's doctrines. Or they may be instances in which Hobbes is, in his own words, "a forgetful blockhead." But Hobbes's texts actually suggest another possibility, namely, that practical reason grasps bodily life and health as a—indeed, the—basic reason for action. Hobbes indicates as much when he lays down two postulates of human nature in the dedicatory epistle to *De Cive*: first, the postulate *cupiditatis naturalis*, whereby man demands private use of common things, and second, the postulate *rationis naturalis*, which teaches man to avoid violent death or to "fly contra-natural dissolution" as the greatest natural evil.[23]

While cupidity is the principle of covetousness in man—which, unchecked, leads to widespread destruction and misery in the state of nature—the rational principle "teaches every man to fly a contre-naturall Dissolution, as the greatest mischiefe that can arrive to Nature." It has appeared to some that Hobbes here identifies reason with the passion of fear.[24] Yet I contend that the tenor of the passage is to distinguish between reason and desire sufficiently to indicate that they are at cross purposes in man—and this suggests that reason is not, or need not be, a slave to the passions. On this reading, the goal of practical reason, to avoid violent death and pursue preservation, is independent of the contingent desires of natural cupidity.[25] In other words, reason grasps life, which Hobbes refers to as the *bonum maximum*, as the basic reason for action.[26] I suggest that Hobbes's contrast with the classical natural law tradition lies not in the sheer instrumentality of practical reason but in his thin theory of the good. Nor does the thinness of Hobbes's notion of the good disqualify his theory from being a natural law theory—but it does mark it off as novel in relation to the older tradition.[27] If correct, the impotent thesis may be what Adrian Blau has called a "Humean anachronism."[28]

Such a reading saves both the psychological diversity principle and the bindingness principle because, while all persons may not actually take the good of life as basic in their practical reasoning, they rationally ought to. The laws of nature can then be understood as so many practical necessities that conduce to the basic good of life. Moreover, Hobbes's texts indicate how he understands his claim that these practical necessities are eternally, immutably, and universally binding *in foro interno* with the force of law to be warranted on his own terms—because God commands them. Hence, I argue that God does play an essential role in Hobbes's natural law theory because God's command secures the legal character of the laws of nature.[29] In other words, Hobbes is a member of what Elizabeth Anscombe called the "law tradition of ethics" since his ethical and political theory rests on a conception of God as a lawgiver.[30] Upon these grounds I offer a rereading of Hobbes's theory of commonwealth and positive law. At the outset, it is necessary to set forth the reasons I think I am warranted in taking Hobbes's theology as sincerely proffered and relevant to his moral and political theory.

Fifty years ago, Hobbes scholars were reconsidering the traditional secular interpretations following the work of A. E. Taylor, Howard Warrender, and F. C. Hood, all of whom had built cases for the view that Hobbes was a theist and that God played an essential role in his political theory.[31] The "Taylor-Warrender" thesis, as it came to be called, engendered a lot of discussion. While, as late as 1968, Brian Barry was able to write that a decade of criticism engendered by Warrender's thesis "has found critics united in rejecting many of Warrender's conclusions, but it has not produced a generally accepted alternative,"[32] by 1990 Edwin Curley was recounting that the attack on the Taylor-Warrender thesis had been "vigorous":

> It came from many sides; and while there may not have been any consensus among the critics about the best way to account for Hobbes' talk of obligation, a consensus does seem to have emerged that the Taylor-Warrender account is hopeless.[33]

But, since Curley's judgment, the work of A. P. Martinich has mounted a serious challenge to whatever consensus had developed and built an impressive case for the proposition that not only was Hobbes a theist and not only did his theism matter for his moral and political thought, but also he was an English Calvinist, orthodox by the criterion of the Nicene and Apostle's Creeds.[34] Accordingly, his work has challenged each of the secular theses.[35] First, the historical thesis does not seem to be decisive when one considers that the epithet "atheist" was a term of opprobrium used to label any generally objectionable religious views.[36] Hence, Hobbes's contemporaries' use of that term would be not paradoxical but expected if he espoused teachings that purported to be orthodox in terms of the language of the creeds but were novel as theories or explanations of them: for example, Hobbes's application of his theory of personation to the Trinity. Moreover, there is simply no consensus among Hobbes's contemporaries about his belief or unbelief in God. Some of Hobbes's most intelligent readers took him to be a theist. I join the company of Leibniz in interpreting Hobbes as sincerely believing that God exists as "ruler of the world" and as the "common monarch of all men."[37]

As for the concealment thesis—which, in my judgment, is a more challenging and interesting interpretation—Martinich has raised a number of potential difficulties for reading Hobbes's religious statements as ironic.[38] In making the case that Hobbes was a theist and a Christian, Martinich does not facilely assume Hobbes's complete sincerity in his theological and religious statements. Rather, as he explains, his project begins by taking the concealment thesis seriously and going on to show that, "given the cultural context of early and mid-seventeenth-century England, Hobbes's own upbringing, his actual religious practice, and his writings, the more plausible interpretation is that he was sincere."[39] While his case may not ultimately persuade those convinced by the concealment and/or the historical theses, it seems that one must admit at least that Martinich has made no mean argument.

The point here is not to rehash Martinich's argument, the secularist responses, the counterarguments, and so on. However, I mention a couple pieces of historical evidence that seem to me important for raising doubts about the secularist thesis in general and the concealment thesis in particular. The concealment thesis builds on the claim that Hobbes feared being completely sincere about his religious views for fear of persecution. Hobbes's cowardice also seems to be self-attested when Hobbes writes in his autobiography that the impending invasion of the Spanish Armada hastened his mother's pregnancy such that he was born the twin of fear. Moreover, he quickly fled to France at the outbreak of the civil war. Yet it has been pointed out that Hobbes's cowardice seems to be diminished by his tenacity and intellectual courage in his disputes with the likes of Bramhall and Wallis.[40] Another important biographical point seems to weaken the concealment thesis. When Hobbes returned from exile in 1652, he could not find satisfactory worship services because, following the church reforms of the Long Parliament and the

Rump Parliament, episcopacy had been outlawed. The legally permitted churches had Reformed liturgy along Independent or Presbyterian lines, which Hobbes indicates he thought were riddled with sedition and blasphemy. Hobbes preferred episcopacy to these other religious forms: "For my own part, all that know me, know also my opinion, that the best government in religion is episcopacy."[41] There is strong evidence based on his own testimony in his "Prose Life" that Hobbes attended St. Clement of East Cheap, where services were conducted by John Pearson, a high churchman who, in spite of the law, conducted the liturgy according to the more traditional Anglican rite and liturgy.[42] But if true, it seems inconsonant with the portrait of a priest-fearing, insincere Hobbes, considering that episcopacy had been outlawed and that compulsory church attendance had been abolished. In short, if Hobbes had been a scared secret atheist feigning faith, it seems that it would have been a better strategy to attend a Reformed church or no church at all.[43]

At a minimum, it seems that Martinich has opened the door to Hobbes scholarship that builds on the assumption that "for the most part, Hobbes meant what he said," including his theological and religious doctrines.[44] To readers of Hobbes more inclined to see him as a religious skeptic, I would say that, at the very least, it seems that a suspension of judgment on this question is warranted. For such readers my argument can be seen as showing the ways in which Hobbes's natural law theory can and cannot be seen as rhetorically continuous with the older theistic natural law doctrines. My argument proceeds by taking as sincere, *ex hypothesi*, Hobbes's natural and revealed theology. A theme of this book is that the theistic interpretation of Hobbes's moral and political theory makes better sense of Hobbes's texts as an integral whole than do rival interpretations.[45]

Throughout this book I suggest that key features of Hobbes's moral and political thought are illuminated by the Aristotelian-Thomistic tradition. In this my approach has been anticipated in some ways by the work of such scholars as Francis Oakley, Mark Murphy, Michael Gillespie, and Timothy Fuller, although, as will become apparent, my own interpretation differs from that of each of the latter in many important respects. It is fitting to address at the outset an immediate objection to this approach: that Hobbes's whole demeanor is deeply antischolastic. This objection deserves elaboration.

In *Leviathan*, Hobbes equated Christian Aristotelianism with the "Kingdom of Darkness." He thought the "tenets of vain philosophy," derived "partly from Aristotle, partly from blindness of understanding," had infected Christian doctrine.[46] As Hobbes narrates it, the early Christian doctors had endeavored to defend Christian faith by means of arguments from natural reason and had begun to make use of pagan philosophy, "and with the decrees of Holy Scripture to mingle sentences of heathen philosophers."[47] First they intermingled "some harmless ones of Plato," but later "also many foolish and false ones out of the physics and metaphysics of Aristotle."[48] It was thus that they let their enemies through the gate and "betrayed unto them the citadel of Christianity."[49] Hence, what was held by the followers of Thomas Aquinas to be *sacra doctrina*—a science that made use of "extrinsic and probable authorities" like Aristotle to elucidate the truths of Christian faith grounded in the "canonical Scriptures as an incontrovertible proof"[50]—looked to Hobbes like a hideous Empusa: "walking on one foot firmly, which is Holy Scripture, but halted on the other rotten foot, which the Apostle Paul called *vain*, and might have called *pernicious philosophy*."[51] It was pernicious because it led to endless doctrinal controversies, "and from those controversies, war."[52] In *Leviathan*, a work Hobbes professes is about "nothing but what is necessary to the doctrine of government and obedience," he takes pains to emphasize that Aristotelian teachings tended to rupture civil peace.[53] The Aristotelian "jargon" of substantial forms and essences was used to "fright [men] from obeying the laws of their country, with empty names; as men fright birds from the corn with an empty doublet, a hat, and a crooked stick."[54]

If these reflections weren't enough to raise doubts about finding any continuity in Hobbes's thought with the Aristotelian tradition and its wedding to Christian doctrine in general, Hobbes gives us reason to doubly doubt that he has anything in common with specifically Thomistic thought. In his controversy with Bishop Bramhall, Hobbes mentions Aquinas by name, and his words are less than praiseworthy:

> I know St. Thomas Aquinas calls eternity, nunc stans, an ever-abiding now; which is easy enough to say, but though I fain would, yet I could never conceive it. They that can, are more happy than I. But in the mean time his Lordship alloweth all men to be of my

opinion, save only those that can conceive in their minds a nunc stans, which I think are none. I understand as little how it can be true his Lordship says, that God is not just, but justice itself; not wise, but wisdom itself; not eternal, but eternity itself; nor how he concludes thence that eternity is a point indivisible, and not a succession, nor in what sense it can be said, that an infinite point, and wherein is no succession, can comprehend all time, though time be successive. These phrases I find not in the Scripture; I wonder therefore what was the design of the School-men to bring them up, unless they thought a man could not be a true Christian unless his understanding be first strangled with such hard sayings.[55]

In reply to Bishop Bramhall's complaint against Hobbes that "it is strange to see with what confidence now-a-days particular men slight all School-men, and classic authors, and philosophers, and classic authors of former ages," Hobbes says:

> It troubles him much that I style School-learning jargon. I do not call all School-learning so, but such as is so. . . . But because he takes it so heinously, that a private man should hardly censure School-divinity, I would be glad to know with what patience he can hear Martin Luther and Philip Melancthon speaking of the same? . . . Luther in another place of his work saith thus: "School-theology is nothing else but ignorance of the truth, and a block to stumble at laid before the Scriptures." And of Thomas Aquinas in particular he saith, that "it was he that did set up the kingdom of Aristotle, the destroyer of godly doctrine."[56]

Hobbes's reference to Aquinas by name in *Leviathan* comes in the same breath as a reference to Aristotle and is no less derisive. The reference appears when Hobbes is explaining how, by words, men can become "excellently wise" or "excellently foolish." Those in the former category see words as "counters" because they do but "reckon" by them—that is, they perform the mathematicized reasoning process of adding and subtracting words or composing and dividing names generally agreed upon. But the "excellently foolish" are those that value counters "by the authority of an *Aristotle*, a *Cicero*, or a *Thomas*, or any other doctor whatsoever, if but a man."⁵⁷ In short, it seems clear that Hobbes references Aquinas as at best a stranger from a bygone era and at worst a mortal enemy who set up the very kingdom of darkness Hobbes's project is meant to bring down. Therefore, the objection goes, there ought to be a presumption that the thesis of this book is stillborn.

Yet such a conclusion is too strong for the following reasons. First, nothing in my argument stands on the claim that Hobbes consciously sought to mimic his scholastic forebearers, and nothing turns on whether Hobbes's knowledge of Aquinas was derivative or not.⁵⁸ My analysis seeks to draw out the essential continuities and discontinuities of ideas in the natural law tradition, with particular attention to those of Aquinas and Hobbes. Second, Hobbes's references to Aquinas don't necessarily entail a stance of wholesale intellectual hostility. In his controversy with Bramhall, Hobbes expresses puzzlement over Aquinas's view of eternity. But, given Hobbes's materialist metaphysics, this is one of the points at which we should most expect Hobbes to disagree with Aquinas. For Hobbes, since corporeity is the touchstone of all being and instantaneous motion of the body is impossible—and since eternity is a state of activity—eternity must be an everlasting succession of moments. The same can be said for Hobbes's rejection of Aristotelian "essence," which he protests throughout his works is not a word used in the Bible. Hobbes is rejecting immaterialistic dualism and hylomorphism—but, as I shall argue, he does want to retain the Aristotelian four causes, including a doctrine of substantial form, to formulate a sort of materialistic hylomorphism. Nor is Hobbes's reference to Aristotle and Aquinas as doctors of the "excellently foolish" evidence that he rejects them wholesale. There Hobbes is critiquing Aristotle's and Aquinas's *followers* downstream, who merely repeat their doctrines without critically reflecting on the meaning of the words they are repeating. If their followers reflected critically in light of the new physics, Hobbes thinks, they would do away with any words or phrases incompatible with the truth of materialism, like "immaterial substance," which is absurd speech. Furthermore, inasmuch as the proliferation of arcane and stale words in later scholasticism sparked its rejection by Hobbes and his contemporaries in favor of getting back to reality, Hobbes is deeply in the spirit of Aquinas, because for Aquinas it is not the words of authorities but the object that is sovereign.⁵⁹

Finally, Hobbes explicitly points out that he does not reject all school learning as jargon, which suggests that he does retain some of the doctrines of the older natural law tradition. While I shall seek to draw these continuities out, in this book I do not intend to suggest that Hobbes did not break with the classical natural law tradition in important ways. My aim is to elucidate how Hobbes broke with that tradition, which I believe most scholars have misunderstood. My argument is that Hobbes's breaks with the classical natural law tradition proceeded amid a number of fundamental agreements with it.

Let me now set forth in brief the outline of the argument I want to develop, in which I broadly seek to follow the order of Hobbes's own presentation. In chapters 1 and 2 I seek to lay the groundwork for my interpretation of Hobbes's natural law theory. On my reading, Hobbes's metaphilosophy should be understood in essential continuity with the realistic tradition of political philosophy. Chapter 1 sets the stage for this argument by limning the realistic foundations of Hobbes's natural law philosophy. Realistic political philosophy has a particular understanding of theoretical science and knowledge in relation to practical science or knowledge in that it takes moral and political truth to essentially rest on truth claims about the structure of reality. The chapter outlines Hobbes's metaphysics, epistemology, theism, and teleological philosophical anthropology. Chapter 2 shows how Hobbesian civil philosophy, while enjoying a certain autonomy, essentially rests on a particular conception of human nature as existing and knowable and on a particular conception of God's causal relation to the world. Chapters 3 and 4 constitute the heart of my positive account of Hobbes's natural law theory. Chapter 3 defends an interpretation of Hobbes's natural law theory as meeting the first requirement of natural law theory in expressing an account of life as the basic good, since self-preservation is desirable for all rational persons. Chapter 4 articulates how Hobbesian natural law meets the second criterion and shows how the pursuit of the good of life and the necessary means thereto attain the force of law by their divine pedigree. In this chapter I seek to shed new light on the divine pedigree of natural law and moral obligation in Hobbesian natural law and contend that Hobbes's solution should be understood in light of the scholastic dialectic between God's absolute and ordained power. The directive of Hobbes's fundamental law of nature to seek peace binds practically reasonable persons as the means to secure the good of life. To secure the good of life, it is necessary to make that good common through incorporation into commonwealth. Chapter 5 argues that Hobbes's theory of commonwealth is properly a common good account. It shows how the distinctiveness and novelty of Hobbes's theory of the common good as the peace of security is illuminated in comparison to the Aristotelian-Thomistic tradition. It also argues that the common good account helps clarify confusion in Hobbes scholarship over the nature of the person of the commonwealth. In chapter 6, which considers Hobbes's theory of civil law, I show that Hobbes's account of the common good provides sovereignty with its end or purpose and, as such, imports a content-based limitation on what the sovereign can effectively command into civil law. The chapter criticizes positivist interpretations of Hobbes and contends that Hobbes has a properly natural law account of civil law inasmuch as the moral validity of civil law turns on its order to the common good. I conclude the book by reflecting on how Hobbes should be thought of in the natural law tradition. I argue that Hobbes should be considered a member of the tradition of natural law liberalism, and I illumine the argument with reference to that tradition in American political thought.

The structure of the book is not only inspired by the order of Hobbes's own *Leviathan*, which, with some exceptions, it broadly follows by beginning with the foundations of his natural law philosophy in his metaphysics and philosophy of the sciences, then proceeding to his account of the natural law, commonwealth, and civil law. The structure is also inspired by common approaches to disputed questions in medieval universities. As Josef Pieper recounts, first a question is posed for discussion, with a proposed answer. Then the poser becomes silent and listens to the positions and objections of his opponents. Their positions are stated as concisely and charitably as possible before reasons for disagreement are offered; a full statement of one's own position is then proffered before turning to answer further objections.[60] This approach is deeply inspired by Socrates in the belief that, through dialectical conversation about a disputed question, one can come to knowledge of the truth of the matter—in this case, a disputed question about the true character of Hobbes's political philosophy.

The method deployed in this book is conversational not only with respect to other Hobbes commentators, but also in that it deploys the political theorist's methodology of studying past political ideas. J. G. A. Pocock identifies three kinds of approaches to the study of past political ideas: those of the historian, the political scientist, and the political philosopher.[61] The political theorist takes his or her inspiration from political philosophy. Whereas the historian focuses on how language is used in specific historical contexts to discuss political problems and the political scientist studies the rise and role of language in organized political activity, the political philosopher has a different approach. As Leo Strauss helpfully articulated, political philosophy is deeply normative in that it sprouts from questions of fundamental human concern: What is the good or best life for man? Can this good be common? In taking as his aim the knowledge of the human good or well-being, the goal of political action (the "complete political good"), the political philosopher is concerned with knowledge of the political things. Political philosophy is then a branch of philosophy that can be provisionally defined as a quest for wisdom or knowledge of all things. Philosophy seeks to know the truth about God, the world, and man—and therefore political philosophy, as a branch of philosophy, cannot avoid making claims (whether implicit or explicit) about knowledge of all these things, what Strauss calls "the whole."[62] The approach of this book is that of the political theorist: to study past political ideas through the lenses of our subject, one of the greatest political philosophers.[63] The political theorist is inspired by classical political philosophy in his or her attempt to understand and elucidate past political philosophers' ideas about political things and to compare those ideas with those of the other great Western political philosophers, with whom the subject of study (and oneself) is engaged in a conversation about these things.[64]

This book is therefore not a rational reconstruction of Hobbes. In it I do not seek to "update" Hobbes to align him with some favored school of philosophy or to enlist some or all of his principles in service of my own views of the moral and political truth. This book is held forth as chiefly an interpretive endeavor. Hence, the point of this book is to defend a theistic natural law interpretation as the most accurate and plausible, that is, the interpretation that is warranted by a close reading of Hobbes's texts. So, while I argue that Hobbes's moral and political philosophy is best understood as a (peculiar) natural law theory, my goal is not to provide an independent defense of that theory.

But, as already indicated, a proper understanding of Hobbes's moral and political theory is of enduring interest because he offers an undeniably rich and challenging account of God, the world, man, morality, and politics. Moreover, inasmuch as his thought played a foundational role in modernity, understanding what Hobbes has to say can help us to better understand ourselves, because we cannot understand ourselves unless we understand where we have come from. Finally, an accurate interpretation of Hobbes's natural law theory is a prerequisite to assessing whether it is the "true moral philosophy."

CHAPTER 1

The Foundations of Hobbes's Natural Law Philosophy

Wisdom, says Hobbes, is *the perfect knowledge of the truth in all matters whatsoever*. But what is it to have perfect knowledge of the truth? In the passage following this definition of wisdom, Hobbes explains that wisdom is the knowledge of *things* through the medium of words:

> Which being derived from the registers and records of things; and that as it were through the conduit of certain definite appellations; cannot possibly be the work of a sudden acuteness, but of a well-balanced reason; which by the compendium of a word, we call philosophy.[1]

What, then, is political wisdom or political philosophy? If we say that political wisdom is perfect knowledge of political things or political truth, what does political truth have to do with truth *in all matters whatsoever*? The question can be recast in terms of the relationship between the sciences. If knowledge of political truth comes through *civil science*, what relationship obtains between civil science and the other sciences or branches of knowledge?

Hobbes makes different statements about his view of the relationship between the sciences in *De Cive*, *De Corpore*, and *Leviathan*.

This has generated a range of perspectives in the Hobbes literature about how it all may or may not fit together. One can discern a spectrum of emphasis in the scholarship between two polar views. On the one hand, there are those who emphasize the unity of Hobbes's moral and civil science with his materialistic, mechanistic, and determinist metaphysics and/or his philosophy of human nature and/or his theology.[2] On the other hand, there are those who contend that Hobbes's moral and civil teachings are essentially severable from his natural philosophy, his theology, and even his philosophical anthropology. Call this latter contention the *autonomy thesis*. The heart of this thesis is that Hobbes holds forth his political doctrines in such a way that they *need not* rest on any other science or knowledge.

The tradition of realistic philosophy understood the practical (moral and political) sciences to have an ultimate grounding in the speculative or theoretical truth about the world. Yet, within that tradition, it was thought that this could be compatible with a certain kind of autonomy for political philosophy. In this and the following chapter I argue that Hobbes's conception of moral and civil science should be understood in essential structural continuity with the tradition of realistic philosophy. With John Wild, I define realistic philosophy to line up with three basic beliefs of human "common sense":

(1) There is a world of real existence that men have not made or constructed.
(2) This real existence can be known by the human mind.
(3) Such knowledge is the only reliable guide to human conduct, individual and social.[3]

In realistic philosophy, each of these basic beliefs corresponds to one of three sciences: first, an account of the world *qua* being or inasmuch as it *is* (metaphysics and theology), second, an account of how we know the world (epistemology), and third, an account of the human good and its pursuit individually and in common (ethics and political philosophy). These are the metaphilosophical principles of natural law philosophy, which as a tradition is united by the golden thread articulated by Paul Sigmund: "the belief that there exists in nature and/or human nature a rational order which can provide intelligible value-statements independently of human will, that are universal in application, unchangeable in their ultimate content, and morally obligatory on mankind."[4]

I argue that Hobbes should be considered a member of the tradition of natural law philosophy in that Hobbesian civil science essentially rests on wisdom about man, God, and the world. And yet Hobbesian civil philosophy does have a certain autonomy in that it is severable from some of his theoretical doctrines, such as his mechanistic physics. In this chapter I lay out the twofold realistic foundation of Hobbes's natural law philosophy: (1) a particular moral conception of human nature as existing and knowable and (2) a conception of God as existing and as causally related to the world in a specific way. Hobbes offers a proximate epistemological ground for (1) and (2) in unaided reason. Yet he intends reason to work in partnership with faith to secure his doctrines on the ultimate foundation of revelation, which we shall consider in the next chapter.

Several scholars who have contributed to the twentieth-century revival of natural law philosophy—Jacques Maritain, Yves Simon, John Wild, Henry Veatch, Anthony Lisska, Ralph McInerny, Russell Hittinger, J. Budziszewski, Elizabeth Anscombe, Paul Sigmund, Mark Murphy, Jean Porter, and (the later) Alasdair MacIntyre—have insisted that a properly natural law theory of morality and politics must rest on a philosophical anthropology and even a natural theology. Meanwhile, Robert P. George, who is one of the foremost defenders of the "new natural law theory" of Germain Grisez, John Finnis, and Joseph Boyle—which aspires to reformulate natural law philosophy in a way that accepts a version of Hume's fact/value dichotomy—has conceded that the ontological foundation of natural law is in human nature. As George puts it, the new natural law theorists are *not* asserting that "basic human good or moral norms have no connection to, or grounding in, human nature."[5] On the contrary, as George points out, for the new natural lawyers the basic human goods and moral norms "are what they are because human nature is what it is."[6]

My argument is that Hobbes's metaphilosophy and natural law theory of morality and politics stand in stark contrast with the post-Humean and post-Kantian approaches. Hume had vigorously argued that an "ought" cannot be derived from an "is," and Kant's moral theory can be understood as an attempt to generate obligation without appeal to the *is* of human nature. The belief that Hume and Kant were basically right has animated a dominant strain of moral and political philosophy. Essentially, it has generated the notion of normative ethical and political philosophy as *autonomous* disciplines in that the doctrines of these sciences do not rest upon factual claims about the world. John Rawls's "political, not metaphysical" conception is the most sophisticated and articulate descendant of this tradition. My contention is that Hobbes's natural law philosophy should be set in contrast with the Rawlsian view, which is probably the most influential conception of political philosophy promulgated in the twentieth century.

I shall postpone more detailed consideration of Hobbes's theory of commonwealth, social ontology, and regime typology until chapter 5. Like the Aristotelian tradition, Hobbes is concerned with identifying regime types and which regime is best to secure the unity of peace. Yet Hobbes's transformative vision of the good entails a distinctive understanding of regime types. The postponement of a detailed consideration of this aspect of Hobbes's civil science is due not only to our deference to the logical order of *Leviathian*, which we are broadly striving to follow, but also to the fact that Hobbes's thoughts on these matters rest on his account of personhood, which merits extended treatment. This entails that my realistic interpretation of Hobbesian civil science will be deepened in chapter 5, where I consider how Hobbes continues the realistic tradition's mimetic principle in making commonwealth, along with the function of identifying regime types, including the best regime.[7]

HOBBES'S REALISTIC PHILOSOPHY: THE WORLD AND OUR KNOWLEDGE OF IT

Hobbes begins the introduction to *Leviathan* in a memorable way:

> Nature (the art whereby God hath made and governs the world) is by the art of man, as in many other things, so in this also imitated.

Politics is a mimetic science because it seeks to establish a social order in imitation of the order God has established in the world. Hobbes refers to this order by the general term "nature." More precisely, politics imitates the order evident *in man*:

> Art goes yet further, imitating that rational and most excellent work of nature, man. For by art is created that great Leviathan called a commonwealth, or state, (in Latin *civitas*) which is but an artificial man.

Hobbes has already introduced the "three foci" of classical natural law theory identified by Yves Simon: order in the divine mind, order in nature, and order in man.[8] To conceive of God as maker and governor necessarily implies order in the divine mind. The product of the divine art has an excellence that is counterposed to disorder and chaos, and man is Exhibit A.

Hobbesian civil science takes commonwealth as its formal object. In order to understand what the commonwealth is, Hobbes considers it in its various parts to see how it comes into being. In *Leviathan* Hobbes follows the same resolutive-compositive or analytic-synthetic method he laid out in the preface to *De Cive*: first to be considered is the "very matter" of government, namely, man. A philosophy of man is necessary, then, in order to understand the causes that generate government. But man is a part of the world, and therefore an account of what man is depends on an understanding of the world man finds himself in. Thus civil science rests at least in part or in some respect upon natural philosophy.

Natural philosophy, and therefore political philosophy, has suffered, Hobbes thinks, from want of a proper scientific method. Application of the proper method yields scientific knowledge. The way of analysis begins with effects and moves back to possible causes. The way of synthesis starts from causes and moves to possible effects. Hobbes applies this method to the investigation of the natural world to arrive at a materialistic and mechanistic picture of the real. He remarks in the first chapter of *Leviathan* that an elaboration of the materialistic foundations of the thoughts of man "is not very necessary to the business now in hand." However, Hobbes deems it fitting to "briefly deliver" the details of the account, and in this section I follow his lead. I draw upon his elaboration in other works of his materialistic and mechanist picture of nature to illustrate how Hobbes supposes this picture informs the workings of human psychology.

Our knowledge of the world begins in our senses, and from our sensory knowledge we arrive at knowledge of causes in external reality by analysis. A cause is the total aggregate of accidents in the agent and the patient that concur in the production of an effect. To arrive at knowledge of the cause, the natural philosopher examines "singly every accident that accompanies or precedes the effect."[9] Then Hobbes proceeds to consider various combinations of accidents in agent and patient, subtracting these out until he arrives at a combination of accidents the combination of which he cannot but conceive conduces to the propounded effect. At the most fundamental level, Hobbes believes it is inconceivable that the standard sensory experiences of the sense powers can be conceived apart from the accidents of *extension* and *motion*.

The world is made up of bodies in motion. A body for Hobbes is something that occupies *space*. His ideas of body and space are closely interconnected. In order to understand what space is, he offers a thought experiment in which he subtracts away all of the accidents that concur in the effect of sensory experience, save those in the patient. Imagine that all of a sudden everything was annihilated except you. Hobbes claims that you would still retain all of your memories of your sense perceptions. Suppose you remembered your cat, and you bring your sense image of your cat before your mind's eye. Hobbes says that you can imagine that cat having existence outside of your head. You can further imagine that cat existing outside of your head without considering any of its particular qualities or the image of the body insofar as it exists. Now you have the notion of space, according to Hobbes, but it is still only a phantasm, an image in your head—in a word, imaginary. Now take the thought experiment another step and imagine that your cat is created *ex nihilo* and placed in the world anew. Once created in the world anew, your cat is an existent, which is to say that it *subsists of itself*, without any dependence on your subjective thought. Thus Hobbes arrives at a definition of a body as "that, which having no dependence upon our thought, is coincident or coextended with some part of space."[10] Hobbes's conception of real space, then, is evident. Real space is the property of true extension or magnitude in external reality.[11] In short, a body is something subsisting in external reality that occupies space and is thereby measurable in length, depth, and width. Corporeity is the touchstone of reality—this is *materialism*.

Bodies are in motion, which Hobbes defines as the "continual relinquishing of one place and acquiring of another."[12] The universe, considered as the aggregate of all finite bodies, is a massive process of relinquishment and acquisition. How does all of this shifting happen? Hobbes accepts Galileo's principle of inertia.[13] A body at rest will remain at rest unless or until some other body gets into its space and suffers it to remain at rest no more, thus displacing it.[14] In other words, bodies act upon one another through contact—this is *mechanism*.

The beginning of sensation in human beings therefore comes from the operation of external bodies on human bodies or, it might be said, from the action of existents on persons. This happens either mediately or immediately. The former is the operation of bodies upon persons through various media such air or water, and it corresponds to the sense powers of sight, hearing, and smelling. The latter takes place by direct impressions of bodies on persons, as in the case of tasting and touching. Through such contact, pressure is exerted upon the relevant sense organ and the impulse travels by way of motions through the nerves and is "continued inwards" to the brain or the heart.[15] There it generates "a resistance, or counter-pressure, or endeavour of the heart"—in Latin, *conatus*—which in turn generates a phantasm or fancy of something without. *Conatus* is an imperceptibly small and invisible motion that cannot be measured and is the internal principle of our experiences of qualia and, as we shall discuss later, the passions.[16]

If Hobbes were apprised of contemporary science, he might fill out his account this way: You perceive your cat lying on the deck. Light waves arriving from the sun traveled at a velocity of 186,000 miles per second to bounce off of the feline body and toward your retinas; upon contact, the light waves impress motion there that in conjunction with the operation of the heart generates an impulse in your optic nerve.[17] This generates, in turn, a specific kind of neural activity in your brain. That neural activity considered in relation to the various sense organs is named accordingly:

> to the eye, in a *light*, or *colour figured*; to the ear, in a *sound*; to the nostril, in an *odour*; to the tongue and palate, in a *savour*; and to

the rest of the body, in *heat, cold, hardness, softness*, and such other qualities as we discern by *feeling*.[18]

One of Hobbes's themes from his earliest writings forward is that the neural activity generated in the brain by existents is a *representation* of external objects.[19] Hobbes uses various terms to denote representations of external objects: *phantasms, seemings*, or *fancies*. He is not entirely clear about the relationship between the object in external reality and its representation in the brain. How much of a gap between mind and reality does Hobbes open by claiming that "the object is one thing, the image or fancy another"? We might first ask, why is there any gap introduced at all?

Hobbes wants to formulate a theory that does not fall prey to the possibility of deception by optical illusions. He relates one particularly strange phenomenon of what might have been an optical illusion, namely, an experiment in which fir tree resin in a convex piece of glass gave the appearance of many fir trees "better designed than they could be done by any painter."[20] He gives various other examples of optical illusions, including seeing a candle double, or seeing the reflection of the sun in a glass. Take a case of the latter. A man, call him Luke, is working on a chain gang to pave a road on a hot and sunny afternoon. An overseer wearing mirrored sunglasses, call him Boss, accosts Luke. When he looks at Boss's face, Luke does not see Boss's eyes, but sees two suns shining off of his sunglasses. If Luke were to say to Boss, "There are two suns on your face, shining out from where your eyes ought to be," then, this would be, on Hobbes's terms, insignificant speech—a failure to communicate anything significant. Why? Because, Hobbes would say, "*colour* and *image* may be there where the *thing seen* is not."[21] Upon this basis, Hobbes will go on to formulate his distinctively modern theory that colors are merely motions in the mind and do not inhere in the thing.

But notice how Hobbes himself indicates the restricted application of the mind-reality gap. In order to even formulate the problem of the optical illusion of the sun reflected in glasses—the problem of seeing an object in a space where it is not—he must suppose that he knows that the object *really* isn't there, but somewhere else. And, apparently, properly functioning human faculties are reliable. As Hobbes puts it,

"Natural sense and imagination are not subject to absurdity," and "all men by nature reason alike, and well, when they have good principles."[22] Human beings perceive objects correctly with sufficient frequency to be able to develop useful arts and pursue their interests. However, fabulous traditions of speech and snares of words perpetuated by bad books can and have obscured the real from people.

As commentators have noted, Hobbes seems to waffle between conventionalist and correspondence theories of truth.[23] A conventionalist theory of truth holds that "true" is nothing more than the proper composition and division of names. The conventionalist theory seems to fit with the notion that all we really know are the motions buzzing around in our heads. The correspondence theory of truth holds that the truth value of propositions consists in their adequation of the intellect to the real: *adaequatio intellectus ad rem*. The correspondence theory holds that we really know things in the world. While acknowledging that Hobbes at times uses conventionalist-sounding language, his deepest commitment seems to be to the correspondence view. How else can we make sense of Hobbes's entire protest against the absurd and insignificant speech of the schools if not because their propositions have no correspondence to reality? If Hobbes were a *deep* conventionalist—believing that truth is just convention all the way down—his protest against insignificant speech could ultimately be only the bluster of one who prefers his own arbitrary definitions of words to the arbitrary definitions of others. This strikes me not only as an uncharitable interpretation of Hobbes but as a misreading of all the relevant texts. Hence, the conventionalist-sounding language in *Leviathan* should be read with the caveat of the *De Cive* definition of philosophy already quoted: words are a conduit to knowledge of things.[24] Hence, on the realistic reading, the Hobbesian universal proposition "man is a rational animal" is true in virtue of its correspondence with the character of all particular substances that constitute the resemblance class "man."[25] It is *not* true just in virtue of an arbitrary definition of the universal word "man."

Hobbes is a shallow conventionalist in his theory of language. The actions of bodies on our senses leave impressions that linger in "the internal parts of man" and "decay" over time.[26] The store of decaying sense impressions in the brain constitutes one's memory.[27] And the assortment of phantasms constitute imagination, such that imagination and memory are not really distinct things. Language presents itself as a solution to the problem that decaying sense presents for philosophy. Philosophy needs some device to recall prior thoughts and to signify those thoughts to others since, Hobbes recognizes, science is normally a social practice. Thus *naming* is the imposing of a word to serve as a mark "which may raise in our mind a thought like to some thought we had before, and which being pronounced to others, may be to them a sign of what thought the speaker had, or had not before in his mind."[28] Hobbes is "conventionalist" in that he believes the original imposition on this or that utterance to signify that something is always arbitrary. Supposing the truth of the Genesis account, Hobbes concedes that "some names of living creatures and other things, which our first parents used, were taught by God himself."[29] However, even the forms of these utterances were arbitrarily imposed by God because they no more specially signified the thing named than another language might have. And Hobbes points out that those original names used by Adam and Eve were lost after the confusion of languages at Babel.

So far, it might sound odd to call Hobbes a "realistic" philosopher—after all, doesn't he unabashedly aver nominalism, and isn't that the opposite of "realism"? As explained in the next section, Hobbes does not believe in the external existence of universals. He is "realistic" in his belief that the human mind has knowledge of reality. And he rejects the doctrine of universals and in its place posits a form of resemblance nominalism.

Hobbes's Resemblance Nominalism

As we have seen, for Hobbes the matter and form of utterances have no essential relationship to the thing named. Hence, he calls "childish" the view that "names have been imposed on single things according to the nature of those things."[30] But it should be noted the reason for his denial of an essential relationship between words and things is crucial for understanding his point. It is because languages everywhere are different, *"while the nature of things everywhere is the same."*[31] Hobbes is not denying that names track the natures of particular things but simply asserting that the "first names" to be used as "marks or notes of remembrance" were arbitrary from place to place. For example, it was arbitrary in the first instance if one imposed the name "shoe" instead of "zapato" to signify a foot covering. But it does not follow from this that when we talk about a shoe we are merely manipulating vibrations in our heads—the word marks off a real object in the world. As Hobbes puts it, "Names cannot be considered without supposing there is some real thing to which they are attributed."[32] And, as Philip Pettit points out, for Hobbes the common name enables us to "address ourselves to an object, not in its particularity, but under its general aspect."[33]

But still, how can these remarks be squared with Hobbes's raw assertion of nominalism? Doesn't nominalism render impossible any such thing as "natures"? Here is Hobbes in his own words:

> Of names, some are *proper*, and singular to one only thing, as *Peter, John, This man, this tree*; and some are *common* to many things, as *man, horse, tree*, every of which, though but one name, is nevertheless the name of divers particular things, in respect of all which together, it is called an *universal*, there being nothing in the world universal but names; for the things named are every one of them individual and singular.[34]

Hobbes's claim that there is "nothing in the world universal but names" has been taken as an unsentimental statement of nominalism. In the first instance, Hobbes seems concerned with rejecting a Platonic conception of universals. According to the Platonic conception, a thing is called beautiful or just or large by partaking in supremely self-same Forms such as Beauty, Justice, Largeness, and so on. These Forms are postulated as separate from the particular things and enjoying their own unity. Hobbes would seem to want to reject this, not least because the Platonic conception considers Ideas to be immaterial realities, which is ruled out by Hobbes's materialist metaphysic.[35] But to reject Platonism, what might be called an extreme realism about universals, is not yet to reject a conception of "natures" as existing and knowable. We need to get a better understanding of what divides nominalists and realists about universals.

According to Michael Loux, the divide between realists and nominalists about universals arises in trying to explain "the phenomena of similarity or attribute agreement":

Realists claim that where objects are similar or agree in attribute, there is one thing that they share or have in common; nominalists deny this.[36]

Another way to put this is that the realist wants to explain the basic phenomena of similarity between objects by grounding *character*.[37] Universal properties or qualities are held out as determinants and therefore grounds of character. So consider, for example, three objects: a hammer, a nail, and a frying pan. Call the hammer, nail, and frying pan *H*, *N*, and *F*, respectively. *H*, *N*, and *F* resemble each other in that they are resistant to pressure or solid. The realist claim is that *H*, *N*, and *F* are similar in virtue of their characters—and the property or quality of *hardness* is so closely connected with these objects' characters as to shape them. The quality of hardness grounds the characters of these objects such that *H*, *N*, and *F exemplify* the universal "hardness." In other words, it is *because H*, *N*, and *F* are *hard* that they are said to resemble each other in solidity.[38] The explanatory principle of resemblance is the universal, which each thing exemplifies. This, in very few words, is the story that metaphysical realists give to account for similarity in terms of universals.

Hobbes's theory of naming rejects this understanding of universals. Immediately following the already quoted passage, Hobbes writes:

> One universal name is imposed on many things for their similitude in some quality, or other accident; and whereas a proper name bringeth to mind one thing only, universals recall any one of those many.[39]

For Hobbes, particular bodies are metaphysically fundamental. The really real things in our world are individual substances, and materiality is the touchstone of being. *To be* is to be a particular body. The qualities that distinguish this body from that body are also fundamental, and therefore, the resemblance between particulars is fundamental. I suggest that Hobbes should therefore be understood as a resemblance nominalist in contemporary metaphysical parlance. For resemblance nominalists, particular objects are what are really real, and among them there are resemblance relations that are metaphysically fundamental. Some things fundamentally resemble some other things more than things that are not in the same class. The fundamental resemblance relation between things is what grounds similarity.

To explain this, consider two objects, coin C_1 and a second coin, C_2. C_1 and C_2 fundamentally resemble each other and, in virtue of that fundamental resemblance relation, they are said to be members of a resemblance class of coins. The coin-y character of C_1 and C_2 is explained by the fundamental resemblance they bear to one another. Resemblance nominalism can be illuminated by contrasting it with class nominalism. For class nominalists, it is membership in a class that grounds character. C_1 and C_2 are coins *because* they are members of the class of coin-y things. Class nominalists say that attributes or properties are just classes. When we say that C_1 and C_2 have the property of *being coins*, what we mean by *being a coin* is just that they belong to the class of coins.

Class nominalists face a number of objections. Suppose that class nominalism is correct that the property of *being a coin* is one that belongs just to the set of all coins that exist. Let us call the set of all coins that exist CoinVault. If we say that N coins exist, CoinVault is constituted by its members $(C_1, C_2, C_3 \ldots C_N)$. Now suppose that C_1—a shiny 1-ounce gold American Eagle—gets melted down and made into jewelry. What has happened to CoinVault? With one member of CoinVault destroyed as a coin, CoinVault no longer exists. CoinVault is *just* the set constituted by $(C_1, C_2, C_3 \ldots C_N)$. If even one member is destroyed, the set no longer is CoinVault. But remember that the property of being a coin is identical with CoinVault. Hence, when C_1 got melted down, its property of *being a coin* was destroyed. Resemblance nominalism can avoid this extensionality problem by denying that coins are coins because they are members of CoinVault. Rather, for the resemblance nominalist, the members of the set of things $(C_1, C_2, C_3 \ldots C_N)$ are coins because they resemble each other more closely and in a certain way than they resemble other things. Shareable properties are grounded on the resemblance relation such that the destruction of one member of the resemblance relation does not destroy the property. Hobbes might have wanted to avoid the extensionality problem just sketched by seemingly rejecting class nominalism.[40]

We shall have occasion to return to Hobbes's resemblance nominalism and consider how it fits with his natural law theory and the nominalist tradition of natural law. For the moment, suffice it to say that, if the best contemporary analytic metaphysics is any guide, the debate between realists and nominalists is far from over, and each side has developed quite sophisticated replies and counterarguments for their interlocutors.[41] For his part, Hobbes seems to be wielding Ockham's razor to do away with metaphysical entities that he believes are unnecessary to explain attribute agreement.

Moreover, it must be repeated that Hobbes's philosophy is "realistic" in that names are always conduits to particular things. The proper name "John" is a conduit to the individual thing John. The common name *man* is a conduit to the group of particular things that fundamentally resemble each other in their respective qualities, such as "quantity, motion, sense, reason, and the like," which compounded together "constitute the whole nature of man."[42] To restate the claim in slightly different terms, the fundamental resemblance of particular things picked out by the universal "man" consists in their having a basically similar (or exactly similar) sum of "natural faculties and powers," such as "the faculties of nutrition, motion, generation, sense, reason, etc."[43] When giving an example of how reason's computative function operates, Hobbes indicates that to be a member of this class is to be a *body*, an *animal*, and *rational*. The faculty of reason or the power of rationality is then the most specific quality that particular things picked out by the word *man* are said to possess in similitude (or exact similitude).[44] Thus, as we discuss Hobbes's philosophical anthropology, we must remember that whenever Hobbes uses words such as "man," "human nature," "mankind," etc., each should be understood to designate a class of particulars standing in a fundamental resemblance relation.

In his classic reflections on natural law, Yves Simon remarks on the importance of the question of the existence of universals in discussions of natural law theory. Simon points out that nominalism diverges from natural law in the Aristotelian-Thomistic realist mold and argues that a strict and consistent nominalism would "probably" render natural law theory impossible.[45] The worry is that nominalism would conflict with the supposition of natural law theory that there is some shared human nature that grounds the rules of conduct. Or, to put it in the form of a rhetorical question Hobbes himself asks, "Have not all men one kind of soul, and the same faculties of mind?"[46] Simon's argument against nominalism goes like this:

> If by the word "man" . . . we mean the set of all existent men, or the set of all men that have existed or are existent or will exist—then clearly, man no longer can be predicated of Socrates. One can say that Mr. Douglas is a member of the Senate, but one cannot say that he is the Senate, or that he is senate.[47]

However, notice that Simon's argument is directed against *class* nominalism. As we have seen, Hobbes rejects this form of nominalism. To be decisive, Simon would have to lay out Aquinas's subtle and difficult doctrine of essence considered absolutely and show how it is not a positive, subsisting unity outside of the mind and why only such a conception can ground a theory of natural law. While Hobbes errs on this point from the Thomistic perspective, he does not think it is logically necessary to affirm a Thomistic doctrine of essence in order to affirm the reality of natural law.

There are at least two more reasons that Hobbes rejects the existence of universals in the world to explain attribute agreement. First, it is apparent that he wants to reject any form of metaphysical dualism, which the theory of universals was tied to in the Platonic and Aristotelian traditions. Second, Hobbes is convicted for theological reasons that fundamental ontology cannot restrain God's power. William of Ockham had given this as a reason for rejecting universals: they would constrain God's power. Ockham contended that God is radically free in his omnipotence to annihilate particular substances.[48] But, Ockham contended, if universals existed, God would not be able to annihilate an instantiation of the universal without destroying all other individuals that instantiate that universal. Hobbes seems to be concerned in a similar spirit when he writes:

> The doctrine of natural causes hath not infallible and evident principles. For there is no effect which the power of God cannot produce by many several ways.[49]

This statement provides a theological foundation for Hobbes's analytical method, which, as we have seen, moves from effects to *possible* causes. It also provides a reason for the rejection of universals. For the realist says that for any object O, it is red if, and only if, it exemplifies the universal, red. But if that is true, it follows that the quality of *being red* could be brought about in a thing only in virtue of this exemplification relation. By hypothesis, God is not constrained to bring about the effect of redness in any particular way, since God "can make and change all species and kinds of body as he dareth."[50] It is apparent, then, that we shall need to consider Hobbes's conception of God in more detail in order to fill out his understanding of the real. What we shall discover is that Hobbes offers a particular answer to the question *an sit deus* (whether God exists) and formulates a conception of God's causal relation to the world that plays an essential role in his natural law theory.

The Immortal God

Hobbes's civil science is aimed at formulating a correct doctrine of "government and obedience," which he argues requires authorization of a very powerful sovereign, the Leviathan, or, in Hobbes's words, "that *Mortal God*, to which we owe under the *Immortal God*, our peace and defense."[51] What are the grounds for theistic belief in Hobbes's philosophy?

We have seen that philosophy is reasoning about causes and effects—and, accordingly, the drawing out of consequences of affirmations and negations. The subject or province of philosophy is "every body of which we can conceive any generation, and which we may, by any consideration thereof, compare with other bodies, or which is capable of composition and resolution; that is to say, every body of whose generation or properties we can have any knowledge."[52] Hobbes's division of the sciences springs from this definition. So where there is no generation or property, there cannot be *philosophy*. Hence *theology* is excluded: "The doctrine of God, eternal, ingenerable, incomprehensible, nothing to divide or compound, nor any generation to be conceived."[53] Taken in conjunction with what Hobbes says in his critique of Thomas White, isn't Hobbes denying that there can be a science of theology?[54]

Hobbes is not saying that we cannot know by natural reason that God exists. While Hobbes's method works from empirical data to move back to *possible* causes, Hobbes thinks that natural reason can judge with a very high probability or accuracy about the existence of a first cause.

And indeed, Hobbes offers a natural theology packed with arguments that were standard in the older tradition of Christian philosophy.

After claiming that theology is excluded from philosophy proper, Hobbes continues to affirm the argument from motion—a version of Aquinas's "first way"—for God's existence: "From this, that nothing can move itself, it may be rightly inferred that there was some first eternal movement."[55] So the statement is not a denial of the possibility of a natural theology. For Hobbes, it is God's *incomprehensibility* that cordons off the *divine nature* from philosophical investigation. In other words, "we understand nothing of *what he is*, but only *that he is*."[56] So stated, the teaching is identical to that held throughout the Christian tradition and in Aquinas.[57] Because we have finite minds, we can have only finite conceptions or ideas: "When we say any thing is infinite, we signify only that we are not able to conceive the ends and bounds of the thing named, having no conception of the thing, but of our own inability."[58] Moreover, there is more of an echo in Hobbes of Calvin's indictment of the effects of man's vain curiosity when he rashly speculates about God, effectively picturing God in man's image. Hobbes sounds Calvin's essentially Pauline theme in his relentless attack on the absurdities of Gentile religion, which conceptualized God by deifying particular things found in nature.[59] The name "God" does not imply a conception of God in our mind but is a name of honor. So, Hobbes says, "We ought not dispute about God's nature; he is no fit subject of our philosophy." He goes on to suggest that true religion "consisteth in obedience to Christ's lieutenants, and in giving God such honour, both in attributes and actions, as they in their several lieutenancies shall ordain."[60] It is notable that this claim is Augustinian and Thomistic *in structure*. Hobbes's difference is in his Erastian-Anglican conception of lieutenancy as lodged in the civil sovereign of England, whereas Aquinas and Augustine believe lieutenancy is lodged in the Roman church.

Robert Arp has developed a generally persuasive case that Hobbes actually has throughout his texts arguments embedded with elements of each of Aquinas's five arguments or ways that reason judges that God exists.[61] While I think the thrust of Arp's argument is correct, I emphasize the interdependence of Hobbes's arguments on one another and his natural philosophy for his judgment that God exists and is omnipotent. Moreover, Arp does not properly connect Hobbes's arguments with the divine pedigree of natural law, which I shall elaborate in chapter 4. We have just seen a glimpse of Hobbes's first-way style argument from motion in *De Corpore*. Aquinas believed this way was the "most evident" way to prove God's existence, and Hobbes tended to favor this way throughout his writings.

Early in Hobbes's career, he rejected the ontological argument for God's existence that had been formulated by Anselm and revived by Descartes. In response to Descartes's Third Meditation, Hobbes argued for an alternative proof of God's existence, in the spirit of the Thomistic tradition, of *a posteriori* reasoning from effect to cause:

> Just as a person is born blind, who has often come close to the fire and felt himself grow hot, recognizes that there is something by which he is heated, and hearing it called 'fire,' concludes that fire exists, yet does not know what shape or colour it is, nor has any idea or image of fire arising in his mind; so man realizing that there must be some cause of his images or ideas, and that this cause too must have another cause prior to it, and so on, I finally led to an end-point, or to the supposition of some eternal cause that, since it never began to be, can have no cause prior to itself. He necessarily concludes that something eternal exists. Yet he has no idea what he could call the idea of this eternal being, but gives this thing he believes in or acknowledges the name or label "God."[62]

Hobbes's statement of the first-cause argument in *Leviathan* is similar in flavor but actually seems to combine the first way with the second way, the argument from efficient causation:

> But the acknowledging of one God, eternal, infinite, and omnipotent, may more easily be derived from the desire men have to know the causes of natural bodies, and their several virtues and operations, than from the fear of what was to befall them in time to come. For he that from any effect he seeth come to pass should reason to the next and immediate cause thereof, and from thence to the cause of that cause, and plunge himself profoundly in the pursuit of causes, shall at last come to this: that there must be (as even the heathen philosophers confessed) one first mover, that is, a first

and an eternal cause of all things, which is that which men mean by the name of God.⁶³

As we saw earlier, Hobbes understands causation in terms of agents acting on patients. No body can bring itself into being, for such would be to say that it is self-created, that is, that it is the efficient cause of itself. But, says Hobbes, this is impossible.⁶⁴ All finite substances have existence *in* themselves but not *from* themselves. Therefore, one cannot proceed to infinity in the order of efficient causation—of bringing things into being. There must be something that has existence in itself *and from itself*, and Hobbes tells us that this is God.⁶⁵ Hobbes synthesizes the first and second ways because he conceives of all finite being as matter in motion. So an efficient cause is just a motive cause.

How is God the cause of a body in motion, if mechanism is true?⁶⁶ To answer this question, we will need to take a detour before coming to consider the third, fourth, and fifth ways in Hobbes's writings. If a body remains at rest or in motion unless acted on by another body, how does God act upon the world? Hobbes cannot conceive of God as incorporeal, not only because incorporeality is inconceivable but also because that would render God powerless to cause any effect in the world. Hence Hobbes conceives of God as material, albeit no ordinary matter. God is "an infinitely fine Spirit," and by "spirit" Hobbes means "thin, fluid, transparent, invisible body," which is the equivalent of a "perfect, pure, simple, infinite substance."⁶⁷

Does Hobbes sincerely believe in a corporeal God? Or is this an example of Hobbesian irony that reveals his deep skepticism? Edwin Curley and A. P. Martinich debated Hobbes's theological sincerity in a famous exchange in 1996.⁶⁸ In 2002, George Wright reassessed the debate, coming down on the side of Martinich.⁶⁹ More recently, Patricia Springborg has entered the fray and argued that the skeptical reading of Hobbes can be rescued if it is considered in light of such works as Hobbes's *Answer* to Bramhall (just quoted) and his *Historia Ecclesiastica*.⁷⁰ While conceding that Hobbes can be understood as carrying forward the general goal of Protestantism to de-Hellenize and simplify Christianity, Springborg believes that Hobbes's deepest commitment is to skepticism of both Christianity and theism. Says Springborg, "Hobbes's ontology and epistemology do not permit a personal God

... and the banality of his concept of 'fluid matter' was designed to mock even Deists."[71] In support of this claim, Springborg rehearses Bramhall's arguments that Hobbes had effectively eliminated God from the real. Bramhall quotes from Hobbes's *Leviathan*, chapters 34 and 41, and argues that atheism is the consequence:

> *The universe being the aggregate of all bodies, there is no real part thereof that is not also body.* And elsewhere, *Every part of the universe is body, and that which is not body, is no part of the universe. And because the universe is all, that which is no part of it is nothing, and consequently nowhere.* How? By this doctrine he maketh not only the angels, but God himself to be nothing.[72]

Springborg then quotes from another argument of Bramhall's, that if God is corporeal, he is made of parts and divisible, since parthood and divisibility are features of matter.

> My next charge is, that [Hobbes] destroys the very being of God, and leaves nothing in his place, but an empty name. For by taking away all incorporeal substance, he taketh away God himself. The very name, saith he, of incorporeal substance is a contradiction. And to say that an angel or spirit, is an incorporeal substance, is to say in effect, that there is no angel or spirit at all. By the same reason to say, that God is an incorporeal substance, is to say there is no God at all. Either God is incorporeal; or he is finite, and consists of parts, and consequently is no God. This, that there is no incorporeal spirit, is that main root of atheism, from which so many lesser branches are daily sprouting up.[73]

Springborg maintains that Bramhall got it right. But did he? Unfortunately, Springborg does not develop Bramhall's argument but simply restates his claim that the denial of immaterial substances necessarily entails atheism before moving on to consider Hobbes's doctrine of the Trinity. Since we are concerned here with Hobbes's natural theology—and the concomitant "Kingdom of God by Nature," accessible by unaided reason—we can set Hobbes's Trinitarian doctrine to one side. I take it, then, that the thrust of Springborg's claim is that

Bramhall's argument, that a materialist conception of God entails atheism, is sound. We can discern two arguments that Bramhall makes for the conclusion that Hobbes's principles entail atheism:

(1) The universe, an aggregate of all bodies, is all that exists. [Implicit premise.] But God is not a part of the universe. Therefore, God is nothing.
(2) Matter has the features of parthood and divisibility. But God is without parts and indivisible. Therefore, the "material God" is no God.

Springborg ignores most of Hobbes's replies to these arguments. After quoting one line of his reply, she immediately jumps into the thicket of Trinitarian doctrine, as if Bramhall's arguments had already demonstrated that Hobbes's doctrine entails atheism. Let us take the second argument first, as that is the order in which Bramhall and Hobbes debate it and the first argument. Of the divisibility-parthood argument, Hobbes writes:

> God is indeed a perfect, pure, simple, infinite substance; and his name incommunicable, that is to say, not divisible into this and that individual God, in such manner as the name of man is divisible into Peter and John.[74]

We have seen that for Hobbes, names are always conduits toward individual things. The proper names Peter and John pick out *this* or *that* man. Meanwhile, the name "man" picks out the class of particular things that fundamentally resemble each other in possessing a certain set of faculties. But the name "man" is not divisible into *parts*. That would be more akin to class nominalism, where *being a man* is just belonging to the entire set of existing human beings. Hobbes draws an analogy from the name "man" to God's name. It also picks out an *individual*: "And therefore God is individual; which word among the Greeks is expressed by the word indivisible."[75] Hobbes wants to affirm the Nicene doctrine that *God hath no parts*. But he continues to point out that this proposition does not forbid the faithful to speak of God according to the common practices of piety. For example, it is common for the faithful to say that "God is in every part of the church." But,

Hobbes points out, surely speaking this way is acceptable and does not *divide* God, as if by speaking in this way someone were to deny that God is also in the churchyard. In short, one can affirm both that God in his essence is indivisible and that one can consider God by parts.

Hobbes continues to develop arguments from scripture and church tradition. Regarding the former, he returns to his principal argumentative strategy throughout his controversy with Bramhall: to out-Protestant Bramhall. Hobbes claims that Aristotelian philosophy—or at least a version of it that he deems "Aristotelity"—was brought, like a Trojan horse, into the citadel of Christianity by Christian doctors under false pretenses. Christian doctors like Aquinas thought it would be helpful in expounding Christian doctrine. However, "Aristotelity" turned out to pervert the learning of "school divinity" rather than enhance it. The perversion largely consisted in introducing Aristotelian metaphysical distinctions to philosophize about God's nature and interpret scripture. And Hobbes relishes pointing out that such terms as "indivisible" and "incorporeal" are not found in scripture. Bramhall has set up a false dichotomy based on his unbiblical metaphysical dualism: *either* incorporeal substances exist *or* there is no God. Having fended off the charge of atheism, Hobbes then considers Bramhall's charges regarding his Trinitarian doctrine, and there he enlists patristic church authorities Tertullian and Athanasius to his cause, which, to repeat, is beyond the scope of our considerations here.[76]

Continuing to argument 1, that God is excluded from existence by the definition of the universe as the aggregate of all bodies, Hobbes makes the point that Bramhall continually urges dualism, which Hobbes believes he has already provided good reasons for rejecting. Hobbes draws a comparison between Bramhall's argumentative strategy and a story in Greek mythology:

> I wonder he so often rolls the same stone. He is like Sisyphus in the poet's hell, that there rolls a heavy stone up a hill, which no sooner he brings to day-light, than it slips down again to the bottom, and serves him so perpetually. For so his Lordship rolls this and other questions with much ado, till they come to the light of Scripture, and then they vanish; and he vexing, sweating, and railing, goes to it again, to as little purpose as before.[77]

Again Hobbes leans on scriptural authority to oppose metaphysical dualism. Such, he thinks, is to introduce alien pagan ideas into the Hebrew texts. Hobbes then replies by denying the minor premise of argument 1:

> From that I say of the universe, [Bramhall] infers, that I make God to be nothing: but infers it absurdly. He might indeed have inferred that I make him a corporeal, but yet a pure spirit. I mean by the universe, the aggregate of all things that have being in themselves; and so do all men else. And because God has a being, it follows that he is either the whole universe, or part of it. Nor does his Lordship go about to disprove it, but only seems to wonder at it.[78]

Isn't this passage another example of Hobbes's subversiveness and impiety? How can God be part of the universe, or how could the universe be predicated of God? And doesn't this directly contradict Hobbes's notion of God as the first efficient "eternal cause of all things"? The language just quoted suggests that God is *outside* of the universe, as it were, upholding it. Indeed, in the course of the reply to the second argument sketched earlier, Hobbes argues that "God is properly the hypostasis, base, and substance that upholdeth all the world."[79] Moreover, Hobbes explicitly affirms in *Leviathan* and again in his controversy with Bramhall that God is not confined to some place, because that would entail that God is finite. What are we to make of this puzzle?

It may be the case that, at the end of the day, a corporealist conception of God is simply ridden with irresolvable contradictions and *aporia*. Yet this does not mean that Hobbes did not sincerely believe it or himself think it aporetic. How could he hold these apparently contradictory propositions consistently? Hobbes often points out that trying to harmonize certain propositions requires the kind of investigation into the divine nature that the human mind is incapable of. However, he does venture a hypothesis that presents at least an initial attempt to solve the puzzle of the corporeal God's causal relation to the universe. Hobbes recalls his empirical experience, which he believes is readily imaginable by his readers, of mixing river water and mineral water in a clear container. When they were put together, the entire substance appeared milky. But it could not be that the murkier water so imbued the clearer water as to completely occupy the whole container, since two bodies cannot be in the same place. Somehow, the murkier water was able to significantly change the clearer substance without displacing or annihilating it. (Notice how Hobbes's empirical example supposes that the mind can breach the mind-reality gap.) We might more readily imagine what Hobbes is getting at if we imagine putting a few drops of dye into a glass of water and consider how the water then appears to be wholly colored. Hobbes then says:

> If then such gross bodies have so great activity, what shall we think of spirits, whose kinds be as many as there be kinds of liquor; and activity greater? Can it then be doubted, but that God, who is an infinitely fine Spirit, and withal intelligent, can make and change all species and kinds of body as he pleaseth?[80]

We should read Hobbes's doctrine of God's causal relation to the universe in light of this passage. As an infinitely fine spirit, a fluid, invisible, subtle body, God encompasses all finite substances and operates upon them through a subtle contact that does not displace or annihilate them. As Cees Leijenhorst has shown, such a conception of God's causal interaction with the world is compatible with Hobbes's conception of *primum fluidum* as a sort of subtle ether that permeates and fills the whole universe.[81] As another substance created by God, *primum fluidum* is not prior to God as unformed matter is prior to Plato's Demiurgos, nor as prime matter is it prior to substantial form, nor is it pantheistically identified with God, as in Spinoza's philosophy.[82] As with other bodies, God can causally interact with it without annihilating it.

According to Hobbes, God is "part" of the universe when that term is defined as the aggregate of all particular material things, because God is a material being who is "particular" in that he is an individual distinct from individuals who do not have existence from themselves (i.e., all created things). It can also be said that, if we consider the aggregate of all created things together, God is *present* to them all as a "part" (as God is present "in part" in the church), but God is not confined to them (as God is not confined to the church), because God is infinite. *Pace* Edwin Curley, Hobbes is no more "uncomfortable" in understanding God as one material object among others than Bramhall is uncomfortable in positing God as one immaterial object among others (i.e., individual souls and angels). Neither need the notion of an infinite entity's being a part of a whole present a special problem for Hobbes vis-à-vis mereological principles stated in earlier works.[83] On this solution, the "universe," defined as the set of things including God, is of infinite magnitude, because God's being is infinite. That Hobbes thought this way, but tentatively, is suggested by his denial that philosophers can resolve the question of the finitude of the universe, at least when supposing the technical definition of the universe that he does.[84]

If this interpretation is correct, why does Hobbes allow for the possibility that God *is* the whole universe? This option, Hobbes himself says in *De Cive*, entails atheism.[85] However, in this passage Hobbes is simply recognizing that these are two logical possibilities that his definition of universe and corporealist conception of God would entail, neither of which Bramhall addressed but just "wondered at." He is not saying that both possibilities are equally valid.

Springborg does not even attempt to make sense of Hobbes's replies to the arguments she rehearses. My point is that it is insufficient to prove the proposition that Hobbes was really a subversive atheist who ironically mocked deism (and, by implication, theism) in his corporeal deity hypothesis *just because* Bramhall thought so. Of course Bramhall thought the corporeal God hypothesis was silly. In his critique he echoed Aquinas, who conceived of God as simple and immaterial, and mocked David of Dinant as *stultissime* for conceiving of God as prime matter.[86] We shall resist the temptation to speculate as to whether Springborg is ironically indicating her own muted belief that Thomistic metaphysics is the objectively correct standard of judgment for philosophical and theological truth.

As I read Bramhall and Hobbes's debate, it was doomed to be an exercise in talking past one another, because for Hobbes metaphysical dualism is a nonstarter as is metaphysical materialism for Bramhall. But readers of Hobbes should not be so dazzled by Hobbes's antischolastic polemics that they miss his own renegade scholasticism.[87] Hobbes is engaged in a scholastic overthrow of scholasticism if we understand the heart of scholasticism to be the Boethian project of synthesizing natural reason and Christian faith. Hobbesian thought is an iteration of that project. He wants to wed the new materialist science with a minimalist reading of the Bible in the *sola scriptura* tradition of Protestant hermeneutics. In this project he is willing to take over and/or modify scholastic principles and arguments in their "lucid" moments, especially when they serve his purpose, which is ultimately a civil science that can secure a sound doctrine of government and obedience.

Proofs of God's Existence

We have seen how Hobbes combines the first and second ways to prove that God exists as an argument from natural reason for God's existence, and we have seen how Hobbes posits an understanding of God as corporeal in order to explain how God could be the first mover in a mechanistic world. The third way moves from possible being to necessary being. Possible or contingent beings come to be and pass away. An infinite regress of possible beings cannot be affirmed, because contingent things cannot get being from contingent things for the same reason that one cannot proceed to infinity in efficient causes. There must needs be some noncontingent or necessary being:

> A man cannot imagine anything to begin *without a cause* ... but if he try, he shall find as much reason, if there be no cause of the thing, to conceive it should begin at one time as another, that he hath equal reason to think it should begin at all times, which is impossible, and therefore he must think there was some special cause why it began then, rather than sooner or later; or else that it began never, but was eternal.[88]

This eternal cause is conceived as *necessary*.[89] Hobbes should be understood to posit the cause as "necessary" with the analytical caveat hinted at in the passage just quoted, that is, that no other cause is conceivable. As we have seen, its necessity consists in having existence from itself rather than another. In other words, God is *the* metaphysically independent being. Thus Hobbes declares that metaphysical dependence is a sign of imperfection in a thing.[90] This leads us to the fourth way, which is the argument from the gradation of perfection in things.

Hobbes has judged by natural reason that a necessary first efficient cause of motion exists, and this is what all men call God. Like Aquinas, Hobbes sees in the world that some things are more honored and some less. And, again like Aquinas, Hobbes is willing to draw an analogy between how persons of different grades relate to the civil sovereign and how the whole realm relates to God as, for example, when the civil sovereign is said to be a "*Mortal God* to which we owe obedience, under the *Immortal God*, our peace and defense."[91] And Hobbes points out that "we ought to attribute nothing to God but what we conceive to be honourable, and we judge nothing honourable but what we count so amongst ourselves."[92] In his discussion of the eminence of the civil sovereign, Hobbes points out that there are greater and lesser dignities in the social order, such as "lord, earl, duke, and prince," and he observes that some shine more and some shine less.[93] But, in the presence of the civil sovereign, who is the fountain of civil sovereignty and honor, "they shine no more than the stars in [the] presence of the sun."[94] In other words, it is apparent in our experience that greater and lesser dignities and titles attach to persons and things. From the fact of various grades of dignity, it is a valid inference that there is a "fountain of [civic] honor," namely the sovereign. One can reason analogically about all finite things that have existence from another in relation to the infinite first cause that surpasses those things in perfection, dignity, and honor inasmuch as it has existence in itself, that is, is the fountain of all existence and therefore all perfections. While Hobbes does not explicitly infer God's existence in this way, he does affirm the necessary premises. At the very least, supposing the unity between his different ways of arguing to God's existence, his fourth-way language works in tandem with his other arguments to judge that the first cause must be denied all imperfections and terms that imply any lack of honor. Thus reason demands that God be referred to by titles in the superlative—"most good, most great, most powerful, etc."—or indefinite—"good, just, strong, creator, king, and the like."[95] As Hobbes puts it in *De Homine*, "They sincerely honour God who believe not only that He exists, but also that He is the omnipotent and omniscient creator and ruler of all things."[96]

Hobbes again asserts that such judgments constitute not quidditative knowledge of God's essence but signs of a will to honor God. This should not be taken to imply that such titles are mere mental fictions that have no correspondence to the reality of God's being, for Hobbes's whole harangue against "Aristotelity" aims to show that some of the scholastic claims (such as, e.g., "God is eternity") are insignificant speech, *even when* coupled with an honest desire in the speaker of the insignificant speech to honor God.[97] In short, I take Hobbes's fourth-way language to constitute a distinct argument for his claim that God is the omnipotent creator, because titles of God signify that which makes God honorable, namely, God's dignity or perfection.

Thus Hobbes's affirmation that the world is created—a claim he repeatedly makes in the philosophical parts of *De Cive* and *Leviathan*—is warranted by his natural theology.[98] By the "light of nature" we can know that the first attribute of God is *existence*.[99] This is a view similar to Aquinas's view that existence is the first of the divine perfections.[100] This is so because something cannot *be* a subject of an attribute except insofar as it exists. But, by the "commands" of reason to honor God in the superlative fashion, if God exists, there is no perfection that can be denied of him—indeed, all perfections are *maximally* so in God.[101] Therefore, the judgment that God exists entails that God is maximally, or, as Hobbes prefers to put it, *irresistibly* powerful because power is a perfection.[102] God is omnipotent. And if God is omnipotent, he has complete power over all of nature. But God could not have maximal power over nature unless he *created* it, because if he didn't create it, its existence would not depend on God's power, and then he would not have complete power over nature. Hence, if a first efficient cause exists, it created the world and is sovereign over it.

These considerations bring us to the fifth way to prove God's existence, which for Aquinas is "taken from the governance of the world."[103] We saw at the beginning of the chapter that Hobbes begins *Leviathan* taking for granted that God is governor of the world. Those who claim that God does not govern the world by imputing idleness to Him have a "wretched apprehension."[104] What evidence is there in nature for inferring the governing God? Recalling that nature is the "art of God," Hobbes points us to that "most excellent work of nature, *man*." There is an order in man that is evidence of a purposiveness or directedness implanted by a mind: "For what is the heart, but a *spring*; and the *nerves*, but so many *strings*; and the *joints*, but so many *wheels*, giving motion to the whole body, such as was intended by the artificer?"[105]

Aquinas's fifth way emphasizes the apparent purposiveness in things that *lack* intelligence as evidence of their workmanship by God. For Hobbes, too, the order we observe in the human organs, which are not subject to imagination and reason for their operation, is evidence that they were fashioned by an artificer's mind: "It is very hard to believe that to produce male and female, and all that belongs thereto, as also the several and curious organs of sense and memory, could be the work of anything that had not understanding."[106] The human organism is a focal instance of "the order of [God's] work, the world, wherein one thing follows another so aptly as no man could order it by design."[107] Indeed, when Hobbes writes about the mechanics of human generation and embryology, which are processes not subject to human intelligence, he goes so far as to say that the person who says the process is undirected by a mind is himself mindless.[108]

Pace Strauss, Hobbes's teleological statements are not merely vestigial.[109] If it's true that Hobbes's teleological language is sparse, it might imply only that he does not feel the need to argue at length for a proposition widely shared by his contemporaries. Moreover, it may be, assuming that the earlier passages are sincerely stated, that many of Hobbes's other passages are *implicitly* teleological. For example, the passages suggest that Hobbes implicitly considers purposive animal motion—"begun in generation, and continued without interruption through their whole life; such as are the course of the blood, the pulse, the breathing, the concoction, nutrition, excretion . . ."—as evidence of divine workmanship.[110]

In sum, Hobbes seeks to retain traditional arguments for God's existence within the power of natural reason while reconceptualizing how God must be (or not be) in a corporeal universe. I have argued that Hobbes retains elements of each of the five ways to prove that God exists. Hobbes thus maintains the classical realistic idea that God makes the things of this world and imbues them with purpose. Perhaps most controversial for readers of Hobbes is my suggestion that Hobbes retains a notion of teleology. How can Hobbes maintain teleology alongside materialism, mechanism, and the principle of inertia? I discuss this issue further in the next section, where I fill out in more detail Hobbes's philosophy of man or philosophical anthropology, including the two postulates of human nature.

That Most Excellent Work of Nature: Man

The standard interpretation of Hobbes holds that he jettisons final and formal causality from his picture of the world. This view is shared even by interpreters who take his theology to be sincere. As Robert Arp puts it, Hobbes "subverts the formal and the final into the efficient and the material."[111] Some of the closest readers of Hobbes in relation to the Aristotelian tradition do not deny that he retains teleology in the sense that acts of human will are purposive.[112] But does Hobbes really *restrict* teleology to the sense of willed purposes? Or is the world, and therefore man, imbued with purpose prior to human willing?

Certainly Hobbes wants to jettison immaterial forms from nature and from the human mind. The Hobbesian universe admits neither of Platonic forms in a metaphysical heaven nor of Aristotelian immaterial substantial forms that animate matter. Yet Hobbes does not take himself to be rejecting formal causes *tout court*. He takes the paradigm example of a chair to explain his view: "The matter of a *chair* is *wood*; the form is the figure it hath, apt for the intended use."[113] The formal cause is radically immanent in the matter and thus is not severable from it. Moreover, the form renders the matter "apt" for its purpose, which is another way of saying that the formal cause organizes matter in such a way as to orient it toward its proper function or end.

What Hobbes opposes is Bramhall's view that substances are *compounded* of matter and form, as if of two different substances: "Does his Lordship think the chair compounded of the wood and the figure?"[114] What then is the principle that organizes the wood to be a *chair* rather than a block? Hobbes wants to retain the notion of form as an explanatory principle. In the case of material, inanimate objects, the matter is informed by a particular assortment of accidental forms of figure, magnitude, and the like.

In the case of human beings, Hobbes also wants to deny that *man* is compounded of two substances, of a material body and a rational, immaterial soul. He opposes all forms of anthropological dualism, Platonic, Aristotelian, Cartesian, and otherwise. Yet Hobbes believes that some sort of notion of formal causation is absolutely essential to include in his philosophical anthropology. He is famous for saying that life is but motion. Less discussed is his belief that the motion of the individual organisms picked out by the word "man" begins in generation. But one might object that even if Hobbes recognized that one's life begins when one's motion begins, that is not sufficient to prove that Hobbes thought that (say) the adult man called Socrates was the self-same thing that he was from the moment of his generation until Hobbes's time. Indeed, Socrates' matter as a grown man was evidently completely different from his matter as an embryo. And, given Hobbes's materialism, on what grounds could he maintain Socrates' identity over time? Hobbes points out that the claim that Socrates was not the self-same being over time because of the complete change of his matter would be open to a devastating objection. According to this view, the Socrates who committed the crime of corrupting the youth of Athens several years before would not have been the same man who was later executed for the crime.[115] So, Hobbes's answer is that, while Socrates' matter changed because his bodily dimensions changed, he was the same man because that name was given for the form. And "if the name be given for such as is the beginning of motion, then, as long as that motion remains, it will be the same individual thing; as that man will always be the same, whose actions and thoughts proceed all from the same beginning of motion, namely, that which was in his generation."[116]

In short, Hobbes's view is that the proper name Socrates picks out the self-same being by the form or principle of its vital motion, from the infinitesimal beginnings of that motion until the time that vital motion ceases.[117] It is somewhat surprising to find this crucial point overlooked in treatments of the contrast between Descartes's and Hobbes's philosophical anthropologies.[118]

Hobbes's doctrine has some similarities with the distinctive materialist, essentialist, and teleological account of living substances in the work of Peter van Inwagen. In van Inwagen's formulation, the root question driving our ontology of material objects is the special composition question which, stated simply, is this: What is it for some objects designated x to constitute (form a proper part of) some object y. Van Inwagen's answer is that some xs constitute some y if and only if the activity of the xs constitutes *a life*. Van Inwagen's doctrine is obviously a very sophisticated account that is indebted to hundreds of years of advances in science and philosophy since Hobbes's time. But I believe that van Inwagen is driving at essentially the same idea Hobbes is when he speaks of biological life as the kind of event that is distinct in kind from other events (such as waves and flames) in that it is well individuated and self-directing, even if its material parts completely change over time. In his words:

> If a life is at present constituted by the activities of the *x*s and was ten years ago constituted by the activities of the *y*s, then it seems natural to identify the two events if there is a continuous path in space-time from the earlier to the present space-time location, along which the life of ten years ago has propagated itself.[119]

The idea is that Socrates was the self-same being through space-time due to having a unique principle of vital motion. It is, of course, an open question from the perspective of the older tradition of hylomorphism whether Hobbes or any kind of materialism has paid the metaphysical price necessary to get personal identity over time.[120] The point here is that the evidence in Hobbes's texts indicates that he is retaining a thinned-out teleology: the telos of each particular substance picked out by the word "man" is its own well-individuated and self-directing life, and therefore acts of will must accord with continued vital and voluntary motion for them to be reasonable. The basic end or good drawing the appetite is life. Thus Hobbes is willing to retain the language of teleology, and he does not restrict it to human willing:

> As *appetite* is the beginning of *animal* motion toward something which pleaseth us; so is the *attaining* thereof, the *end* of that motion, which we also call the scope, and aim, and final cause of the same ... so that *bonum* and *finis* are different games, but for different considerations of the same thing.[121]

Meanwhile, Socrates is said to have been a *man* in that he stands in a fundamental resemblance relation to other things with a particular assortment of faculties, including sense and reason. These are the key faculties for Hobbes's civil science. Accordingly, Hobbes lays down two most certain postulates of human nature: first, the postulate *cupiditatis naturalis*, and second, *rationis naturalis*. In the next chapter, the two postulates are taken up in greater detail. Here they are briefly introduced.

Hobbes identifies "wrong definitions" as the "first abuse" of speech.[122] Hence, he distinguishes two broad categories into which statements can fall: *abuses of speech* or *not abuses of speech*. Therefore, the two postulates of human nature are either abuses of speech or not abuses of speech. For felicity of expression, this can be restated thus: the two postulates are either abusive or nonabusive. I have already argued that the criterion for nonabusive speech is whether it is warranted by the real. Abusive speech is *absurd* or *insignificant*, because it does not signify anything that actually exists. For example, according to Hobbes, there is no rational warrant for speaking of "immaterial substance." The locution "immaterial substance" is an abuse of speech, because to *be* a substance is to be material or a body.[123] Hobbes understands his two postulates of human nature to be *nonabusive* speech because they have a rational warrant in the powers of reason and desire in actually existing individual human beings. The word "man" picks out the set of individual things that resemble one another in being endowed with a particular assortment of powers that distinguishes them from other things in the world, including beasts, plants, and inanimate objects. Moreover, the distinguishing feature of man, the power of reason, is that which makes man "apt" for a particular end.

On my interpretation, the conjunction of the powers of reason and desire in man constitutes the nature or "form" that is *radically immanent* in man, making him "apt" for his purpose or function.[124] This function or purpose is *life*. When someone rightly reasons—when the faculty of reason functions properly—the person judges the good of life to be basic in his or her plan of life.

Having sketched the lineaments of Hobbes's realistic foundations of metaphysical materialism, resemblance nominalism, theism, and teleological philosophical anthropology, we can reconsider the role of these foundations in Hobbesian moral and civil science. As we shall see in the next chapter, Hobbes will build his civil philosophy on his particular conception of this resemblance class of things called "men" or "rational animals," who are fashioned and ordered in this way in virtue of their creation by God.

CHAPTER 2

Hobbesian Moral and Civil Science

Rereading the Doctrine of Severability

In this chapter I argue that Hobbes's moral and civil philosophy rests upon the realistic foundations outlined in the previous chapter.[1] My argument can best be understood in contrast with two alternative accounts of Hobbesian moral and civil science as essentially autonomous, an interpretive claim that we can call the autonomy thesis. The first version of the autonomy thesis we shall consider is the sophisticated account developed in the recent work of Sharon Lloyd, who has argued that Hobbesian civil science is proto-Rawlsian in that it is independent of philosophical anthropology. My critique of Lloyd's argument at the outset also serves as an introduction to the issues and texts in dispute. I then outline my own reading of Hobbes on severability and introspection on the passions before considering a second version of the autonomy thesis in the work of Leo Strauss. Strauss believes that Hobbesian moral and civil science is grounded in philosophical anthropology, but that it is severable from theology. I advance a number of arguments against Strauss's secularistic interpretation of Hobbesian philosophical anthropology before turning to outline my account of how the theistic and anthropological foundations of Hobbes's natural law philosophy are enlarged and enhanced by his ultimate foundations in biblical revelation and faith.

Lloyd's Interpretation of Hobbesian Civil Science as Free-standing

One of the most eminent Hobbes scholars in the world, Sharon Lloyd, has advanced the most interesting comprehensive rereading of Hobbes's moral and political theory attempted in recent years. There is much to be learned about Hobbes in her work and much that I agree with. But here I take issue with her version of the autonomy thesis.

In Lloyd's view, "Hobbes steadfastly operates to show the independence, not only of moral theory from metaphysics and epistemology, but also of political theory from moral theory."[2] Hobbes saw no problem in offering an independent political philosophy, "or as we would now say after Rawls, . . . a 'free-standing' doctrine."[3] Lloyd has not been the only commentator to see this similarity between Hobbes and Rawls. To give just two other prominent examples: in his book review of *Political Liberalism*, John Gray argued that Rawls's ideas were essentially Hobbesian, and Hobbes scholar Rosamund Rhodes has argued that, in many details, one hears Hobbes while reading Rawls.[4] Lloyd's argument offers a recent defense of this view. She contends that Hobbes sharpens the free-standing character of civil science in at least three ways. First, "his insistence that we have no scientific knowledge of human nature (nor the nature of the 'smallest creature living')" means we "*cannot* found a civil philosophy on that."[5] If we can't even know the nature of a fly, how can we know (and ground a civil philosophy upon) the nature of man? Second, Hobbes purports to settle political rights and duties "solely out of the *definition of a commonwealth*."[6] Third, Hobbes's chart of the sciences appears to corroborate this in making civil science independent of the other sciences.[7] In that chart "civil philosophy" is defined as the consequences from the accidents of political bodies, in distinction from "natural philosophy," which is defined as the consequences from the accidents of natural bodies. Lloyd concludes that "indubitable introspection" suffices to do whatever work a science of human nature would do and approvingly quotes Kavka's claim that Hobbesian political theory is not committed to materialism, mechanism, or determinism: "It can remain neutral with respect to these ontological and metaphysical positions."[8]

I contend that each of these three supports for reading Hobbes's civil science as free-standing buckles upon closer examination. I shall consider them momentarily. At first blush, it seems unlikely that Hobbes has a proto-Rawlsian conception of civil science if my argument in the previous chapter was sound. To recall my discussion in the last chapter, Rawls's political liberalism takes its first principles from four historically contingent facts and takes its goals to be eminently historical. Political liberalism begins with a political culture from which justice as fairness is "worked up." For the elements of his political philosophy, Rawls turned to liberal democratic culture and history, eschewing the philosophy of nature, metaphysics, and theology. If my reading is at least broadly on track, there are prima facie good reasons to doubt that Hobbes is a (proto-) political liberal in the Rawlsian sense. Rather, Hobbes follows Descartes's methodological break from Plato and Aristotle—whose methodology took the *doxa* of the day as provisional starting points—inasmuch as he begins by doubting received wisdom and common opinion. Doctrines of the laws of nature have, before Hobbes, been "built on air." Hence, the Aristotelian doctrines prevalent in the schools of Hobbes's day are the frequent object of Hobbes's frontal assault. Besides being duped by "erroneous doctrines," man's heart is confounded with "with dissembling, lying, [and] counterfeiting."[9] Inasmuch as common opinions are tainted by lies, counterfeits, and parroted erroneous doctrines, they would be unstable elements whence to work up a civil philosophy. Hence, insofar as the political culture of Hobbes's day was animated thus, it seems doubtful that he worked up an autonomous political theory from merely historical-cultural elements. Still, civil history has an important place in Hobbesian civil philosophy since civil histories provide an "abundance of evidence" upon which rest the demonstrations of moral and civil science.[10] Later in this chapter I suggest that, indeed, the knowledge delivered in sacred history has a crucial place in the ultimate foundation of Hobbes's moral and civil doctrine.

Let us consider each of the supports Lloyd offers for her version of the autonomy thesis. Lloyd's first support for her argument regards Hobbes's view of our ability to know the nature of a fly. To recall Lloyd's contention in full:

> Hobbes insists that "in this naturall Kingdome of God, there is no other way to know any thing, but by naturall Reason; that is, from the Principles of naturall Science; which are so farre from

teaching us any thing of Gods nature, as they cannot teach us our own nature, nor the nature of the smallest creature living." [*EW* III, 354] ... Hobbes's natural science ... cannot in practice ground *any* conception of human nature, nor through it a political philosophy.[11]

Importantly, Lloyd wants to reject the secularist thesis, the claim that God plays no essential role in Hobbes's political philosophy. In fact, she has spent a fair amount of her scholarship defending an interpretation that takes Hobbes's theology to play an important role in his thought. We can proceed, then, on the basis of the shared assumption that Hobbes is sincere in his theology and that he offers his arguments for God's existence nonironically. But if we take Hobbes's natural theology seriously, Lloyd's first support crumbles. It becomes apparent that the passage may only be expressing a point that Aquinas took to be axiomatic: the weakness of the human intellect is manifest in that no one has yet been able to know the nature of a single fly.

For how is it consistent to say, on the one hand, that we cannot know the nature of even a single fly and, on the other hand, that reason can assert true propositions concerning the natures of things? In other words, how could one hold a correspondence theory of truth while denying that the human intellect has been able to know the nature of a fly? I suggest that the point is not to deny the power of reason to penetrate and reveal truths about real things but to deny that our knowledge can be final or exhaustive. Hobbes may only be affirming an epistemic humility due to his belief in the *createdness* of natural things. The constitutions of creatures are based on—and hence likenesses of—the plan of artifice in the mind of the divine artificer. As we have already seen, for Hobbes, nature is "the art whereby God hath made and governs the world."[12] Hobbes sees an analogy between man-made artifacts that are based on a plan in a human mind and man, that "most excellent work" of God, who is based on a plan in the divine mind: "For what is the *heart*, but a *spring*; and the *nerves*, but so many *strings*; and the *joints*, but so many *wheels*, giving motion to the whole body, such as was intended by the artificer?"[13] But the divine mind itself is radically unfathomable. Hobbes maintained with Aquinas that "we understand nothing of what [God] is, but only that he is."[14] The infinite can never be comprehended by a finite mind. Hence, men "cannot have any idea of him in their mind, answerable to his nature."[15] The suggestion seems to be that our ideas of finite things *are* answerable to their individual constitutions—but they are answerable only in a limited way since we cannot know them *as likenesses* to the plan in the infinite mind of the divine artificer. In short, a correspondence theory of truth is compatible with the essence-of-the-fly axiom.

It seems then that once we carefully consider Hobbes's natural theology, Lloyd's first support for reading Hobbes's civil philosophy as free-standing is by no means unshakable. Now let us consider Lloyd's second support. Lloyd finds a second support in Hobbes's definition of commonwealth. Hobbes seems to derive his civil teachings just from the definition of a commonwealth, as if this were offered independently of any conception of human nature. To recall, Hobbes defines the commonwealth in this way:

One person, of whose acts a great multitude, by mutual covenants one with another, have made themselves every one the author, to the end he may use the strength and means of them all, as he shall think expedient, for their peace and common defence.[16]

Notice that Hobbes deploys the concepts of person, multitude, covenant, and authorship. These make sense only in light of the previous section of *Leviathan*, "Of Man," because a group of men constitutes the multitude that incorporates itself into the person of the commonwealth through peculiarly human covenantal and authorial acts. As Hobbes puts it, man is the "matter" and the "artificer" of the commonwealth. Hence, the definition on its face relies on a conception of man or human nature because, at the very least, it supposes that man can be a material part of a whole, namely the commonwealth. We shall explore this point further when we take up Hobbes's theory of the commonwealth in detail in chapter 5. It is sufficient for the moment to point out that Hobbes's complex definition synthesizes a range of conceptions of human nature and personhood (not to mention authorship, covenant, and peace).

Finally, Lloyd's third support is based on Hobbes's chart of the sciences. This chart does not seem decisive as to whether his civil philosophy is free-standing or not because Hobbes was apparently not wed to it. Hobbes's schema of the sciences significantly changes in the Latin *Leviathan*.[17] In the Latin version, Hobbes claims that "from the study of man and his faculties arise the sciences of *ethics, logic, rhetoric,* and at last *politics* or *civil philosophy.*"[18] Here Hobbes claims that civil philosophy depends on the study of man and his faculties. We need not decide whether the English or Latin *Leviathan* should be considered more authoritative.[19] It is enough to say that the Latin version of *Leviathan*, chapter 9, seems to vitiate the force of Lloyd's third argument.

Yet the autonomy thesis need not be jettisoned altogether. For Kavka, Lloyd, and others are onto something when they point out that Hobbes's moral and civil philosophy is held forth in such a way that it need not rest on a materialistic-deterministic mechanism. This actually is true because, most fundamentally, Hobbes's moral and civil philosophy rests on these realistic claims: that there are particular substances constituted in such a way as to stand in a fundamental resemblance relation to one another, that they are existentially dependent on a Creator God, and that these truths about the world are knowable. These particular substances fundamentally resemble one another in that they are endowed with an order toward the good of life—and these value-laden anthropological facts are available to be affirmed through introspection. The mechanistic *explanation* of those facts is actually not essential to the claim. It may be that there is a nonmechanistic and nonmaterialistic account of the "mechanics" of bodily organs and motions that corresponds to the operation of reason and the passions. It seems, then, that it would be fitting to reread Hobbes's doctrine of severability in this light.

Rereading Hobbes on Severability

In this section I reconsider some of the passages in which Hobbes appears to advocate some version of the autonomy thesis. I argue that a close rereading of the relevant passages from *De Cive*, *De Corpore*, and *Leviathan* suggests the dependence of civil philosophy on the ontological truth that there is a definite human nature and that we can know it. In effect, in this section I seek to reinforce the conclusions of the previous section by presenting a foundationalist interpretation of the texts in which Hobbes indicates that civil philosophy is in some sense severable.

Hobbes asserts the severability of civil science in the preface to *De Cive*. There he makes his well-known claim that he had planned three sequential treatises on, first, body and its general properties; second, man and his special faculties; and third, civil government and the duties of subjects. These three parts are supposed to correspond to physics, moral philosophy, and civil philosophy. Yet Hobbes tells us that the boiling controversy and approaching war in England "plucked from me this third part."[20] Hence, "what was last in order, is yet come forth first in time, and the rather, because I saw that grounded on its own principles sufficiently known by experience it would not stand in need of the former sections." Hobbes seems to confirm this point in *De Corpore*. There, "moral philosophy" is said to consider "the motions of the mind, namely, appetite, aversion, love, benevolence, hope, fear, anger, emulation, envy, etc.; and what causes they have, and of what they be the causes."[21] Hobbes says this comes after physics, since the cause of the passions is in sense and imagination, which are objects of physics. But "*Civil* and *moral philosophy* do not so adhere to one another, but that they may be severed."[22] How is this so if "the principles of the politics consist in knowledge of the motions of the mind"?[23]

Hobbes's answer is that the causes of appetite, aversion, and the passions are known not only by "ratiocination"—that is, by his analytic-synthetic method—but also by "the experience of every man that takes the pains to observe those motions within himself."[24] But Hobbes seems to think that *he* is the first one to have set forth the scientific fruit of taking such pains, since he thinks civil philosophy is no older than *De Cive*.[25] These points would seem to be confirmed in the introduction to *Leviathan*. By *nosce teipsum*—that is, by rigorous self-reflection on one's experience—one can affirm the teachings of Hobbes's civil science. Hobbes invites the reader to affirm the fruits of Hobbes's own rigorous self-reflection.

But a careful reconsideration of the *De Cive* and *Leviathan* passages suggests the dependence of civil philosophy on the ontological truth that there is a definite human nature—a resemblance class of particular substances picked out by the universal word "man"—and that we can know it. Hobbes suggests as much in the same breath that he lays down the principle of experience:

> In the first place I set down for a principle by experience known to all men, and denied by none, to wit, that *the dispositions of men are naturally such*, that except they be restrained through fear of some coercive power, every man will distrust and dread each other, and as by natural right he may, so by necessity he will be forced to make use of the strength he hath, toward the preservation of himself.[26]

This passage is the sequel to Hobbes's profession of resolutive-compositive method:

> Concerning my method, I thought it not sufficient to use a plain and evident style in what I had to deliver, except I took my beginning from the very matter of civil government, and thence proceeded to its generation, and form, and the first beginning of justice; for every thing is best understood by its constitutive causes; for as in a watch, or some such small engine, the matter, figure, and motion of the wheels, cannot well be known, except it be taken in sunder, and viewed in parts; so to make a more curious search into the rights of states, and duties of subjects, it is necessary, (I say not to take them in sunder, but yet that) they be so considered, as if they were dissolved, (i.e.) that we rightly understand *what the quality of human nature is*, in what matters it is, in what not fit to make up a civil government, and how men must be agreed among themselves, that intend to grow up into a well-grounded State.[27]

This passage indicates the importance of attaining knowledge of human nature and its fitness for civil government. How can that knowledge be attained in a nonratiocinative mode? To see the rights of the state and the duties of subjects requires dissolving the state into its constituent elements and recomposing it. Hobbes suggests that this is not an actual sundering in reality but a mental consideration, to see these elements "as if they were dissolved." Is the state of nature intended as a merely mental construct, then? Rawls, for his part, populated the room behind the veil of ignorance with fictional persons who would act as our representatives. Hobbes sometimes suggests that his covenanters in the state of nature are merely fictional, as when he says, "Let us return again to the state of nature, and consider men as if but even now sprung out of the earth, and suddenly, like mushrooms, come to full maturity without all kind of engagement to each other."[28] The consideration of human beings as mushroom men suggests that the contractors in the state of nature are not real.

Yet Hobbes more often maintains that the state of nature obtains in reality. In *Leviathan*, the state of nature is said to obtain *in rerum natura*: among the American savages, in civil war, and in international relations.[29] Crucially, all of these conditions are social states of affairs in which there has been engagement between actual persons. Accordingly, as Laurie Johnson has lucidly demonstrated, the presence of intrinsically other-related passions such as pride, envy, shame, and honor in the state of nature logically presuppose that it is a social condition.[30] Returning to *De Cive*, Hobbes relies on the third state of affairs in reply to those who would deny that that which he had just said was "denied by none," namely, that without fear of a coercive power, men will distrust and dread one another. Those who deny Hobbes's claim with their lips confirm the same with their actions:

> We see all countries though they be at peace with their neighbors, yet guarding their frontiers with armed men, their towns with walls and ports, and keeping constant watches. To what purpose is all this, if there be no fear of the neighboring power? We see even in well-governed states, where there are laws and punishments appointed for offenders, yet particular men travel not without their sword by their sides, for their defences, neither sleep they without shutting not only their doors against their fellow subjects, but also their trunks and coffers for fear of domestics. Can men give a clearer testimony of the distrust they have each of other, and all, of all? How since they do thus, and even countries as well as men, they publicly profess their mutual fear and diffidence.[31]

The defensive posture among nations is evidence of the sort of mutual fear and mistrust that is characteristic of a state of affairs void of law and authority. Moreover, fear and mistrust are evident "even in well-governed states" that are constituted by the rule of law when men carry weapons and lock their doors. The suggestion is that the inchoate fear and mistrust evident in civil society would be exacerbated if or when the rule of law was dissolved and states ceased to be well governed (as in, e.g., a civil war). In short, Hobbes's mature picture of the "state of nature" is a condition of actual persons that is void of human positive law and authority.

So Hobbes appeals to our experience of how men really act in our day-to-day experiences living in a world of more or less well-governed states in order to fix our imagination on how men in all likelihood would act if that actual state of affairs devolved into a lawless condition. He seems to assume something like the Aristotelian principle of knowing potency through act. If men are actually fearful and mistrusting of others in a lawful state of affairs, their potentiality for fear and mistrust in a lawless condition is manifest. Such a state of affairs is a "state of men without civil society, which state we may properly call the state of nature."[32] Hobbes's contention is that by considering men in this condition, we rightly understand what the quality of human nature is and its fitness to be incorporated into a commonwealth. Hobbes seems to think that we can observe "particular men" acting defensively from external and internal threats—guarding the borders of their country, carrying weapons, locking their doors, and so on—and that, on the basis of this observation, we can arrive at a universal feature of human nature by induction: "Can men give a clearer testimony of the distrust they have each of other, *and all, of all*?"[33] Observation of regularities among members of the resemblance class "man" can yield knowledge of those not observed, since they stand in a fundamental resemblance relation.

As Hobbes has already pointed out in the epistle dedicatory, the whole point and promise of philosophy is to move "from observation of individual things to universal precepts."[34] The possibility of the truth of the claim depends on the prior ontological truth that "particular men" have sufficiently similar constitutions that the induction is valid.[35] Moreover, it presupposes that we can have such knowledge. Hobbes's *nosce teipsum* tack in *Leviathan* buttresses the point. Since one is a member of the resemblance class of men oneself, it follows that introspection can yield knowledge about human nature.

Hobbes contends in his introduction to *Leviathan* that by rigorous self-reflection—by *nosce teipsum*—we can "read" other men. One can carefully reflect on the character of one's desires when, for example, one hopes or fears. Such a clear-headed reflection on one's own passions is, in turn, the cipher that teaches one the passions of other men in similar circumstances. As Hobbes puts it, *nosce teipsum* teaches us

> that for the similitude of the thoughts and passions of one man to the thoughts and passions of another, whosoever looketh into himself and considereth what he doth, when he does *think, opine, reason, hope, fear*, &c, and upon what grounds, he shall thereby read and know, what are the thoughts and passions of all other men upon the like occasions.[36]

Notably, self-reflection on the movements of one's appetite includes reflection on *the grounds* upon which one's appetite is moved. Presumably, one will have the key to knowing the passions of other men when the grounds are similar. Already Hobbes's claim that one's introspection about one's own passions can shed light on another individual's inner life suggests that individuals are sufficiently similar to one another so as to provide a warrant for the induction. How else could we explain the fact that distinct individual substances are moved in identical or similar ways on similar occasions? The validity of the claim depends on the prior ontological truth that they have sufficiently similar constitutions. But that is another way of saying that these individuals constitute a class that is picked out by the word "mankind." The suggestion becomes explicit when Hobbes continues to point out that "he that is to govern a whole nation must read in himself, not this or that particular man, but mankind."[37] The principle of *nosce teipsum* is thus an invitation to the reader to affirm Hobbes's teaching about human nature and, on that basis, what must follow for the formation of a well-ordered commonwealth.

To sum up, the introductory passages of *De Cive* and *Leviathan* indicate that the truth of Hobbes's civil science teachings requires, first, that there be a peculiarly *human* constitution of some particular substances prior to our thinking about it, and, second, that it play a role in grounding the notions of the good and the just. The second condition requires that knowledge of human nature be available—but it need not require the citizen or the statesman to be a metaphysician. In other words, the warrant for Hobbes's two postulates of human nature is that the powers of reason and desire *are* in every individual substance picked out by the word "man"—and we can *know* this by observation of others, introspection, and induction.

Tom Sorell is correct to insist that "Everyman" can affirm these teachings through his own experience.[38] The statesman need not be trained in physics, metaphysics, or the Paduan school. Hobbes indicates that knowing in those ways is not a necessary condition for one to "read" mankind. Hobbes's moral and political philosophy are "severable" from his metaphysics inasmuch as they have an independence in the *epistemic* order. One can know things about human beings and the things about morality and politics that flow therefrom without having scientific knowledge of metaphysics—particularly Hobbes's own materialistic-mechanistic metaphysics. But this does not imply that the doctrines are free-standing. Hobbes is making a distinction between the order of knowing and the order of being. This is compatible with maintaining that his civil and general metaphysical claims are connected in such a way that the full demonstration of the truth of his civil doctrines depends on the connection.

INTROSPECTING ON THE PASSIONS

It is fitting to now make an initial attempt to unlock Hobbes's human nature teaching by considering his doctrine of *nosce teipsum*. *Nosce teipsum* can yield knowledge of passion descriptions. However, I shall argue that this knowledge is insufficient to ground Hobbes's civil science because mere passion descriptions do not yield knowledge of an object that is capable of universally moving appetites. Such an object is required by the key teachings of Hobbes's civil philosophy, including his theory of the commonwealth and natural law.

We have just seen the passage in which Hobbes's suggestion that individual members of a natural kind are moved in identical or similar ways on similar grounds and occasions. That suggestion is immediately complicated in the following passage:

> I say the similitude of passions, which are the same in all men, *desire, fear, hope,* &c, not the similitude of the objects of the passions,

which are the things *desired, feared, hoped,* &c: for these the constitution individual and particular education do so vary, and they are so easy to be kept from our knowledge, that the characters of man's heart, blotted and confounded as they are with dissembling, lying, counterfeiting, and erroneous doctrines, are legible only to him that searcheth hearts.[39]

As Edward Earl of Clarendon observes, here Hobbes seems to completely reverse what he had just said. Hobbes makes

a judgment of the Passions, and Nature of all other Men by his own observations of Himself, and believes, that by looking into himself, and considering what he doth when he do's think, opine, reason, hope, fear, &c. and upon what grounds, he shall thereby read, and know what are the thoughts and passions of all other men upon the like occasions. And indeed by his distinction in the very subsequent words between the similitude of passions, and the similitude of the object of the passions, and his confession, that the constitution individual and particular education, do make so great a difference and disparity, he reduces that general Proposition to signify so very little, that he leaves very little to be observed, and very few Persons competent to observe.[40]

Indeed, if individual constitutions are radically disparate from individual to individual, that which moves a person's appetite—that which he or she calls "good"—will be radically relative. In that case, how could the grounds of one's passions ever be the grounds of another's passions? What can serve as the "like occasion" so that the inner lives of others can be unlocked by *nosce teipsum*?

The kernel of all passions is *conatus*, an invisible tiny motion that is either *toward* or *away from*. Motions toward are appetites, and motions away from are aversions. Passions are generated when appetites are conjoined with opinions as to the goodness or desirability of some object. As suggested by the introduction to *Leviathan*, Hobbes's initial move is to elude common objects by opting for an abstract description of appetite + opinion as a common principle of the passions. Call this a passion description. This move implies that the external object is necessarily refracted through the prism of the individual's reckoning. There is something commonsensical about this move because the principle of the same passion in disparate persons need not be the same external object. For example, a person might have an appetite with an opinion of attaining the presidency as, say, Michael Dukakis did in 1987. Meanwhile, another person might have an appetite with the opinion of attaining an appointment to the Supreme Court as, say, Robert Bork did in 1987. While the presidency and a Supreme Court justiceship are different objects that are refracted through the prisms of disparate individuals, each individual's judgment can be picked out by an identical passion description: an appetite for some good with an opinion of attaining it, or "hope." If Bork and Dukakis continued to desire those respective positions after being denied them, they would have had an appetite for an object without the opinion of attaining it, which is *despair*. Moreover, since the respective experiences of Dukakis and Bork that this passion description picks out are not solipsistic dreams but are experiences common to (and verifiable by) both men, it must be the case that each individual does have similar (or exactly similar) powers of appetite and reason.

Now, suppose that we alter the previous example to compare two persons who state their desire for the same object. Replace Dukakis with Anthony Kennedy, and let the object desired be a Supreme Court justiceship. Hobbes's account indicates that Kennedy and Bork experienced the desire of hope. Doubtless Bork and Kennedy would be examples of persons with "particular educations that do so vary" as to significantly alter their judgments about what is desirable. However, this does not mean that the two persons cannot be said to experience a similar (or exactly similar) movement of their respective appetites. By *nosce teipsum*, Bork can know what Kennedy felt when he received Ronald Reagan's nomination.

Crucially, as we have seen, what makes this judgment possible is the prior ontological truth of resemblance nominalism (to which, in the order of knowledge, we may infer based on our experience) that each individual is made up of sufficiently similar powers of appetite and reason. Indeed, Hobbes holds forth this truth as a crucial premise in his account of the state of nature.[41]

Hobbes does not deny that the occasion or remote principle of the same passion in disparate persons might be the *same* object. Indeed, conflict in the state of nature arises from competition over the same good.[42] In the state of nature, Steve and Adams might both have an appetite with an opinion of obtaining the same apple grove. Hence, they would both hope for the apple grove. In this case, the object is not a good necessarily drawing persons to it, because Steve and Adams might or might not have liked the taste of apples (setting aside the grander sense of necessity held by Hobbes that all events are necessitated by God's decree). The nature of the apple grove does not determine the character of the passion for another reason. If the apple grove is in fact attainable by Adams but, for whatever reason, Adams misjudges that he is unable to get it (by, e.g., misjudging his own or Steve's strength, perhaps because of Steve's "wiles"), Adams might have the opinion of not attaining, in which case he would experience despair. Persons receive their experiences "from the natural objects of sense, which work upon [them] without passion or interest of their own."[43] Yet because of human fallibility, the actually obtaining state of affairs is refracted through the fallible prism of individual opinion.

But, even if similar or identical appetite-opinion combinations can serve as "like occasions," independent of any common object, does it follow that this is a sufficient foundation for Hobbes to build his civil science on? It would seem not because, in Hobbes's view—as indicated by his definition of the commonwealth—what distinguishes the condition of men in the commonwealth from the condition of men in the state of nature is not merely having sufficiently similar constitutions of appetite and reason. Rather, it is the collective pursuit of a common object, that is, the common good of peace and security. For the good to be truly common, it must be an object capable of universally moving human appetites. The challenge is to find an object that can draw all men in spite of their diverse individual passions.

Similar appetite-opinion combinations, considered independently of the object moving the passion, cannot sufficiently ground Hobbes's civil science for another reason. If our knowledge of human nature extended only to objectless passion descriptions and to no *normative* object of the appetite, we would not be able to distinguish between rational and irrational passions. But Hobbes does think we can make such a distinction because he maintains that there is a distinction between correct and absurd opinions. For example, Hobbes discusses the "absurd opinion of the Gentilism" in which there has been

> almost nothing that has a name that has not been esteemed amongst the Gentiles, in one place or another, a god or devil, or by their poets feigned to be inanimated, inhabited, or possessed by some spirit or other.... Men, women, a bird, a crocodile, a calf, a dog, a snake, an onion, a leek [were] deified.[44]

Fear, let us recall, is a complex negative passion: aversion with the opinion of hurt. So Hobbes would call irrational any person who feared a leek deity more than he feared violent death. Inasmuch as the state of nature invites us to imagine a massive worst-case scenario in which all positive law and human authority are dissolved, it seems intended to uncover a normative, universal end upon which to reconstruct authority and law. In such a condition, says Hobbes, the end of persons, for all their diverse individual constitutions and education, would be "principally their own conservation."[45] Why is that?

One possibility suggested by Hobbes is that this is due to a certain impulsion of nature "no less than that whereby a stone moves downward." But if that were true in the state of nature, wouldn't experience in civil society confirm it, as our experience of civil society confirms the fear and mistrust of the state of nature? The quick answer is arrived at by comparing the number of cases we have heard of rocks flying to the number of cases we have heard of people committing suicide. Hobbes indeed recognized cases of men desiring death. For example, he tells us the story of an ancient Ethiopian society that was a sort of ecclesiocracy in which priests had the power to anoint kings as chosen by the god.[46] Strikingly, priests would command kings to put themselves to death, and the kings would obey. This is just one example in which Hobbes admits that real persons have what Lloyd has called "transcendent interests"—interests for which they may be willing to lay down their lives.

One might object that the Ethiopian king example is atypical. Moreover, one might point out that the Ethiopian kings were "mastered by superstition" and so are not fitting examples for confirming what man's principal end in the state of nature would be. Granting the force of this objection, it would be more fitting to find an example of Hobbes recognizing more common cases in which men are willing to lay down their lives and which might obtain in the state of nature. Indeed, we do find such an example regarding slander: "Most men would rather lose their lives (that I say not, their peace) than suffer slander." "All signs of hatred, or contempt, provoke to fight; insomuch as most men choose rather to hazard their life, than not to be revenged." "Life itself, with the condition of enduring scorn, is not esteemed worth the enjoying, much less peace."[47] Indeed, the desire for honor plays a key role in generating conflict in the state of nature. Hence, Hobbes seems to recognize that whatever empirical necessity of desiring life obtains must be compatible with uncertain outcomes for any particular individual.

Another possibility may be that it will be *predominantly the case* that men will desire life in such a condition. Gregory Kavka has offered an interpretation of Hobbesian agents along these lines.[48] The trouble is that Hobbes's civil science requires an object capable of moving desire not predominantly but universally. Hobbes's natural law teaching suggests as much. Since Hobbes's laws of nature are so many precepts directing human actions toward the good (the good that can be made common through commonwealth), and since the common good is an object capable of moving universally, the natural law must bind universally. Hence Hobbes holds that the laws of nature are not only immutable and eternal but also *universal*.[49] They are binding on all rational persons as such. Therefore, the laws of nature cannot depend on contingent, albeit predominant, desires for their universal validity.

What is needed is an object that is objectively good independent of contingent desires. Not only can such an object meet the universality criterion indicated by the laws of nature and the end of the commonwealth, but it can also function as the principle distinguishing rational and irrational passions.[50] That is, it can function as the criterion by which Hobbes can distinguish between normal and abnormal passions.

In this section I have briefly sketched how Hobbes thinks *nosce teipsum* can yield knowledge of passion descriptions. Hobbes contends that we can introspect on our own passions and describe with a passion description what another is feeling when he says he hopes, fears, and so on. But we saw that this sort of knowledge is not in and of itself sufficient to ground Hobbes's civil science. We have suggested that his definition of commonwealth and his understanding of the laws of nature require an object that is objectively good independent of contingently felt passions.

A central argument of this book is that this object is identified by the basic judgment of right reason that life is good. Hobbes suggests as much when he identifies his two postulates of human nature, which are the deep, basic principles of the passions, the conjunction of which constitutes the immanent, nonseverable "form" of man (see chapter 1). The two postulates pick out the bare-bones positive content of Hobbes's conception of human nature: the powers of reason and desire. It is necessary to consider directly Hobbes's two postulates of human nature, which, because more fundamental than complex passions, are deeper foundational principles of Hobbes's moral and political philosophy.

I want to argue that Hobbes's two postulates of human nature and their function in the state of nature indicate that the two postulates are not absolute beginning points but must be understood within Hobbes's theistic and Christian framework. In other words, Hobbes's imprimatur on experiential knowledge of human nature is qualified. He is supposing that the person with experience of the world is implicitly holding, de minimis, theistic beliefs. Furthermore, he thinks that the grounds of his civil science are enhanced or most securely held by those who hold specifically Christian beliefs about man, God, and the world. If severed from these theological and religious background assumptions, experience will be at best a shaky foundation for civil science, in Hobbes's view.

David Johnston seems correct in saying that *Leviathan* is united by a single cultural-political aim, which is to secure the doctrine of government and obedience with a wide audience in mind.[51] Johnston takes Hobbes's metaphysical and theological doctrines as being connected to his political aims not by logical deduction but by political effect, that is, he believes Hobbes's concern is to polemically critique certain metaphysical and theological views because of their adverse political effects. It is true that Hobbes wants to ridicule specific theological views (particularly Roman Catholic, Presbyterian, and Independent) that he believes pose a threat to civil peace. But an argument can be rhetorical without being *merely* rhetorical. For all of its literary and rhetorical flourish, the argument in *Leviathan* does, of logical necessity, rest upon particular realistic claims: there is a set of particular substances that stands in a fundamental resemblance relation to one another; these substances were created and ordered by God, and Hobbes's propositions are affirmable by unaided reason. To continue building my argument, I consider Leo Strauss's influential statement of the view that Hobbes's philosophical anthropology is autonomous from theology and mechanistic science.

Strauss's Interpretation of the Two Postulates

Leo Strauss advanced a foundationalist interpretation of Hobbesian political philosophy on the basis of a particular "moral view" of human nature. But Strauss argued that Hobbes intended his philosophical anthropology and political teaching to be autonomous from natural and revealed theology. In this section I outline Strauss's interpretation and offer a critique. I first recount Strauss's secularist interpretation of the two postulates of human nature. Strauss fails to make sense of the two postulates for a number of reasons that turn on a misinterpretation of Hobbes's teachings on human evil. I develop the *argument from evil* for the legal character of the natural laws and suggest that Hobbes's belief that there are evil people in the state of nature is better explained by the theistic interpretation. The character and role of the two postulates in the state of nature depends on a theistic framework. These considerations open the door to reconsidering the two postulates in light of Christian revelation, which I will argue provides Hobbes's ultimate foundation for the two postulates. Let us recall Hobbes's two postulates of human nature. Hobbes says that he obtained first the postulate *cupiditatis naturalis*, whereby man demands private use of common things, and second the postulate *rationis naturalis*, which teaches man to avoid violent death or "fly contra-natural dissolution" (*mortem violentam*) as the greatest natural evil.[52] I have argued that the warrant for these two postulates is actually obtaining a condition of reason and desire in all individual substances picked out by the word "man."

Hobbes's two postulates of human nature take center stage in Leo Strauss's well-known interpretation of Hobbes in his early *The*

Political Philosophy of Hobbes, which sought to show the "moral basis" of Hobbes's political philosophy.[53] The heart of Strauss's argument is that Hobbes's political philosophy should not be taken as simply a deduction from the materialistic and mechanistic doctrines of modern science.[54] Hence Strauss sought to show how Hobbes's teachings about the nature of man stand on their own. The true basis of Hobbes's political philosophy was not modern science but his "fundamental view of human life." Animated by a particular "moral attitude" throughout his corpus, Hobbes formed his view of human life by reflection on his "actual experience of how men behave and in 'public conversation'" and his "first-hand experience of human life."[55] Strauss identified some strong textual bases for this conception of Hobbes's moral and political thought as independent from modern science (or their explanation in terms of modern science), particularly Hobbes's repeated appeals to the reader's own experience to confirm his teachings.[56]

According to Strauss, the first postulate of human nature should not be understood as a faculty simply jerked this way and that by external sensory stimuli. Natural desire cannot be explained by the mechanisms of matter in motion successively operating on sense perception. Whereas animals can desire only finite particulars, human appetite is spontaneously infinite in itself.[57] As such, human appetite cannot be identified with bestial animal appetite since the latter can desire only finite particulars, while man spontaneously desires infinitely. In making this interpretive claim, Strauss leans on the following passage from Hobbes's *Decameron Physiologicum*:

> But know you not that men from their very birth, and naturally, scramble for every thing they covet, and would have all the world, if they could, to fear and obey them?[58]

Whereas a child's desire for this toy or that cup of juice can be explained by the child's sense impressions of those objects, the impressions of finite particulars cannot explain a desire to rule the world because beasts also perceive and desire particular objects and do not desire this dominion. Hence Strauss concludes that this desire is fundamental and sui generis—it "arises from the depths of man himself."[59] Moreover, this irrational desire for power after power is based not in successive sense impressions but "in the pleasure which man takes on the consideration of his own power, i.e. in vanity. The original of man's natural appetite is, therefore, not perception, but vanity."[60] Vanity is the true "root of natural appetite."[61] For Strauss's Hobbes, then, vanity is a basic feature of human nature, independent of man's contingent sense experiences. Unchecked, vain or prideful man is apt to get caught up in the struggle to be first in the race of life and forget about his basic bodily fragility. Man manifests his vanity particularly in his own dream-world:

> Living in the world of his imagination, he need do nothing, in order to convince himself of his superiority to others, but simply think out his deeds for himself; in this world, in which indeed 'the whole world obeys him,' everything is accomplished according to his wishes.[62]

In other words, "man by nature lives in the dream of the happiness of triumph."[63] Man needs a jolt to shake him out of this dream.

The second postulate of man's reason provides the needed jolt. By this postulate, reason sees life as the primary and most urgent good. But for Strauss's Hobbes, reason is itself impotent and must serve at the altar of the passions. I have called this the impotent thesis. On this reading, reason could not even see the goodness of life "if the passion of fear of death did not compel [man] to do so."[64] More precisely, it is the present, powerful fear of *violent* death—a mutual fear of all men of each other as their potential murderers. Men come to feel the powerful pull of this passion once the *bellum omnium contra omnes* has obtained in the state of nature that, on Strauss's retelling, is generated by a series of events following from the vain man's stepping outside of his own imagination to demand recognition of his superiority in reality. As a passion, the fear of violent death is nonrational in origin but is rational in effect inasmuch as it tempers or quashes the desire to dominate and serves as the first premise whence Hobbes deduces all of morality and constructs a rational state. The upshot is that fear of violent death is the postulate of natural reason—Hobbes "identifies reason with fear."[65]

In sum, Strauss understands the two postulates that ground Hobbes's political philosophy as the antithesis of irrational vanity and rational fear. Strauss's Hobbes intends this polarity of basic features of human nature as a moral judgment such that his political philosophy flows from the antithesis between fundamentally unjust vanity and fundamentally just fear.[66] These antithetical postulates characterize Hobbes's fundamental moral outlook.[67] As mentioned, the postulates ultimately depend on self-knowledge and self-reflection for their corroboration.

Notably, Strauss maintains that Hobbes "could not make up his mind explicitly to take as his point of departure the reduction of man's natural appetite to vanity."[68] Hobbes's indecision was supposedly due to the fact that the proposition that "man by nature finds his pleasure in triumphing over all others" entails that "man is by nature evil"—and Hobbes "did not dare to uphold this consequence or assumption of his theory."[69] Yet Hobbes in fact held, by the first postulate, that man is by nature evil; without this postulate Hobbes's political philosophy "would lose all its character."[70] So it was only rhetorically that Hobbes sought to obscure the implications or true character of his premises. Man's natural vanity and hence natural evil is put "more and more in the background in favor of innocent competition, innocent striving after power, innocent animal appetite," but Hobbes finally is unable to "make us forget that man does not happen to be an innocent animal."[71] In the *De Cive* passage in which Hobbes defends himself against the charge that his teaching would imply that man is by nature evil, he says that such a claim "cannot be conceded without impiety."[72] Strauss's suggestion is that, in the context of religious scrutiny, Hobbes exercised caution by gilding the poison ivy. While Strauss's view of Hobbes's theological views seemed to evolve over time,[73] he was convicted in his early work of Hobbes's unbelief and the political reasons for which Hobbes "hid his true opinions and was mindful of the maintenance of theological convention."[74] The suggestion is that Hobbes's professions of Christian theism were offered not as genuine constituents of his political philosophy but as a genuflection to the religious authorities of his time. This is a clear statement of the concealment thesis.

The point is significant for understanding Hobbes's two postulates inasmuch as they are laid bare in man's natural condition, that is, the state of nature. In Strauss's view, Hobbes's unbelief "is the necessary premise of his teaching about the state of nature."[75] Strauss tells us that everyone knows that the antithesis between vanity and fear is the secularized version of the antithesis between spiritual pride and fear of the Lord. But, so far from being the mere residue of the Christian tradition, the state of nature and its sister human nature teachings are intended to overthrow the biblical teaching of God's creation of man in a state of perfection because Hobbes drops the division between a state of nature in the condition of grace and a state of fallen nature. Hence, whether or not Hobbes denies the fall of man in fact, he denies its importance.[76] Let us now consider the problems with Strauss's interpretation.

A Critique of Strauss's Interpretation

There are three problems with Strauss's reading that flow from the claim that Hobbesian man is by nature evil. First, man is not by nature evil in Hobbes's notion of the natural as the infantile, because the desire for absolute dominion is not even minimally acted out from birth. Second, vainglory is not a universal feature of people in the state of nature. Third, Hobbes believes that there are evil persons in the state of nature, a claim that requires a theistic framework because evil presupposes breach of law, and God secures the legal character of the laws of nature *in foro interno*.

We are initially struck by Strauss's claim that Hobbesian man is vain by nature when the natural is understood as the innate or infantile (Hobbes uses "by nature" in the sense of the infantile in his preface to *De Cive*). Besides Hobbes's own denial that his teaching entails this proposition (we shall examine Hobbes's denial momentarily), the initial trouble with the claim is that the desire for the kind of preeminence and recognition suggested in the notion of having the "whole world" fear and obey one cannot be *in act* from birth. Such a desire depends on the active capacity to reason. Let us see why.

In Hobbes's terms, the notion of absolute command over the whole world logically presupposes a peculiarly human understanding of effects and causes. That is, when imagining absolute dominion, humans "seek all the possible effects, that can by it be produced; that is to say, we imagine what we can do with it, when we have it."[77] This sort of quality distinguishes the nature of man from "the nature of any living creature that has no other passion but sensual, such as are hunger, thirst, lust, and anger."[78] Hobbes's suggestion is that such imagining presupposes the active capacity to reason about effects. The distinctive nature of man is also manifest in his inquisitiveness or "desire of knowing causes"—a "peculiar quality" that is "not to be found in other living creatures."[79] Knowledge of causes, Hobbes indicates, is sought by the dominion-seeker inasmuch as he seeks to order affairs to his advantage.[80] But since for Hobbes knowledge of causes comes through the distinctively rational power of ratiocination—in distinction from the knowledge available through "sense and memory of things, which are common to man and all living creatures"—the fulfillment of the desire to know causes presupposes active reasoning capacity.[81] Moreover, the desire to know causes presupposes that the agent reckons such knowledge good.[82] There is a hint of this in Hobbes's comment that it is "anxiety of future time" that "disposeth men to enquire into the causes of things, because the knowledge of them maketh men better able to order the present to their best advantage."[83]

By connecting anxiety with ordering one's affairs, Hobbes indicates that the active desire to know causes depends on the ability to reason, since infants and madmen are not able to order their own affairs.[84] Therefore, Hobbes's view is that the peculiarly human desire to know causes and effects cannot occur until the age of reason or the age at which one can be provident for oneself and others. In short, the desire for absolute rule over the whole world could be actual only in one who can imagine the possible effects of dominion and inquire into the causes of things in order to better order things toward one's dominion. The desire for absolute dominion could be actual only in those who can actively reason.

But if this is the case, the cupidity innate to man from birth cannot be equated with an actual desire for absolute rule over the world.[85] It cannot even be inchoate, since that would be a desire of the same kind minimally in act. And, if it depends on being able to actively reason, inasmuch as one rightly reasons, one will not have this vain desire. Thus I contend that there is an interpretation of the desire-for-dominion passage that is more fitting. To recall that passage:

> But know you not that men from their very birth, and naturally, scramble for every thing they covet, and would have all the world, if they could, to fear and obey them.[86]

By the spark of cupidity men have from birth, they scramble for *every thing* they covet. Because one cannot actively reason from birth, one's desires are going to be similar to those of irrational animals. Actual desires will always be for basic human needs and will take immediate goods and immediate evils for their objects. They will be very much like the beasts' desires for "quotidian" objects like food and ease.[87] This is not a whitewashing of cupidity but simply recognition that the very young lack the habits of virtue (as picked out by the laws of nature) necessary to check cupidity inasmuch as they lack the active capacity to reason. Hence, the first part of the sentence expresses a coherent thought in itself and is compatible with what Hobbes thought must be true of creatures without the active capacity to reason. The "and" in the preceding passage signifies the beginning of a conjoined but distinct thought regarding men who have the active capacity to reason—and hence are able to form the desire to dominate the world—but who are childish. Those whose spark of cupidity is not tamed and educated by right reason will, in Hobbes's words, be "rather like a sturdy boy, or a man of childish mind."[88] One who has the vain and tyrannical desire to rule the world is, in other words, a childish person whose reason is dominated by his cupidity or unruly passions.[89] According to Hobbes, such a person is "an evil man."[90]

Nor does Hobbes claim that men are evil by nature when "by nature" is taken in the sense of men in the state of nature, that is, without the rule of law. If Hobbes thought men were by nature evil because they were by nature vainglorious, we would expect vainglory to be a universal feature of men in the state of nature. But Hobbes's presentations of the state of nature never make this claim. Recall that Hobbes says: "There be *some* that taking pleasure in contemplating their own power in the acts of conquest, which they pursue farther than their security requires...."[91] Hobbes thus distinguishes between the "temperate" or "moderate" man and the vainglorious one in the state of nature.[92] If, as I shall argue, reason is not the mere calculating slave of the passions, this distinction tracks the reasonable and unreasonable residents in the state of nature.

Moreover, if all men were living in a vainglorious dreamworld in the state of nature, conflict would never be generated. To take pleasure in *imagining* one's own power and ability is glorying. If this imagining is "grounded upon the experience of his own former actions," it "is the same with *confidence*."[93] When it is "only supposed by himself, for delight in the consequences of it," it is *then* called vainglory. Hobbes distinguishes between confidence and vainglory in this sense because "*confidence* begetteth attempt, whereas the supposing of power does not, and is therefore rightly called *vain*."[94] Taken in conjunction with Hobbes's account of the state of nature, it would seem that it is not *vainglory* in the sense of mere imagining of one's own power but confidence that begets further acts of conquest.[95] A condition made entirely of such vainglorious men would never become a war of all against all.

Let us now recall the passage in which Hobbes denies that men are by nature evil:

> Still less does it follow that those who are evil were made so by nature. For although they have from nature, i.e. from their birth itself, from the fact that they are born animals [*animalia*], this characteristic, that they immediately want what pleases them and do whatever they can, in fear or anger, either to flee or to ward off the evils that threaten them, they are not normally thought to be evil on that account. For the passions [*affectus animi*] which arise from animal nature are not themselves evil, though the actions that proceed from them sometimes are, namely, when they are harmful and contrary to duty.[96]

As we have seen, Strauss maintains that Hobbes conflates man's natural vanity with innocent animal appetite. But Strauss's interpretation does not account for the immediate sequel to the passage, in which Hobbes indicates the conditions in which the notions of blame and innocence are applicable.

Infants, Hobbes tells us, are apt to cry, get angry, and even strike their parents unless they get whatever they want. But they are free from *culpa* because they are not subject to duty. They are not subject to duty because they have not reached the age of reason. Hence, they are not naturally evil. Blameworthiness and evil are concepts inapplicable to infants. Therefore, it makes no sense to say that man by nature, in the sense of infantile, is evil. Blame and evil presuppose breach of the law. And before the age of reason, neither positive law nor natural law binds man: "Over natural fools, children, or madmen there is no law, no more than over brute beasts."[97] Hence, "The desires and other passions of man are in themselves no sin. No more are the actions that proceed from those passions, till they know a law that forbids them."[98] Man becomes evil when passion is not well educated or subject to the dictates of right reason or the natural law. Such a person's reason is dominated by unruly passion: "Thus an evil man is rather like a sturdy boy, or a man of childish mind, and evil is simply want of reason at an age when it normally accrues to men by nature governed by discipline and experience of harm."[99] Hobbes concludes that unless we are willing to say that "men were made evil by nature simply because they do not have discipline and the use of reason from nature, it must be admitted that they can have greed, fear, anger, and all the other animal passions from nature but still not be made evil by nature."[100]

Strauss denies that the laws of nature are really laws prior to civil law and so would deny that passion need come under the guidance of law at the age of reason.[101] But such a view cannot explain the existence of evil persons in the state of nature. The existence of such persons is supposed in Hobbes's presentation of the state of nature in the preface to *De Cive*:

> For we cannot tell the good and the bad apart, hence even if there were fewer evil men than good men, good, decent people would still be saddled with the constant need to watch, distrust, anticipate, and get the better of others, and to protect themselves by all possible means.[102]

I suggest that the only way we can make sense of Hobbes's claim that there are evil people in the state of nature is by realizing that the laws of nature—the dictates of right reason—are truly laws. Since there are good reasons to think Hobbes held his theological views sincerely, we ought to take seriously his repeated assertions that the laws of nature are immutable and eternal and that God's command secures their legal character. They bind immutably and eternally *in foro interno*, "to a desire that they should take place."[103] And since the fundamental law of nature is to seek peace, man is always bound to desire peace *in foro interno*. When peace cannot be had, the natural law permits defensive measures that would include a measure of aggression on the best-defense-is-a-good-offense principle. But one is always bound to seek peace when it can be had, and warlike measures must be instrumental to establishing security. Those who desire war to sate their rapacious appetites or their lust for glory are in breach of this basic duty to will peace when it can be had—they are evil. In subsequent chapters I build the case for the legal character of the laws of nature and explain further how Hobbes understands God's command to secure the legal character of the dictates of right reason.

For the moment, the point is that when people are at the age of reason, they are subject to the natural law in a way such that they can be evil and subject to blame. Hence, Hobbes includes among the sources of crime a "sudden force of the passions."[104] The suggestion is that man is evil only when passion is untamed by right reason.

My explanation of why man is not naturally evil has suggested that Hobbes gives reason a greater dignity in human nature than Strauss allows. Indeed, the immediate sense of the two-postulates passage is that the untutored spark of concupiscence generates war, while the direction of reason leads to peace. Is not Hobbes distinguishing between reason and desire in a way that indicates reason is not or need not be a slave to the passions? As Bernard Gert has argued, the passage may just as faithfully be taken to express the judgment of practical reason as the goodness of human life, that *bonum maximum*.[105] On this reading, the goal of practical reason, to "fly contra-natural dissolution," is independent of the contingent desires of natural cupidity. Contrary to Hobbes interpreters who claim that reason is merely computative, I claim that reason also has the function of judging that life is a good to be pursued. Fear—a complex negative desire (aversion with the opinion of hurt)—in the form of fear of violent death is then parasitic on the (reasonable) desire to preserve one's life. The role of the passion of fear can be understood as derivative of right reason's judgment. Moreover, that which right reason judges to be good is pursued with right.[106] Since right reason in the lawless condition judges the good of life to be basic, it is "not therefore absurd, nor reprehensible, nor contrary to right reason, if one makes every effort to defend his body and limbs from death and to preserve them," as long as one desires peace when it might be had.[107] Hence, the right of nature is defined as "the liberty each man hath to use his own power, as he will himself, for the preservation of his own nature, that is to say, of his own life."[108] Hobbes's moral and political doctrines can be deduced from the fundamental judgment of reason as to the primary goodness of life.

For the moment, notice that Hobbes's moral view of human nature is intended to pass a moral judgment on vanity or pride. If the postulates of human nature were taken to be beginning points full stop, nothing would warrant such a moral judgment. As Strauss recognizes, Hobbes intends to pass moral judgment on vanity or pride. Hobbes condemns the prideful man in the state of nature, who supposes himself superior to all others and seeks dominion with the intention of glory; in contrast, the temperate man's willingness to commit acts of violence is not condemned because it derives from an intention to defend himself, his family, and his goods.[109] In contrast with the temperate man, the prideful man is evil because he intends war, in breach of natural law.

It should be apparent now why Strauss's secularist reading fails as a sound interpretation of Hobbes's two postulates and their role in the state of nature. Strauss's interpretation cannot explain why the condemnation of the prideful man as evil is warranted on atheistic grounds. In the atheistic interpretation, morality does not bind with the force of law (*in foro interno*) in the state of nature, that is, the condition in which human law has been dissolved. Indeed, the dictates of reason that bind one *in foro interno* to seek peace (and forbid pride) could never be more than recommendatory prior to or independent of human positive law. Such a view cannot explain Hobbes's moral condemnation of vanity in and out of the state of nature. Neither can it explain Hobbes's condemnation of the fool, whose denial of any immutable and eternal standard of justice entails his willingness to commit acts of injustice if he calculates that the consequences are to his advantage. The force of this point is not diminished by the fact that Hobbes condescends to argue with the fool on his own terms (see chapter 4).

In contrast, the interpretation of Hobbes as sincere in his profession of Christian theism can explain his moral convictions. The legal character of the dictates of right reason, prior to civil law, has a rational warrant, in Hobbes's own terms, in the notion of God's "rational word," to which corresponds the hearing of right reason. Meanwhile, Hobbes's theory of God's "prophetic word," to which corresponds the hearing of faith, offers a suprarational warrant or ultimate ground for the two postulates of human nature. Hobbes insists that, while God's prophetical word is above reason, it is not contrary to reason.[110] Since God's prophetic and rational words are harmonious—God does not speak with a forked tongue—it follows that faith does not contradict or annul reason. Thus Hobbes enlarges the sphere of what can count as knowledge to include sacred sources. For the Hebrews, God's prophetic word consists in the words of the old law and the prophets, and for Christians it also includes (and terminates) in the words of Christ and his apostles as recorded in Holy Scripture. Accordingly, the only way that scripture and reason can conflict is by "erroneous ratiocination."[111] On the "Judeo-Christian" view, the basic postulates of human nature are not mere fact-judgments or the ineradicable features of human essence in a godless universe. Rather, in the next section I shall argue that Hobbes holds a biblical anthropology that indicates that the principles in man were created in harmony under God's law and became disharmonious after man's rebellion.

Reason and Desire after the Fall of Man: The Biblical Foundation of the Two Postulates of Human Nature

If Hobbesian practical reason is not a mere slave to the passions but capable of taming cupidity in line with its own goals, and if Hobbes is sincere in his theology (natural and revealed), then for all of his vociferous criticism of scholasticism, his teaching has striking similarities with the view held in the older Christian tradition. In this section I offer a brief sketch of how a rereading of Hobbes's two postulates in light of the Christian tradition would look. Helen Thornton has persuasively written that Hobbes's account of the state of nature should be seen to have parallels to the broadly Augustinian tradition of the interpretation of Genesis.[112] Thornton has emphasized the Calvinist and Lutheran elements in Hobbes and suggested that Hobbes combines elements of prelapsarian and postlapsarian conditions into his state of nature. While there is much to recommend in Thornton's study, I believe Thornton misses a crucial point about Hobbesian biblical anthropology. The state of nature is unqualifiedly a postlapsarian condition, and this is evident in his formulation of the two postulates of human nature. I suggest that, in limning the unruly spark of appetite when it is not subject to reason, Hobbes is in his own way making an essentially Pauline point that was fruitfully developed by Thomas Aquinas.

Paul famously remarked, "I see another law in my members, fighting against the law of my mind and captivating me in the law of sin that is in my members."[113] Aquinas was concerned to make sense of the apostle's claim that he found a *law* in the movements of sensuality or the *fomes* (kindling) of sin. How could there be a "law of sin" if law is essentially *aliquid rationis*, or something of reason?[114] Aquinas's solution was that the "law of sin" was a punishment for man's disobedience. To understand Aquinas's answer, recall that, while both Aquinas and Hobbes affirm God's providence over all things, they both distinguish the character of God's rule over man from his rule over irrational things. For Aquinas, man's subjection to God's reign is the focal case of rule by law, since to be properly subject to law requires knowledge of the precept.[115] Aquinas and Hobbes are in full agreement that promulgation is a necessary condition for something to be law—"Law made, if not also made known, is no Law."[116] Aquinas points out that one of the effects of knowledge of the precept will be fear of punishment, "which the law makes use of in order to ensure obedience."[117] But the notions of precept, obedience, and punishment cannot be addressed to irrational animals or to any nonrational being. Hence irrational animals are subject to the eternal law only *per similitudinem*.[118] Hobbes makes the same point this way:

> But to call this power of God (which extendeth itself not only to man, but also to beasts, and plants, and bodies inanimate) by the name of kingdom is but a metaphorical use of the word. For he only is properly said to reign that governs his subjects by his word, and by promise of rewards to those that obey it, and by threatening them with punishment that obey it not. Subjects, therefore, in the kingdom of God are not bodies inanimate, nor creatures irrational (because they understand no precepts as his).[119]

So it is only by way of similitude or metaphorically that there is said to be a "law" of the beasts, because God governs or moves these creatures but not by way of commanding precepts.[120] Aquinas points out that we observe variegated orders of human positive law that may have conflicting demands. For example, the demands and permissions of local criminal law differ from the demands and permissions of diplomatic law. Similarly, as we observe variegated and even rival behavior in the animal kingdom, we can speak of, say, fierceness as the "law" of the wolf or meekness as the "law" of the sheep. But, inasmuch as irrational beasts are *generally* under the impulse of sensual appetite, animal appetite has the character of law in the way described.

Now, it is the law of man, in distinction from all the beasts, in his proper condition (which for Aquinas is also his primordial condition), to order his actions in accord with reason.[121] In the Christian tradition it had been held that man's proper condition was a state of original justice, a condition in which man was perfectly subject to God and the lower powers of the soul were perfectly subject to reason.[122] When man turned away from God,

> he fell under the influence of his sensual impulses: in fact this happens to each one individually, the more he deviates from the path of reason, so that, after a fashion, he is likened to the beasts that are led by the impulse of sensuality, according to Psalm 48:21: "Man, when he was in honor, did not understand: he hath been compared to senseless beasts, and made like to them."[123]

Man comes to be compared to the beasts inasmuch as he acts on his sensuality unreasonably. But where the impulse of animal appetite has the *rationem legis* directly from God's movement of irrational animals, it has the character of law in man indirectly as a deviation from the law of reason. This is because the sovereign can deprive one from the dignity of some higher order of law and thereby place him under a lower order of law. For example, a sovereign could strip his diplomat of his status and hence the protection of diplomatic immunity. Analogously, by God's just sentence, man is punished for his disobedience by being deprived of his proper dignity such that the spark of cupidity now has in man the *rationem legis* by way of penalty.

Since the fall, man has been in a wounded condition. For Aquinas, revelation illuminates the insights into human nature available to unaided reason. Without the aid of revelation, Aristotle had observed that reason has a royal and politic rule of the passions in distinction with a despotic rule.[124] Aquinas explains Aristotle's insight as follows. Despotic rule is that sort of rule exercised over slaves, "who have not the right to resist in any way the orders of the one that commands them, since they have nothing of their own."[125] But subjects in a royal or politic order are free. They are subject to the command of the sovereign, but they retain something of their own by which they can resist his commands. Analogously, appetite can resist the dictates of reason inasmuch as we sense or imagine something pleasant that reason forbids or something unpleasant that reason demands. By expounding Aristotle's insight in the context of commenting on Paul's *fomes* dictum, Aquinas suggests that, by grace, reason ruled the passions despotically in Eden and that it was the fall that liberated sensuality.[126] Aquinas captures the idea of liberated sensuality using various terms: concupiscence, the *fomes* of sin, or *cupiditas*.[127] The consequence of original sin is the inordinate spark of desire.

Hobbes also took on faith the creation of man in a condition of happiness and the subsequent fall of Adam and Eve:

> From the very creation, God not only reigned over all men *naturally* by his might, but also had *peculiar* subjects, whom he commanded by a voice, as one man speaketh to another. In which manner he reigned over Adam, and gave him commandment to abstain from the tree of cognizance of good and evil; which, when he obeyed not, but tasting thereof took upon him to be as God, judging between good and evil (not by his creator's commandment, but by his own sense), his punishment was a privation of the estate of eternal life wherein God had at first created him.[128]

Hobbes describes in more detail what the original condition was like:

> Man was created in a condition immortal, not subject to corruption, and consequently to nothing that tendeth to the dissolution of his nature, and fell from that happiness by the sin of Adam.[129]

Hobbes gives us here a strikingly different picture of man's original condition than the picture conveyed by his various presentations of the state of nature.[130] Read in light of the Christian tradition, the passage takes on a significance that has been overlooked. Crucially, Hobbes points out that nothing in that condition *tended to the dissolution of his nature*. Man in the primordial condition stands in stark contrast to man in the state of nature, where natural cupidity seeks "to appropriate to it self the use of those things in which all others have a joint interest"—a desire that, untamed by reason and the rule of law, generates war—while reason is the faculty that teaches every man to fly contranatural dissolution. That is, the state of nature is a condition in which the powers of reason and desire of human nature are at cross purposes and so tend to man's destruction.

Why are the powers at cross purposes? As in the Augustinian tradition, Hobbes's Christian faith taught him that it was due to our parents' "first sin."[131] Original sin doomed the entire human race to forfeit eternal life, paradise, and incorruptibility. In Adam, we are all originally "guilty of disobedience to God's Law."[132] The punishments for original sin are manifold evils and calamities, including "death and misery."[133] Only after our first parents' sin have reason and desire been in a condition that can lead to death and misery, to man's dissolution. Hobbes is indicating that the state of nature—a potential condition of actual persons when positive law is dissolved—is a potential condition of *fallen* persons. In the Latin *Leviathan*, apparently in response to objections that Hobbes's portrayal of the natural condition of human beings was anti-biblical, Hobbes wrote:

> But someone may say: there has never been a war of all against all. What! Did not Cain out of envy kill his brother Abel, a crime so great he would not have dared it if there had at that time been a common power which could have punished him?[134]

Curley wonders at the orthodoxy of this passage, since God, the common power over the natural commonwealth, punishes Cain after the event. However, Hobbes is referring here to the lack of a *civil* common power, since the birth of human cities comes after this, through Cain.[135] As in the Augustinian tradition, the birth of the terrene city comes only after Cain's crime. What is important about this passage is that Hobbes traces an evil act to envy. Envy is a complex passion: a sort of grief or sorrow at the success of a competitor in the pursuit of some good, conjoined with an endeavor to supplant or hinder him. Emotions are enacted that are undirected by right reason.

Hobbes is suggesting that in paradise, where nothing tended to the dissolution of human nature, reason perfectly governed desire. In this reading, the state of nature does not replace the biblical account of the Edenic state but is a potential condition of actual fallen persons when human positive law and authority—the institutions necessary to enforce the demands of reason against those dominated by unruly passions—break down or fail to obtain.[136] For Hobbes, revelation provides insight into why the state of nature is a potential condition of real human beings. Aristotle and Aquinas also recognized that man's potentiality to act like an irrational animal is exacerbated without human authority and positive law.[137] Plato, Aristotle, Augustine, and Aquinas hold a vision of human psychology in which reason has a relation to the passions like that of a rider on a wrecked bike or like a rider on an elephant.[138] Reason can tame and direct the passions but only with difficulty. Plato and Aristotle take this as an almost curious empirical fact, while Augustine and Aquinas offer a theory to explain the fact, based on data from revelation. Hobbes's theological anthropology may thus not be so far from Aquinas's after all. Where they differ is in their rival accounts of the objective good(s) discoverable by human reason.

My reading of the state of nature as a condition of fallen men is buttressed by Hobbes's brief discussion of the fall. To understand his interpretation, recall that, in his view, sovereign authority—divine and human—entails the right to the legislative and adjudicative powers. The sovereign's right to legislate and judge means that the sovereign "prescribes the rules of discerning good and evil [and] which rules are laws." The sovereign is, moreover, the sole judge of cases and controversies. Hence, Hobbes marks off the following as a most poisonous doctrine: *That every man is judge of good and evil actions*. Hobbes immediately points out that this is true of the condition of mere nature, having already argued: "And therefore so long a man is in the condition of mere nature (which is a condition of war) as private appetite is the measure of good and evil."[139] Lloyd helpfully points out:

Note carefully that this passage does *not* say (as the standard interpretation would have it) that *so long as* people are in the condition of mere nature, their private appetites *are* the measure of good and evil; what it says is that so long as private appetite is *the measure* of good and evil, people will remain in the condition of mere nature, which is a state of war.[140]

The upshot is that the state of nature is a *reductio* of the widespread application of the right of private judgment. Hobbes thus traces the English Civil War to the pernicious influence of preachers who taught the doctrine of private judgment to the prejudice of obedience to their rightful sovereign. This is the height of prideful arrogance because it reserves to oneself a right that one would not be content for everyone else to actually have. When each individual effectively usurps the right of judgment proper to the sovereign, it effectively inaugurates a state of affairs in which everyone is his own absolute sovereign, with a right to all things. But that would just be a nasty, poor, brutish, and short state of affairs.

Hobbes argues that Adam and Eve's sin in Eden was actually the first usurpation of the right of private judgment:

> "Ye shall be as gods, knowing good and evil." (Genesis 3:5) And verse 11. "Who told thee that thou wast naked? hast thou eaten of the tree, of which I commanded thee thou shouldest not eat?"[141]

In Hobbes's, view, God's forbiddance of eating of the tree of knowledge was his proscription of "Cognisance or Judicature of Good and Evil." God was essentially proscribing the right of private judgment. Hence Satan's temptation—which "enflamed the ambition of the woman, to whom that fruit seemed beautiful"—holds forth the prospect of Adam and Eve's becoming gods through taking on the right to judge good and evil. Hence, their sin was to usurp what was properly God's office as sovereign. The punishment for our disobedience is a disharmony in our nature that tends toward our dissolution. Whereas reason and desire before the fall were in harmony, desire now has a spark of its own, seeking to make its own that which is common. The unleashed spark of *cupiditas* goes hand in glove with the assertion of the right of private judgment of good and evil—and man's condition is now such that he is all too likely to be dominated by cupidity and assert a right to private judgment.

Hobbes believed that the echoes of the first sin were heard in the sermonizing of the religious dissenters and nonconformists, who preached rebellion in the years before and during the English Civil War. Doubtless Hobbes would consider as a prime example the Independent Hugh Peter, whose chaplaincy to the parliamentarian army in the 1640s and preaching to the unconverted were credited with advancing the parliamentarian cause. Peter and his collaborators sought to overthrow the king and build the kingdom of heaven on earth. Hobbes's strong opposition to this kind of interpretation and political use of Christianity has the flavor of antichiliasm in the spirit of Augustine. Still, Hobbesian anthropology acknowledges that the potentiality to engage in political violence in the name of God is a feature of broken human nature. The state of nature is all too likely a potential condition for us today because of our first parents' sin. Moreover, whereas Adam and Eve lived in a natural condition of peace, we can achieve peace only by erecting a terrifying Leviathan powerful enough to check the potentiality for evil in "all the children of pride."

As we have seen, none of the foregoing entails the proposition that man is by nature evil, because the spark of cupidity in the very young is not sufficient to make them lawbreakers, since they lack the use of reason. On this point Hobbes is in full agreement with Aquinas, for "if the ignorance be such as to exclude the use of reason entirely, it excuses from sin altogether."[142] Hence, "Before a man comes to the age of discretion, the lack of years hinders the use of reason and excuses him from mortal sin, wherefore, much more does it excuse him from venial sin, if he does anything which is such generically."[143] Hobbes is willing to say that all men who have come of age are evil since that proposition is "clearly said in Holy Scripture."[144] But he is not saying that all men are actually vainglorious. He is affirming an axiom of scripture, that no man of reason is without any actual sin or any breaking of the law: "For all have sinned and fallen short of the glory of God,"[145] and "If we say we have no sin, we are deceiving ourselves and the truth is not in us."[146]

I have argued that Hobbes's two postulates of human nature are illuminated when read in light of the older Christian tradition, as expressed in the thought of Aquinas. But, even if it be admitted that the foregoing shows the plausibility of reading Hobbes's human nature teaching as rooted in the Christian tradition, we can reasonably ask: What relevance do any of these putative truths of revelation really have for the foundations of Hobbes's political philosophy? After all, doesn't Hobbes hold forth his theory of human nature to be affirmed by all persons inasmuch as they are rational? And doesn't that mean that Hobbes's teaching is affirmable by introspection and experience on the one hand and, on the other hand, scientifically, by a resolutive-compositive and geometrically modeled method of ratiocination? Aren't these two paths open independent of one's faith tradition or lack thereof?

It is true that, by unaided reason, one might accept the two postulates and even the conclusions Hobbes derives from them (i.e., that due to their capacity to do bad things, human beings will be in a miserable condition without the guidance of reason embedded in positive law and some authority with the power to enforce its demands). But what is it that would warrant Hobbes's supposition that the potentiality in man to bring on death and misery is an *immutable* feature of human nature? One might think, with Rousseau, that this potentiality in man is a mere historical accident that followed upon metallurgy.[147] In other words, one might affirm these postulates as characteristic of man only at a definite point in history beyond which he might progress. One might hold that through the proper sorts of institutions and/or the progress of history, the potentiality for evil in man could be eradicated.

But history does not fundamentally change human nature, according to Hobbes's worldview. This is not because human nature is an eternally existing form being circulated through matter (à la Plato) or because the human species eternally exists through procreation and animation by the immaterial substantial form of man (à la Aristotle). The world and therefore human particulars are created in time. Christian revelation grounds the claim that human potentiality for evil is immutable in the flow of history because man fell from God's grace. Man will not be finally healed except by God's grace through Christ at the Resurrection—what Hobbes calls "salvation absolute."[148] This comes through two articles of faith in Hobbes's simplified salvation formula: belief that Jesus is the Christ and obedience to civil laws, which in Christian commonwealths reflect both natural law and divine positive law, as mediated by the sovereign in his office of chief pastor.[149] Hobbes's Christian understanding of the fall seeks to forestall attempts to immanentize the eschaton by both secular and religious fanatics.[150]

Stephen B. Smith has recently argued that Hobbes is a "modern political theologian" in his recognition of the need for religion to shore up sovereignty. I would express qualified agreement. Hobbes's biblical interpretation is undoubtedly purposed toward propping up the sovereignty of the state. But I would emphasize, first, that Hobbes cannot be seen to be engaged in a wholesale critique of the Christian religion since his theological anthropology has important continuities with the orthodox Christian tradition. Still, this anthropology—partnered with a range of controversial biblical interpretations, including a soteriology and ecclesiology in which civil obedience is paramount—is enlisted for peculiarly modern purposes. Second, while Hobbes's biblical interpretation can be seen as useful to the state, this need not mean that it is *merely* useful, as if its use value were exclusive of its truth value.[151]

Thus the autonomy of Hobbesian moral and civil science is qualified. It depends on the notion that there is a human nature and that we can know it. That is its proximate foundation. Revelation provides an ultimate foundation because the continued definiteness and unchangeableness of human nature for Hobbes depends on Christian teaching that the potentiality for evil is ineradicable on this side of heaven since human nature cannot be so altered apart from salvation absolute.

One might object that by unaided reason we can affirm the immutable character of man's potency for evil as the ancients did, without revelation. One might point in particular to that ancient who preoccupied Hobbes, namely, Thucydides. Notably, Thucydides had keen insight into the potentialities embedded in human nature for unchecked passions to generate death and misery on a massive scale, particularly under conditions of civil war.[152]

But recall, first, that Hobbes does not think that a human act can be called evil unless one is culpable for it—and culpability comes only through breach of law. This means, minimally, that calling human acts evil is unwarranted outside of the theistic framework of a providential lawgiver whose authority secures the legal force of the dictates of reason.[153] We have seen the lineaments of Hobbes's natural theology, which could do this work. But the rather thin character of Hobbes's natural theology suggests that Hobbes intends it to be understood as an integral aspect of a comprehensive doctrine of reason and faith in partnership. Biblical revelation provides the ultimate explanation for (and, for Hobbes, enhances the case for) the moral culpability of pride or the vain desire to make oneself god. Firsthand experience and corroboration by introspection have their place. But it is Hobbes's Christian faith that is the ultimate basis for his moral view of fallen human nature. If this is correct, Hobbes offers us a single comprehensive doctrine of faith and reason that underpins his political teaching.

This point brings us full circle, back to our contrast of Hobbes's realistic political philosophy with Rawlsian political liberalism. While much of the *content* of Hobbes's philosophy and theology is different from that of the ancients and the medievals, Hobbes's metaphilosophy holds more in common with the ancients and medievals than with Rawlsian liberalism. The truth of Hobbes's moral and political teachings essentially rests on claims about what is true of human nature, God, and the world in which we find ourselves. Hobbes's metaphilosophical differences from the ancient and medieval traditions flow largely from his metaphysical materialism and thin theory of the good.

At the beginning of this chapter we looked at Lloyd's three arguments for reading Hobbes's civil science as free-standing. We are now in a position to consider Lloyd's offering of what she takes to be the "best case" that can be made for reading Hobbes as the "first political liberal." Lloyd identifies the following similarity between Hobbes and Rawls, which she thinks may have been what prompted Rawls to wonder whether Hobbes was the first political liberal. According to Lloyd, Hobbes offers a convergence of arguments for the affirmation of his principle of political obligation. These include arguments from narrow self-interest, morality, special prudence for salvation, and religious duty. That is, the narrowly self-interested egoists, nonreligious moralists, egoistic religionists, and dutiful religious can each affirm Hobbes's principle of political obligation from within their respective comprehensive doctrines. Lloyd explains:

> After all, to show one's principles justified without dependence on *any* comprehensive doctrine, and to show them justifiable from within *many* comprehensive doctrines, are different ways of showing one's principles to be not dependent upon affirmation of

some *privileged* comprehensive doctrine ... the justification for [Hobbes's] principle of political obligation will not depend on privileging any particular comprehensive doctrine—just as the justification for Rawls's principles of justice does not—and this is a very big plus under conditions of pluralism.[154]

We have already seen that Hobbes does privilege a comprehensive doctrine held by unaided reason in which (1) there is a human nature and we can know it and (2) God exists and created all of nature, including human nature. That is enough to sharply distinguish his doctrine from Rawlsian political liberalism. Now set aside for the moment the unclear distinction between the egoistic and dutiful religious.[155] Upon what grounds can the narrow egoist or the nonreligious moralist be bound to accept Hobbes's principle of political obligation? If one denies that God exists, one will not take oneself to be bound with the force of law to enter the sovereign-making covenant, according to Hobbes.[156] Keeping one's promises is the most pressing judgment of reason in maintaining the social covenant. But because nontheists don't accept the legal character of the natural law, they cannot be trusted to keep their word. Hence Hobbes contends that it is the atheist in the state of nature who cannot be trusted to keep his word in the sovereign-making covenant since "there is no living in a commonwealth with men, to whose oaths we cannot reasonably give credit."[157]

It is possible that non-Jewish and non-Christian theists could take themselves to be so bound. It could thus be said that a "partially comprehensive" doctrine of God's causal relation to the world is the necessary foundation for any Hobbesian pluralism.[158] Hobbes labors, moreover, to show how his doctrine of natural law does not contradict biblical revelation but is buttressed by it. We have seen how Hobbes's interpretation of man's first sin enriches the character of the two postulates. The next chapter considers the axiological pillar of Hobbes's natural law theory.

CHAPTER 3

Hobbes and the Good of Life

In this chapter I defend my interpretation of Hobbes as a properly *natural law theorist*. Hobbes's theory counts as a natural law theory because he retains two key notions that classical natural law theory considered requirements for a properly *natural law theory*: that the human good, which is grounded in human nature, provides basic *reason(s)* for action and that the norms or precepts that correspond to the human good have a *legal character*. It has so far been suggested that, in his identification of the two postulates of human nature, Hobbes distinguishes between reason and desire in a way that indicates that reason is not and need not be a mere slave to the passions. The basic postulate of Hobbesian practical reason is that *life is good and is to be pursued* and that bodily life and health is a—indeed, *the*—basic *reason for action*. As to the second requirement, Hobbes maintains that the laws of nature are eternal, immutable, and universally binding, *in foro interno*.[1] Their bindingness *as law* depends on their legislative pedigree in God's rational word. This chapter considers the first requirement, and the next chapter will consider the second.

In the first section I explore Hobbes's thin theory of the good. I argue that his teaching should be understood as sifting out what he took to be the grains separated from the chaff of the Aristotelian-Thomistic tradition, which held a thick theory of the good. As already suggested, most interpreters—by, respectively, rejecting God's essential role and/or adopting the proto-Humean reading of Hobbesian practical reason—have missed how Hobbes's thought may be illuminated when read in this light.[2] This section includes discussions of the roles of the virtues and habituation in Hobbes's moral theory, his reasons for rejecting the thick theory of the good, and his theory of conscience. In the next section I consider a range of objections to my interpretation and, in the course of replying to those objections, fill out how Hobbes's axiology is reinforced in various ways, including his interpretation of the Bible and presentation of the laws of nature in *Leviathan*.

The Good of Life

Let us briefly recall the claim of the impotent thesis, which is well put by Michael Zuckert using the helpful metaphor of a computer:

> Reason ... contains no substantive principles within it, not even such vague things as "seek the good"; reason is merely a calculative power ... more or less a kind of computer—a logical processor. It has no content other than what is supplied from elsewhere. It requires input.[3]

The impotent thesis attributes to Hobbes the belief that reason is a purely passive faculty. The "inputs" into the human processor are the passions and the extrinsic principles of the passions, which determine the goals to be sought. Passions are generated by external objects operating on us to stimulate *conatus*, which is the infinitesimal internal motion generating appetite and aversion. The appetite wants what it wants and shuns what it shuns. Reason's function is to compute the means of attaining the appetite's goal, which reason itself plays no role in determining. In this view, reason is confined to the ability to name and compose and divide names but is powerless to set its own goals.

Against the impotent thesis, I have argued that Hobbes speaks of reason and desire as distinct faculties with distinct functions. While Hobbes emphasizes reason's calculative function throughout his writings, none of Hobbes's accounts of reason ever restrict reason's functions to *mere* calculation. Since the calculative operation takes center stage in *Leviathan*, it might be easy to miss Hobbes's fundamental assumption, stated in various places across his writings, that reason judges life to be good. The assumption becomes explicit in Hobbes's account of madness, which I shall elaborate on later in this section. To begin this section, I argue that Hobbes's axiology should be understood in comparison and contrast to the Aristotelian-Thomistic tradition. For Hobbes, the objective, basic good grasped by Hobbesian practical reason is life. Therefore, Hobbes's doctrine is best understood as a thin theory of the good in comparison to the ideas of Aristotle and Aquinas. Such an interpretation faces a number of objections based on familiar passages in Hobbes that allegedly support the impotent thesis and value subjectivism. These and other objections are considered later in this chapter.

Hobbes carries forward the Aristotelian-Thomistic tradition when he takes it as axiomatic that one must act under the aspect of the good. In formulating his first principle of practical reason—that good is to be done and pursued and evil is to be avoided—Aquinas made a fundamental axiom of Aristotle's his own. The principle "is founded on the notion of good, viz. that 'good is that which all things seek after.'"[4] Aquinas's explanation of Aristotle's axiom is the occasion for him to enunciate the famous *sub ratione boni* thesis.[5] He explains that the appetite of the agent and the good are mutually implicating concepts because the good provides the term of the appetite as that in which the agent finds rest. Hence it is a natural necessity that the appetite desires whatsoever it desires, *sub ratione boni*.[6] The necessity of desiring the good is intrinsic to the nature of the will just as it is intrinsic to the nature of a triangle that its three angles be equal to two right angles.[7] Aquinas maintains, moreover, that this natural necessity is not repugnant to the will since the good is as a principle moving or drawing the appetite. Hobbes formulates the principle this way: "A necessity of nature maketh men to will and desire *bonum sibi*, that which is good for themselves, and to avoid that which is harmful."[8] Hobbes also calls this necessity of desiring good for oneself an "impulsion of nature, no less than that whereby a stone moves downward."[9] For Hobbes this necessity is neither repugnant to the will nor incompatible with uncertain outcomes for any particular agent.

If the *sub ratione boni* thesis is true, it follows that objects both beneficial and harmful are desired under the aspect of the good. It is not surprising, then, that Hobbes also retains the Aristotelian-Thomistic distinction between the merely apparent good and the genuine or real good. It is only by right judgment or the correct exercise of practical reason that one identifies beneficial or real goods and aligns one's desires accordingly. As Aquinas puts it:

> Not only is the good desirable, but even the apparent good [is desirable]. Since every enjoyment from the fact that it is an enjoyment, is a good. However much it is rendered bad by something added to it, an enjoyment is and is able to appear good, and as a consequence is able to be desired. But it is thus desirable to one not having right judgment; but to one having right judgments some enjoyments are not desirable. Accordingly, the prudent and temperate man does not desire intemperate enjoyments.[10]

Hobbes concurs that good is "divided into *real* and *apparent*."[11] The distinguishing features of actual goods are those objects that are on the whole good in the long run, while the merely apparently good are those that have evil annexed to them in the long run: "Whence it happens that inexperienced men that do not look closely enough at the long-term consequences of things, accept what appears to be good, not seeing the evil annexed to it; afterwards they experience damage."[12]

Yet, in the immediate sequel to the passage, Hobbes's own winnowing fork threshes with vigor: "Moreover, the greatest of good [*bonum maximum*] for each is his own preservation."[13] It is this good, what we might call the basic good of life, that Gert has identified as the primary goal of practical reason. In our discussion of the two postulates of human nature in chapters 1 and 2, we saw that, in the epistle dedicatory to *De Cive*, Hobbes indicates he is distinguishing between reason and cupidity in a way that reason is not, or need not be, a mere slave to the passions. Hobbes's two postulates of human nature, as nonabusive speech, correspond to two powers of human nature: cupidity and reason. Cupidity demands gain and private use of common things, while reason teaches man to flee violent death as the *summum malum*. Hobbes's formulation of reason's judgment is thus stated in terms of both a desirable good and an undesirable evil. The good of life and the evil of violent death are two sides of the same coin.

The basic goodness of life does not entail that the rational agent's goal is *merely* to stay alive—but it does mean that the criterion of distinguishing between real and apparent goods is whether the object or course of action would conduce to one's destruction, "that greatest of evils."[14] Aquinas, too, had identified life as basic. But, developing Aristotle's political animal anthropology, Aquinas formulated a hierarchical account of objective goods knowable by unaided reason, ascending from self-preservation to marriage and childrearing to life in society and the pursuit of truth, to which correspond the precepts of natural law.[15] These goods, Aquinas tells us, correspond to essential *inclinationes*. In his words:

> Since, however, good has the nature of an end, and evil, the nature of a contrary, hence it is that all those things to which man has a natural inclination, are naturally apprehended by reason as being good, and consequently as objects of pursuit, and their contraries as evil, and objects of avoidance. Wherefore according to the order of natural inclinations, is the order of the precepts of the natural law.[16]

There is debate among Thomists over what Aquinas means by this. Jacques Maritain has argued that the inclinations generate "connatural" knowledge of an object's goodness that is spontaneous and not conceptualized. Others have argued that the goods have to be cognized in some way, and they differ as to whether and to what extent theoretical knowledge of human nature is required to see an object as good. However, as Stephen Brock has pointed out, most interpreters have supposed that the inclinations are "pre-rational," such that reason's seeing the objects of the inclinations as good is posterior to the inclinations. I believe that Brock is correct to insist that Aquinas actually holds that the inclinations *follow* upon the operation of reason.[17] Indeed, Aquinas recognizes a range of subrational inclinations in human beings without denominating their objects as human goods. As Aquinas says in the same passage quoted above: "All the inclinations of any parts whatsoever of human nature, e.g., of the concupiscible and irascible parts, in so far as they are ruled by reason, belong to the natural law."[18] But this claim is compatible with the idea that moral knowledge comes entirely through a connatural grasp of genuine human goods, and the moral agent need not have a theoretical grasp of axiology in order flourish.

In other words, natural inclinations toward objects—including objects that are easily obtained and those obtained only with difficulty—may or may not correspond to genuine human goods. To put the issue in more familiar terms, someone might have a genetic predisposition to alcoholism. This "inclination" of the appetite to overindulge in that particular substance does not thereby render the object good. Hence, Aquinas's account of the human good stands or falls on whether, upon reflection, human reason really does apprehend life, marriage and childrearing, friendship and political life, and knowledge and religion as genuine and objectively desirable human goods. Hobbes believes that human reason grasps *life* as such a good. His comparison of human desire for the good of life to a stone's movement does not indicate an empirically false necessitarianism or monolithic psychology. It may suggest a Hobbesian version of connaturality in that all properly functioning agents intuitively grasp the goodness of life. Hobbes's break from tradition is to lop off the other goods from his axiology *qua objective*. Hobbes holds forth a thin theory of the good.

This is not to say that Hobbes rules out marriage or childrearing or friendship or knowledge or religion as "goods." He is saying that life has primacy of place in relation to other goods: "Of things held in propriety those that are dearest to a man are his own life and limbs; and in the next degree (in most men) those that concern conjugal affection; and after them riches and means of living."[19]

Why does Hobbes hold that man's bodily life and health is said to be the "dearest" good and the *bonum maximum* of man? Does its goodness lie only in its instrumentality to getting other things one wants? The good of life seems to answer to goodness in all three modes that Hobbes identifies: *pulchrum* (good in life's promise), *jucundum* (delightful or pleasing), and *utile* (profitable or useful).[20] Life is good in its promise and usefulness, necessary preconditions of felicity. But it is also delightful in itself. In *Leviathan* Hobbes identifies the *bonum jucundum* with what corroborates vital motion, and in *De Homine*, the pleasing good is said to be good *propter se*. How can Hobbes maintain this view when he also recognizes a range of acts that are destructive but can be pleasurable, such as drunkenness and other acts of intemperance? Here is where the virtue ethicist's interpretation of Hobbes is on target.[21]

Virtue, Habituation, and the Good

Hobbes defines "habit" in *De Corpore* as follows: "a motion made more and more easy and ready by custom; that is to say, perpetual endeavour, or by iterated endeavours in a way differing from that in which the motion proceeded from the beginning, and opposing such endeavours as resist."[22] Habit is a particular pattern of motion that is made easier by practice. Thus Hobbes's example of a beginner learning to play an instrument. A beginner pianist will not be able to move his hands with ease to strike the keys. Every note and stroke of the key will be a distinct endeavour of interrupted motion, over and over again, "till at the last, by doing this often, and by compounding many interrupted motions or endeavours into one equal endeavour, he be able to make his hand go readily on from stroke to stroke in that order and way which was at the first designed."[23] Once the motions proper to playing the piano have become easy and second nature, they have become *habitual*. This definition of a habit is broad enough to constitute a genus under which the several moral virtues can be grouped. Virtue in this understanding is broadly Aristotelian: it is a quality by which a thing performs its work well.

As David Boonin-Vail recounts, Hobbes develops his understanding of how habits function in the moral life in *De Homine*. When actions are new to a person, they "offend" when the nature of that person resists. But "more often than not [such actions] whet that same nature when repeated; and those things that are at first merely endured soon compel love."[24] Early in *De Homine*, Hobbes indicated that, through habituation, things previously displeasing can be rendered pleasing and vice versa.[25] Like Aristotle's virtuous person, the Hobbesian person of virtue takes pleasure in acting virtuously. This is how we should understand the *bonum jucundum* to be "helping and fortifying" in corroborating the actual good of human substances. A person whose character is formed by the virtues is one who takes pleasure in those acts and objects that Hobbesian moral science shows to be immutably and eternally constitutive of peace and life and/or permitted by it.

Aristotelian virtue is couched within a teleological conception of human nature that is imbued with purposiveness toward objects that fulfill man in virtue of the kind of thing he is. Hobbes accepts this *structural* account of virtue, but he differs from Aristotle in thinning out human teleology and the objective good knowable by unaided reason to conservation or the good of life (see chapter 1). Virtuous activity in Hobbes's view can be (and, for the just person, *is*) desirable in itself inasmuch as it is pleasurable. Yet being pleasurable is not sufficient for something to count as actually good or as an objective end in Hobbes's system. Hobbes gives the example of those who love wine because they have become accustomed to drink it from their youth. Such persons, if they lack the virtue of temperance, may indeed find it pleasurable to drink excessively, to the point of drunkenness. The criterion of actual good as an end thus cannot simply be felt pleasure in choosing an object. There must be some criterion of goodness that, strictly speaking, is independent of felt pleasure in order to know whether objects—pleasing and displeasing—ought to be desired or not. Like the pianist who plays with ease, the one well habituated practices the virtues with pleasure. Yet righteousness or justice in the broad sense is better described as *constitutive* of the Hobbesian person's happiness. The virtues are endlike in their pleasantness, but they also have the note of the *utile* in that they conduce to peace and therefore to one's conservation.

For his part, Boonin-Vail did not trouble to consider whether Hobbes might have a theory of virtue more in common with that of Thomas Aquinas than with Aristotle's, inasmuch as the former synthesizes an account of the moral virtues within a framework of divinely sourced natural law. (For Aquinas, the inclinations not only correspond to the precepts of natural law but are also the seedbed of the virtues.[26]) This was probably due to Boonin-Vail's acceptance of the practical severability thesis—that even if Hobbes was a sincere believer, God does not play an essential role in his theory. I shall say more on the legal character of Hobbes's theory in the next chapter. For the moment, it is notable that Boonin-Vail finally cannot show why persons are *obligated* to live virtuously—and that he drives a wedge between an ethics of virtue and an ethic of natural law, which is foreign to Hobbes's moral philosophy.

Let us return to the question: what makes life basically good? As I shall discuss in the next chapter, the ultimate explanation is God's ordained will, which assigns to each thing its proper motions, its telos. Reason grasps this as a basic reason for action, but it can also reflect on its goodness. Hobbes suggests that life is good in the mode of *jucundum* in that delight attaches to the very experience of having desires.[27] In other words, Hobbes seems to posit the view that the very *having of desires*, the substantial reality of being a desiring self, is itself the central aspect of the basic good of life. The virtues are constitutive of this good, inasmuch as the virtues are per se ordered toward the good of life. Moreover, I suggest that this is how we should understand why Hobbes describes the evil of the "terrible enemy of death" in terms of both loss of all power and great bodily pain. Death entails both the cessation of life's good in the modes of *pulchrum* and *utile* as the loss of minimum power to pursue the fulfillment of one's desires and in the mode of *jucundum* as cessation of a particular substantial reality of being a desiring self. The substantial reality of being a human substance—and thereby having the radical powers of reason and desire—is the fundamental *ratio* of the good of life.

In *De Homine*, Hobbes offers an extended discussion of various goods that answer to "good" in its various modes. Several goods are useful in that they foster security and protection, such as power, friendship, and wealth. Various fields of study, such as the arts, sciences, and letters, are also good in their usefulness for economic progress and commerce but can also be pleasing. Work is good in that it is more pleasing than idleness, and the aesthetic experiences of music, painting, and poetry are three different modes of the pleasing good of imitation. Wisdom is a good in all three modes as well: it is pleasing, useful, and pulchrum. Thus the good of philosophic contemplation comes closest to being a basic reason for action alongside life in Hobbes's axiology. Yet even wisdom is finally a good relative to individual subjective desire because, as Hobbes implicitly acknowledges in the same passage, some people are stupid and reckon it a good. Moreover, Hobbes closes his discussion with a reaffirmation that life's basic goodness consists in the substantial reality of being a desiring self, to which the enjoyment of all other things reckoned as good is subordinate:

> For of goods, the greatest is always progressing toward even further ends with the least hindrance. Even the enjoyment of a desire, when we are enjoying it, is an appetite, namely the motion of the

mind to enjoy by parts, the thing it is enjoying. For life is perpetual motion that, when it cannot progress in a straight line, is converted into circular motion.[28]

There are at least two important factors in Hobbes's rejection of the thick theory of the good. First, he thought that sociological dissensus in his time provided a window into the nature of man and therefore the true nature of the good. Second, he rejected the notion of happiness as a kind of rest. Let us consider each in turn.

Rejecting the Thick Theory of the Good

Hobbes was not convinced that reason really does grasp Aquinas's thicker account of the goods and the common good as objectively good. The first reason for this was Hobbes's firsthand experience of the effects of the breakdown of a rational consensus about the good life: Diverse persons differ in their judgment "of what is conformable or disagreeable to reason in the actions of common life."[29] The thought seems to be that if reason really does apprehend an Aristotelianlike account of the good life, why is there so much disagreement over how one ought to live? This is a familiar objection to the classical natural law picture of eudaimonia, one that Aristotle and Aquinas were aware of and one that has been voiced in the modern and postmodern traditions, from Locke to Alasdair MacIntyre. There is a complex historical-cultural story about how relative consensus about the good life in Aquinas's day evolved (or devolved) into relative dissensus is Hobbes's day. Doubtless there were factors gradually eroding whatever consensus obtained through the Renaissance, not least of which was the decline in the church's prestige and perceived moral authority due to a number of factors, including the Black Death and the profligacy of the papacy. Yet it is hard to underestimate the sociopolitical effects of the Reformation as a watershed event.

One of the chief rallying cries of Luther, Melancthon, Calvin, Zwingli, and the other Reformers was that the Bible was the sole rule of faith and that it ought to be shorn of mere human customs, traditions, and accretions that had obscured its meaning. But this emphatically did not mean that the patriarchs of Protestantism affirmed a right of private judgment. To the contrary, they explicitly affirmed that individual opinion—about the good, the true, the beautiful, indeed all things—must conform to scripture. As Luther put it in a treatise defending the real presence of Christ in the Eucharist, "This is not Christian teaching, when I bring an opinion to scripture and compel scripture to follow it, but rather, on the contrary, when I have first got straight what scripture teaches and then compel my opinion to accord with it."[30] Yet, as Brad Gregory documents, the Reformers immediately found themselves in heated disagreement about what the Bible actually taught about non-peripheral doctrines, such as the Lord's Supper and Baptism. William Chillingworth, with whom Hobbes spent time in the Great Tew circle in the 1630s, recognized this disagreement but denied that the various Lutheran and Reformed confessions constituted the "religion of Protestants." Rather, Chillingworth famously declared that "The *Bible*, I say, the *Bible* only, is the religion of Protestants! Whatever else they believe besides it, and the plain, irrefragable, indubitable consequences of it, well may they hold it as a matter of opinion."[31] Unfortunately, this declaration ultimately raises the question of proper interpretation anew: what counts as a "plain," "irrefragable," and "indubitable" deduction from scripture? Luther battled with the early Reformers over the doctrine of the real presence. Zwingli fought it out with the Anabaptists over infant baptism. The interlocutors in these debates sincerely believed their positions were plain deductions from scripture and were able to marshal an assortment of biblical proof texts. The historical evidence indicates that there never was a unified Protestant church that then fractured into various denominations. While it was entirely apart from the intentions and desires of the Reformers, the Protestant principle so passionately articulated by Chillingworth was itself the generative *cause* of exponential religious dissensus from the get-go, what Gregory calls a "pattern of fissiparous disagreement."[32]

The advance of Reformation principles and their consequences in England under Henry VIII, then their acceleration under Edward VI, Elizabeth, James I, and Charles I, provide the sociopolitical backdrop for Hobbes's observation that diverse men disagree over what is the reasonable way to live. The latter question and others like it—"What should I live for?," "What should I believe?," "What kind of person should I be?—are what Brad Gregory calls "Life Questions."³³ The Reformation has the sociological effect, apart from the intentions of its intellectual leaders, of generating deep dissensus with regard to how the Life Questions ought to be answered. Hobbes's report that diverse men disagree over what is a reasonable way to live—and indeed, that the same man at different times is in disagreement with himself about how to live—reflects this social fact. However, it would be incorrect to conclude that Hobbes is *merely* modeling the contingent seventeenth-century English man, as C. B. Macpherson argued.³⁴ Rather, Hobbes is making a paradoxical claim about human nature: it is somewhat malleable, inasmuch as appetites and aversions are shaped by "different tempers, customs, and doctrines of men."³⁵ Hobbes thus recognizes the great power of custom and education in shaping the passions or affections of people.³⁶ Custom may or may not be rational or informed by reason. For Hobbes, the six-hundred-year custom of the English people "unquestionably" taking the monarch for their sovereign is a reasonable custom.³⁷ Adherence to immaterialist scholasticism in the schools and what Coke called the "artificial reason" of the common law among lawyers are examples of unreasonable customs. While custom has the power to set people stubbornly in their ways, it is not so powerful that people can't set themselves against custom when they think it in their interest to do so. In the same passage in which Hobbes makes this point, he tells us that people are just as likely to set themselves against reason as in accord with it in pursuit of their interests (another implicit denial of the impotent thesis).³⁸ Thus Hobbes's philosophical anthropology leaves the door open to persuading people to adopt customs informed by the distillation of right reason taught in *Leviathan*.

It must be noted that Hobbes is not reasoning from the fact of disagreement over what is good and conformable to reason toward the conclusion that private appetite is therefore *the measure* of good and evil. At any rate, this would be an invalid inference, because it would conflate the *valued* with the *valuable*. On the contrary, such is the state of affairs that generates and defines war. While Hobbes was broadly within the Protestant tradition, he was keenly aware of the problems for civil peace that came from the rejection of religious authority. A central theme of *Behemoth*, in which Hobbes traces the causes of the English Civil War, is that the common English people were prey to contesting religious parties. Presbyterians, Catholics, Independents, Anabaptists, and "diverse other sects" became enemies of the king and "arose against his Majesty from the private interpretation of the Scripture."[39] Hobbes's answer to the central Life Question, intimated throughout his writings, is that which he finds rival sects rationally agree on: the good of life is basic to any reasonable plan of life.

Hobbes's strategy for arguing against religious warfare in *Leviathan* is twofold. First, he argues for a conception of the common good as security that is proximately grounded on the good that is practically reasonable for all sects (preservation). Second, Hobbes argues from the shared basis of Protestant religion, the Bible, for the unquestionable religious authority of the civil sovereign as the necessary curative for sectarian threats to the peace of the realm. Of course there remains the implicit problem of interpretation: why should Hobbes's private interpretation of scripture justifying an absolutist conception of civil sovereignty and an Erastian picture of church-state relations bind anyone else? This is a question always lurking in the background of Hobbes's controversies over his biblical interpretations, particularly with Bramhall. Yet, as to the key doctrine he wants to defend, civil sovereignty over religious doctrine, Hobbes repeatedly appeals to the Elizabethan and Stuart custom of maintaining regal sovereignty over the church, an instance in which he believes his rational interpretation of scripture is actualized in Anglican ecclesial structure. The nod to the power of custom to shape passions and beliefs is implicit when Hobbes expresses hope that *Leviathan* will "fall into the hands of a sovereign" and "convert this truth of speculation into the utility of practice"—which will, in part, be done by introducing *Leviathan* as required reading at universities, since "instruction of the people dependeth wholly on the right teaching of youth in the universities."[40] The learned will have the *science* and the proper rule of faith—the knowledge of the truth of morality and politics in terms of its first causes and right understanding of the scriptures—while those citizens who are unlearned in civil science and biblical scholarship will take as the rule of right and wrong what has been established as customarily so by the learned. Hobbes hopes his doctrines will trickle down from the sovereign and the schools to pulpits, parents, and pupils.

A second reason that Hobbes rejects the Aristotelian picture of happiness is his rejection of its picture of eudaimonism as a kind of contemplative rest: "Felicity of this life, consisteth not in the repose of a mind satisfied. For there is no such *Finis ultimus* (utmost aim) nor *Summum Bonum* (greatest good) as is spoken of in the books of the old moral philosophers."[41] This denial flows from one of his first principles: life is but motion. But a necessary condition for fulfillment is being alive. Therefore, happiness cannot be cessation of motion.

Hobbes is famous for this denial of the classical *summum bonum*. Interpreters have often taken this to be a denial of any objective ends *simpliciter*. But a closer reading indicates that nothing in this passage requires such an interpretation. Hobbes clearly qualifies his claims to be about felicity *in this life* and the *summum bonum as is spoken of in the books of old moral philosophers.* Indeed, in the very same chapter Hobbes speaks nonironically about the "unspeakable joys of heaven."[42] Moreover, in *Leviathan* a few chapters later, Hobbes argues that keeping covenant is a necessary condition for "gaining the secure and perpetual felicity of heaven," an argument that explicitly countenances the possibility of eternal felicity.[43] When he discusses this issue in *De Homine*, Hobbes again denies that a *summum bonum* is attainable "*in the present life.*"[44]

A clear-eyed reading of these passages indicates that Hobbes is not rejecting the existence of a final end per se. Rather these passages present a standard Christian view that perfect beatitude is not available in this life. So stated, Hobbes is actually in complete agreement with Aquinas.[45] Hobbes leaves it open as to whether some sort of ultimate fulfillment can come in the next life. He seems to have left open the possibility of eternal life as revealed in Christianity or the order of grace. Hobbes forestalls considering the claims of Christian revelation until parts III and IV of *Leviathan* because in the first two parts he is mostly concerned with reasoning on the basis of unaided reason. The point Hobbes is making in these passages is more limited: he is denying that unaided reason discovers Aristotelian eudaimonia, Aquinas's *beatitudo imperfecta*, or any form of the contemplative life as the objective content of temporal happiness. Accordingly, neither do these passages indicate an outright jettisoning of teleology from human substances. To recall a passage quoted in chapter 1, Hobbes writes:

> As *appetite* is the beginning of *animal* motion toward something which pleaseth us; so is the *attaining* thereof, the *end* of that

motion, which we also call the scope, and aim, and final cause of the same ... so that *bonum* and *finis* are different games, but for different considerations of the same thing.[46]

The necessity for Hobbesian men to will *bonum sibi* means that, necessarily, men seek happiness. We have just seen that the *objective* content of happiness discoverable by reason is not Thomistic imperfect beatitude. But, whatever felicity consists in, *not being dead* is the *sine qua non* of living a felicitous life. Therefore, reason judges *life* to be the primary good.

Hobbes, Synderesis, and Conscience

In this way I suggest that Hobbes's first postulate of human nature and the corresponding power, *rationis naturalis*, function to direct the agent to seek the good of life and avoid the evil of death. Recalibrated by the thin theory of the good, this operation of reason is Hobbes's functional equivalent of Aquinas's synderesis, or habit of first indemonstrable principles of moral reasoning.

While my account differs from his in various ways, Mark Hanin has recently offered a helpful discussion of the issues that finds some continuities with the Thomistic tradition.[47] For Aquinas, synderesis is a fundamental habit of first principles, and the most basic principle of practical reason is that good is to be done and evil is to be avoided. What this means is that human persons are ordered to the good in general, to their integral flourishing. This is "habitual" since, although reason grasps human goods and appoints the precepts of morality, one may or may not reflect upon the first principles as first principles.

Aquinas draws an analogy to the theoretical order, which is governed by the first principle of noncontradiction (PNC). Being is that which colors the theoretical order, and good is that which colors the practical order. By the power of reason *qua* its order to contemplation, we have an intuitive grasp of being and therefore PNC when we compose and divide, when we assert and deny. But we usually don't reflect on the PNC in mundane affirmations and negations. Similarly, by the power of reason *qua* its order to action we have an intuitive grasp of good as that which is fulfilling, completive, or perfective when we wish, desire, want, will, and the like. A thing cannot be and not be at the same time and in the same respect. The analogate to this principle governing all practical reasoning is that good is to be done and evil avoided because being stands to nonbeing as good stands to evil, which is a kind of negation or privation of what is actually good. Every knower has, minimally, a general and confused knowledge of being and goodness as governors of the theoretical and practical orders. Aquinas's claim is that there is an essential core of goods that is common to all human beings—goods including bodily life and health, family and childrearing, friendship (including civic friendship), knowledge, and religion (according one's will with God's)—in that they are desirable objects of pursuit for all persons. Synderesis is thus a habitual grasp of and ordering toward one's complete good, toward one's integral flourishing.

Discussions of synderesis were ample directly after Aquinas's classical expression. Yet, in the works of Scotus and Ockham, the discussion of synderesis is scant or entirely lacking.[48] Scotus's brief discussion indicates his acceptance of the Thomistic view of synderesis as a habit of the intellect. Ockham retains a view of conscience as an act of practical reason, but the concept of synderesis drops out of his account.[49] Luther, who was strongly influenced by Ockham, came to discard the concept of synderesis and enveloped the idea into his distinctive theory of conscience, which played such a central role in his theology.[50] As Michael Baylor recounts, for Luther conscience became "an autonomously functioning power or faculty of the soul rather than, as [in] the scholastics, the product or manifestation of one."[51] Its primary function became the judgment of one's salvation status. Yet Luther did acknowledge the existence of natural law and implicitly allowed conscience as a witness to its principles. Calvin also maintained that, even in the postlapsarian condition, conscience endures as a witness to natural law: "The law of God which we call moral, is nothing else than the testimony of natural law, and of that conscience which God has engraven on the minds of men."[52] As Stephen Grabill points out, Calvin retains the functional equivalent of synderesis as a natural knowledge of basic principles of morality that persists in the postlapsarian condition.[53]

Hobbes does not enter into scholastic debates over the relationship of synderesis to conscience, whether it is a power, habit, or act, whether it resides in the intellect or the will, and so on. It suffices for him to note in the margin of the chapter 15 *in foro interno* passage that "the Lawes of Nature oblige in Conscience alwayes." Accordingly, his postulate of human nature implies a root function of reason to grasp and incline human beings toward the (thin) goods of preservation and peace, as is evident in the definition of the law of nature and the fundamental law of nature. Preservation as the primary good in the practical order corresponds to the Hobbesian first truth of the theoretical, that *life is but motion*. Aquinas had held that the first precepts of natural law are at some level known to all, while secondary precepts may not be. Hobbes's differentiation of the most basic duties to preserve oneself and seek peace from the other laws of nature may suggest a similar distinction. Hobbes does not believe that all twenty-one of the laws of nature are held "habitually" by the reasoning agent. He remarks that "this may seem too subtle a deduction of the laws of nature, to be taken notice of by all men; whereof the most part are too busy in getting food, and the rest too negligent to understand." Still, he does go on to suggest that there is a habitual understanding of the immediate corollary of the first principle, "one easy sum, intelligible even to the meanest capacity, and that is *Do not that to another, which thou wouldest not have done to thyself*."[54]

In chapter 14 Hobbes had already suggested that the golden rule in its positive formulation is a deduction from the fundamental law of nature to seek peace. Putting these passages together, it looks as if by the faculty of reason, *in foro interno*, the reasoning agent has knowledge of at least these principles: to seek the good of life and shun the evil of death, to seek or endeavor peace, and to do unto others as one would have others do unto oneself. In the very act of creating man with reason, God gave these principles to him to provide a "rule for his actions."[55] A. E. Taylor missed this point in his discussion of the sense of the imperative as evidence of promulgation of the natural law.[56] Thus, "whatsoever any man doth against his conscience is a sin; for he who doth so, contemns the law."[57] As in Aquinas, an erring conscience binds; but those who act from an erring conscience are not blameless. For Hobbes, it is possible that "the conscience may be erroneous"—as indeed he believes it was in the minds of the rebels in the English Civil War—and this entails the need for a massive program of civic education ordered toward civil peace and guided by a true account of the natural law.[58]

The "Hobbesian moment" in the history of synderesis and conscience is not in jettisoning it as a divinely sourced universal and certain rational guardian in the moral life. It is, rather, in thinning the moral good to bodily life and health and attaching to the pursuit of this good the corollary practical necessities of willing peace and reciprocity. Moreover, my account suggests that Hobbes is more scholastic in spirit inasmuch as he believes more weight can be placed upon reason and natural law than Luther and Calvin thought they could bear.

Hobbes's account of the good of life and the evil of death provides the grounds of what I call Hobbes's *felicity pluralism*.[59] Hobbes's felicity pluralism is widely inclusive of many diverse life plans as long as they are reasonable—and the fundamental requirement of practical reasonableness in the pursuit of felicity is to take the good of life and the evil of death as basic. Only peaceful life plans will count as exercising the "harmless liberty" that the sovereign is bound to protect. Another way to put the point is this: when an agent takes on some (reasonable) end or conception of happiness, a number of practical necessities (the laws of nature) ensue that forbid him from doing that which is destructive of his life or which takes away the means of preserving his life, because being alive is a necessary constituent of pursuing felicity. Hobbes agrees with Aquinas, moreover, that these practical necessities will only have the force of counsel unless they are commanded by God—only then do they bind as *laws* of nature.[60] With this sketch of Hobbes's axiology in hand, we can turn to a number of important objections.

Objections and Replies

How is such an interpretation of Hobbes's doctrine of the good compatible with his texts that suggest the radical subjectivity of the good? Consider Hobbes's claims in his well-known passage accompanied by the side note "Good. Evil.":

> But whatsoever is the object of any man's appetite or desire that is it which he for his part calleth *good*; and the object of his hate

and aversion, *evil*; and of his contempt, *vile* and *inconsiderable*. For these words of good, evil, and contemptible are ever used with relation to the person that useth them, there being nothing simply and absolutely so, nor any common rule of good and evil to be taken from the nature of the objects themselves, but from the person of the man (where there is no commonwealth) or (in a commonwealth) from the person that representeth it, or from an arbitrator or judge whom men disagreeing shall by consent set up, and make his sentence the rule thereof.[61]

A common interpretation of this and similar passages is that Hobbes is a value subjectivist. That is, he believes the valuable or the good is nothing other than what one personally or subjectively desires. For example, commenting on this passage, David Gauthier writes:

Where the contemporary value subjectivist says that utility is the measure of individual preference, Hobbes says rather that "private Appetite is the measure of Good, and Evill" (L 15), thus exchanging measure and measured. But it is evident that both treat value as dependent on choice or appetite.[62]

For Gauthier's Hobbes, good is synonymous with "desired by me" or "desired by the agent."[63] But a closer reading suggests that Gauthier's interpretation is too quickly arrived at and ultimately incorrect. The object of some individual's appetite is that which, *for his part*, he calls good. Hobbes is claiming nothing more than that the common way people speak is to "call good" what they in fact desire. So far, Hobbes has not denied that there are objects that are *actually* good. Still, doesn't Hobbes deny that there are any objects that are actually good in the immediate sequel when he claims that the word "good" is "ever used with relation to the person that useth them, there being nothing simply and absolutely so," and that there is no "common rule" of the good in the object itself?[64] If we read these passages in light of what Hobbes is and is not rejecting in the Aristotelian tradition, a more nuanced interpretation presents itself.

Once we see that Hobbes has not adopted the impotent thesis, it becomes clear that his claim that nothing is simply or absolutely good need imply only that there is no actually good object that is not *in fact* being desired. I suggest that Hobbes is trying to express a point that one influential Aristotelian philosopher of the twentieth century (and an admirer of Hobbes), Peter Geach, made. Geach argued that "there is no such thing as being just good or bad, there is only being a good or bad so and so."[65] Geach argued for the point by reflecting on how we talk about "good." In the common way we speak about objects, good is an attributive adjective—it "sticks" to the noun that it modifies, as in "x is a good car." In contrast with the proposition that "x is a red car," the former proposition does not split up into "x is good" and "x is a car." Whereas I can see that the distant object is red and my color-blind friend can see that it is a car, "there is no such possibility of ascertaining that a thing is a good car by pooling independent information that it is good and that it is a car." Similarly, Hobbes is reflecting on the way people talk about good. He is saying that to claim that some object or state of affairs is *good* cannot be said simply independent of the object's relation to human desire. So when an agent says, "That car is good," the agent is typically saying something relative to his or her purposes—for example, it is good *for* transporting me to work or good *for* driving the kids to soccer practice or good *for* off-roading, and so on. In these examples, the agent's purposes align implicitly with what the car was designed to do, that is, locomote.

But, consider a case in which the agent's purposes do not align with a car's locomotive purpose. In 1974 the art design group Ant Farm searched for cars that were "good," picked out ten Cadillacs, and proceeded to create Cadillac Ranch in Amarillo, Texas.[66] By calling each of the chosen cars "good," they were not referring to "goodness" in the sense of fulfilling its designed purpose of locomotion. In fact, many were chosen from junkyards. Rather, each was "good" in that it was fit to be buried hood first in a straight line, at about a 50 degree angle, in imitation of the Great Pyramid of Giza, which was the purpose of the artists. Hobbes wants a notion of good that is supple enough to capture examples like this—but does not deny that (1) there is an inbuilt purpose to the human organism or (2) the good of life is basic, and appetite may or may not align with this goal. Thus Lloyd seems correct that Hobbes's peculiar way of speaking does not undermine the objectivity of the good, even if it makes it rather opaque.[67] In short, Hobbes does not maintain that "good" is just synonymous with "desired by the agent." The power of reason to grasp the good of life as basic still seems to be a better interpretation.[68]

The diversity of tastes in the agent does not negate the basicality of the good of life. In *Leviathan* Hobbes first broaches the topic of the good in chapter 6 in the context of his differentiation between vital and animal motion (a full eight chapters before he formulates the laws of nature). The smallest beginnings of animal motion or "voluntary motion, as to go, to speak, to move any of our limbs" is endeavor. Endeavor considered as stretching out toward "something which causes it" is called appetite.[69] In Latin, *appetitus* is a compound of *ad* (toward) and *petere* (to aim at or desire). The "something which causes" appetite thus has a sort of magnetic pull on the Hobbesian agent. Of those objects that draw the appetite, only "some are born with men" as appetites for food, excretion, exoneration, "and some other appetites, not many."[70] But notice that the natural appetites common to all men—for food, excretion, and exoneration—logically presuppose the natural purpose *to live*.

Again, beyond the good of life, objects that draw the appetite are widely diverse. The reasons Hobbes gives for this can be divided into two different types: biological and cultural. Under the first, Hobbes notes the material flux both of the body and of various temperaments.[71] He tries to strengthen this reason on the basis of his materialist metaphysics, suggesting that our bodies are in constant flux and therefore constant mutation. I have already discussed the cultural reasons for diversity of appetite. The cultural reason Hobbes is most interested in are the effects of custom and doctrine—presumably including civil and religious law. Which objects will draw one's appetite at any given time will depend on the variables of one's bodily makeup, the civil and religious customs in which one was reared, and one's experiences of tasting and trying.

But nothing here has undermined right reason's grasp of the intrinsic desirability of life. Being alive is intrinsically desirable, in the three modes of the good, as the necessary precondition for having and seeking to fulfill any desires at all and the delightful condition of *experiencing desire*. Hence Hobbes can maintain that conservation of one's life is identified by reason as the *bonum maximum*, to which the desires of any particular agent may or may not conform.[72] The natural necessity or impulsion of nature is compatible with uncertain outcomes in the case of any particular agent. Hence Hobbes also distinguishes between the apparent and the actual good. That is, the merely apparently good is that which, while perhaps conducing to some immediate benefit, is annexed to evil in the long run, while the really good is that which is, on the whole, good. *Pace* Michael Oakeshott, the actual good has a *moral* connotation.[73]

One might object: fine, the good of life is basic in the three modes of the good—but that need not imply that *reason* grasps the goal of self-preservation as desirable. It might just be the case that, inasmuch as contingent desires seek different objects, desire always sets life as a necessary proximate end, since life is a necessary precondition for attaining the object. The following passage might be cited in support:

> For the thoughts are to the desires as scouts and spies, to range abroad and find the way to the things desired; all steadiness of the mind's motion, and all quickness of the same, proceeding from thence; for . . . to have no desire is to be dead.[74]

The first point to be noted about this passage is that it doesn't seem concerned primarily with claiming that reason is and only can be a slave to the passions. Rather it appears in the context of Hobbes's arguing that a man who does not have great passions for riches, knowledge, or honor cannot have "great fancy or much judgment," since Hobbes had defined "good fancy" as insight into the likenesses of things and "good judgment" as distinguishing, discerning, and judging well of things.[75] The immediate context of the passage suggests that Hobbes is primarily thinking of objects like riches, honor, or knowledge—objects of desire for which reason judges of the means. In my interpretation, the goodness of riches, honor, and knowledge *are* subjective when the agent judges on the basis of unaided reason. Hence this passage presents no special difficulty for my interpretation.

Moreover, Hobbes's use of the image of a spy does not necessarily support the impotent thesis's claim that reason is a *slave* of the passions. Hobbes understands a spy to be someone who carries out the will of a sovereign in secretly collecting information on his behalf.[76] But a spy is not an *enslaved instrument* of his sovereign's will. The spy *concurs with* the will of his sovereign. Hobbes suggests that a spy's concurrence is not merely instrumental, as a hammer is to a craftsman. Rather the spy's concurrence is personal, which is to say intentional, since a spy who gets caught can be justly put to death, and culpable crimes are intentional.[77] So while this image suggests that the desire has a sort of sovereignty regarding *riches*, *honor*, or *knowledge*—suggesting diversity of desire regarding such objects necessitates a felicity pluralism—it does not entail reason's impotence to concur or not in the end sought. This is important because, if I am right that Hobbes does not adopt the impotent thesis, reason can tame the passions in line with its own goal of preservation. The desire for riches, honor, or knowledge at the wrong place, the wrong time, in the wrong respect, or to the wrong degree may be incompatible with the goal of preservation. Various virtues picked out by the laws of nature (dictates of reason) are supposed to tame the passions to seek the subjective goods in the right way, that is, the way that is compatible with the common good of security and one's own preservation. When riches, honor, and knowledge are desired and pursued according to the limits of reasonable actions imposed by the virtues, reason concurs as to their goodness.

But suppose it were conceded that the spy image is intended to communicate the notion of a mere instrument or a slave. Even then, nothing in the passage we are considering constitutes a defeater of my thesis. For it is conceivable that reason could at once function to grasp the basic good of life and as a mere instrument to desires for specific goods under the genera of riches, honor, and knowledge.

My interpretation would also help make sense of Hobbes's remarks in the review and conclusion (R&C) of *Leviathan*. There he considers afresh whether human nature is fit for civil duty. Hobbes wonders whether the "severity of judgment" is compatible with the "celerity of fancy," because the former makes men censorious and the latter makes them unable to distinguish right from wrong. Hobbes connects judgment to the "faculty of reasoning," without which sentences would be unjust, and he connects fancy with eloquence, without which "the effect of reason will be little."[78] Hobbes then strengthens the connection between judgment and reason when he aligns judgment with truth while aligning fancy with the opinions and passions of men, which are contingent and potentially false:

> But these are contrary faculties: the former being grounded upon principles of truth; the other upon opinions already received (true or false) and upon the passions and interests of men (which are different and mutable).[79]

Hobbes then points out that judgment and fancy "may have place in the same man—but by turns."[80] The claim seems to presuppose that the faculty of reason is of sufficient dignity that it can have pride of place in man and can tame passion in accord with its dictates. Hobbes here sheds light on how he understands his whole project in *Leviathan*: it is a piece of right reasoning about the true grounds for and character of civil duty, stated so eloquently that it can't fail to capture the hearts and imaginations—the passions—of his countrymen. Reason cloaked in eloquence has the power to educate passion:

> For all men are by nature provided of notable multiplying glasses (that is their passions and self-love), through which every little payment appeareth a great grievance, but are destitute of those prospective glasses (namely moral and civil science), to see afar off the miseries that hang over them, and cannot without such payments be avoided.[81]

The Argument from Madness

My interpretation makes the best sense out of Hobbes's account of madness, in a way that even Bernard Gert, who enlists it in his rejection of the impotent thesis, does not. Whereas Gert suggests that by "madness" Hobbes means the equivalent of what we would call "mental disorders," this explanation seems too restrictive. We don't necessarily call someone "mentally disordered" who is habitually intemperate, but Hobbes does call such people "mad."

Hobbes defines "madness" as a sort of vehemency of passions. The vehemency of the passions and the ill constitution of the bodily organs are interdefined:

Whereof there be almost as many kinds [of madness] as of the passions themselves. Sometimes the extraordinary and extravagant passion proceedeth from the evil constitution of the organs of the body or harm done them; and sometimes the hurt and indisposition of the organs is caused by the vehemence or long continuance of the passion. But in both cases the madness is of one and the same nature.[82]

An example of passion vehemence that Hobbes gives is what is observed in the bodies and behavior of drunk people. Again Hobbes points out that the passions of drunk persons proceed from "evil disposition" of the bodily organs. Drunkenness puts on display a smorgasbord of passions wholly ungoverned by reason, which is madness. It is fitting to quote the whole passage, as these passages are not often cited and analyzed in the Hobbes literature:

For the variety of behaviour in men that have drunk too much is the same with that of madmen: some of them raging, others loving, others laughing, all extravagantly, but according to their several domineering passions; for the effect of the wine does but remove dissimulation, and take from them the sight of the deformity of their passions. For (I believe) the most sober men, when they walk alone without care and employment of the mind, would be unwilling the vanity and extravagance of their thoughts at that time should be publicly seen; which is a confession that passions unguided are for the most part mere madness.[83]

Gert enlists that last line, stating that unguided passions are "mere madness," to great effect. He is correct that Hobbes's notion of madness indicates that reason must set limits to what can be the content or aim of the passions. If it did not, habits and mental disorders that generate desires to perform self-destructive actions could be called rational. If it did not, the sober decision to get drunk could be considered rational in instrumentalist terms if the potential drunkard had some deeply felt desire he wanted to fulfill but his inhibitions prevented him from acting to fulfill it, and drunkenness might provide the most fitting or only available means. Upon such reasoning in an entirely plausible scenario, the drunkard would act rationally, contrary to what Hobbes explicitly says.

So far, Gert and I are mostly in agreement. However, I don't think Gert's acceptance of the practical severability thesis can ultimately make sense of what Hobbes is saying here. While Gert sees no reason to doubt Hobbes's theological sincerity, he contends that God plays "no essential role" in his philosophy.[84] But if God plays no essential role, God's existence, creation, and ordering of the world are not essential presuppositions to Hobbes's account of madness. What, then, is the Hobbesian warrant for calling some dispositions of the bodily organs "evil"? As noted in the previous chapter, evil is a breach of law, according to Hobbes. What is the law that governs the operations of the organs? Can it be anything other than the order willed by God in artificing man, in Hobbes's terms? In other words, can it be anything other than the "common laws of their creation" that bind all men as one of the species of natural obligation?[85] It certainly cannot be a normative standard set by Platonic Ideas or Aristotelian substantial forms. The order of the body prior to our thought and will is apparent in the way people in the medical profession speak about the human body. The function of the heart is to pump blood. The function of the lungs is to oxygenate the blood. The function of the liver is to clean the blood. And so on. A *good* heart is one that performs its function well, one that operates according to the purpose for which it was made. An evil heart is one that performs its function poorly, against the purpose for which it was made. It is not enough to say that there is no is-ought gap in Hobbes's thought. It is essential to this account that the nonrational order in man have something of the measure of law, inasmuch as man was made and ordered by a being with the right to make and order him.

Hobbes indicates that the organs are functioning properly when a person's desires are regulated by reason's judgment of the goodness of life and the evil of death. Organs not so functioning are of an "evil constitution." The prior evil constitution of the organs generates passions against the order of reason, and the causal arrow can go the other way; that is, repeated acts based on passions inclining one against the order of reason can be the cause of evil constitution in the organs. The point about organ function can be illuminated by what we know today about the human brain. The ventral tegmental area (VTA), also referred to as the "reward system," is located in the midbrain.[86] When it is activated it releases dopamine to other regions in the brain, which is thought to alert the cortex that something important is happening that requires focus. The subsequent neural activity is thought to underlie the feeling of pleasure. Many addictive drugs trigger the release of dopamine, causing the "high" that is sought in future ingestions of the substance.

Taking Hobbes's example, modern science illuminates how people with an ill-constituted reward system in their brains are at greater risk of alcoholism. Recent cutting-edge research indicates that those predisposed toward alcoholism have an abnormally higher brain dopamine response to the consumption of alcohol than do those not so predisposed.[87] Since there is a strong correlation between increased dopamine release and reward-seeking behavior, persons with this condition are much more likely to seek another drink, then another and another. This provides an explanation for why some people are predisposed toward alcoholism: their brains are not functioning properly, inasmuch as dopamine release in the VTA is imbalanced. It is not hard to imagine how the causal arrow could go the other way as well, given what we know about the plasticity of the brain.[88] The repeated ingestion of alcohol (and other intoxicating substances) can forge new neural pathways and circuits in the brain, altering the matter such that the associated pleasure can be triggered only by ingesting alcohol (or the intoxicating substance). In this way, one's own actions can change one's organic dispositions from "good" to "evil" in the sense of functional to dysfunctional. In the practical severability thesis, there is no Hobbesian warrant for the good-evil terminology to refer to organ disposition. But the theistic interpretation can make sense of this, because it takes seriously Hobbes's claim that the proper motions of our irrational parts constitute the "common laws" of our creation.[89] The next chapter will elaborate on how the "common laws" are grounded in God's power.

When these patterns of motion become entrenched (Hobbesian habits), they can properly be called diseases, according to the American Society of Addiction Medicine's (ASAM's) definition of "addiction" as

> a *primary, chronic disease of brain reward, motivation, memory and related circuitry*. Dysfunction in these circuits leads to characteristic *biological, psychological, social and spiritual manifestations*. This

is reflected in an individual *pathologically pursuing reward and/or relief* by substance use and other behaviors.[90]

Inasmuch as consumption of alcohol (and other intoxicating substances) renders one unable to reason properly, it is an act of intemperance and forbidden by the dictate of reason or natural law. Modern science thus indicates that Hobbes's insight into vehement passion and organ dysfunction was fundamentally sound. Moreover, it completes the story in a way that Hobbes would accept, since addictions to intoxicating substances are the sorts of diseases of the body, accompanied by vehemence of passion, that Hobbes would classify as species of "madness." While addictions are obviously destructive of one's bodily health and integrity, today we do not use the term "madness" as a genus for different species of addiction. Still, the point here is not to quibble over semantics but simply to point out that Hobbes's account of madness as vehemence of passions/organic dysfunction is strong evidence against the impotent thesis. The dispositions of the organs are evil and the acts they incline one toward are evil when they are contrary to the proper order of the body and reason, which have a lawlike and a legal character, respectively. This is how terms such as "diseased," "dysfunctional," "healthy," "functional," and their cognates are, in Hobbesian philosophy, normative concepts. The rational necessity to pursue the good of life provides the objective criterion by which to judge whether organs and systems, such as the VTA, are functioning properly or dysfunctional.

One might object at this point that the argument unduly emphasizes the virtue of temperance, which Hobbes arguably downgrades in importance, placing it at the end of his catalogue of virtues in *Leviathan*, and which he declines to discuss at length as being not "pertinent enough in this place."[91] Let us set aside, *arguendo*, the influence of intoxicating substances and consider a hypothetical *sober* person who desires death. I take this hypothetical to be a *reductio ad absurdum* against the impotent thesis because, supposing the complete enslavement of reason to the passions, such a person is rational as long as he calculates fitting means to achieve his end. But according to Jean Hampton, whose earlier interpretation of Hobbes attributed to him the impotent thesis, "little or nothing" can be called rational in a death-desiring person. Why not? If reason is a slave to the passions, a person's rationality will turn on whether he can connect a universal premise with a particular premise in a practical syllogism. We can take Hampton's own example. Suppose a human being tries to drown himself because he desires death. And he does not have any "higher-order desire" to be alive. He reasons thus:

Death is good.
This maelstrom is death-causing.
I will enter the maelstrom.

Such a person is completely rational according to the impotent thesis. Hampton tries to escape the entailment by arguing that death-seekers are diseased, the subjects of some biological error or misfiring. She argues that such people have a damaged "desire-formation mechanism"—a "completely noncognitive biological 'error' in the process of forming a desire."[92] The desires in such a person are "wrong." Calling them "wrong," Hampton suggests, is a criticism of the desire but not a moral evaluation. I maintain that this argument is confused.

If the desire is not *morally* wrong, the "diseased" formulation has absolutely no normative punch at all, since the normative is morally charged. In that case my argument holds that the death-desirer is completely rational. If, on the other hand, the "diseased" formulation *is* supposed to have a normative punch, the problem of normativity remains: what is the criterion for distinguishing what counts as normatively valuable (biologically healthy and well-functioning) and normatively disvaluable (biologically diseased and malfunctioning)? *It cannot be contingently felt desires*. Mere desires cannot tell us *which* desires the body ought to produce, according to the impotent thesis. My interpretation can answer the normative question just where Hampton's cannot. The judgment of reason that the good of life is basic and objectively good can tell us which bodily conditions are healthy and which are diseased.[93]

Hampton rejects the view that Hobbesian reason is capable of grasping its own ends because of its Aristotelian overtones: "The constant disparaging of Aristotelian ethics in Hobbes's writings shows that he didn't intend an Aristotelian theory."[94] It is of course true that Hobbes is critical of Aristotle. But it isn't correct that Hobbes "constantly" disparages Aristotle's *ethics*. Hobbes directly addresses Aristotle's ethics only a few times in his writings. In *Leviathan* he remarks that Aristotelian ethics agrees with his own in acknowledging some of "the same virtues and vices."[95] However, he notes, Aristotelian ethics differs in basing the goodness of the virtues on the "mediocrity of the passions."[96] At one point in *Behemoth*, there is a short discussion about Aristotle's ethics per se in which "A" says that the doctrine of Aristotle has not done any good, having only generated disputes about virtue and vice. Hobbes here interprets Aristotle to be saying that the goodness of virtue consists only partly in the mediocrity of the passions and partly in the fact that they are praised. The first point to be made is that, on the basis of these remarks, Hobbes either deliberately misconstrues or belies a misunderstanding of Aristotle's teaching.[97] For Aristotle a virtue is good neither *because* of the mean it aims at between two passions nor *because* it is praised. Rather, for Aristotle (and Aquinas) the goodness of a virtue is due to its disposing an agent toward its proper function or good as determined by the kind of thing it is. One of the *effects* of possessing a virtue is that a person performs actions within the golden mean because actions outside of the mean are defective in reference to authentic human fulfillment. Similarly, praise of the virtues is an effect of their praiseworthiness, not the other way around.

Still, it is notable that in Hampton's later work she came to acknowledge that "the long shadow of Aristotle is cast upon Hobbes."[98] Hampton seemed to recognize that Hobbes was not able to build up a theory of *morality* on a purely naturalistic basis if "nature" is taken to be an aggregate of nonmoral facts about the world. She ingeniously argued that even the neo-Hobbesian theorists such as Kavka and Gauthier, who want to construct a moral theory in terms of prudential rules to satisfy preferences, cannot do what a moral theory is supposed to do—namely, *evaluate* action—without smuggling in a normative conception of rationality. To tell someone who wants some object A that the practically necessary means to achieve A is to do B, is to hold forth a criterion of right reason. Suppose the person fully understands the means-end connection but maintains that he doesn't desire to do B. As Hampton puts it, drawing upon Bernard Williams's distinction between internal and external reasons, the agent refuses to take this instrumental reason to be an internal reason. The neo-Hobbesian can reply, "Well, it *ought* to be an internal reason" only at the price of introducing an authoritative conception of reason, a normative standard of instrumental rationality. And this is to make an appeal to something outside of or irreducible to subjective desire. The best a sheer instrumentalist view of reason can do is to offer a purely *descriptive* moral theory in which human action is "rational" or "irrational" depending on whether the means chosen fit the preferred end desired, full stop. But, as Hampton points out, such would be a moral theory without prescription and therefore no moral theory at all.

In sum, for Hobbes "mad" persons include those with irrational passions and/or bodily dysfunctions when they overrule the judgment of right reason. Vehemence connotes "long continuance" of the passion, but it is not merely that. After all, the person who fears a violent death his whole life is not a madman. Such passions are intense and long-enduring passions that incline persons to actions *against the order of reason*. The criterion for the reasonableness of the passions is whether they incline one toward actions compatible with self-preservation and the common good of security or not. The passions, when not checked and governed by reason, have the potential to lead individuals and society to destruction. This is compatible with Hobbes's attempt to enlist some passions that incline men to peace.[99]

There are three more objections to my interpretation of Hobbes's axiology. Inasmuch as my account suggests that life is the basic good and that taking life as good is a requirement of practical reasonableness, it must explain a range of Hobbes's doctrines that might appear to be in tension with such an account. First, it is alleged that my account cannot explain transcendent interests in Hobbesian philosophical anthropology, for which Hobbesian persons might rationally lay down their lives. Second, it is alleged that it can't give an account of the twenty-first law of nature, which requires the sacrifice of civil service. And third, it is alleged that it cannot account for what Hobbes says about suicide.[100]

Transcendent Interests, the Twenty-First Law of Nature, and Suicide

Lloyd advances a couple of Hobbes's texts in which he seems to declare the "rationality of our concern for our eternal over our merely temporal prospects":[101]

> If the command be such as cannot be obeyed, without being damned to eternal death; then it were madness to obey it [*L*, 43.2, 398].

> Eternal life is a greater reward than the life present; and eternal torment a greater punishment than the death of nature [*L*, 38.1, 301].

Lloyd contends that an interpretation of Hobbesian practical reason as judging the good of life to be basic cannot account for *transcendent* interests, for which Hobbesian agents might be willing to lay down their lives. On the basis of these and other passages, Johan Olsthoorn powerfully argues that the *summum malum* for Hobbes is not violent death but the loss of eternal life.[102]

But notice that these texts of Hobbes (as well as those that Olsthoorn summons) come in part III of *Leviathan*, in which Hobbes begins consideration of the claims of Christian revelation. Unaided natural reason knows nothing of eternal beatitude: "There is no natural knowledge of man's estate after death."[103] These passages, then, would only seem to support the loss of eternal life as the *summum malum*, supposing the truth of Christian revelation.

As was seen in chapter 2, Hobbes declares that the claims of Christian revelation do not conflict with or annul the dictates of natural reason. He explains that parts I and II of *Leviathan* "derived the rights of sovereign power, and the duty of subjects hitherto, from the principles of nature only," while parts III and IV handle "the nature and rights of a Christian Commonwealth, whereof there dependeth much upon supernatural revelations of the will of God."[104] Hobbes then proclaims that reason and faith are harmonious:

> Nevertheless, we are not to renounce our senses and experience, nor (that which is the undoubted word of God) our natural reason. For they are the talents which he hath put into our hands to negotiate till the coming again of our blessed Saviour; and therefore not to be folded up in the napkin of an implicit faith, but employed in the purchase of justice, peace, and true religion. For though there be many things in God's word above reason (that is to say, which cannot by natural reason be either demonstrated or confuted), yet there is nothing contrary to it; but when it seemeth so, the fault is either in our unskillful interpretation or erroneous ratiocination.[105]

Hobbes indicates that revelation does not contradict reason—and this claim would seem to entail the principle that the order of grace does not destroy nature. Hence, if my interpretation is correct—that in the order of nature, the basic goodness of conservation of one's life is discovered by Hobbesian practical reason—we would expect that the claims of Christian revelation would not contradict this claim. In fact, we find that Hobbes's interpretations of Christianity's promise of eternal life and its requirements to witness to Christ do not annul the fundamental good of life.

Grace builds on nature in the Hobbesian theory of eternal life. For Hobbes, the eternal life made possible by faith in the mystery of Christ's passion comes through God's grace alone—it is a free gift that cannot be earned.[106] Grace thus makes available a good that men naturally desire—that is, the good of everlasting vital and voluntary motion—though they could not have known it was possible by unaided reason. But the possibility of eternal life turns on its compatibility with unaided reason's judgment—and unaided reason judges that "life itself is but motion."[107] Hence Hobbes rejects Aquinas's doctrine of eternity as a *nunc stans*.[108] Since corporeity is the touchstone of all being and instantaneous motion of body is impossible—and since eternal *life* is a state of activity—eternity must be an everlasting succession of moments. Seen in this light, the passages Lloyd and Olsthoorn advance do not annul the basic good of life; the knowledge made available by grace *enlarges* the agent's notion of that good to countenance an eternal possibility.

Furthermore, Hobbes pursues a number of strategies to minimize the occasions on which Christianity would actually require giving up one's life, including interpreting the story of Naaman to permit a Christian to bow to idols while believing in the true God in their hearts when "he is desirous to save himself from death or from a miserable life."[109] However, the promise of eternal life for those who die for Christ's sake would make martyrdom reasonable. "For an unlearned man that is in the power of an idolatrous king or state, if, commanded on pain of death to worship before an idol, he detesteth the idol in his heart, he doth well (though if he had the fortitude to suffer death, rather than worship it, he should do better)."[110] Notice that these will be cases of Christians witnessing under non-Christian governments.

Still, Hobbes is concerned to undercut contemporary Catholic claims to martyrdom since they threaten the security of the realm:

"For he that can allure foreign subjects with so great a reward, may bring those who are greedy of such glory, to dare and do anything."[111] Hobbes undercuts Catholic claims by attributing only to direct witnesses of Christ the status of martyr in the first degree while attributing second-degree martyrdom only to those who die bearing witness to the article that *Jesus is the Christ*. Hobbes maintains that to die for any further Christian tenet is to die for some opinion that most likely serves the profit or ambition of clergymen. Hence, such are not authentic transcendent interests because they are not required by faith in Christ. The suggestion seems to be that the Catholics put to death by the Tudors and the Stuarts—Thomas More, John Fisher, and Edmund Campion being the most famous—were not martyrs because they were not being asked to deny that Jesus was the Christ.

According to Hobbes, only the transcendent interests of Christianity so understood can rationally motivate because Christianity is unique in introducing authentic transcendent interests. For Hobbes, Jesus alone spoke truly in his claim to be Christ.[112] Whatever interests were introduced by the founders of pagan religions were only putatively transcendent. In reality pagans deployed "pretended revelation" and "innumerable other superstitious ways of divination" to secure temporal order:

> And therefore the first founders and legislators of commonwealths among the Gentiles, whose ends were only to keep the people in obedience and peace, have in all places taken care: first, to imprint in their minds a belief that those precepts which they gave concerning religion might not be thought to proceed from their own device, but from the dictates of some god or other spirit (or else that they themselves were of a higher nature than mere mortals, that their laws might the more easily be received).[113]

So when Hobbes tells us in *Behemoth* that some Ethiopian kings used to obey when priests pretending to have divine authority commanded them to commit suicide, the explanation of their obedience that he gives is that the kings' reason was "mastered by superstition."[114] By Hobbes's lights, their suicides were irrational and unreasonable. Hence this and other pagan examples of "transcendent interests" that

Lloyd advances do not count as evidence against the primary goodness of life in Hobbes's thought. This includes the pagan interest in posthumous glory.

Hobbes mentions the Roman Decii as an example of dying for glory: "For what was it but an honourable name with posterity which the Decii and other Romans sought after, and a thousand others who cast themselves upon incredible perils?"[115] As Hobbes puts it elsewhere, the "good to themselves" was a "good fame after death."[116] But the case of the Decii is an instance of vainglory in Hobbes's terms. For Hobbes, the exultation of the mind called glorying is properly confidence when "based upon the experience of [one's] *former* actions."[117] But when it is "only supposed by himself, for delight in the *consequences of it*, it is called Vain-Glory."[118] While the Decii may have enjoyed a measure of confidence while alive, Hobbes is suggesting that their acts of casting themselves upon incredible perils were due to their vainglorious delight in the thought of the fame that their names did not yet have but that they imagined would accrue to their names as a consequence of their deaths.

Nor can we say in Hobbes's terms that the Decii had a transcendent interest in the afterlife. We have seen that in the order of nature there is no knowledge of the afterlife. Hobbes sharpens the point when he maintains, against Aquinas and on the authority of the Bible, that there is also no knowledge of an immortal soul: "That the soul of man is in its own nature eternal, and a living creature independent on the body, or that any mere man is immortal otherwise than by the resurrection in the last day (except Enoch [Hebrews 11:5] and Elijah [2 Kings 2:11]) is a doctrine not apparent in Scripture."[119] To hold such a view, says Hobbes, is to be deceived by Aristotelian dualism.[120] Hobbes goes on to argue that eternal life begins only after the Resurrection, as promised by Christian revelation. The upshot seems to be that dying on the battlefield for one's commonwealth is ultimately rational only for a Christian who has an authentic promise of resurrection.

Hence the objection that my interpretation would be unable to account for the law of nature requiring civil service, which potentially requires sacrifice. Hobbes formulates this law as follows: "*that every man is bound by nature, as much as in him lieth, to protect in war the authority by which he is himself protected in time of peace.*"[121] But Hobbes conspicuously omits the deduction of this law in chapter 15, which is situated in the first half of *Leviathan*, the half concerned with the dictates of unaided reason. This law comes only after Hobbes has considered the order of Christian grace in parts III and IV—and then in the review and conclusion when he is directly addressing his fellow Christian countrymen. So I suggest that Hobbes's *placement* of this law is consistent with his denial that personal immortality is demonstrable philosophically. The order of Christian grace makes reasonable a demand that would have left unaided reason in *aporia* since personal immortality is not knowable by unaided reason. Only supposing the truth of Christianity's promise of resurrection can Hobbes make good on his earlier claim that "gaining the secure and perpetual felicity" is had only by "keeping of covenant"—even to the point of death in defense of the realm.[122] Here is another example of how the ultimate foundation of Hobbes's moral and political theory in biblical faith supplements and strengthens the proximate foundation in unaided reason.

To sum up our replies to objections from (1) transcendent interests and (2) the twentieth law of nature: neither pagan glory nor pagan religion introduces transcendent interests that are reasonable in Hobbes's terms. According to Hobbes's interpretation of scripture, the primacy of the good of life in Hobbesian practical reason is not annulled but rather confirmed and enlarged by Christianity. The Christian promise of resurrection to eternal life underwrites the law of nature requiring civil service because it makes sacrifice for the realm reasonable.

It is notable that, if Hobbes sincerely took the Christian promise of resurrection to eternal life as confirming and enlarging the primacy of the good of life, and if the sovereign's *raison d'etre* is to secure the good of life, we might expect that the sovereign is cognizant of the final end, at least in Christian commonwealths. Aquinas had argued that the king should be cognizant of the last end, but he reserved the direction of spiritual matters to the Roman ecclesiastical authority. Hobbes's difference is not in rejecting a divine politics but in uniting temporal and spiritual authority in the king. Indeed Hobbes expends much effort defending the English sovereign's headship of the Anglican Church, whose ultimate aim is to lead its flock to eternal life. The sovereign's cognizance and leadership toward this end are *exclusive*. In other words, Hobbes defends an Erastian ecclesiology in which the church's body is united, quickened, and made lawful by the head of the Christian civil sovereign, and by him or her alone.[123] Hobbes thus constantly seeks to fend off two ecclesiological enemies: Protestant dissenters and nonconformists to the Anglican Church (Brownists, Puritans, Presbyterians), on the one hand, and Roman Catholics, on the other.[124] Hobbes's solution is a sort of civil authoritarianism in matters of religion.[125] His attempts to ground this conception in the Bible are instances of a general rationalizing thrust of parts III and IV of *Leviathan*, which seek to show how the Bible complements, confirms, and enlarges the philosophical doctrines of parts I and II rather than ironically critiquing Christianity as unreasonable.

Finally, is it true that suicide is justifiable in Hobbes's view, as the final objection alleges? The foregoing interpretation suggests that suicide is unreasonable because of the foundational judgment of practical reason that life is objectively good and the legal force with which God's command binds the theist to act in accord with reason's judgment. It is true that Hobbes says, "The pains of life can be so great that, unless their quick end is foreseen, they may lead men to number death among the goods."[126] Yet his observation of the possibility that men will count death as a good need not count as an endorsement of such a view. The fact that this passage follows immediately after Hobbes distinguishes between apparent and actual goods and after enumerating conservation of life as the *bonum maximum* suggests that death for the suicidal is only apparently good. Moreover, when Hobbes directly addresses suicide in his dialogue on the common law, he denies that suicide is good for the agent and says that it is to be presumed that the suicidal agent is "not compos mentis."[127]

It seems unlikely that Hobbes would countenance the blamelessness of suicide in the commonwealth because he is concerned to forbid acts that would weaken the sovereign. Since the strength of a sovereign consists in the strength of the sovereign's subjects, sovereigns can expect neither delight nor profit but only damage in the weakening of their subjects.[128] Prima facie, suicide seems to be a dismembering of oneself from the body politic—and hence, a weakening of it. Actions that weaken the sovereign violate the law of nature: "And it is a dictate of natural reason, and consequently an evident law of nature, that no man ought to weaken that power the protection whereof he hath himself demanded, or wittingly received against others."[129] This law of nature alone provides sufficient grounds for the sovereign justly to deny subjects the right of suicide.

The basicality of the good of life seems not only to fit the texts but to provide the key to understanding a whole range of Hobbesian doctrines and even the structure of *Leviathan* itself. But the account of Hobbes's natural law theory remains incomplete until we demonstrate how Hobbes's theory meets the second requirement, that the precepts of natural law have a *legal* character. In the next chapter we take up the second pillar of Hobbes's natural law theory, its divine pedigree.

CHAPTER 4

The Legal Character of the Laws of Nature

Some scholars would emphasize an evolution in Hobbes's theory of natural law, including defenders of the theistic interpretation. For example, A. P. Martinich contends that Hobbes evolves from *De Cive* to *Leviathan*, the latter of which expresses a divine command theory. In contrast, I suggest that Hobbes's fully formed teaching in *Leviathan* is not of a different kind, even if it was present in embryonic form in his early work. In his *Elements of Law, Natural and Politic*, Hobbes had identified the law of nature with reason.[1] Hobbes added that "forasmuch as law (to speak properly) is a command, and these dictates, as they proceed from nature, are not commands; they are not therefore called laws in respect of nature, but in respect of the author of nature, God Almighty."[2] Later, in *De Cive*, Hobbes defined the law of nature as a "dictate of right reason."[3] These dictates of right reason were the content of the natural, moral, and divine law, which citizens and sovereigns have a duty to obey.[4] He went on to suggest that knowledge of the laws "depends on knowledge of the kingdom" and that God rules the natural kingdom "by the tacit dictates of right reason."[5] In *Leviathan* Hobbes brought together these threads to express his view in mature form. A law of nature became "a precept or general rule, found out by reason, by which man is forbidden to do that which is destructive of his life or taketh away the means of preserving the same, and to omit that by which he thinketh it may be best preserved."[6] From this definition Hobbes deduced a catalogue of nineteen natural laws and claimed that their legal character was secured by God's command.

In my interpretation, life is grasped by reason to be the basic good or fundamental, not merely instrumental, reason for action, and the goodness of life underpins all the laws of nature. In this chapter I seek to show how the dictates of reason attain the force of law by God's command. Such an interpretation indicates that the most basic duty in Hobbes's system is to preserve one's life. In the first section I demonstrate that self-preservation is a fundamental duty in Hobbes's scheme and outline how God's word grounds the legal character of this law. The most influential defense of this interpretation in the work of Martinich has been subjected to a powerful epistemological objection that, if decisive, would undercut Hobbes's entire theory. With this objection in view, I then seek to throw new light on how irresistible power grounds the legal force of the natural law. In the second and third sections, I seek to place Hobbes's doctrine of divine power within the scholastic dialectic between the absolute and ordained power of God. Reading Hobbes in this light, I contend, indicates how Hobbes offers a distinctive solution to the epistemological difficulty of knowing the natural law *as law*. In the course of considering further objections to my reading, the third section also reconsiders the role of computational reasoning in deriving the propositional content of the laws of nature. I then offer my solution to the epistemological objection raised against the divine command interpretation of Hobbes's natural law theory. In the final section of the chapter, Hobbes's two consent conditions of moral obligation are considered. Hobbes's replies to the Foole and the Atheist are discussed in this light.

It is fitting to give a summary list of Hobbes's laws of nature for the ease of reference of the reader. In some cases I have offered my own suggested names where Hobbes left the laws nameless or clunky. My list also blends the accounts of *De Cive* and *Leviathan* to include the precept against intemperance as the twentieth law of nature. I also include the law of nature derived in the review and conclusion of *Leviathan*, which, even though not listed in chapter 15, is sometimes mistakenly left out by commentators.⁷ This brings the list to twenty-one laws of nature, but this should not be understood as a rigid number since Hobbes himself acknowledges that other laws of nature can be validly derived from these. The twenty-one laws of nature are as follows:

1. Peaceableness: Seek peace, and follow it when it can be had.
2. Reciprocity: Be willing to lay down one's right to all things, and reserve only as much liberty to oneself as one permits others to reserve to themselves.
3. Justice: Don't break covenants made.
4. Gratitude: Be thankful for benefits received.
5. Sociability: Strive to be accommodating to others.
6. Clemency: Forgive offenses repented of.
7. Proper punishment: Intend the good of the offender in his correction and the good of others by direction.
8. Avoidance of contumely: Do not speak, write, or act hatefully toward others.
9. Avoidance of pride: Acknowledge other human beings as one's equals.
10. Modesty: Don't desire more than one's fair share.
11. Equity: Don't be partial in judgment or a respecter of persons.
12. Usufruct: Enjoy indivisible and common goods in common.⁸
13. Equitable distribution: Determine the right of first possession or alternate use of indivisible and noncommon goods by lot.
14. Equitable lot: Allot rights to indivisible and noncommon goods by primogeniture or first seizing.
15. Diplomatic immunity: Allow safe conduct to mediators of peace.
16. Arbitration: Submit to an impartial judge disputants over claims of right and fact under the law.
17. Avoidance of private arbitration: Ensure that human beings are not judges in their own cases.
18. Recusal: Ensure that disputants are not bound by judgments of judges who aren't impartial, who have interests tied up in the victory of a party.
19. Impartial assessment of testimony: Ensure that judges hear the testimony of witnesses impartially.

20. Temperance: Act so as to preserve the proper functioning of the faculty of reason.
21. Civil service: Defend the commonwealth that has secured your preservation according to your capacity.

The Duty of Self-Preservation

At first blush, it seems evident that self-preservation is an obligatory duty in Hobbes's definitions of the right of nature and the law of nature. While Hobbes's right of nature has been frequently taken by scholars as prior to and conditioning all law and duty, his definition seems to suggest otherwise: "The Right of Nature . . . is the liberty each man hath to use his own power, as he will himself, *for the preservation of his own nature*, that is to say, of *his own life*."[9] If Hobbesian natural right connoted an *absolute* liberty, why is there any object specified at all? I suggest that the curiously telic feature of Hobbesian natural right becomes clearer when considering that the essence of a law of nature is a discovery by reason of precepts forbidding man from doing that "which is destructive of his life or taketh away the means of preserving the same, and to omit that by which he thinketh it may be best preserved."[10] Hobbes is indicating what we have already seen regarding reason's judgment as to the primary goodness of life—there is a foundational rational necessity or duty to preserve one's life that underpins the laws of nature. If there is a basic duty to preserve one's life, we would expect that the duty would come coupled with a right to the means necessary to fulfill the duty, since Hobbes strongly believed in the principle that a duty comes with the means to fulfill it.[11] But the right of nature just seems to be that one have the means necessary to preserve one's life. The fundamental law of nature and the catalogue of natural laws can be derived from the foundational duty to pursue the good of life.

There is historical support for my interpretation in that a number of Hobbes's contemporaries and critics read his text to indicate that self-preservation is a precept in Hobbes's natural law theory. Thomas Tenison believed that the law of self-preservation was fundamental to Hobbes's scheme, and he protested in favor of a Thomistic account of the good and corresponding precepts.[12] Samuel Parker also lambasted

Hobbes for his claim that self-preservation is the "first Reason and Foundation of all Natural Right."[13] Meanwhile, one J. Shafte articulated Hobbes's view in more detail. While examining Hobbes's definition of the right of nature, Shafte writes:

> Now according to the definition it self, the Right of Nature is only a liberty that each man hath to use his power for his own preservation, not his own destruction; for this should be really to infringe the Law of Nature and Reason, to the breach of which no rational man will ever pretend to any Right, which commands Self-preservation.[14]

Shafte seeks to confute Hobbes by arguing that the right of nature cannot provide a rule of action since doing what *in one's own judgment* conduces to one's preservation sometimes in fact conduces to one's destruction, thereby violating the rule.[15] Clarendon, for his part, was also critical of Hobbes's doctrine of natural law, but he focused his criticism on various of Hobbes's deductions, including the ninth law, requiring acknowledgment of others as equals, and the fifteenth law, mandating safe conduct for mediators. But Clarendon did not challenge the law that he took to be fundamental to Hobbes's scheme, namely, that man acts rightly when he defends himself from violence.[16] In other words, Clarendon, too, understood the law of preservation to be basic in Hobbes's scheme.

Robert Filmer famously said of Hobbes's doctrine that he admired the edifice but not the foundations. Filmer liked Hobbes's absolutism and monarchism but did not like their basis in natural liberty and equality, since Filmer held that the sovereign right of kings was rooted in a paternal authority inherited from Adam. When Filmer assesses Hobbes's definitions of the right and law of nature, he points out that, since the right of nature is a liberty aimed at preserving one's life, "nature must teach [man] that life is to be preserved." But if the law of nature is a rule of reason enjoining and forbidding acts conducive to and destructive of man's life, it follows that the right of nature and the law of nature "will be all one." Filmer believes that the right of nature and the law of nature collapse into one another, and he denies that Hobbes would say the right of nature is a liberty "to destroy one's own life."[17] The point here is that Filmer takes self-preservation to be a duty that is basic in Hobbes's scheme. To Filmer's testimony might be added George Lawson's and John Bramhall's examinations of Hobbes's doctrine of commonwealth. Lawson implicitly recognized preservation as the fundamental law of nature in Hobbes's scheme in his criticism of Hobbes that one's right of self-defense is not absolute but that he who is convicted of a capital crime resists punishment unjustly.[18] Bramhall took Hobbes's commonwealth to be built on a catalogue of laws of nature that boiled down to the laws of "self-interest, and self-preservation."[19] Likewise, Samuel Pufendorf took Hobbes's catalogue of natural laws to be deduced from "the Principle of Self-preservation."[20]

I should immediately add that I am not suggesting that historical testimony is decisive evidence of the correctness of textual interpretation, for indeed I believe that these interpreters misunderstood Hobbes in several ways. However, on this score I think that they were right. Yet, against the testimony of some of Hobbes's contemporaries already discussed, Martinich has denied that the "law of self-preservation" is a law in Hobbes's scheme.[21] The reason he gives is this: the definition of a law of nature is not a law of nature, just as the definition of a horse is not a horse; therefore, there is no law of preservation. Martinich's argument is tantamount to denying that Hobbes believed that the human agent is bound to preserve his life. While Martinich may have a point about the duty of self-preservation not being a "law" according to Hobbes's technical definition, this does not imply that it is not the first principle or most basic duty underlying his account. In light of our discussion, a different argument seems available to prove that, according to Hobbes, the human agent is bound to preserve his life. I offer the following arguments, first, to establish that the laws of nature bind all human agents to preserve the means necessary to preserve the objective good of life. (For the moment, I abstract from the *force* with which they bind—they bind universally, but for Hobbes the force will differ between theists and atheists; for theists they have the force of law, but for atheists they have the force of recommendation or counsel.) The second set of arguments is to prove that every human agent is bound to preserve his life.

To prove: The laws of nature bind all human agents to pursue the means necessary to preserve the objective good of life.
1. The laws of nature specify the means necessary to obtain an object of desire for all human agents. (From the definition of a law of nature)
2. If the laws of nature bind *universally*, either they depend on a desire that does not fail to obtain in all human agents or they depend on no contingent desires at all.
3. The laws of nature are universally binding. (*L*, 26.40, 186)
4. Therefore, the universal bindingness of the laws of nature is either dependent on a desire that human agents cannot fail to obtain or depends on no desire at all. (From 3 and 2 by *modus ponens*)
5. But there is no such desire that cannot fail to obtain, since human agents are psychologically diverse. (From Hobbes's own empirical and historical observation and verifiable by introspection)
6. Therefore, the universal bindingness of the laws of nature does not depend on a contingent desire. (From 5 and 4 by *modus tollendo ponens*)
7. But the laws of nature specify *preservation of life* as the object of desire for all human agents. (From the definition of a law of nature)
8. An object of desire that is good independent of any particular contingent desire is objectively good.
9. The laws of nature specify preservation of life as an objective good. (From 7 and 8)
10. Therefore, the laws of nature bind all human agents to pursue the means necessary to preserve the objective good of life. **QED**

To prove: Every human agent is bound to preserve his life.
1*. Suppose that the laws of nature bind all human agents to pursue *only the means necessary* to the objective good of life. (Supposition for *reductio*)
2*. Human agents are bound to *always* perform promises made. (From the third law of nature, one of the necessary means)

3*. Human agents that always perform promises made are tractable. (*L*, 15.36, 99)
4*. Human agents are bound to be tractable. (From 3* and 2*)
5*. Human agents are bound to make themselves prey to others. (From the meaning of "tractable" [*L*, 15.36, 99])
6*. Human agents are bound to pursue the means of their own certain ruin. (From the meaning of making oneself prey to others [*L*, 15.36, 99])
7*. The laws of nature bind all human agents to pursue the means to the objective good of life, and all human agents are bound to pursue the means of their ruin. (From 6* and 10 by conjunction)
8*. Therefore, every human agent is bound to preserve the objective good of life. **QED**

It might be said that this argument actually shows that Hobbes contradicts himself since, by the conjunction of (10) and (6*), one seems to be bound and not to be bound to pursue the means to the good of life. (My argument for the *reductio* accepts the truth of premises (2*)–(5*), from which (6*) is validly derived.) A further distinction is needed to save the argument. Hobbes's distinction between *in foro interno* and *in foro externo* validity saves the conclusion of the first argument (10) while qualifying (6*) in a way that is compatible with (10) but incompatible with the supposition for the *reductio* argument, hence rendering (8*) sound.

The agent is always bound by the laws of nature *in foro interno* but not always *in foro externo*, because one would make oneself prey to others if one always put the laws of nature into act *in foro externo*. This is because, *in foro externo*, there may or may not be sufficient security to sanction noncompliance with the laws of nature. Moreover, while the catalogue of the laws of nature always bind *in foro interno*, "that is to say, they bind to a desire they should take place," they can fail to bind *in foro externo* when they would conduce to one's destruction which is "contrary to the ground of all laws of nature."[22] Hence, the conclusions of both arguments (10) and (8*) should be understood with the *in foro interno–in foro externo* proviso. The *in foro interno–in foro externo* distinction also indicates how conclusion (6*) of the second argument can be true only *in foro interno*—and this distinction is not available to the interlocutor who claims that only the means necessary to life are binding. This is because, if we suppose that the laws of nature bind only the agent, and not the object at which they aim (the supposition for *reductio*), it would effectively make the *in foro interno–in foro externo* distinction pointless. The whole point of that distinction is lost if one denies that the ground of all the laws of nature is the objective good of life, which one is always rationally bound to pursue. Without that referent, one would be unable to distinguish between acting rationally and irrationally, in Hobbes's terms. (This is why the *in foro interno–in foro externo* distinction is implicitly deployed as true in the *reductio*.)

The definition of the law of nature presupposes Hobbesian reason's most basic grasp of the good to be done. I have argued that Hobbes's postulate of *rationis naturalis* functions similarly to the Thomistic idea of synderesis, recalibrated to the thin theory of the good. It is a basic function of reason, the practical judgment of which is the act of conscience, to grasp and incline human beings toward the (thin) goods of preservation and peace, as is evident in the definition of the law of nature and the fundamental law of nature.

So the laws of nature bind one to preserve one's life and the means necessary thereto. Can the autonomous operation of practical reason suffice to bind an agent? Hobbes explicitly denies this: "Nor is it possible for any person to be bound to himself, because he that can bind, can release; and therefore, he that is bound to himself only is not bound."[23] In Hobbes's view, obligation is an essentially *relational* notion. For example, in a covenant, when A gives up his right to φ to B for some determinate time in exchange for something from B now, A forms a promissory obligation that he fulfills by not φ-ing or by B's releasing him from his promise.[24] How, then—apart from any covenant (or a contract)—does one have a natural or rational obligation? Autonomous practical reason cannot self-impose a duty, because one who is bound to oneself only is not really bound, since he can release himself. In other words, a person cannot legislate a law for himself by the mere activity of his autonomous practical reason. While A might say he is legislating a law for himself, such an act would not generate an obligation because A would be both promisor and promisee—and whatever he decides to do would satisfy the "obligation."[25]

Pace Kant, Hobbes denies that one can bind oneself with the force of law. Hobbes's relational theory of obligation is evident horizontally, in covenants, and vertically, in God's command of the laws of nature. The vertical relationship between man and God does not spring from contract but from nature. Prior to man's thinking and willing there is a natural order of superiority and inferiority in terms of power:

> God in his *natural kingdom* hath a right to rule, and to punish those who break his laws, from his sole *irresistible power* ... if God have the right of sovereignty from his power, it is manifest that the obligation of yielding him obedience lies on men by reason of their weakness.[26]

After Hobbes has deduced the catalogue of laws in *Leviathan*, he notes the following:

> These dictates of reason men use to call by the name of laws, but improperly; for they are but conclusions or theorems concerning what conduceth to the conservation and defence of themselves, whereas law, properly, is the word of him that by right hath command over others. But yet if we consider the same theorems, as delivered in the word of God, that by right commandeth all things, then are they properly called laws.[27]

Hobbes maintains that the dictates of reason considered in themselves do not have the force of law because "law, properly, is the word of him that by right hath command over others." But if we consider the dictates of reason "as delivered in the word of God, that by right commandeth all things, then are they properly called laws." The right by which God commands all things is his irresistible power. More on this later.

This passage is frequently cited as evidence that Hobbes thought the laws of nature are not really laws.[28] But such an interpretation really doesn't make sense of what Hobbes says. As Martinich points out, Hobbes's remark that "these dictates of reason men use to call by the name of laws, but improperly," *presupposes* that *he* is using the word "law" correctly, that is, that law *is* properly the say-so of the one who "by right commandeth all things." Otherwise Hobbes would have said something like, "These dictates I (like men before me) call 'laws' but improperly."[29]

By "word of God" Hobbes does not mean the Bible. He means God's "rational word," to which corresponds the "hearing" of "right reason."[30] Clearly, the hearing of "right reason" is not a form of "prophetic knowledge." As Hobbes explains:

> God declareth his laws three ways; by the dictates of natural reason, by revelation, and by the voice of some man, to whom by the operation of miracles, he procureth credit with the rest. From hence there ariseth a triple word of God, rational, sensible, and prophetic: to which correspondeth a triple hearing; right reason, sense supernatural, and faith.

Hobbes clearly distinguishes knowledge gained by unaided reason from prophetic knowledge. Prophetic knowledge corresponds to faith, which comes from God, coupled with the instrumental cause of "some man." But what is it for God to command the laws of nature? In Martinich's interpretation of Hobbes, God performs speech acts of the form "I command you to x," where the propositional content ("x") is provided by the dictates of reason in Hobbes's catalogue of natural laws.

To this interpretation an understandable objection has been raised: that it constitutes an epistemological problem.[31] Doesn't such an interpretation imply that Hobbes is saying that addressees of the laws of nature must cognize God speaking to them—not unlike a human superior speaking to a human inferior—to command them to obey the laws of nature? This would seem to set the epistemological hurdle for securing the legal character of the natural law very high. The objection could be pressed phenomenologically. Who among common religious believers who affirm the reality of the natural law has ever been so bold as to claim that he hears God's voice in his conscience in this way? Martinich's explanation of the divine command looks more like how Hobbes conceives of *prophetic* knowledge. It has been pointed out that this problem would undermine the normativity of the laws of nature if not resolved. The theistic interpretation still seems in need of an account of how God's *rational* word is known.

Hobbes offers us an alternative way of understanding how God commands the laws of nature by the right of his irresistible power in light of the medieval dialectic of absolute and ordained power. This alternative, I argue, does not fall into the epistemological problem of prophetic knowledge that Martinich's account faces. My discussion is intended to advance the *conclusion* of the Taylor-Warrender-Martinich thesis that obligation in Hobbes depends on its divine pedigree. But it seeks to improve upon that thesis as to the details of the argument. Meanwhile, my account constitutes a new challenge to the many Hobbes scholars who, while agreeing that self-preservation is a duty in Hobbes's scheme, would concur with J. P. Sommerville's judgment that "the idea that all obligation in Hobbes stems from God's will cannot be vindicated."[32] This judgment, my account suggests, fails to account for the dialectic in Hobbes and how the createdness of the world endows the dictates of reason with legal force.

Hobbes locates the source of all moral obligation and therefore moral and civil law in God's irresistible power. Irresistible power binds with the force of law. As Hobbes puts it in his controversy with Bramhall, "Power irresistible justifieth all actions really and properly, in whomsoever it be found."[33] And, in the discussion of the divine pedigree of obligation in his *De Cive*, he observes that God has the "right of sovereignty from his power" such that the "*obligation* of yielding him obedience lies on men by reason of their weakness."[34] But how is this to be understood? In the following sections I argue that we should understand Hobbes's doctrine in light of what Francis Oakley calls the medieval "dialectic" between God's absolute and ordained power—*potentia absoluta et ordinata*.

The Dialectic in Aquinas, Scotus, and Ockham

As William Courtenay has shown, a distinction can be made between God's absolute power—that which God can do, considered in the abstract—and God's ordained power—what God can do supposing what he has in fact done in establishing the orders of nature and grace. Another way to state the distinction, in Courtenay's helpful language, is the contrast between God's *capacity* and his *volition*.[35] The former is what God is theoretically capable of. The latter is what God actually wills to do. The distinction has its roots in the scriptures themselves in the Augustinian interpretive tradition. In his *On Nature and Grace*, Augustine distinguished between what God was able to do and what he wished to do.[36] This passage was picked up by Peter Lombard in his *Sentences*, which became the standard textbook for scholastic theologians. Oakley points out that the distinction between God's capacity and his volition stated in the precise terms of *potentia absoluta et ordinata* was not formulated before the work of Albertus Magnus.[37] Albert the Great was the teacher of Thomas Aquinas, and it is in Aquinas that we find the locus classicus for the distinction.

Aquinas continues the Augustinian tradition by citing the Bible as his foundation for the distinction.[38] He cites Matthew 26:53, where Jesus asks rhetorically if his listeners think he cannot call upon legions of angels. But since he did not, it follows that God can do what he does not. Aquinas then develops his philosophical-theological account of the distinction. God does not act from natural necessity. In other words, God is radically free in his omnipotence. This belief that God is free from necessity has been the orthodox position throughout the history of Christian doctrine, as implied in the Nicene Creed and the doctrine of creation ex nihilo. God is free to create or not to create. We might call this position divine libertarianism.

Aquinas holds a strong form of divine libertarianism because he believes that not only is God not necessitated to act but God is not constricted to effect *this* order of nature and grace if he indeed wishes to create.[39] While in God power and goodness and wisdom are simply one—Aquinas affirms the doctrine of divine simplicity—it does not follow that the order God wills in making creatures is commensurate to his infinite goodness and wisdom. The created order does not exhaust God's goodness, if for no other reason than that his goodness is infinite, and a finite created order cannot perfectly reflect that. Therefore, it is within God's absolute power to do other than he has done. The chief limit on God's absolute power is that he cannot will formal contradictions to be true at the same time and in the same respect. This includes the constraint to respect the necessities in the natures of things *ex suppositione*, that is, on the supposition that God wills them to be.[40]

The dialectic between absolute and ordained power in scholastic thought after Aquinas is a complex story. We are heavily indebted to the works of Courtenay, Oakley, and Heiko Oberman, among others, who have traced this story in detail in recent decades. My reading of the scholastic and early modern intellectual history of the *potentia absoluta/ordinata* dialectic draws in part from their work, but a recounting of the story in full detail is beyond our scope. Here I briefly discuss two subsequent Franciscan scholastics and voluntarists who are particularly important in the story: John Duns Scotus and William of Ockham.

The intellectual climate after Aquinas's death fertilized the soil in which theological voluntarism and nominalism would grow. In 1277 Archbishop of Canterbury Robert Kilwardby and Bishop of Paris Etienne Temper handed down condemnations of a number of Thomistic theses, including propositions that were thought to constrain the divine liberty. This was due to the perception that Aristotelian essentialism imposed necessity on the deity.[41] As Oakley points out, the condemnations "marked the beginning of the theological reaction that was to dispose Christian philosophers to vindicate the freedom and omnipotence of God at any cost."[42] This reaction might be characterized by what Heiko Oberman calls a "common attitude" of preoccupation with divine freedom and omnipotence—and, indeed, this attitude is the essence of theological voluntarism and nominalism.[43] A key conceptual dynamic that framed subsequent discussion and debate of God's liberty and power was the distinction between God's absolute and ordained power.

John Duns Scotus took up the distinction and explicated it in the spirit of some earlier canon lawyers who had used the distinction to analogize to human sovereignty, particularly the nature of papal power. In Scotus's discussion of the twofold power, he breaks from Aquinas's understanding to formulate what can be characterized as an operationalized understanding of *potentia absoluta* to be a presently active power.[44] Aquinas had held that that which is within God's absolute power was initially open to him.[45] However, once God chose to create the way that he did, those possibilities are now only hypothetical. In contrast, Scotus treats absolute power and ordained power as present active capacities and treats the God-man analogy univocally. In Scotus's words:

> In every agent acting intelligently and voluntarily that can act in conformity with an upright or just law but does not have to do so of necessity, one can distinguish between its ordained power and its absolute power. The reason is that either it can act in conformity with some right and just law, and then it is acting according to its ordained power ... or else it can act beyond or against such a law, and in this case its absolute power exceeds its ordained power. And therefore it is not only in God, but in every free agent that can either act in accord with the dictates of a just law or go beyond or against that law, that one distinguishes between absolute and ordained power; therefore the jurists say that someone can act *de facto*, that is, according to his absolute power, or *de jure*, that is, according to his ordained legal power.[46]

When God or the civil sovereign acts in accord with posited law, he acts according to his ordained power. When the sovereign acts outside the confines of the law, he acts according to his absolute power. In short, in Scotus's thought absolute power becomes a form of action actually available to the sovereign within the constituted order rather than a theoretical possibility.

Courtenay considers the subsequent late medieval discussion of the dialectic as operating in "the shadow" of Scotus. And yet William of Ockham's subsequent treatment indicates that he sought to extricate himself from the shade. In one of his *quodlibetales* he explains his understanding of the distinction more in the spirit of Aquinas.[47] Reaffirming divine simplicity, Ockham maintains that the two powers are not really two in God, but we can consider them separately according to our finite capacity. By God's ordained power, he is able to do things in accordance with the laws he has ordained and instituted. God's absolute power is the power to do anything that does not involve a formal contradiction. This set of actions are those things that God can do but does not wish to, which tracks the distinction between capacity and volition. In this same matter, Ockham argues that God could save without created charity according to his absolute power. But this is not possible given what God has actually ordained. In other words, God binds himself to the de facto order of grace (and nature). As Courtenay notes, a growing number of scholars have recognized that Ockham's distinction is much more conservative and closer to Aquinas's than has been recognized.[48]

I would argue that this entails a qualified similarity in the metaphysical-theological foundations of Ockham's and Aquinas's respective natural law theories that is not often recognized. Armand Maurer voices one example of the standard radical voluntaristic reading of Ockham:

> Because God is omnipotent and absolutely free, he is not bound to impose a given set of laws upon men. We should not imagine him as ruled by an eternal divine law from which human laws flow as necessary conclusions from premises. The laws he imposes on men are completely arbitrary, so that he can annul or change them at will.[49]

Some recent scholarship has sought to reread Ockham's moral theory to reject the radical voluntarist interpretation.[50] I am somewhat sympathetic with the spirit of this scholarship, particularly if we consider Ockham's natural law theory in light of his rejection of a Scotist picture of absolute and ordained power. I contend that Ockham agrees with Aquinas that the legal character of the natural law flows from God's command, inasmuch as God can be said to command in the very act of creation.

For Aquinas, law—an ordinance of reason, for the common good, made by a proper authority and promulgated—is, properly speaking, a *command*. How, then, does God "command" the natural law, which is properly law? According to Aquinas, God is said to command the natural law in the very act of creating man. By creating man and endowing him with essential inclinations—a sort of impression of a particular substantial form—God orders man toward his proper good. Thus the practical necessities requisite for pursuit of human good have the character of law. In this intellectualist manner Aquinas can be understood to hold what Gerald Postema calls the "command model" of law.[51]

Ockham is often portrayed as a radically voluntaristic divine command theorist because God is unqualifiedly free in his omnipotence to command any action, including those actions that were considered intrinsic evils in traditional Christian ethics. Ockham claims that evil is nothing other than doing the opposite of what one is obligated to do. God's will is the supreme source of law and obligation, such that evil is a breach of God's command. In the context of discussing the condition of fallen angels, Ockham remarks that hatred, theft, adultery, and the like are evil according to the *communi lege*, the common law, promulgated by God. But, Ockham points out, God himself could perform any of these actions without committing evil. And God could make such acts meritorious if he commanded them to be performed.[52] Do these passages imply that Ockham is a radical voluntarist?

To get at this question, one must ask, What is the common law referred to here if not the natural law? While Ockham does not author a treatise on the natural law, he does affirm that it exists. In his *Dialogus* he identifies the dictates of right reason, such as the precepts against adultery and lying, as one mode of the natural law.[53] This mode of natural law is "*immutabile et invariabile ac indispensabile.*"[54] The features of immutability, invariability, and indispensability indicate that the precepts of natural law are exceptionless. The other two modes of natural law that Ockham identifies are tailored to unfallen and fallen human nature and as such consist of precepts *ex suppositione*, or hypothetical imperatives. We can set aside these modes for our purposes.[55] After drawing this distinction, the student in the dialogue asks the master to explain the doctrine that every natural law is a divine law. In response, Ockham says that natural law is from God in that he is the creator of nature. It is in this light that I suggest we should understand Ockham's remark that the dictate of right reason binds one to will some action because the "divine will wishes it."[56] The dictates of right reason have the force of law inasmuch as God created man and willed man to act according to the dictates of right reason.[57] Hence, when Ockham distinguishes between positive and nonpositive moral science, and sources the former in divine commands and the latter in *per se nota* first principles, he seems to be referring to divine positive law in the former, and not denying God's legislation of the latter (in the broad sense of creation) is essential to the legal character of the dictates of right reason.[58] Such a reading suggests an intellectualist element in God's command of the natural law. Indeed when Ockham discusses creation he makes the point that the will to create is an act in which the will *and the intellect* cooperate.[59] For Ockham, will and reason in God is only a distinction of reason: in God they are simply one.

Thus I maintain that for Ockham, God's *potentia ad ordinata* in the moral order is confined by, because actualized in, the natural law, which was the order, reflective of his wisdom, established in the very act of creating and ordering man. In short, Ockham's remarks about God making traditionally evil acts meritorious do not seem to refer to any actualizable possibility. Hence Maurer's suggestion that moral obligation is continuously subject to God's arbitrary diktat must be rejected. Like Aquinas, Ockham grounds the moral obligation in God's creation and order of nature.

Still, Ockham's continuity with Aquinas must be immediately qualified, for a few reasons. First, because even while Ockham strove to maintain the Thomistic or "classical" understanding of the dialectic between absolute and ordained power, he at times spoke in a Scotistic way, succumbing to the temptation to analogize from the divine to human sovereignty and locating within the temporal sovereign's authority and absolute power posited law. Hence it might be said that Ockham cannot entirely eclipse the shadow of Scotus on that point. Second, in contrast with what the passage about intellect and will cooperating indicates, Ockham elsewhere holds forth an indifferentist theory of freedom and willing. For Ockham, to be free is to be able to will something indifferently and contingently.[60] This not only implies that the will has priority over intellect—it can resist the dictates of reason—but it can even will evil under the aspect of evil. The defender of a more Thomistic reading of Ockham's natural law theory might reply that Ockham is speaking only of *human* willing, which is distinct from divine willing, since in God intellect and will are simply one. In this spirit, J. Kilcullen appeals to divine simplicity in his defense of his natural law interpretation of Ockham.[61] It is true that by his ordained power God in fact wills man toward his proper good and happiness, which Ockham indicates is reflective of his wisdom. However, Ockham maintains that it is theoretically within God's power to command a person to hate God—and Kilcullen does not recognize how this weakens the divine simplicity fallback, that is, Ockham's own doctrine of simplicity.[62] To this characterization of God's power the Thomist would respond by asking, In what sense could it be reflective of God's wisdom and goodness that in his absolute power God could command a person to hate God himself, who is goodness itself? As Francisco Suárez would later put it, it would be incongruous with God's nature for God to command hatred of anything that is intrinsically maximally loveable.[63]

Ockham was eager to protect God's freedom from Averroistic Aristotelian necessitation. However, in his eagerness he upset the delicate balance Aquinas achieved between immanent law and imposed law, between *lex indicans* and *lex praecipiens*, between intellect and will, between God's power and God's goodness. The voluntarist interpretation of Ockham seems correct to insist that moral obligation ultimately is grounded in God's sheer will, since the moral order actualized in creation was itself only one of a set of possibilities open to God initially, some of which included performing what traditional morality or right reason takes to be intrinsically evil acts.

Third, Ockham is a nominalist, in contrast with Aquinas's moderate realism about universals. Deploying the principle that entities should not be needlessly multiplied—the famous razor—Ockham holds that the phenomenon of attribute agreement does not require positing universals. Ockham argues at length, giving various reasons why he thinks the doctrine of universals is unreasonable. One argument is specifically theological and flows from the dialectic of absolute and ordained power in his thought. God's power includes the power not only to create but also to annihilate.[64] Here Ockham is referring to God's ordained power, because creation ex nihilo and annihilation are actionable (albeit extraordinary) capacities within the ordained framework. But, as noted in chapter 1, this power would be incompatible with the existence of universals that exist in every particular as constituting it. For to annihilate something would be to entirely unmake the thing so that its "metaphysical parts" would cease to exist, including the universal. In other words, annihilating Socrates would annihilate the universal "man." But, if universals exist, this would mean that God could not annihilate Socrates without maintaining Plato and all other men in being according to their entire essence, since thereby the universal "man" would no longer be a constituent of their being. But annihilation of one individual in a species is an ability within God's ordained power. Hence Ockham rejects the doctrine of universals and posits a form of resemblance nominalism to explain attribute agreement.[65] In short, I maintain that Ockham should be understood as a sort of voluntaristic and nominalistic natural lawyer—but one who has "intellectualist" or "rationalist" elements, *ex suppositione*, that is, supposing the order that God in fact has willed.

The medieval dialectic between absolute and ordained power was inherited by the later scholastic and many early modern thinkers, including early modern English thinkers. In particular, Scotist and Ockhamist doctrines made their way through later scholastic conduits to the Reformers, post-Tridentine scholasticism, and the early modern philosophers and scientists. The details of this story have been the subject of groundbreaking intellectual history in the work of Oakley and need not be rehashed here.[66] A few remarks about the dialectic in the work of the founders of Protestantism, Luther and Calvin, are fitting, however. Luther at times affirmed a doctrine that carried forward the Scotistic understanding, conceptualizing God's absolute power as an actionable capacity to suspend the physical laws operative by his ordained will, as when God protected Shadrach, Meschach, and Abednego from the flames of the Babylonian furnace.[67] At other times Luther seemed to reject the distinction altogether.[68] However, Calvin was less sanguine about the distinction, and he denounced *la puissance absolue de Dieu* as a decadent tool of popish theologians.[69] Calvin maintained that the absolute-ordained distinction would sever God's power from his justice, since all he in fact ordains is perfectly just.[70] Still, as Oakley notes, later Reformed theologians would defend the distinction, and as we shall see, Hobbes himself would as well.

The absolute-ordained distinction made its way into English theological discourse and was deployed by Tudor and Stuart sovereigns in their characterizations of sovereign power, and more or less explicit traces of the distinction have played an important role in the thought of many of the most influential philosophers and scientists in England and on the Continent, including many with whom Hobbes interacted, such as Francis Bacon, René Descartes, Marin Mersenne, Pierre Gassendi, and Robert Boyle.[71] The general influence of the operationalized understanding of absolute power is apparent in these authors. The dialectic was, moreover, transmitted in the Jesuit iteration of the post-Tridentine scholastic tradition, including in the work of Francisco Suárez, with whom Hobbes interacted. Suárez acts as a kind of sieve for the older scholastic learning.

Suárez retains the absolute-ordained distinction, maintaining God's initial freedom to create in a variety of ways, but believes that God in fact established a certain physical and moral order according to his ordained power. Suárez makes statements that suggest a full-blown Scotistic understanding of God's absolute power as operationalized, an active capacity to dispense from the law he has ordained.[72] However, Suárez softens the doctrine in insisting that, while God's absolute power is not bound by the ordained moral law, any dispensation or departure from that order would necessarily be good, since the act would proceed from the standard of goodness itself. We are now in a position to consider Hobbes's doctrine of irresistible power in light of the scholastic *potentia absoluta/ordinata* dialectic.

THE DIALECTIC IN HOBBES AND THE DIVINE PEDIGREE OF NATURAL LAW

Divine libertarianism is one of Hobbes's first principles. According to Hobbes, freedom is the absence of external impediments. The person who is maximally free is the person "that can be free when he will."[73] The object of Hobbes's doctrine of liberty is to try to understand in what sense man can be said to be "free" in a natural commonwealth ruled by an omnipotent being. Whatever human liberty turns out to consist in, it cannot constitute an "impediment to the omnipotence and *liberty* of God."[74] God is absolutely free because there are no extrinsic impediments or necessities binding him to act or not to act. Hobbes takes divine libertarianism to be a philosophically necessary inference regarding "the first of all causes," because to be first in a chain of causes is to be free from prior necessitation. Thus Hobbes maintains that it is natural to believe that "the Almighty can do all things."[75] He also takes divine libertarianism to be the orthodox Christian position. In the context of considering the question of universal salvation, he remarks: "It is not Christian to think, if God had the purpose to save all men, that any man could be damned; because it were a sign of want of power to effect what he would."[76] Radical freedom is a principal feature of irresistible power.

Hobbes's distinction between absolute and ordained power in God is difficult to see because he strains to find nonscholastic terminology to communicate the idea. In one of his formulations he distinguishes between God's *will* and God's *command*. The latter is God's revealed will, and the former is God's secret "decree" or inner purpose. For example, God commanded Abraham to sacrifice Isaac, but it was his secret decree or purpose, later revealed, that Isaac was not to be sacrificed. These are special cases in salvation history that concern God's prophetic word. Hobbes later approves of the distinction between God's twofold wills that was made by Protestant divines:

> The Protestant doctors, both of our and other Churches, did use to distinguish between the secret and revealed will of God; the former they called *voluntas bene placiti*, which signifieth absolutely his will, the other *voluntas signi*, that is, the signification of his will.[77]

Hobbes thus notes that the Protestant doctors used a different term to refer absolutely to God's will and another term to refer to his revealed will or command, but the basic notion is similar to the older absolute-ordained distinction. Hobbes draws this distinction in referring to God's special revelation, which in his theory of divine communication corresponds to God's prophetic word. But it is important to recognize that Hobbes indicates that the distinction of absolute and ordained power also applies with respect to God's rational word.

Hobbes's implicit recognition of the distinction's applicability to God's rational word is supposed when he continues to insist that God's revealed will, "which is his word," must be known beforehand, since "it ought to be the rule of our actions."[78] God's word rules human actions both by special revelation in the Bible (God's prophetic word) and by general revelation through the dictates of right reason (God's rational word). These two expressions of God's word roughly track the orders of grace and nature. My point is that Hobbes recognizes God's absolute and ordained power not only with respect to the order of grace but also with respect to the order of nature. This is apparent a few paragraphs later when Hobbes speaks of God's ordained will as evident in creation: "To the order of his work, the world, wherein one thing follows another so aptly as no man could order it by design, he gives the name will and purpose."[79] In the *Historia Ecclesiastica*, this *opus* of God, which manifests the natural law, is said to be knowable by man.[80]

As in the older Christian tradition, God in his radical freedom is not only able to create or not create but is also able to create otherwise than he does—a point Hobbes insists upon against Thomas White.[81]

The order of the world God actually chose to create is the product of God's ordained power. In Hobbes's words, that which proceeds from nature "is not the immediate, but the ordinary work of God."[82] While Hobbes does not use the scholastic turn of phrase *potentia ad ordinata*, the idea is clearly there when he distinguishes God's operation "by the way of nature, ordained in the creation."[83] He implicitly refers to God's ordained power when he discusses the proper function of philosophical reasoning, "busily flying up and down among creatures, and bringing back a true report of their order, causes and effects."[84] The order in creation, in conjunction with order in the mind, is a generative principle of philosophy. As Hobbes puts it, philosophy is "the child of the world and your mind."[85] He takes the proper method of philosophy to be mimetic of the order of God's ordained power. It has often been remarked that Hobbes offers a Baconian definition of knowledge as power. I would suggest that Hobbes's similarity to Bacon is deeper. Like Bacon, Hobbes wants to baptize modern science's aspirations to relieve man's estate. The scientists' goal to understand causes and effects sufficiently that we might produce such effects as the nature of things permits, for the commodity of human life, is thus not only permitted by Christianity, in Hobbes's thought, but the scientific project also takes on the character of a sort of share in God's power.

Meanwhile, Hobbes's conception of God's absolute power, the exercise of which Hobbes refers to as "extraordinary work," is operationalized in the shadow of Scotus and Ockham.[86] Yet Hobbes seems to be only partly in that shade since, for instance, he never says that God can command his subjects to hate him (which makes sense in light of his fourth-way language; see chapter 1). Rather, by his absolute power, God brings about effects in many different ways outside the natural course of affairs, including miracles.[87] For example, on Hobbes's principles, if the biblical testimony of Balaam's donkey is credible, it would count as a miracle, because "both the thing is strange, and the natural cause difficult to imagine."[88] In contrast with the ordinary work of God, the extraordinary work of God is incomprehensible to the human mind.[89] Hobbes will also apply the analogy of absolute power as operationalized in application to the power of the civil sovereign.[90] Few scholars of Hobbes have recognized the absolute/ordained distinction at work in Hobbes's theology.[91] Even those scholars that have recognized the distinction have not properly connected it to Hobbes's natural law theory.

It was within God's absolute power to create otherwise than he did. Again, Hobbes explicitly affirms this when he asserts that "God by his right might have made men subject to diseases and death, although they had never sinned."[92] However, we know what God in fact willed, inasmuch as that is apparent in his "ordinary work," namely, nature. In the de facto natural kingdom, God orders man not toward death but toward life, in both his prelapsarian and postlapsarian conditions. An order toward life is still apparent even in the postlapsarian condition, where the dissonance between appetite and reason sparks a tendency toward destruction (see chapter 2). Yet human nature is not so damaged that God's willing of our good is not apparent in our nature. "For there is no kind of substance in the world now, that was not at the first creation, when the Creator gave to all what natural and special motion he thought good."[93] And "there is no good inclination that is not of the operation of God"—including both supernatural and natural inclinations.[94] As already noted, generally speaking, the special motions that God imparted to things according to their kinds constitute the "common laws of their creation."[95] The operations of the bodily parts for the good of man's substantial life thus have a lawlike character. They are not mere facts in a godless and purposeless universe. Most properly speaking, the motions special to man, *those of right reason*, constitute the "hearing" of God's rational word: the laws of nature. This is what Hobbes means when he avers, "From the very creation, God ... reigned over all men *naturally* by his might."[96]

Now, as we saw in chapter 2, in parts III and IV of *Leviathan* Hobbes offers a biblical anthropology, affirming the Genesis account of God's gift of speech to man. But, even within his proximate foundation in unaided reason, by his philosophical theology, specifically by means of the fourth way, an agent reasoning by Hobbesian lights can affirm that God is the "first author" of speech. Since we cannot deny a perfection to God, we must affirm that God is maximally rational. And speech is the mark of rationality. But since God is the first cause of all of nature, including man, and man is a rational animal, God must be the author of speech. Hence Hobbes's philosophical theology warrants his claim that God's "rational word" corresponds to right reason. It is by the rational faculty that we grasp life to be good and that we rightly reason about the means necessary to preservation.

This is how God's irresistible power grounds the foundational rational obligations to preserve one's life and endeavor to fulfill the precepts of the natural law. By creating and ordering man in his bodily parts and reason the way that he in fact did, the rational necessity to preserve oneself and the practical necessities requisite to secure that goal are thereby endowed with legal force, because God is the only being with the sovereign right to will such an order. Hobbes contrasts his omnipotence-based foundation for the legal force of natural law from gratitude-based foundations, even though both conceptions imply a relationship of dependence.[97] Thus Hobbes clarifies in a footnote what he means by subjection to God from weakness: man is not omnipotent.[98] By this Hobbes means that man is a metaphysically dependent being. As such he is part of an order that he did not make and cannot unmake.[99]

God's ordained power constricts man's liberty by "hope or fear," precisely in how God artifices man, by ordering him toward his proper good.[100] These are two of the most basic complex passions. Hope is a positive appetite with an opinion of attaining the object desired; fear is a negative appetite with an opinion of enduring hurt from the object. Reason's foundational grasp of the goodness of life and the evil of death, the dictate to endeavor peace, and the catalogue of virtues are the practical requirements for the pursuit of human fulfillment. The virtues are constitutive of the goods of peace and life. Agents are bound to shape their passions, including fear and hope, by the virtues, such that they fear and hope in the right way at the right time and in the right degree. It follows that some fears and hopes are unreasonable and vicious. For example, the hope to rule the entire world is vicious.[101] It is vicious precisely because it is a vainglorious attempt at self-deification and as such is a rebellion against one's nature, which is to say God's irresistible power in the ordained mode. Hobbes believes that, by God's ordained power, there is an intrinsic directedness of the action types and character traits picked out by the laws of nature toward a contented life, and he appeals to this order in his reply to the Foole (which will be discussed further later in this chapter). Yet that intrinsic order is hardly a guarantee of human happiness under conditions of anarchy, since the untutored spark of concupiscence in even a few people is enough to generate war and misery on a massive scale. There is a manifest need for human art to assist postlapsarian nature in the construction of commonwealth, positive law, and the threat of sanction to the vicious.

Does Hobbes's emphasis on God's power imply that the order of nature, including the moral order, was just arbitrarily imposed from the initial possibilities open to God? In other words, was God's power prior to God's goodness? Such is the Scotistic-Ockhamistic impression Hobbes often gives. And yet Hobbes at times speaks in a more Thomistic voice, as when he is also willing to speak in the same breath of God's "power and goodness." Hobbes denies that anything can be said of God that would "breach [the] unity in God that reigneth."[102] Moreover, we saw in our discussion of Hobbes's fourth-way language that God is properly called "most good" and "most powerful." These attributes cannot introduce any real distinctions or divisions in his being.[103] So when Hobbes speaks in the same breath of God's "power and goodness," he cannot be introducing rival attributes into God's nature if he is consistent.[104] Hobbes's God is also a God of reason, whose "rational word" corresponds to the dictates of right reason. Thus there is a hint of a Hobbesian iteration of the Augustinian and Thomistic idea of God as *Summa Ratio*.

Hobbes has a rationalist theology. As already discussed, in the *Behemoth* Hobbes identifies religious extremism and fanaticism—that is, violence in the name of religion—as the chief source of the English Civil War. There were many millenarian sects who fancied they had a mandate from God to act violently in his name to overthrow the government. They wanted, in Eric Voegelin's words, to immanentize the eschaton.[105] Hobbes sees this as a major threat to peace, the response to which demands a rationalist theology. But he also recognizes that religion can be a source of noble acts, including sacrifice for civil service to the commonwealth, and therefore a force for good.[106] So he wants to harness the energy of religion to put it in service of peace while defanging it, or rescuing it from its worst impulses. This is how we should understand Hobbes's doctrine of God as reasonable. Publicly reasonable comprehensive and religious doctrines must affirm that the first cause is a God of reason and the first dictate of reason is to will peace. It follows that, if God does not act contrary to his nature, he cannot act contrary to his goodness and reason. These elements in Hobbes are strengthened given Hobbes's adherence to the *sub ratione boni* principle. Thus Hobbes outright rejects the idea that an agent could will evil for the sake of evil.[107] When we speak of God's goodness, it "his goodness to us"—and my suggestion is that Hobbes is claiming that this is apparent in his ordinary work of nature, God's ordained power.[108]

These reflections can shed further light on how Hobbes should be understood in the natural law tradition and in the debate between proponents of *lex indicans* and *lex praecipiens*, which corresponded to intellectualist-voluntarist debates. As Suárez summarized it, the *lex indicans* camp championed by Gregory of Rimini argued that the natural law was demonstrative—that is, it indicated what was intrinsically good and evil. In this view, what is good for a thing according to its nature is not rationally grounded on God, even if it depends on God for its existence. For example, the goodness of truth telling and the badness of lying flow from the nature of rational animality itself and do not depend on the will of God. Long before Hugo Grotius's famous *etsiam daremus* counterfactual, Gregory and his followers held that the natural law did not depend on the will of God and that even if God did not exist, the dictates of right reason would still have the same legal character *qua* indicator of what is good or evil for rational animals.[109] Meanwhile, the *lex praecipiens* camp insisted that reason's indication of action as good or evil is insufficient in and of itself to prescribe law. This camp insisted that law, properly speaking, is the command of a superior to an inferior. This view Suárez takes to be initiated by Ockham in passages already examined and carried forward by later voluntarists such as Jean Gerson and Pierre d'Ailly.[110]

Suárez professes dissatisfaction with the two camps. He rejects *lex indicans* because law properly speaking is a binding relationship between an inferior and a superior whose superiority consists in the authority to bind. But the mere judgment of practical reason could be done by an equal or an inferior. Therefore, Suárez seeks to find a middle way. His idea is that legal precepts of natural law must contain two properties: an essential order toward the good/away from evil and being commanded by God. The precepts of natural law do indicate what is intrinsically good and evil according to the measure of reason, but this is insufficient to render them laws because God must command the precepts for them to have a legal character. Suárez holds not only that this must be true in the order of being in order for the command condition to be satisfied, but he also holds that the addressee of the command must have some knowledge of the precepts *as commanded* by God. Thus Suárez posits the idea that the precepts themselves carry with them a *sign* of the divine volition. In doing so, he ups the ante for the kind of knowledge the human agent must have in order to be bound by natural law vis-à-vis Aquinas. For Suárez, the moral data of conscience is itself a preeminent indication not only of the goodness or badness of an act but of God's volition itself.[111] Aquinas more clearly kept the orders of being and knowing distinct.[112]

Hobbes also seeks a middle way between the *lex praecepiens* and *lex indicans* camps. He retains the element of divine pedigree in his doctrine of God's irresistible power ordering man toward the good of life by the normative standard of reason and declaration of the natural law by his rational word. Meanwhile, Hobbes retains the element of reason's indication of what is intrinsically good and evil (as modified by his thin theory of the good) by its dictates of what is good and the practical necessities to achieve that good. The dictates of reason are "immutable and eternal" because it can never be that they aren't the way of peace and preservation, and peace and preservation can never fail to constitute the human good. For Hobbes, the role of God's commanding will and the role of reason as its measure are thus two necessary conditions for some data to be a precept of natural law.

My suggestion has been that God's irresistible power is operative in the very work of creation, in artificing human nature as such, such that the judgment that human nature is created is sufficient to endow the dictates of practical reason with a legal character. If I am right, on the issue of promulgation of the natural law, Hobbes's doctrine can be understood as a middle way between Suárez and Aquinas. Aquinas had deemed it sufficient for the promulgation of natural law that, in the order of being, man in fact be created with the light of reason.[113] Meanwhile, Suárez insisted that the moral agent must be aware that his will is bound by that of a superior in order for him to be *legally* bound. In order to secure the legal character of natural law, Suárez insisted that there is a sign of divine pedigree in the precepts of natural law themselves. Hobbes agrees with Suárez that acknowledgment of divine pedigree is a necessary condition for the promulgation condition of natural law to be met: "The knowledge of all law . . . dependeth on the knowledge of the sovereign power."[114] However, he rejects the Suarezian claim that the divine volition must be indicated by some sign in moral consciousness.[115] This is fairly evident if we consider the propositional content of the laws of nature themselves, as summarized at the beginning of this chapter. For example, when one deduces the fourth law of nature, gratitude, nothing in its propositional content is indicative of the precept's divine pedigree. And so on with the rest of the laws of nature. Hobbes seems to recognize with Aquinas that the Suarezian solution would overburden the capacity of moral consciousness and is phenomenologically dubious. Therefore, Hobbes is in agreement with Aquinas in holding that the act of judgment that a first cause exists as artificer and governor is essentially distinct from acts of reasoning in the practical-moral order.

One objection to this line of reasoning is that it is not compatible with Hobbes's apophaticism. To know *that* God is, but not know *who* God is, would seem to empty the divine pedigree of any guidance for action. A. E. Taylor, who contends that the legal character of the laws of nature is epistemically secure apart from special revelation, makes an interesting argument that seeks to stave off this objection. The incomprehensibility of the divine nature, rather than counting against the legal character of the laws, counts in its favor since that very incomprehensibility makes it "impossible to use our inability to understand *how* God commands us as any argument against the fact that He does so command us, provided that the fact appears to be sufficiently authenticated."[116] Taylor points to one candidate witness to this fact: the sense of the imperative itself. Here he is gesturing at the witness of conscience in the knower, which was discussed in the previous chapter. This is helpful but could be strengthened. Hobbes's apophaticism is not a sheer negative theology. Recall Hobbes's fourth-way language of God as most good and so on, and his belief that the fact that God declares his laws by reason indicates that God is *Summa Ratio*. But, having wielded Ockham's razor, Hobbes has lost the doctrine of the *analogia entis*, which Aquinas believed was an essential metaphysical doctrine to justify our limited "positive" knowledge of God by analogy and the idea of right reason as a participation in the eternal law. Hence, from this perspective, a more satisfactory answer to this question would require a richer metaphysical apparatus that Hobbes has jettisoned. While he does not use the language of participation, he does speak of human right reason as a "hearing" of the divine reason, which does imply a sharing in the divine rule and measure, thus indicating that the divine will is not utterly obscured in the *Deus absconditus*.[117]

It should also be noted that Hobbes's remarks at the end of chapter 15 of *Leviathan* are not at all aberrant from the perspective of the scholastic tradition. Hobbes believes that the precepts can be considered apart from God's existence, simply as reason measuring human acts, and as such they have the force of suggestion, exhortation, or theorems of prudence.[118] But when considered in light of God's power, they are properly laws. Aquinas speaks in a similar way when he points out that sin can be considered in two ways: merely in relation to human reason and in relation to God.[119] Suárez also believes reason is subtle enough to consider dictates of reason in different lights. What Aquinas, Suárez, and Hobbes all agree on—not to mention Scotus, Ockham, and most later members of the schools they spawned—is that, in the order of being, there must be a divine source of nature in order for the dictates of right reason to have a legal character.

The dialectic between absolute and ordained power is essential to make sense of moral obligation in Hobbes's natural law theory. For Hobbes, belief in the existence of God endows the dictates of reason with a legal character for the person who so believes. This is because the judgment that God exists and providentially governs the world would make a difference, if true. In Hobbes's terms, if we find ourselves in a godless universe, any "order" we discover in the world or in ourselves toward the good, and the means necessary to the good, will not be willed by a being with the right to will it. That order, then, will not have the character of law. As we have seen in the discussion of Hobbes's fifth-way language, there is an order in the world that is apparent in the operations of our subrational bodily parts and in the process of human generation. If God exists, the order of man's body and reason toward the good of life is an order *willed* by one with the right to order things by his command (and the order itself is evidence of such an ordering artificer). This is the explanation of why dictates of reason have the character of law for theists, according to Hobbes.

Computational Reasoning

It is worth pausing to note an objection that proponents of the practical severability thesis would raise at this point. Gregory Kavka, one of the most influential proponents of this thesis, contends that God's role is severable precisely because God plays no role in the derivation of the propositional content of the laws.[120] Kavka seems to mean that in the deductions of the laws of nature, by the geometrical or computational use of reason, God plays no role. The acting agent performs these deductions. It is true that God is not performing through the instrumentality of persons as if, in Averroistic fashion, God were *the* Agent Intellect and human beings so many occasions for the operation of divine reason. But that admission does not warrant the judgment that God plays no substantive role in Hobbes's moral and political philosophy. God is the author of human nature, including reason.

Kavka's claim is like saying that Shakespeare plays no substantive role in Romeo and Juliet's romance and tragedy. It is true that Shakespeare does not author an acting role for himself into *Romeo and Juliet*. Analogously, in God's natural kingdom, God is not represented by a prophet or incarnated. But the divine-command interpretation being outlined here does not understand God's role in securing the legal character of the laws of nature in this way. God is the author of reason and speech—he creates and orders man. This means that God is the author of all the powers of reason, including the computational function:

> And therefore in geometry (which is the only science that it hath pleased God hitherto to bestow on mankind) men begin at settling the significations of their words; which settling of significations they call *definitions*, and place them in the beginning of their reckoning.[121]

God authored man with reason, thereby bestowing upon him the computational power deployed in deducing the laws of nature. Kavka might admit this but still maintain that God plays no substantive role. To see why such a reply is not persuasive in Hobbesian terms, consider an analogy. Over the course of a few years in the mid-1990s, a team of engineers at IBM built Deep Blue, a supercomputer designed to win at the game of chess. The three designers were Murray Campbell, Joe Hoane, and Feng-hsiung Hsu.[122] In 1997 Deep Blue played in a six-game chess match against Garry Kasparov—whom many still consider the best chess player alive—losing the first match; winning the second; drawing in the third, fourth, and fifth; and winning the sixth.[123] This marked the first time that a computer had ever beaten a reigning world-champion Grandmaster. As Campbell, Hoane, and Hsu recount, Deep Blue was programmed and built to calculate millions of positions per second and generate the whole range of possible moves—including checking, check evasion, attacking, and retreat—and then choose one. The language of computational function is replete in the authors' account of Deep Blue: "The move generator, although it generates only one move at a time, implicitly computes all the possible moves and selects one via an arbitration network."[124] Through their creative genius, these engineers bestowed on Deep Blue idoneous principles of tractation.

Would it make any sense to say that Campbell, Hoane, and Hsu "played no substantive role" in Deep Blue's victory over Kasparov? While it is true that the men did not themselves perform the move calculations during each match, that hardly implies that they played no substantive role in Deep Blue's victory. Such an assertion would be patently false. They designed the machine with a specific end in mind and provided it with the means to achieve that end, testing, modifying, and fine-tuning it over time to complete the work. Analogously, God artificed man, making all of man's organs and powers to function for the good of his bodily life, including the power of reason, which functions properly when it judges preservation of life to be a fundamental goal and when it composes and divides well-defined words to generate a correct (if subtle) catalogue of the laws of nature. What more substantive role could there be?

Another school of Hobbes scholars, which holds what can be called a definitivist interpretation of Hobbesian natural law, interprets the computational function of reason in a different way. A brief discussion of this school will help elucidate the role of geometrical reasoning in my interpretation. Argued for by F. S. McNeilly and developed by John Deigh, this form of reasoning emphasizes *Leviathan* as a formal deductive system that is modeled on geometry. Hence *Leviathan* presents moral and political propositions "which are *definitionally* true, which are not to be interpreted as purporting to state truths *about human nature*, and which would remain true, if well constructed, regardless of what we might suppose the actual nature of human motivation to be."[125] McNeilly thus presents a definitivist interpretation of the laws of nature as *a priorical* and necessary as opposed to empirical and probabilistic. They are true just in virtue of their formal deduction, not in virtue of their connection to or dependence on human psychology. McNeilly thus segregates the "formal" from the "material" components in Hobbes's definition and deduction of the laws of nature.[126]

John Deigh sought to develop the definitivist view, contending that the operations of Hobbesian reason are "entirely formal."[127] Hence the branch of science that deals with the laws of nature, the science of ethics, begins with axioms and deduces theorems. The fundamental law of nature is the axiom whence the several theorems or laws of nature are deduced. Deigh maintains that it is a betrayal of Hobbes's understanding of reason and science to import a "material criterion" into Hobbes's conception of reason. Using language reminiscent of McNeilly, who referred to the "material concept of self-preservation," by "material criterion," Deigh means the good of self-preservation. This is "introduced" in Hobbes's definition of a law of nature: "a precept, or general rule, found out by reason, by which a man is forbidden to do that, which is destructive of his life." Deigh argues that to include within reason the "material criterion" would throw the early chapters of *Leviathan* into "war" with chapters 14 and 15 because it is set against the purely formal-computational conception of reason. Moreover, it runs afoul of Hobbes's nominalism because it "implies either universal concepts that inhere in the human mind or a world of universals that exists independently of any particulars and is accessible to reason alone, and either implication contradicts Hobbes's thesis that nothing universal exists independently of speech."[128]

Unfortunately, the springboard for Deigh's whole argument lacks bounce. Deigh cites the following passage of Hobbes: "Reason, in this sense, is nothing but reckoning (that is adding and subtracting) of the consequences of general names." Deigh seems to breeze over this passage without reading it carefully. Hobbes explicitly qualifies his statement of the computational function: "Reason, *in this sense*, is nothing but reckoning." Thus this passage is weak evidence that Hobbes intends to promulgate an understanding of reason as entirely formal. On its face, the passage seems to indicate a broad conception of reason that includes other noncomputational functions.[129] Reason has a computational function, but that does not exhaust its abilities. As the first postulate of human nature and other passages already discussed indicate, reason has a directive or originative function of grasping life to be good and worthy of pursuit and death to be undesirable.

Moreover, how should we interpret the fundamental law of nature, which seems to import the good of life as the object to be secured by the laws of nature? Deigh wants to deny that this object is imported by the goals of desire or the dictate of practical reason. What, then, is the warrant for its place in the definition of a law of nature? In other words, what is the criterion for "well-defined" terms? Deigh contends that what makes definitions correct are "facts about the linguistic usage of competent speakers," not facts about the human good (whether that is determined by reason or desire). But none of the passages Deigh cites are sufficient to justify his deep conventionalist reading of Hobbes's theory of language. Nor does he offer any extratextual evidence for the claim that Hobbes's definition of the fundamental law of nature was the conventional understanding of the term "fundamental law of nature" in 1651 English society.

Deigh's dismissal of the theistic natural law interpretation is premised on the extremely thin basis that Hobbes says we cannot have a thought of God in our heads. Hobbes believes a person can judge that God exists and predicate a range of titles in the superlative. He maintains, with the older Christian tradition, that none of this implies that the person has quidditative knowledge of God or an image of God in his head, much as a blind person does not have quidditative knowledge or an image of fire in his head but infers its existence from its effects.

Perhaps the biggest problem with this interpretation is that it is not clear how conventionally understood words shuffled about in various compositions and divisions could in and of themselves have any normative or binding force for human beings. Why should anyone care about abstract geometrical cogitations when faced with the question How should I live? Deigh can win pure logical independence of the science of ethics only at the price of entirely severing reason from the needs of embodied human existence. He attempts to walk back this implication when he admits that the science of morals will bear a "trace" of the material or bodily interests it serves. But this admission betrays the dilemma he has written himself into. To say, as Deigh does, that the material-bodily interest provides an "explanation" for the laws of nature is to smuggle back in human nature and its needs as grounds for the normative force of natural law.[130] In other words, the criterion for distinguishing between "well-formed" linguistic conventions and poorly formed linguistic conventions in Hobbesian ethics is the real condition and needs of human nature.

When Hobbes goes into synthetic mode, clearly he wants a deduction that is logically valid in light of the definitions he has given. However, it makes more sense of Hobbes's texts to see his manifest failure to present an entirely formalistic and *a priorical* deduction as an indication that he did not intend to strictly apply the geometrical method to his moral science. Hobbes manifestly rests his moral philosophy on first principles that the geometric method he pays lip service to does not itself yield. Thus, on this point I would concur with Kavka: we must interpret what Hobbes says in light of what he *does*—and, plainly, he imports empirical and probabilistic reasoning into his moral philosophy.[131] Such an admission need not entail that Hobbesian moral norms aren't of universal force, just as the universality of Aristotelian moral virtues and moral norms is not undermined by an account that moves from the empirical and particular to the universal and necessary and just as the universality of general principles of natural law in Aquinas's account can fail in some particulars as to rectitude and knowledge.[132]

What the definitivist interpretation ends up doing is subordinating the good and happiness of man to the logical relationships between words. Of course Hobbes wants to give logically rigorous deduction of the laws of nature. But he takes on principles delivered by the basic judgment of practical reason, introspection, empirical experience, theoretical reason, and even faith. Hobbes's background assumptions must be taken into account when considering why Hobbes settles on the definitions of words the way he does. To deny this is to get oneself "entangled in words; as a bird in lime twigs, the more he struggles the more belimed."[133]

Hobbesian moral philosophy is a science of good and evil, an account of practical necessities that must be observed individually and collectively in order to achieve human happiness. The laws of nature are premised on their order toward peace, because peace is a necessary condition of human happiness. They derive their proximate normative force from the human good, particularly the good of life, which is an objective constituent of any reasonable plan of life. Its ultimate legal force derives from God's ordained power. Hence, flowing from created human nature is the basic rational necessity to pursue the good of life, whence derives the rational necessity to endeavor toward or desire peace (the fundamental law of nature). A *crime* against the natural law is the commission by word or deed of that which natural law forbids or omission of that which natural law requires.[134] The whole natural law can be summed up in the golden rule: to do unto others as you would have them do unto you. This is a principle that guides all human conduct, including philosophical writing, the end of which is the benefit of mankind.[135] It follows that a maxim of philosophical writing is the requirement to aim at human happiness. Hence I believe that Hobbes would judge accounts of his moral theory that sever it from human happiness, the goods of life and peace, inasmuch as such accounts are held forth for our assent, to be themselves failures by word and deed to act as the natural law requires. Therefore, in Hobbes's own terms, McNeilly and Deigh appear to be guilty of *word crimes*.

Reply to the Epistemological Challenge

Having clarified the role of computational reasoning in Hobbesian moral knowledge, we are now in a position to return to the epistemological challenge noted earlier in this chapter. Notice that nothing in this account requires that the addressee of the natural law cognize a divine command in the form of "I command you to *x*," as Martinich suggested. The judgment that creation is existentially dependent upon an omnipotent creator and endowed by that creator with order is not a judgment of prophetic knowledge—in either the classical natural law tradition or in Hobbes's thought. It should also be apparent now why the practical severability thesis—the claim that God plays no substantive role in Hobbes's political thought—fails as a sound interpretive key to Hobbes's natural law theory. The practical severability thesis downplays or misunderstands how transformative the judgment that God exists is for the Hobbesian practical reasoner and, hence, Hobbes's vision of morality and politics. Hobbes does not make these claims merely to "multiply men's motives for following them" or merely to show that they are compatible with Christianity in order to persuade his Christian audience.[136] Rather, God's legislative activity evident in his ordinary work is essential to the dictates of reason being laws. To hold otherwise would be to attribute to Hobbes systematic distortion because he would have been warranted only to deduce a catalogue of "counsels of nature" when in fact he purports to deduce a catalogue of *laws* of nature.[137]

So far I have argued that the binding force of the laws of nature flows from God's irresistible power in its ordained mode. Obligation in Hobbes's system springs "*either* from nature, or from *contract*."[138] The former instance is special in that the obligation springing from nature flows from God's power, which is not taken away. While that would be sufficient to ground the legal character and binding force of the laws of nature, Hobbes is not consistent on the point. In fact, he often wants to include a foundational liberal consent condition in all obligation, which complicates the picture.[139]

Ockham had insisted, in his discussion of the third mode of natural law noted above, that rulers must be elected by consent. Paul Sigmund remarks that this is "probably the first time in the history of political thought that governmental legitimacy was defined as derived from consent based on natural law."[140] Suárez would push this line of thought further, arguing for a fundamental political liberty equality of all human beings by natural law, and therefore for the necessity of a kind of transfer of authority from the people to rulers, which he calls a "special volition" and "common consent."[141] Suárez again enlisted Aquinas as the source of his view. But, while Aquinas maintains that the best regime has a substantive participative role for the people, the passage Suárez cites does not necessitate any particular mode of consent as a criterion for the justice of government.[142]

Hobbes's natural law theory represents a continued radicalization of the idea of consent as a necessary (but not sufficient) condition for obligation, including even the natural duties that bind man, as picked out by the laws of nature. When such texts are taken into account, it appears that consent in two modes is a necessary condition of the legal force of natural law: first the agent's assent to reason's dictates regarding the means to one's proper good and second to the divine pedigree of nature. To the first Hobbes remarks that the law of nature "is the assent itself that all men give to the means of their preservation."[143] In other words, in the very act of rightly reasoning about the practical necessities to secure the good of life, one performs the necessary act of consent. To the second it is necessary to assent to God's dominion over the natural kingdom, and this is actualized in the act of judging God to exist. What if one withholds assent in either of these modes? Those who refuse assent in the first mode are fools. Those who refuse assent in the second mode are atheists. I discuss each in the next section.

Replying to the Foole and the Atheist

Hobbes's reply to the Foole has garnered as much attention as any passage in his corpus. I do not intend to do justice to that vast literature here. I would, however, like to suggest that the Foole is a particular character who withholds assent to the practical necessities that reason dictates are the means of preservation. In this way the Foole fails to meet the first consent condition for the natural law to have legal force. Those who deny God's existence fail to meet the second consent condition for natural law to have legal force. While these two modes of consent are logically distinct, the Foole of *Leviathan* also fails to meet the second consent condition because he is an atheist. Hobbes's reply to the Foole thus throws light on his natural law theory of morality and indicates that Hobbes's laws of nature are not mere maxims of prudence to satisfy the desires of egoistic or predominantly egoistic agents.

The Foole questions the goodness of justice. This challenge to justice has a long pedigree in political philosophy that can be traced to Plato. Glaucon put to Socrates the challenge of the Myth of Gyges. If a person, P, could don a ring of invisibility and sneak into the castle, kill the king, bed his wife, steal his riches, and make himself tyrant, wouldn't P do it? The Foole's objection to justice is similar. The Foole reasons that if a kingdom can be gotten by unjust violence, then why not do it?

> He questioneth whether injustice, taking away the fear of God (for the same fool hath said in his heart there is no God), may not sometimes stand with that reason which dictateth to every man his own good; and particularly then, when it conduceth to such a benefit as shall put a man in a condition to neglect, not only the dispraise and revilings, but also the power of other men. "The kingdom of God is gotten by violence; but what if it could be gotten by unjust violence? were it against reason so to get it, when it is impossible to receive hurt by it?"[144]

The antecedent of the last "it" appears to be "unjust violence." The Foole's reasoning can be restated like this

> P1. Reasonable persons act for their preservation and contentment.
> P2. Sometimes injustice conduces to preservation and contentment.
> SP1. Injustice never conduces to eternal discontentment because neither God nor eternal punishment exists.
> Therefore, reasonable persons should sometimes be willing to act unjustly when it conduces to their preservation and contentment.

By this reasoning, "successful wickedness hath obtained the name of virtue," but Hobbes maintains that the reasoning is specious and false.[145] The Foole's reasoning looks pretty similar to the reasoning that animates Machiavelli's portrait of the new prince of *virtù*. Machiavelli's understanding of virtue can be briefly recounted.

Machiavelli jettisons the ancient ideal of virtue as a perfective habit of man and redefines *virtù* as the quality by which one maximally controls one's environment and tames or minimizes *fortuna*. By *fortuna* he means the whole set of forces of nature and other wills that opposes one's own will. Machiavelli paints a new portrait of the virtuous prince whose *virtù* is a sort of effectiveness in gaining or holding onto power and glory. And, to be effective in acquiring and holding onto dominion, one must be willing to get one's hands dirty. This means that *virtù* requires overcoming the scruples of conscience to do things that traditional morality condemns, such as lying or even killing when necessary.

Hobbes's reply to the Foole is a rejection of the Machiavellian understanding of virtue.

Hobbes condescends to take on the Foole on his own terms and accepts his subpremise (SP1) for the sake of argument. A few observations can be made on Hobbes's reply. His overall strategy is to argue against premise 2 (P2). In the first part, Hobbes supposes that actions have an intrinsic order either toward preservation/contentment or toward destruction/discontentment in this world. This is what makes justice good for Hobbes. Thus just actions (promise keeping) have an intrinsic order toward good results such as peace and preservation, and unjust actions have an intrinsic order toward bad results such as war and destruction. The Foole then must rely on accidental causality or chance (what Machiavelli would call *fortuna*) for the success of his wickedness. Elsewhere Hobbes relates his view that there is a causal chain that links breach of the natural law with natural punishment:

> There are few things in this world but *either* have mixture of good and evil *or* there is a chain of them so necessarily linked together, that the one cannot be taken without the other: as for example, the pleasures of sin, and the bitterness of punishment, are inseparable.[146]

Thus, for example, excessive drinking of wine brings with it pleasure. But drunkenness also brings with it evils attached to it such as the impairment of the faculty of reason, the unleashing of extravagant passions and the vicious behavior associated with them, and a painful hangover. Gluttony as well brings pleasures of the belly but carries the bitter punishment of obesity and bodily disease. Temperance is especially a self-regarding virtue in such a way that Hobbes indicates that it binds persons both *in foro interno* and *in foro externo* even in the state of nature since intemperate acts are intrinsically ordered to destruction.

Do acts of injustice carry with them evil consequences in the way that intemperate acts do? Hobbes argues that unjust actions can result in good consequences only provided that accidental causation—cause and effects that could not be expected—intervenes to turn the unjust act to one's benefit. As one cannot reasonably expect to hit upon a treasure chest by digging dozens of holes in one's backyard, so one cannot reasonably expect to gain and keep dominion by injustice.[147] Yet, even if by accident what was intrinsically unjust turns to one's benefit, "such events do not make it reasonably or wisely done."[148]

The second part of Hobbes's reply focuses on the consequences of promise breaking in the state of nature. His argument boils down to a claim that foolish promise breakers will develop a bad reputation in the state of nature, a condition in which it is practically reasonable to confederate with others for one's safety and defense. The risk of being publicly known as a promise breaker and therefore untrustworthy of covenant is a chief evil attached to injustice. Now accidental causality may intervene such that the Foole is not found out by his benighted allies. But the Foole cannot reasonably expect the security he seeks through covenant. His allies' false belief about his being trustworthy "cannot reasonably [be] reckon[ed] upon as the means of his security."[149] The Foole's allies' false belief at the very least entails that they forbear him only out of ignorance and only so long as he is not found out. It also may indicate a more general ineptness of his confederates, such that they are less likely to be reliable confederates to secure the good of the group.

So far, Hobbes hasn't taken on the Foole's objection that it is sometimes reasonable to break covenant "for the getting of a kingdom."[150] In other words, Hobbes's reply so far has focused on situations of war and trying to show the reasonability of promise keeping. The principle that promise keeping has an intrinsic order toward preservation and peace applies in commonwealth as well. But what about the possibility of successful wickedness in the form of a treacherous and accomplished coup d'état, of which history is not lacking in examples? Take, for example, Cesare Borgia, whom Machiavelli holds out as the new prince of *virtù*. In one of his exploits Cesare treacherously took the Italian city-state Urbino. Cesare wrote to the reigning prince, Guidobaldo de Montefeltre, requesting his military assistance for a feigned attack on Camerino and professing his love for and friendship to Guidobaldo. For his part, Guidobaldo had a reputation as a kindly, just, good ruler and was loved by his people. Guidobaldo agreed to help Cesare and, believing Cesare's word and promise, did not prepare any defenses of Urbino. After a few days of forced march, Cesare swept into Urbino at the head of his army and took the city before Guidobaldo was even aware of the treachery.[151] This is a prime example of successful wickedness that Machiavelli lends the name *virtù*.

Machiavelli ostensibly distinguishes Cesare Borgia's princely virtue from that of other princes who have gained dominion by treachery, such as Agathocles of Syracuse. Through cunning Agathocles rose from rags to praetor in Syracuse before calling together the influential Syracusan people and senators on the pretense of discussing important matters and butchering them. Machiavelli tells us, "It cannot be virtue to kill one's fellow-citizens, betray one's friends, be without faith, without pity, and without religion; by these methods one may indeed gain power, but not glory." Yet we have to wonder how serious Machiavelli is here, since in the very next sentence he speaks of the "virtues of Agathocles." Indeed, Machiavelli has just been praising the virtues of Cesare Borgia, who was irreligious, betrayed his friends, and was without faith. As Harvey Mansfield points out, Machiavelli uses the term "virtue" "in two contradictory senses as to whether it includes or excludes evil deeds."[152] On my reading, it is the inclusive sense that Machiavelli believes is truly virtuous. If Agathocles lacked virtue, it wasn't because he did evil but because he did not do evil according to necessity to secure his good and the good of the city. Indeed Machiavelli seems explicitly to countenance the initial coup as cruelty well used inasmuch as it secured Agathocles. It was only Agathocles' persistence in cruelty that was unnecessary and therefore unvirtuous.

Hobbes's reply to the Foole shows us that he is not impressed with this picture of virtue. Agathocles' actions were rebellious because they were a treachery from within. Even though successful to acquire dominion, Hobbes would maintain that such actions are unreasonable because "it cannot reasonably be expected (but rather the contrary), and because (by gaining it so) others are taught to gain the same in like manner, the attempt thereof is against reason."[153] The latter is a principle that flows from the fundamental premise that unjust actions are intrinsically disordered. Even if successful, they have a tutelary and expressive character that renders the dominion gained intrinsically flimsy.

The English maxim "turnabout is fair play" colloquially captures the essence of the principle. The principle seems to find empirical verification time and again in turbulent English political history, where those who break troth to take the throne by violence themselves meet a violent end. Mortimer deposed and killed Edward II and was himself executed by Edward III. Henry IV invaded England and deposed Richard II. This generated the Epiphany Rising, which failed to restore Richard II to the throne but was not a surprising consequence. Henry Bolingbroke's act was later seen by supporters of Richard Duke of York (the Yorkist party) as a Lancastrian usurpation. If Richard II's incompetence justified Henry's invasion, why didn't the incompetence of Henry VI—under whose reign England lost many treasured French possessions won by Henry V—justify his deposition in favor of the highly competent and accomplished Duke of York? The Yorkist argument was bolstered by the fact that he was the great-grandson of Edward III and, besides Henry VI, the only other unbroken male descendant of Edward III. The cycles of bloody violence in the various civil wars of English history demonstrate that getting the throne by violence has a tutelary effect on the friends, family, and supporters of the vanquished, who in their turn exact bloody vengeance on the vanquishers. As Shakespeare wrote:

> England hath long been mad, and scarred herself;
> The brother blindly shed the brother's blood;
> The father rashly slaughtered his own son;
> The son, compelled, been butcher to the sire.[154]

That horror story was a not-too-distant memory in Hobbes's time, and alongside the story of Charles I, it is probably tacitly referred to when Hobbes points out that English kings would have had the means "to defend their people against foreign enemies, and to compel them to keep peace among themselves ... if they had never given their rights away, and their subjects always kept their oaths and promises."[155] Promise breakers cannot reasonably be free from fear of treachery. *Turnabout is fair play*. Thus Shakespeare's Henry IV remarks: "Uneasy lies the head that wears a crown."[156] Hobbes's point is that uneasy will be the head of any person who got the crown by promise breaking. Cromwell himself felt the force of this principle when, after he had conquered England and executed the king, he was immediately beset by the Leveller mutinies. Even Machiavelli seems to acknowledge the truth of the principle when he wonders how those who have gotten dominion by cruelty can hang onto power against external threats, since one's first act by its nature has the potency to generate internal conspiracy against the usurper and with his enemies.[157]

So Hobbes's reply to the Foole focuses on getting him to assent to the first consent condition, that the laws of nature really are the means of self-preservation. By arguing that the Foole relies on accidental causality and ignores the expressive character of "successful" injustice, Hobbes is implicitly deploying the truth of God's ordained power, which establishes a certain regularity of cause and effect between virtue and vice. This would be expected if my interpretation is correct, namely, that Hobbes regards God's ordained power as establishing a regularity of cause and effect in the world.

An objection arises: what about the possibility of a "happy traitor" and, more generally, that of a "happy crook"? The objection is formulated by Ernest Fortin thus: by unaided reason, we cannot rule out the possibility "that some lucky person might commit a single undetected crime by means of which he obtains the fortune or the position on which his heart is set and then, without repenting or surrendering any of his ill-gotten gains, live 'honestly' and happily thereafter."[158] The belief that such a possibility cannot be ruled out without appeal to revelation gives rise to an interpretation of Hobbes's reply to the Foole as unserious, that Hobbes didn't really believe it.[159] To this objection it is replied that Hobbes does believe that affliction is not necessarily preceded by sin. He takes this to be the orthodox biblical position, as seen in Job, who suffered afflictions in spite of his righteousness. Moreover, he takes it to be the orthodox position that wickedness can precede prosperity, since the Psalmist laments that the wicked live in prosperity. Moreover, as discussed in the previous chapter, while unaided right reasoners can affirm the existence of a providential God, by unaided reason there can be no knowledge of the afterlife, which at the very least raises doubts about the unaided Hobbesian practical reasoner's ability to factor in sanctions in the afterlife. All of this can be understood in harmony with Hobbes's natural law theory.

As in the Aristotelian-Thomistic tradition, that which is accidental in the sense of "by chance" is something that attaches to a thing, but not necessarily, which was taken to be usually or for the most part. So the person digging holes in her backyard to plant trees who strikes upon treasure discovers it "by accident" because tree planting is not usually accompanied by discovery of treasure. However, Hobbes agrees with Aquinas in rejecting the Aristotelian explanation of accidental causality inasmuch as it rules out providence.[160] How, then, can one speak of both accidental causality and providence as if they are compatible concepts, as Hobbes and Aquinas do? The solution is that things are said to be "accidental" in reference to lower, particular, and proximate causes but are not so spoken of when considered in relation to God, the *causa causarum*. Initially, all Hobbes needs to say is that the Foole cannot reasonably expect to get dominion by breaking troth because successful treachery happens in a minority of cases—it is "accidental" with reference to the relevant particular causes. Does this mean that Hobbes recognizes the theoretical possibility of a "happy traitor"? If by "happy" is meant simply that there can be cases in which somebody gets and holds onto the position of power one desires, then yes. However, authentic happiness in Hobbes's scheme of felicity pluralism requires that agents take the good of life as basic and have a will to abide by the practical necessities to secure that good. Condescending to the Foole's own terms, there can't really be "happy traitors" because, even within the small set of treacheries that are successful, the promise breaker cannot reasonably expect to be safe from treachery and violent death himself. Even if there is a minority subset of cases in which the usurper does not experience treacherous plots to overthrow him, he fails to be practically reasonable if he does not always fear such plots.

Another objection could be raised. If Hobbes really regarded God's existence in the order of being and assented to that proposition in the order of knowing as essential conditions of being bound by the natural law, then why didn't he engage in a metaphysical refutation of the atheist's failure to "reason aright"?[161] To address this objection we should recall that Hobbes deploys at least five different kinds of argument for theism throughout his writings such that he is not uncritical of atheistic reasoning. Still, why not make such an argument here? My reply is a sort of riff on Kinch Hoekstra's interpretation of Hobbes as replying to the "Explicit Foole," who loudly declaims justice and/or flagrantly violates agreements.[162] I would suggest that Hobbes's Foole is a Silent Atheist.

The Foole says *in his heart* that there is no God. Hobbes seems to recognize that there are Fooles who profess theism while their atheism is known only "to him that searcheth hearts."[163] Consider the possibility that the Foole is a Silent Atheist in conjunction with desiring to get the kingdom of God by violence. Hobbes may be insinuating that the rebels stoking insurrection against the king in the name of God and Christ—certain Presbyterians, Catholics, Independents, Anabaptists, and individuals from other sects who Hobbes explicitly calls out in *Behemoth*, years after the Restoration—did not really believe in God but cloaked their ambitions for temporal power in the garb of their religious piety and (private) interpretation of scripture. The dissenting sects pretended that regicide was necessary to establish the kingdom of God. But Hobbes insists that the felicity of membership in God's kingdom can be gotten in "one way imaginable, and that is not breaking, but keeping of covenant."[164] This suffices for his purpose here: to suggest that the people who rebelled against Charles I and unjustly murdered him were fools and silent atheists.[165] The hint is subtle, and intentionally so, given the Cromwellian context in which *Leviathan* was published. At any rate, Hobbes's reply to the Foole hardly seems evidence against the theistic natural law interpretation of Hobbes's moral and political theory.

Hobbes does not think that the necessity to pursue the end of life or the means thereto has the force of law for the atheist because he denies that God has any being. So even if the atheist seeks preservation, and seeks peace as the means thereto, seeking peace can be only recommendatory. This is why Hobbes points out that it is dangerous to covenant with Explicit Atheists: "There is no living in a commonwealth with men, to whose oaths we cannot reasonably give credit."[166] Hobbes's reply to the atheist thus seems to be that he ought to remain silent about his metaphysical convictions and ought to behave in a way that, according to Hobbes, his worldview doesn't ultimately warrant, namely, that there is a causal order in the world—in fact established and maintained by God's power—that generally rewards virtuous action and punishes evil behavior.[167]

Having shown how Hobbes secures the legal character of the natural law on the metaphysical-theological foundation of God's irresistible power, in the mode of *potentia ad ordinata*, and how this grounds the basic duty to preserve one's life, whence the laws of nature are derived, I have now demonstrated that Hobbes's moral theory is properly a *natural law theory*. The human good of life provides the most basic reason for action, and the norms that it proximately grounds have a legal character. According to Hobbes, the foundational judgment of right reason is that life is good—indeed, it is the *bonum maximum*. The need to desire the good of life has the character of rational necessity. This necessity is universal inasmuch as all human beings have the power of rationality. But the force of the necessity will be variable according to one's beliefs, according to Hobbes. If one is a theist, one takes oneself to be created and governed by God—who by his irresistible power (and maximal goodness) rightly orders the world, including human beings by his rational word—and one takes the dictates of reason to bind with legal force. Because the order of reason directs man to pursue life and the necessary means to life, these rational necessities take on the character of law for the theist. These laws have the status of rational necessity for nontheists who otherwise reason rightly—but they are not, properly speaking, laws. If correct, the tendency of much of modern Hobbes scholarship to discover in Hobbes an entirely secular ethic is deeply misleading.

If the argument is successful, an account of Hobbesian practical reason as grasping the intelligible goal of life as a not merely instrumental reason for action and deducing the necessary means thereto—dictates which, for the theist, bind with legal force—would seem to be the best interpretation of Hobbes's "true and only moral philosophy." The following chapters build on this conclusion and, on these grounds, offer new interpretations of Hobbes's theories of personhood, commonwealth, the common good, and civil law.

CHAPTER 5

The Essence of Leviathan

*The Person of the Commonwealth
and the Common Good*

In this chapter I examine the implications of Hobbes's natural law theory for his theory of commonwealth. I argue that Hobbes constructs a *common good theory* of commonwealth upon his notion of natural law. Accordingly, Hobbes's common good account of commonwealth is grounded on his understanding of goodness. It has been argued that Hobbes's axiology is best understood as a thin theory of the good. The need to desire the good of life has the character of rational necessity. This necessity is universal inasmuch as all human beings have the power of rationality. In the previous chapter I articulated the legal character of the laws of nature, including Hobbes's fundamental law of nature, to seek peace when it can be had, and the second law of nature, to lay down one's right to all things and incorporate into commonwealth through the sovereign-making covenant.[1] Because Hobbes's common good account of commonwealth is grounded in the claim that God, by his rational word, binds human beings to seek peace, we can also say that Hobbes's theory qualifies as a natural law account of commonwealth. The establishment of peace through the sovereign-making covenant transforms the basic good of life into the common good of security.

The argument of this chapter is framed around Hobbes's definition of commonwealth. According to Hobbes, a commonwealth can be defined as follows:

> *One person, of whose acts a great multitude, by mutual covenants one with another, have made themselves every one the author, to the end he may use the strength and means of them all, as he shall think expedient, for their peace and common defence.*[2]

We can break this definition down to its parts:

> (a) One person, (b) of whose acts (c) a great multitude, (d) by mutual covenants one with another, have made themselves every one the author, (e) to the end he may use the strength and means of them all, as he shall think expedient, (f) for their peace and common defence.

Given Hobbes's willingness to deploy the terminology of the Aristotelian four causes, we can make sense of his definition in those terms. Part a indicates the formal cause or "form" of the commonwealth—and it is initially unclear whether it refers to the person of the *commonwealth* or the person of the *sovereign* or both. The central argument of this chapter is that the one person is a truly representative artificial person, marked off by its order to the common good. In virtue of the authorization relation, the sovereign bears this person, and different constitutions of sovereignty by the one, the few, or the many differentiate the different regime types. Part b refers to ordinances and judgments or simply the commands of the one person (civil law), which are authoritative. Consideration of part b is postponed until the next chapter, where we take up Hobbes's natural law theory of civil law. Part c indicates the material cause or "matter" of the commonwealth, which is man. Part d indicates the efficient cause of commonwealth—the acts by which the "matter" makes or artifices the commonwealth. Part e refers to the essential rights of the sovereign, which are for the sake of the final cause of the commonwealth, that for which it is made (part f).

The claim I want to defend is this: the "peace and common defence" referred to in part f is *the common good*, and this marks off the Hobbesian commonwealth as a distinct kind of (social) entity. This will become evident in the analysis of each part of the definition. The common good provides the end of action for (c) the great multitude (the "material" parts) when they (d) covenant and make the commonwealth. The (e) means and strength of those incorporated are used by the sovereign for the common good as he (it) thinks expedient. Full consideration of part e is also postponed until the next chapter, where we address the question of whether the sovereign is unbound in this capacity.

Throughout the analysis of each part of the definition, I suggest that Hobbes's common good account is illuminated in juxtaposition with the traditional Aristotelian-Thomistic account of the common good. I argue that Hobbes's break from the older tradition consists not, as some scholars have suggested, in the rejection of the political animal anthropology, as Aristotle and Aquinas understood it, nor in reason's incapacity to discover a common good, nor in Hobbesian political art's supplanting nature, nor in fictionalizing society. Hobbes holds forth a theory of commonwealth as a real unity that is characterized by common pursuit of a common aim—a truly common good. Hobbes's novelty is in thinning out the common good to security. For Hobbes, the unity attained in society is best understood as a thinned-out version of peace. Peace is still an essentially *shared* and *good* state of affairs. Still, since the only unity available is through security, the Hobbesian theory of peace entails a *unitarist* conception of commonwealth—and herein lies a significant break with the Aristotelian-Thomistic account of the common good. Hobbes, moreover, takes over concepts from the older natural law tradition and enlists them in service of his theory of the common good. This is manifest in his theory of man as maker of the commonwealth, as Hobbes takes over the Aristotelian-Thomistic principle of mimesis. Still, Hobbes agrees with the older tradition inasmuch as the pursuit of what he takes to be the common good marks off the commonwealth from other forms of association. The classical natural law tradition held that a *societas* is a genuine unity and therefore a real thing to be included in any fundamental ontological account of the real. While Hobbes's social ontology is transformative, it is, as a social holist position, in structural continuity with the classical natural law view.

I shall begin by analyzing part a of the definition, and the chapter will build toward the conclusion that the commonwealth is a truly representative artificial person. In the first section I give a preliminary discussion of personhood in which I seek to clarify the different kinds of persons, including natural, artificial, and feigned. This will set the stage to consider the fitness of (c) the "great multitude" of natural persons to incorporate into the artificial person of the commonwealth. The standard reading of Hobbes is that he radically rejects Aristotelian political animal anthropology. In the second section I challenge this interpretation. A close reading of Hobbes's discussion of man and bees and his discussion of man's fitness for community in *De Cive* reveals that Hobbes retains a kind of *zoon politkon* anthropology with stated continuities with how Aquinas understood the dictum. Having shown how man is and is not inclined toward community, I turn in the third section to part d of the definition and consider natural persons as covenanters and makers of commonwealth. Hobbes takes over the Aristotelian mimetic principle that art imitates nature—and this is explicable only on the basis of the theistic natural law interpretation argued for thus far. But Hobbes co-opts it for his own distinctive purpose of thinning out the common good to security and to strengthening the sovereign to be unlimited. For Hobbes, the urgency of this good demands power proportionate to securing it, a notion captured in part e's inclusion of a principle of expediency. The thin theory of the common good, combined with unlimited sovereign prerogative, generates unitarism, which sharply contrasts with the social pluralism of Aristotelian-Thomistic social ontology. Yet Hobbes structurally agrees with the older tradition in that the commonwealth is a distinctive kind of social entity rather than a mere aggregate of individuals considered "one" only by a mental fiction.

Distinguishing between Persons Natural, Feigned, and Artificial

In order to clarify the meaning of the "one person" referred to in the definition of commonwealth, we must turn back to Hobbes's discussion of personhood in chapter 16 of *Leviathan*. Hobbes's definition of a person has been a somewhat vexing object of debate among scholars. The outcome is important because, as David Runciman notes, "What the state is has to be inferred from the text of *Leviathan*" since Hobbes "never states explicitly what kind of person it is."[3] A straightforward reading of the text of *Leviathan*, anchored in Hobbes's own examples, will clear up the confusion and indicate what kind of person the commonwealth is.[4] Hobbes defines person in the following way.

> A person is he *whose words or actions are considered either as his own, or as representing the words or actions of another man, or of any other thing to whom they are attributed, whether truly or by fiction*. When they are considered as his own, then is he called a *natural person*; and when they are considered as representing the words and actions of another, then is he a *feigned* or *artificial person*.[5]

The first thing to notice is that "person" is evidently a genus further divided into the species of natural persons, feigned persons, and artificial persons. The features common to all persons include the capacity for words and actions. Each kind of person is specified according to ownership or representation. Natural persons are those whose words and actions are their own. Feigned and artificial persons are those whose words and actions are representative of an other thing or an other man, whether truly or by fiction. At this point questions naturally arise. Does "or" indicate that "feigned" and "artificial" are synonyms such that feigned persons are identical to artificial persons? Or are "feigned persons" essentially distinct from "artificial persons"? Moreover, does "truly representative" and "fictitiously representative" further specify feigned and artificial personhood?[6]

Prima facie, "feigned" and "artificial" do not seem synonymous in meaning. "Feigned" carries the note of imaginary, while "artificial" need not imply this. If Jones loses his leg in combat, he will find walking around with a feigned leg much more difficult than walking around with an artificial leg. Moreover, the next time "feigned" is mentioned in the discussion is to suggest the difference between an artificial person and a feigned person.[7] For the moment, then, let us assume that feigned and artificial persons are not identical. What, then, is the meaning of "truly representative" and "fictitiously representative" in relation to feigned and artificial persons? One option would be that these introduce further specific differences. Call this the specification thesis.

If we adopt the specification thesis we will now have, in addition to natural persons, the following: truly representative feigned persons, fictitiously representative feigned persons and truly representative artificial persons, and fictitiously representative artificial persons. In order to pursue this line of inquiry, "truly representative" and "fictitiously representative" would have to really add something to "feigned person" and "artificial person." Let us first consider the case of feigned persons.

What would a "truly representative feigned person" or a "fictitiously representative feigned person" be? One possibility would be to take Hobbes's discussion of personation as acting on stage or in conversation in representing oneself or another as shedding light on the meaning of "feigned" in its literary-stage sense—a sense not uncommon in seventeenth-century England. In this sense, an example of a feigned person would be a character in a dialogue. We could then take "truly" and "by fiction" to mean authentic in authorization or act-ownership and not authorized or counterfeit, respectively.[8] Consider that person A in *Behemoth* could thus be an example of a "truly representative feigned person." To recall, A and B are two characters who have a dialogue about the origins of the English Civil War. Person A is certainly a feigned person in the literary-stage sense, and he could be said to be truly or authentically representative of another in his words, namely, the real Thomas Hobbes, because Hobbes *authored* the dialogue himself. Sticking with the literary-stage sense of "feigned," an example of a fictitiously representative feigned person would be a feigned person who does not truly represent the person it purports to but is a counterfeit representation. Such would be an unauthorized representation, and Hobbes might say that Thomas Tenison's "Hobbes" in his dialogue is such an example.[9] So in this interpretation an example of a feigned person truly representing is a literary-stage character that is truly representative because authorized like A's representation of Thomas Hobbes in *Behemoth*. An example of a feigned person fictitiously representing is a literary-stage character representing by counterfeit, that is, without authorization of the real person it represents—for example, Tenison's "Hobbes" representing the real Thomas Hobbes.

But there are interpretive problems with the first option just described. When Hobbes discusses the covenanting powers of artificial persons, he recognizes the possibility that some actors will pretend to authority they do not have when entering into a covenant. In such cases, Hobbes says that the actors' authority is feigned. So here "feigned" means "unauthorized." Acts of a feigned authority "obligeth the actor only, there being no author but himself."[10] So even if "feigned" could have a literary-stage note, it must also include the notion of unauthorized. Now consider again the specification thesis. If we substitute instead "unauthorized" for "feigned," we will have fictitiously representative unauthorized persons and truly representative unauthorized persons. But given this meaning of "feigned," the specification thesis evidently results in absurdity.

Another problem for the specification thesis as applied to feigned persons is how Hobbes later describes representation by fiction: "There are few things that are incapable of being represented by fiction."[11] He mentions bridges, churches, hospitals, idols, and generally "inanimate" things. Due to their inanimation, such things cannot authorize words or actions. But they can find fictional personation by authorization of the owners or governors of those things. Similarly, although animate, children, fools, and madmen lack the use of reason and so can't authorize by words and actions. But they can find fictional personation by authorization of the one who governs them by right. Here "fiction" does not mean "counterfeit" in the sense of being unauthorized but is fiction in the sense of imaginatively invented because the represented cannot self-authorize. The attribution of words and actions to a bridge or a madman is a fiction in the sense of imaginatively invented for the purposes of the bridge's or the madman's representation at civil law. Given that "feigned person" must at least include as one of its meanings "unauthorized person," the specification thesis would lead to "fictitiously representative feigned persons," meaning "self-unauthorizable unauthorized persons," which, in the case of a madman, would mean nothing more than the madman himself and, for a bridge, an absurdity.

So, given Hobbes's own examples of feigned persons and personation by fiction, it does not seem that the specification thesis is true for feigned persons. But perhaps feigned persons are best considered in their own category as pretending unauthorized persons. This definition captures Hobbes's own example of an unauthorized mediator. It seems to capture the common literary-stage sense of feigned persons as well. For example, the person of Julius Caesar in Shakespeare's tragedy is pretending to represent the words and actions of the real Julius Caesar, but his "authorization" flows from the words and actions—the pen—of the Bard, not Caesar himself.[12]

We can now consider the specification thesis as applied to artificial persons. Perhaps "truly" and "by fiction" modifies only artificial persons. Truly representative artificial persons would then be those actually or evidently authorized to speak or act on behalf of some other(s). Artificial persons representative by fiction would be those actually authorized to speak or act on behalf of some other that cannot authorize itself or himself. Here the specification thesis does not lead to an absurdity, and it accounts for Hobbes's own examples. Moreover, because "truly" and "by fiction" add something over and above "artificial"—that is, they specify the character of the authorization—the common equation of "artificial" with "fictional" in Hobbes scholarship must be rejected.[13]

In sum, the genus "person" is divided into the species of natural persons, feigned persons, artificial persons truly representing, and artificial persons representing by fiction. Natural persons are particular substances that have the immediate capacity to perform to speak and act on their own behalf. Truly representative artificial persons are those entities actually or evidently authorized to speak or act on behalf of some other(s). Artificial persons representative by fiction are those entities actually authorized to speak or act on behalf of some other that cannot authorize itself or himself. Feigned persons are unauthorized actors. This interpretation is not elaborate but follows from a straightforward reading of the text.[14] If this reading is right, the best candidate for the kind of which the "one person" is an instance is the truly representative artificial person. Before considering Quentin Skinner's influential rival reading, it is fitting to further build the case for reading Hobbes's theory of commonwealth as a common good account. If Hobbes does in fact hold a common good account of commonwealth, we might expect him to affirm an openness or fitness in men or a multitude of men—the "matter" indicated in part c—to incorporate. But Hobbes seems to deny the latter when he takes a detour in chapter 17—before giving the formula for the sovereign-making covenant—to reject the Aristotelian thesis of man's natural sociality. Does Hobbes really reject the older teaching?

Is Man a Social and Political Animal "by Nature"? On the Fitness of the "Great Multitude" to Incorporate

In the Aristotelian-Thomistic tradition, the claim that society is not a mere aggregate or fiction but rather a group marked off by the common pursuit of a common aim (a good shared by all the members of the group) was grounded on the claim that man is by nature a social and political animal. The claim was that, since man is by nature a social and political animal, his natural good or happiness is attained as a share of the common good through membership in a commonwealth. The standard interpretation of Hobbes is that, since man is not by nature a social and political animal, his happiness is not "by nature" attained as a share of the common good. To the contrary, says the standard interpreter, since what "nature" gives us leads to a war of all against all, we need a purely artificial contrivance, the Leviathan, to keep our radically asocial impulses in check. As Ernest Fortin puts it, it is in the thought of Hobbes that there is a real "watershed" in the history of political thought in "denying that human beings are political by nature ... and by proclaiming the absolute priority of rights and duties."[15] But it has already been shown how the duty to preserve oneself is prior to the right of nature. Moreover, I contend that Hobbes actually does affirm something like the *zoon politikon* anthropology that is broadly within the spirit of how Aquinas understood it. On this basis, Hobbes builds a common good account of commonwealth.

In both *De Cive* and *Leviathan*, Hobbes is particularly concerned with showing how human beings differ from irrational animals like bees, "which are therefore by Aristotle numbered amongst the political creatures."[16] Why don't bees require a fear-inducing sovereign power to compel order? While we observe queens in every hive, the queens don't seem to have the character of little leviathans. But if the distinction between rational animals and irrational animals was but one of a small degree, we might expect to find unruly bees brought into order by so many fearsome apiarian Abaddons. Their natural sociality seems to be enough to order them in the common life of a hive. Hobbes writes:

> It is very true that in those creatures, living only by sense and appetite, their consent of minds is so durable, as there is no need of any thing more to secure it, and (by consequence) to preserve peace among them, than barely their natural inclination. But among men the case is otherwise.[17]

So Hobbes emphasizes six differences between men and bees, each of which is grounded on man's distinct capacity for reason and language. First, because men have speech they are able to contend over the honor due to themselves, whence follows envy, hatred, and finally war. Second, the private good is identical with the common good for bees, whereas it is not so for men because men desire eminence in the possession of goods to the exclusion of others—"positional advantage," to use Philip Pettit's helpful phrase.[18] Third, bees neither find fault with nor question their government, thus instigating others into faction. Fourth, through want of language, bees cannot signify to others their desires and aversions and hence cannot dress up good in the robes of evil and vice versa. Fifth, there is no distinction between injury and damage or harm among bees, but among men this distinction disturbs the peace. And finally, agreement among bees is natural, while agreement among men is by covenant, which is artificial.[19]

At first blush the difference from the Aristotelian principle seems striking. Aristotle, followed by Aquinas, argued that man was the focal case of political and social animality *because of* man's distinctive capacity for reason and speech. (Hobbes obscures the point that, for Aristotle and Aquinas, bees were political to a lesser degree and hence only by analogy.[20]) The faculty of reason and hence speech enabled man to signify the just and the good—and it is association in terms of the just and the good that constitutes the essence of familial and political society.[21] Hobbes flips this argument upside down, making reason and speech the causes of the asocial parade of horribles: self-seeking, discord, faction, dissembling, and war.

Hobbes's inference of the parade of horribles from human reason seems to be in stark contrast with the Aristotelian inference of natural sociality from human reason. What, then, are we to make of Hobbes's six differences between men and bees? Do these points constitute breaking points from the tradition? We need a bit more context for Hobbes's discussion of men and bees. The flow of the chapter is to first identify the final cause of the commonwealth, peace—which is sought by persons due to "the foresight of their own preservation, and of a more contented life thereby"—and then to show why peace requires an unassailable sovereign with the coercive power of positive law.[22] Hobbes denies that peace can be had by (a) the mere direction of the laws of nature, (b) the conjunction of a few families, or (c) by an unincorporated great multitude.

Regarding a, recall our discussion of Hobbes's understanding of the human nature, the good, and natural law. Secured by God's legislative activity, the dictates of right reason bind eternally, immutably, and universally *in foro interno*. But their bindingness in conscience is insufficient to secure peace, for a number of reasons. First, man is a fallen creature. Reason no longer perfectly governs desire, as it did in the Edenic state.[23] The two postulates of reason and desire are now at cross purposes. From the untutored spark of cupidity flows the passions that "carry us to partiality, pride, revenge, and the like."[24] In a condition void of positive law, men will be more apt to be dominated by the passions because in that condition there will be no positive legal sanctions against partial, prideful, and vengeful acts. Hobbes acknowledges that there may be many who would live according to reason even without the sanctions of positive law—many who would "be glad to be at ease within modest bounds"—but there will be some who, by their unruly passions, will seek to increase their profit, power, glory, and dominion. Since the primary good is life, those whose passions are governed by reason act well when they seek to defend themselves, even to the point of augmenting their territory (the best-defense-is-a-good-offense principle).[25] So even if a few virtuous families banded together without inaugurating an order of positive law, it would not be sufficient to secure the peace. Option b is ruled out. Nor can c, an unincorporated great multitude, live in peace because, lacking corporation, they will be divided by rival particular judgments and have no common rule of action, rendering internal and external security impossible. In other words, as we would expect, part c of Hobbes's definition of commonwealth is not sufficient to secure the peace. Hobbes hints that if such a multitude is not already at war with itself, it soon will be, since the war of all against all, as we have seen, is a *reductio* of the practice of the right to private judgment on a massive scale.

In short, the laws of nature in and of themselves are insufficient to ensure peace. Positive law with a sovereign powerful enough to enforce it is needed. But what about bees? After all, they are all directed by their "particular judgments and appetites" and yet live in peace—why can't mankind do the same? In other words, why can't man live peacefully without positive law? We have already seen the root principle of Hobbes's reasons: the spark of cupidity in man leads him to use his power of reason in self-seeking (which spawns hatred and envy), to overvalue his own opinion and judgment (spawning discord and disobedience), and to dissimulate and lie—all of which generate civil war. An order of positive law can enforce the demands of reason (and it can do so credibly when the sovereign has sufficient power to do so).

Strikingly, Aquinas also insists on the need for positive law to enforce the demands of the natural law:

> Laws were made that in fear thereof human audacity might be held in check, that innocence might be safeguarded in the midst of wickedness, and that the dread of punishment might prevent the wicked from doing harm. But these things are most necessary to mankind. Therefore it was necessary that human laws should be made.[26]

Aquinas makes two points that are noteworthy. First, he claims that man has, by nature, a certain aptitude (*aptitudo*) for virtue. Second, he claims that man is especially inclined (*proni*) to undue pleasures, particularly when young. How are these points consistent? We have seen that, in Aquinas's view, fallen man finds himself under the law of sin and consequently the rebellion of his passions against right reason. But man still has the faculties of intellect and will that allow him to retain a natural aptitude (an essential orientation, inclination, or proneness[27]) toward the true and the good—they are the powers by which man knows and responds to the good.[28] Learning to distinguish actual from apparent goods requires training and instruction. And since moral education of (inchoately rational) youth begins principally in training the passions to love and hate as they ought, and since the young tend to be inclined to undue pleasures, they must be educated by others who are fully reasonable. Some of the young are more inclined to virtue—whether by bodily disposition, custom, or the grace of God—and for these paternal instruction is sufficient. But not all the young are so lucky:

> But since some are found to be depraved, and prone to vice, and not easily amenable to words, it was necessary for such to be restrained from evil by force and fear, in order that, at least, they might desist from evil-doing, and leave others in peace.[29]

When force and fear become embodied in a legal order—and, for Aquinas and Hobbes, this is when the dictates of reason become embodied in the law, since reason is the soul of the law[30]—backed up by a credible threat of punishment for noncompliance, the discipline of the laws has come to be. Aquinas agrees with Aristotle's remark that, without the discipline of the laws, man is apt to become a beast. The reason he gives is key: "because man can use his reason to devise means of satisfying his *concupiscentias et saevitias* (concupiscence and savagery), which other animals are unable to do."[31]

In other words, Hobbes and Aquinas both recognize that men are not bees. For Aquinas, the political animal anthropological claim does not entail that man is simply or irresistibly driven toward righteousness or social unity. Aquinas acknowledges that reason is all too easily enlisted in the service of concupiscence and savagery. For him, failing to act according to right reason entails the whole range of sins Hobbes mentions, including the inordinate desire for glory (vainglory); sorrow for another's good, which can be provoked by neighbors who desire vainglory (envy); hatred of one's neighbor; telling falsehoods in order to deceive (lying) and dressing up good in the robes of evil and vice versa (dissimulation); as well as reliance on one's own judgment, with an unwillingness to accept sounder judgment (obstinacy) and refusing to concur with the will of better men (discord).[32] As I argued in chapter 2, Hobbes and Aquinas have a more similar philosophical-theological philosophical anthropology than is usually recognized. Prelapsarian man had no inner tendency to dissolution because reason perfectly governed desire. In postlapsarian man, the two postulates of human nature are at cross purposes. The spark of cupidity, which Hobbes says is the desire to make common things one's own, is now liberated and has potency to generate chaos, misery, and civil war. This is why

Hobbes says that the direction of reason (natural law), either individually or in the mode of families or small confederacies, is insufficient. Taming cupidity requires public power, law, and a credible threat of punishment for breaches of natural law principles. Both Aquinas and Hobbes incorporate these Augustinian claims into their anthropology.

So has Hobbes rejected the *zoon politikon* anthropology? In *De Cive* he identifies the political animal dictum with the claim that man is *aptum natum*, born apt or fit, for society. Hobbes says that this axiom is false and is based on a superficial view of human nature. In a footnote, Hobbes explains that he is not denying that men are by nature compelled (*cogere*) to come together, since infants need the care of others to survive. And adults need society to live well, since life in solitude would be hard to bear. Hobbes distinguishes between *congressus*, a meeting, gathering, or intercourse, and *foedus*, a league or compact. It is the latter that Hobbes denies that men are born fit for because it requires faith and agreement. The idea seems to be that they aren't born fit because they can't perform the acts of right reason and will to enter a covenant. Hobbes then lumps in with infants the uninstructed and says that neither knows the power of society or its usefulness. Hobbes concludes that it is impossible for infants to enter into society and that the uninstructed do not care to. Hobbes even says it is possible that the majority of adults are unfit for society, due to either mental disorder or lack of discipline. But infants and undisciplined adults share a common human nature. Therefore, concludes Hobbes, man's aptitude for society is not by nature but by training.[33]

Notice how Hobbes trades on an understanding of the natural as the infantile, in which the activity of right reason must be lacking. Then notice how he connects the natural as the infantile to adults who are not well instructed or educated. The idea is that infants and undisciplined adults are ungoverned by right reason and ruled by their passions. Hobbes's conclusion is that human aptitude for society must be acquired through discipline and instruction by right reason. But this is the Thomistic position. Aquinas's whole point is that the discipline of the laws, as embodying the dictates of reason in positive law backed up by a coercive power, is necessary to make life in society possible. True, Thomas allows that some of the young will be more inclined toward virtue by bodily disposition, custom, or, more likely, by God's grace, so that paternal discipline will suffice. In this way Aquinas may be more optimistic than Hobbes—but just how much more optimistic is not so clear, since Aquinas maintains in another place that "sensible pleasures are desired by the majority." The reason Aquinas gives is man's material constitution and hence his material way of coming to know: "Vehemence of desire for sensible delight arises from the fact that operations of the senses, though being the principles of our knowledge, are more perceptible."[34] At any rate, Aquinas indicates that, in his view, the proposition that at least some youth will be depraved is sufficient to justify the utility of a coercive order of law. The argument has some similarities with Hobbes's argument in the epistle dedicatory of *De Cive*, which Martinich has aptly termed "The Great Fear and Ignorance Argument."[35] It goes like this:

(1) Some people in the state of nature are dangerous.
(2) It is very difficult to know who these people are.
Therefore, (3) It is necessary to be afraid of everyone.

From these premises Hobbes continues to show how incorporation into society under law is necessary: "And so it happens that through fear of each other we think it fit to rid our selves of this condition."[36] While Aquinas does not use the term "state of nature" in this sense, he is considering a functional equivalent, what we might call a "lawless condition." I call this argument of Aquinas's "The Great Hooligan Argument":

(1) Some youth in a lawless condition are dangerous.
(2) Parental admonition is insufficient to keep them in check.
Therefore, (3) The force and fear of the law is required for peace.

Since Aquinas, in one of his replies in the same article, is willing to speak of the evil disposition in some human beings—and hence acknowledges evil dispositions in both young and adult persons—Premise 1 could be modified to include adults (even adults have parents and elders).[37] The chief similarity between "The Great Fear and Ignorance" and "The Great Hooligan" rhetorical arguments is the first premise. After that, the arguments take different tacks by focusing on different aspects of human beings. Hobbes relies on the fear that would obtain in that condition and the unfittingness of mass fear and war with human well-being; Aquinas relies on the inability of parents or elders to check younger persons by themselves.[38] They arrive at the same conclusion: the need of society and law for human life and happiness.

Let's return to the question of whether man is "by nature" a social and political animal. Hobbes's difference now appears to be chiefly a terminological one: in the *De Cive* passage, he uses the term "natural" in the sense of "infantile," while Aquinas uses the term "natural" in the sense of the "reasonable" and the "teleological." So Hobbes is implying that the unnatural is the noninfantile, while Aquinas is implying that the noninfantile is natural.

But Hobbes is not consistent in holding to this meaning of the natural because he does not restrict the natural to the infantile throughout his writings. To the contrary, in many other places Hobbes repeatedly affirms that what distinguishes human nature from other animal natures is reason. As Hobbes puts it, "Man's nature is the sum of his natural faculties and powers ... contained in the definition of man under these words, *animal* and *rational*."[39] Recall one of the themes of the previous chapters, Hobbes's two postulates of human nature: cupidity and reason. We saw that Hobbes's view is that human nature is not constituted merely by the subrational desires that we have from infancy onward. The definition of man as a *rational* animal suggests that the postulate of reason is what marks human nature as human. The universal "man" picks out the particulars that have sufficiently similar constitutions in being endowed with the distinguishing power of reason. *Natural* persons are those whose powers to speak and act on their own behalf are immediately exercisable. Moreover, the dictates of reason are so many laws of *nature*: "A Law of Nature (*lex naturalis*) is a precept or general rule, found out by reason."[40] Hence Hobbes is willing, when it suits him, to use the term "natural" in the sense of the *reasonable* and that to which the dictates of reason direct us (peace), i.e., the teleological.

In other words, we can conclude the argument of this section with the following inference. On his own terms, Hobbes can say that (a) inasmuch as man is directed by the dictates of right reason to live in society under a rule of positive law, man is "by nature" a social and political animal, since reason is the feature distinguishing human beings from irrational creatures, and (b) inasmuch as the young and the foolish lack the personal guidance of right reason, they require discipline and instruction, including the discipline of the laws. So stated, we can see that Hobbes is a Thomist.

Do not mistake this claim as being more than it is. This is primarily a *structural* point. It would be better to say that, on the question of man's "natural" sociality, Hobbes is structurally Thomistic when he uses the term "natural" in the sense of the reasonable. But we do not yet know what the substantive content of the common good is for Hobbes and how this contrasts with Aquinas. As we shall see later, Hobbes's break from Aquinas lies in his new conception of peace.

So far we have sought to secure the grounds for an interpretation of Hobbes's theory of commonwealth as a common good account. In this section we have considered the fitness of the great multitude to incorporate in light of Hobbes's professed rejection of the *zoon politikon* anthropology. It had been suggested that one could argue that, since Hobbes rejects the political animal anthropology, he could not really have a common good account of commonwealth, since the common good is conceived as a state of affairs in which social animals attain their natural good or happiness. But we have seen that, inasmuch as Hobbes thinks we identify peace as constitutive of our good by reason, and inasmuch as the reasonable is the natural, Hobbes does have a sort of political animal anthropology, and so the common good account is still an available interpretation of Hobbes's theory of commonwealth. Aquinas and Hobbes are in agreement that peace through commonwealth is reasonable and necessary for human happiness or flourishing.

Covenanting and Artificing the Commonwealth for the Common Good

To open this section, recall again our partition of Hobbes's definition of commonwealth:

> (a) One person, (b) of whose acts (c) a great multitude, (d) by mutual covenants one with another, have made themselves every one the author, (e) to the end that he may use the strength and

means of them all, as he shall think expedient, (f) for their peace and common defence.[41]

In this section I argue that Hobbes's common good account of commonwealth is evident in his account of parts d–e: the sovereign-making covenant and the absolutist nature of the sovereign. In the first subsection I analyze the first clause of part d and consider Hobbes's theory of covenant. In the second subsection I analyze part e and consider the unitarist feature of Hobbes's theory of commonwealth. And in the third subsection I analyze the second clause of part d and consider how man is maker of the commonwealth.

Natural Persons as Covenanters: The End of Covenant as the Common Good of Peace

In this subsection I analyze the first clause of part d, "mutual covenants one with another," and its aim of peace. I argue that, within the natural law tradition, Hobbes's view is best understood as a thin version of peace. But this does not annul the truly common character of the goodness of peace.

The fundamental law of nature binds rational agents to pursue peace. As Hobbes defines it:

> *That every man ought to endeavour peace, as far as he has hope of obtaining it, and when he cannot obtain it, that he may seek and use all helps and advantages of war.*[42]

From this Hobbes derives the second law of nature:

> *That a man be willing, when others are so too, as far-forth as for peace and defence of himself he shall think it necessary, to lay down this right to all things, and be contented with so much liberty against other men, as he would allow other men against himself.*[43]

To "lay down" a right is to divest oneself of one's liberty of hindering another from the benefit and use of that right. This happens either by renouncing it, in which case the person cares not to whose benefit it redounds, or by transferring it, in which case the person transferring it intends the benefit to go to a certain person or persons. The sovereign-making covenant is in the mode of the latter because covenanting persons intend to transfer their rights to one man or assembly of men to bear their person, which at once authorizes the sovereign to act in their name and empowers him (it) to do so. As Hobbes puts it, this is a

> covenant of every man with every man, in such manner as if every man should say to every man *I authorize and give up my right of governing myself to this man, or to this assembly of men, on this condition, that thou give up thy right to him, and authorize all his actions in like manner.*[44]

In this way covenanters form a promissory obligation to one another not to hinder the commonwealth, on the pain of injustice. The person to whom the rights are conferred is not a party to the covenant. From the perspective of the person empowered, the rights received are a "free gift." This is one of the ways in which Hobbes can deny that the sovereign can ever do injustice because, in his technical definition of justice, injustice is violation of a contract or covenant. Another way Hobbes can shield the sovereign from injustice is by leaning on authorization. Since covenanters have authorized all acts of the sovereign, they cannot ever accuse him of injustice.

Why do covenanters do this? Hobbes tells us in the opening lines of chapter 17, in which he gives us the above-quoted sovereign-making formula:

> The final cause, end, or design of men (who naturally love liberty and dominion over others) in the introduction of that restraint upon themselves in which we see them live in commonwealths is the foresight of their own preservation, and of a more contented life thereby; that is to say, of getting themselves out from that miserable condition of war, which is necessarily consequent (as hath been shown) to the natural passions of men, when there is no visible power to keep them in awe, and tie them by fear of punishment to

the performance of their covenants and observation of those laws of nature set down in the fourteenth and fifteenth chapters.⁴⁵

God binds man through the laws of nature to pursue their genuine self-interest, which lies in plans of life that take the good of life as basic. This practically entails that reasonable persons are bound to quit the condition of war through the erection of such a common power "as may be able to defend them from the invasion of foreigners and the injuries of one another."⁴⁶ Authorization of the sovereign is thus *for the sake of* securing one's self through securing the peace, understood principally as public safety. Hence Hobbes provides a rider to his authorization formula just a couple lines before:

> and every one to own and acknowledge himself to be author of whatsoever he that so beareth their person shall act, or cause to be acted, *in those things which concern the common peace and safety*.⁴⁷

Hobbes continues:

> and therein to submit their wills, every one to his will, and their judgments, to his judgment. This is more than consent, or concord; it is a real unity of them all, in one and the same Person.

In other words, it is the unity of peace that marks off the commonwealth from the bellicose condition of the disunited multitude. Accordingly, Hobbes considers peace as the set end of the ruler:

> The office of the sovereign (be it a monarch, or an assembly) consisteth in the end for which he was trusted with the sovereign power, namely, the procuration of *the safety of the people*, to which he is obliged by the law of nature, and to render an account thereof to God, the author of that law, and to none but him.⁴⁸

In the marginal note to this paragraph, Hobbes has "The procuration of the good of the people." In another place, Hobbes points out: "There can be a common good, and it can rightly be said of something, *it is commonly a good*, that is, useful to many, or good for the state."⁴⁹

Hobbes's point can be formulated as follows: the office of the sovereign consists in procuring the common good. When covenanters erect the commonwealth, they authorize the sovereign to procure the common good. We can now turn to uncovering the novelty of Hobbes's notion of the common good within the natural law tradition.

Like Hobbes, Aquinas teaches that the benchmark of a society's well-being "lies in the preservation of its unity, which is peace."[50] Such is a set end for the ruler. As the end of the doctor is the health of the body, which consists in the harmony of its material parts, the end set for the ruler of the commonwealth is peace, which is harmony of wills.[51] Aristotle calls such a harmony *homonoia*, or concord—and this denotes a kind of unity. For Aristotle and Aquinas there are four senses of concord, social unity, or peace: (1) the mere absence of civil strife, (2) agreement of citizens on important matters, (3) civic friendship, and (4) complete harmony of persons, of their affections within and choices without.[52] As Michael Pakaluk points out, 1–4 constitute a gradated scale, and hence a political society may find itself more or less perfectly united at any one time. Senses 1–4 denote degrees of unity of peace as a desirable state of affairs. As such it is an object of united action, and its goodness is essentially shared or participated in. It is proper, then, to speak of the pursuit of the common good as the distinguishing mark of society. The common good so conceived has the feature of drawing or attracting. In other words, it has the note of a final cause. Aristotle and Aquinas offer another formulation of the foregoing when they say that society is a *unity of order*—and further consideration of this notion of unity introduces the distinction between the intrinsic and extrinsic good of society.

Aristotle and Aquinas teach that the common good of a society or unity of order is twofold: the intrinsic order among its parts and the order of the whole to an extrinsic end. Consider the example of an army. In the order of the members of the army to one another, there is an intrinsic common good. The well-being of the fighting group shared in by each member is conditioned on the order necessary for the life-together of the whole. Moreover, the whole army is directed toward the goal of victory. Victory is the extrinsic common good that the army aims at, and there is a special sense in which the common good of victory is found in the commander as the directive principle toward that end. So according to this principle, society at large or the *civitas* would also seem to have a twofold common good: its intrinsic order and that to which the whole is directed. What, then, is the twofold common good of the *civitas*?

We have already seen that the answer must lie in the notion of peace. An extraordinarily high degree of civic friendship may approach the fourth sense of concord, social unity, or peace and therefore can function in the way of Aristotle's best regime: as a regulative ideal.[53] In this sense it is an extrinsic common good to which the political community is always striving.[54] But any degree of peace enjoyed along the scale 1–4 within the political order would seem to be the intrinsic common good of the whole as accidental perfections inhering in the members of the whole. It should now be apparent how Hobbes's notion of the common good is novel.

Hobbes's break with earlier views is in the thinning of the common good to mere security. Aristotle and Aquinas had been willing to affirm somewhat higher common ends for man—including the intrinsically social goods of community and friendship. But for Hobbes, concord sets its sights lower. On the scale 1–4, Hobbesian artificial unity aims low: somewhere between 1 and 2. There ought to be absence of civil strife inasmuch as all are agreed about one important matter: security. For Hobbes, civic friendship is not sought for its own sake as perfective of man's rational faculties but as conducive to the good of preservation.[55] Does this thinning out of the traditional notion of the common good really mean that Hobbes is denying that there is any such thing as the common good discovered by reason? John Rawls argues as much. On Rawls's reading of Hobbes, our difference from naturally political animals like bees—for whom the private good differs not from the common good— not only is regrettable, but it suggests that human reason cannot discover any common good: "We are not that fortunate, and there is no common good that we recognize by reason."[56] But, *pace* Rawls, Hobbes's discussion of the differences between men and bees actually indicates that Hobbes is affirming that reasonable persons understand the security of peace as truly a common good. Recall Hobbes's second distinction between men and bees: man's private good differs from the common good. This distinction would be pointless unless there were some real common good.[57] Therefore, that discussion actually supports the common good interpretation.

In *De Cive* Hobbes lays out the substantive features of the common good of security: (1) defense from extrinsic threats, (2) defense from internal strife, (3) economic prosperity, and (4) enjoyment of harmless liberty. Corresponding to each feature is a principle guiding the sovereign. Corresponding to 1 is the sovereign's duty and authority to create (a) a standing professional army and navy that is well armed and such forts and garrisons as are necessary to defend the territory of the realm and (b) a foreign intelligence service and network. Corresponding to 2 is the sovereign's duty to establish and enforce criminal laws and ensure equitable punishment for breaking the law. Since equitable punishment must consider the future good of the perpetrator and the commonwealth, it would seem that the sovereign must establish a criminal justice system that aims at rehabilitation. Also corresponding to 2 is the sovereign's teaching office and the corresponding duty to reform the universities and ferret out doctrines noxious to the common good. Corresponding to 3 is the duty of the sovereign to tax equitably, and Hobbes contends that equity requires a consumption tax rather than an income tax, for the apparent reason that frugality should be encouraged and luxury discouraged.[58] However, as Hobbes formulates it in this passage, the latter argument is not convincing because he does not consider the case of people who are equally frugal but who have radically disparate incomes, and so does not explain why equity and the common good don't require more from the wealthy. Still, in another place Hobbes avers that all property rights are conditional in that they do not exclude the right of the sovereign to their use "when the common good of the people shall require the use thereof."[59] Also corresponding to 3 is the sovereign's duty to make laws regulating and encouraging all fruitful labor that provides the necessities and enjoyments of life, which includes work in the agricultural, mechanical, industrial, and navigational arts and sciences.

Finally, to 4 corresponds the sovereign's duty not to leave a sphere of liberty untouched by law. That portion of natural right not given up by the sovereign is to be retained and acknowledged by the silence of the laws. In practice, this means that the sovereign is bound "by the laws of nature" not to pass more laws "than necessarily serve the good of the magistrate and his subjects."[60] Why is "harmless liberty" an essential feature of the common good? Hobbes teaches that liberty is necessary for the vigor of the people. A commonwealth that legislated every aspect of human existence would behave as if embanking a body of water that was never refreshed. Such a body of water is stagnant. On the other hand, with no banks at all, the water disperses. What is needed are enough laws to direct human action without smothering its energy and motion, as the banks of a river guide the water's flow.

The Hobbesian conception of the common good in many ways anticipates the liberal-constitutionalist vision of the national common good in the U.S. Constitution. The enumerated powers of Congress extend to a defined set of objects that are contemplated as constituent elements of the "general welfare" of the nation. Seven of Congress's eighteen powers flow from the principle of defense from external threats. Five of its powers directly concern the nation's monetary and economic well-being and include specific powers to tax and regulate commerce. Moreover, the powers to promote the progress of useful arts and sciences and establish postal roads and offices indirectly conduce to this feature of the national common good. The very enumeration of Congress's powers is a prime feature of the Constitution intended to secure harmless liberty because, by restricting the scope of congressional authority to a definite set of elements of the common good, it restricts the kinds and therefore the number of laws Congress is authorized to legislate.

Of course the two great structural features of the American Constitution—federalism, or the division of powers between the states and the federal government, and the separation of powers—do not jibe with the Hobbesian conception of sovereignty as undivided. Hence, in the original Constitution, the "internal" peace and security of the American polity is in large measure left to the various states inasmuch as each state reserves the "police power" to legislate regarding local safety, health, morals, and so on. Moreover, as James Madison famously argues in *Federalist* 51, federalism and the separation of powers provide "double security" to the liberty of the people. But it should be noted that Hobbes's disagreement with the Constitution is over the *means* to secure the common good (including the "harmless liberty" feature of the common good). Hobbes believes that constitutional means of limiting authority will risk rebellion. For, emergency circumstances may arise in which the urgency of the common good requires limiting or curtailing freedoms. In the American context, Abraham Lincoln provides an example of a leader deeply committed to liberal principles of government and yet curtailed civil liberties for the sake of security. Lincoln's suspension of habeas corpus was decried as tyrannical and as justification for continued rebellion or secession. Hobbes would take this as empirical evidence verifying the principle that "when the exercise of the power laid by is for the public safety to be resumed, it hath the resemblance of an unjust act, which disposeth great numbers of men (when occasion is presented) to rebel."[61] At any rate, as J. Judd Owen has argued, Hobbes's skepticism about liberal-constitutional *means* of government does not entail that Hobbes is an enemy of liberty or that his commitment to individual liberty is not principled.[62] (Yet, contrary to Owen's suggestion, the sovereign cannot be conceived to be *bound* to respect harmless liberty apart from an account of Hobbesian natural law dissevered from its divine pedigree, because otherwise the laws of nature would not bind the sovereign in conscience as law.[63]) Hobbes's difference from later liberals such as Locke is in his prioritization of security to liberty and his insistence that constitutional limitations on sovereign power are imprudent. While Locke wants constitutional limits, he essentially agrees with Hobbes that the urgency of security justifies acts of executive prerogative outside constitutional limitations.

Still, we can ask whether Hobbes's account really counts as a common good account from the perspective of the older tradition. In the Aristotelian-Thomistic tradition, the social and political animal anthropology entailed that human happiness lies in the social unity denoted by sense 4: complete harmony of persons, of their affections within and choices without.[64] In this conception of the common good, social unity is not merely a means to some extrinsic end or good. In other words, the common good is not *merely* a useful good. Hobbes does emphasize the usefulness of the common good. But I suggest that the Hobbesian common good also has an intrinsic goodness inasmuch as living virtuously is or can (ought to) be pleasurable. It is pleasurable for those who live reasonably and can be pleasurable for anyone who is properly educated and habituated to live by the laws of nature. Let me elaborate the argument.

For Hobbes the common good consists in a state of affairs in which the practice of the moral virtues outlined by the laws of nature is backed up by the command of the sovereign. It is good because all men agree that peace is good—"and therefore also *the way or means* of peace."⁶⁵ The virtues are the means to peace because they enjoin cessation of the kinds of acts that incite violence and war. The goodness of a state of affairs in which the mutual practice of the virtues is ensured by the threat of punishment for their breach is evident. Such a state of affairs is undoubtedly "the good of the state"—it is a good shared by all the members of the commonwealth. According to Hobbes's criterion, its goodness is real (and not merely apparent) because its long-term consequences do not have evil annexed to them for the good reason that it is most likely to conduce to the preservation of all.⁶⁶

The common good constituted by this state of affairs is not properly anyone's private good (as is, say, the balance in one's checking account), but it is each individual's good in the manner of participation inasmuch as everyone has an equal share in the protection of the laws. But its intrinsic goodness is no "thicker" than the features of security laid out earlier—and for Hobbes a good desired *propter se* (for its own sake) is nothing other than the *bonum jucundum* (the delightful good).⁶⁷ Hobbes's conjectures that the criterion for something to qualify as a delightful good sought for its own sake is whether it corroborates vital motion. But the whole point of Hobbes's argument is to show that the practice of the virtues outlined by the laws of nature *in foro externo* is the ultimate corroboration of and help toward continued vital motion since that is constitutive of peace. Presumably, those who are disciplined by good education—an education that should be based on *Leviathan* itself—will understand this, and the practice of the civic virtues will be pleasurable. Hence I see no grounds, in Hobbes's terms, for denying intrinsic goodness to the common good. Hobbes's novelty *vis-à-vis* Aquinas on this point seems to lie chiefly in identifying the good per se with the pleasing.⁶⁸

Of course Hobbes also says that peace is good in the mode of the *bonum utile* (the useful good) as well. The extrinsic aim of membership in society is not any higher degree of unity but rather the individual pursuit of felicity. So while not merely instrumental, the common good is also a good in the mode of the *bonum utile* as conducive to a wide sphere for the individual pursuit of "felicity" or living "well" where these pursuits do not involve breaching the peace—in other words, "harmless liberty."⁶⁹ Felicity is continual success in attaining whatever we happen to desire in accord with the harmless liberty the sovereign is bound to secure. And the boundaries of this liberty cannot be set according to any thicker vision of the common good, because diverse persons differ in their judgment "of what is conformable or disagreeable to reason in the actions of common life."[70]

Hence Hobbes's common good account of commonwealth goes hand in glove with his doctrine of felicity pluralism, which we discussed in the previous chapter. In his chapter on the office of the sovereign in *Leviathan*, the *safety of the people* is declared to be not "a bare preservation, but also all other contentment of life, which every man by lawful industry, without danger or hurt to the commonwealth, shall acquire to himself."[71] Life as the basic good does not mean that the common good is merely survival. It means that the sovereign will facilitate the common good of security as the condition of felicity pluralism—but the filled-out content of individual contentment is left to individual judgment. Here we see a key contribution by Hobbes to the liberal tradition inasmuch as liberalism seeks to be maximally inclusive of diverse pursuits of happiness. Hobbes's felicity pluralism is widely inclusive of many diverse life plans so long as they are reasonable—and the basic requirement of reasonableness in the pursuit of felicity is to accord one's will with the common good. This means that the sorts of acts destructive of life or conducive to violence and war are ruled out as unreasonable pursuits of felicity.

To sum up this subsection, Hobbes's properly common good account of commonwealth is evident in his theory of the sovereign-making covenant because covenanters seek peace. The Hobbesian theory of the common good is best understood as a thin conception of peace. Its intrinsic and useful goodness is common because all members of the commonwealth enjoy security in their pursuits of a contented life. In the next section I show how the second clause of part d of Hobbes's definition of commonwealth also indicates that covenanters act for the common good as makers of commonwealth.

Natural Persons as Makers: How Political Art Imitates Nature

According to Hobbes, artificiality corresponds to the man-made. But how should we understand man as maker? In this subsection I argue that man makes or crafts the commonwealth in pursuit of peace understood as the common good of security—and that, in doing so, man imitates an order in nature: Hobbesian political art imitates nature. In the Aristotelian-Thomistic tradition this meant that political art makes use of material, efficient, formal, and final causality, since these causes are in natural things. Some interpreters have argued that Hobbesian artifice, as the man-made, is doctrine formulated in spite of nature—in radical rejection of the traditional principle that art imitates nature.[72] The implication is that no final cause is apparent in nature; hence, we construct society for the purposes we make up. But, supposing we have good reasons to think Hobbes held forth his theology of a providential, creating God seriously, a rereading of Hobbesian political art is fitting. As I argued in chapter 1, Hobbes should be understood as a realistic political philosopher. Rereading Hobbes in this light reveals that his political art makes use of matter, form, efficient cause, and telos because, as in the Thomistic tradition, God created and ordered man toward his good. Where Hobbes differs is in his thin theory of the good. His new political art co-opts the Aristotelian mimetic principle and the four causes in service of his new conception of the common good. Hobbes then makes powerful use of the mimetic principle to support his unitarist vision of the common good. Therefore, my theistic natural law interpretation is the only one that can make sense of Hobbes's doctrine of political art.

The surface impression of Hobbes's theory of artifice as the man-made is that it is radically breaking from the older tradition. That is, Hobbes shows us how commonwealth is artificial because man-made and not natural, as it is for bees, as those benighted by naïveté would have us believe. But we have already seen how Hobbes is in agreement with Aristotle and Aquinas that men are not merely instinctually driven toward community as creatures in swarms. Aristotle and Aquinas do not understand the "natural" as the irresistibly impelled toward but as the reasonable. (For Aristotle and Aquinas, bees are a peripheral case of political animality.) We saw earlier how Hobbes's criticism of the *zoon politikon* anthropology ended up turning on his use of "natural" in the sense of "infantile." But, inasmuch as Hobbes connects the natural with the reasonable and inasmuch as he agrees with Aristotle and Aquinas that life in society under law is much more reasonable than living as beasts, he isn't so far from the tradition after all. As one might have guessed, Hobbes's notion of political art as man-made is also not so different from the Aristotelian tradition—and this turns out to be a subtle point of agreement regarding the dignity of human agents. Recall the last point of difference he points out between men and bees:

> Lastly, the agreement of these creatures is natural; that of men is by covenant only, which is artificial; and therefore, it is no wonder if there be somewhat else required (besides covenant) to make their agreement constant and lasting, which is a common power to keep them in awe, and to direct their actions to the common benefit.[73]

It turns out to be very important for Hobbes in his criticism of Aristotelianism to sufficiently differentiate between nonrational and rational animals to warrant the apparent rejection of the Aristotelian dictum that man is a *zoon politikon*. But in order for the argument to work, Hobbes must maintain that rational agents enjoy somewhat more dignity in causation than appears in his discussion of liberty and necessity. We see here another continuity with the Aristotelian-Thomistic tradition regarding the dignity of the individual. Human individuals are not driven into concord but must make the commonwealth after reflection and choice. Whether wittingly or not, Hobbes is in agreement with Aristotle and Aquinas that in the order of time, the city is not "natural" in the sense of the primitive, which we might expect if "natural" means irresistibly impelled thereto. The city is, rather, the product of reflection and choice. As Aristotle puts it, "By nature, then, the drive for such a community exists in everyone, but the first to set one up is responsible for things of very great goodness."[74] In short, the city in the Aristotelian tradition is "man-made." In Hobbes's terminology this means that the city is the product of human art—human beings are "makers and orderers" of the commonwealth. Aquinas is also willing to use the term "art" in distinguishing the operation of practical reason that orders the polity.[75]

Hobbes indicates from the start his intent to co-opt Aristotelian language to describe the product of his political art, the commonwealth. In the subtitle to *Leviathan*, "or the Matter, Form, and Power of the Commonwealth," Hobbes signals his intent to take over Aristotelian ideas of efficient, material, and formal causality and enlist them in service of his account of commonwealth. So Hobbes lays out his project "to describe the Nature of this Artificial Man." The first part of the book is concerned with "the matter thereof and the artificer; both of which is Man." As we already have seen in our initial partition of Hobbes's definition of commonwealth, men (or the "natural persons") that make up the great (unincorporated) multitude appear as material and efficient causes.[76] When part I of *Leviathan* culminates in chapter 16, "Of Persons, Authors, and Things Personated," material, efficient, and formal cause come together as Hobbes's propaedeutic to his doctrine of final causation. The final cause of the commonwealth is the common good. Hence, the first chapter of part II is entitled "Of the Causes, Generation, and Definition of a Commonwealth," recalling the subtitle of *Leviathan* and opening with a reflection on the "final cause" of the commonwealth. Hobbes has rounded out the quartet of Aristotelian causes by the time he offers the covenantal formula and definition of commonwealth.[77]

These points are important because Hobbes claims that art—including political art—imitates nature. Therefore, if political art deploys material, formal, efficient, and final causality, and if Hobbes seriously holds the mimetic principle, then these causes must be found in nature. Hobbes indicates as much in his opening comments about artifice in *Leviathan*.

Hobbes's introduction to the Leviathan is the proper place to begin to see what one recent study calls "the often overlooked significance of the concept of artifice in *Leviathan*."[78] We are immediately told that nature is the artifice of God. It is "the art whereby God hath made and governs the world."[79] And Hobbes says that we perceive by our senses and judge by reason that God has made a mechanical world. By God's order of artifice, natural life is an organic-mechanic motion of the various parts within wholes "giving motion to the whole body, such as was intended by the artificer."[80] As I argued in the previous chapter, nature is the product of God's ordained power. Among natural bodies, one stands out. The most excellent work of nature was God's greatest work of art: man. So if man is to be a great artist, he must reflect man in his greatest production. The creation of the artificial person of the state is the ultimate imitation of God's creation of man. In Hobbes's words, the *pacts* and *covenants*, by which the parts of this body politic were at first made, set together, and united, resemble that *fiat*, or the *let us make man*, pronounced by God in the creation.[81]

Since "nature" in Hobbes's system is the manifestation of God's *potentia ad ordinata*, it is imbued with value and purpose prior to our thinking about it. The normative value of proper biological functioning is lawlike, for Hobbes.

Within the Aristotelian tradition, the principle that art imitates nature traces back to Aristotle's *Physics* and later is taken to be axiomatic by Aquinas in his commentary on Aristotle's *Politics*.[82] In the *Physics* passage, Aristotle argues that since art imitates nature, in knowing how an art relates to artificial things we will know how natural science relates to natural things. But in the medical art the doctor knows health as a form and the humors as the matter of which health consists because health is the harmony of the bodily humors. Likewise, the builder knows both the form of the house and the bricks and mortar as its matter.[83] Hence, Aristotle concludes, it belongs to the natural scientist to know matter and form. But why should the axiom that art imitates nature be admitted in the first place?

Aquinas explains that knowledge is the principle of art. But all of our knowledge comes through the senses, through sensible things in nature. Therefore, artificial things are produced in likeness to natural things. But our senses reveal that there is an order in natural things whence it can be inferred that there is an intellectual principle ordering them toward their ends.[84] Art imitates nature, then, by ordering its product toward its end. In the older view, the order in natural things pointed to an ordering intellectual principle, and this ordering is imitated in making artificial things. Hobbes often speaks as if he agrees with the Thomistic tradition on this point. We have seen that Hobbes affirms fifth-way language in several places across his works, including when he remarks that "by the visible things of this world and their admirable order, a man may conceive there is a cause of them, which men call God."[85] In chapter 1 I pointed out that Hobbes believes generation, hominization, and the operation of the bodily organs are processes whence one can validly infer the existence of a creating mind.

Whereas Hobbes's introduction to *Leviathan* invoked his ultimate foundation in revelation by reference to the Genesis account of God's *fiat* in creation, here we are in the (compatible) realm of Hobbes's proximate foundation for his civil science—the knowledge of human nature by unaided reason. Our knowledge of man reveals an order and hence must be the product of something with understanding. Another way to put the point is that reason discovers a plan of artifice of an irresistibly powerful being. Hobbes himself declines to use the term "design" to refer to the products of his ordained power because it implies a discursiveness of thought that is inapplicable to God.[86] However, I suggest that Hobbes's plan of artifice is similar to what Alvin Plantinga calls a "design plan." As Plantinga explains it, a design plan is

> the way the thing in question is "supposed" to work, the way in which it works when it is functioning as it ought to, when there is nothing wrong with it, when it is not damaged or broken or nonfunctional. Both human artifacts and natural organisms and their parts have design plans.[87]

Plantinga goes on to suggest that "we need not take the notions of design plan and way in which a thing is supposed to work to entail conscious design or purpose . . . it is perhaps possible that evolution (undirected by God or anyone else) has somehow furnished us with our design plans."[88] The latter possibility has been taken up and defended by some contemporary philosophers.[89] Hobbes himself does not seem to have countenanced the latter possibility. His own theory is closer to what Plantinga calls "the central and paradigm cases," which "do indeed involve the thing's having been designed by one or more conscious designers who are aiming at an end of some sort, and design the thing in question to achieve or accomplish that end."[90] In creating man, God ordered him to the good of life.

Hence Hobbes's claim that men are "makers and orderers" of the commonwealth should be understood as ordering man on the basis of the order in the most excellent work of God: man.[91] The order in man of his subrational parts and of his reason toward the good of life is an order willed by one with the right to so will it—hence the rational necessity to pursue the good of life and the means necessary thereto have the character of law for the theist. We now see that the order in man is the natural thing that man imitates in making the commonwealth—and this turns out to be an imitation of God's creative act. In the account in Genesis 1, God says, "Let us make man in our image and likeness." So Hobbes says that, in making the commonwealth, man imitates God by creating the state in his own image and likeness.[92]

Hobbes borrows from the Aristotelian tradition inasmuch as, like the doctor or builder, the political artist knows both matter and form. As the manufacturer can resolve the watch into its material parts and compose it again, so the civil scientist can apply the resolutive-compositive method to the body politic to understand how the material parts are in potency to incorporation through a political form.[93] The covenantal acts of will that inform this "matter" bring into being something distinct in dignity and not merely an aggregate of its material parts: a truly representative group-person. A man-made form constitutes or organizes the "matter" of natural substances (natural persons) into a new (social) entity. Once authorized, the sovereign takes on the character of the form or *arche*, giving life and motion to the body politic.[94]

On the ground of his mimetic principle, Hobbes compares the body politic to the human body. The parts function well when they operate for the good of the whole, but they are dysfunctional when they dissolve the whole. Recently Michael Krom has argued that Hobbes's use of the body as a metaphor to describe the polity deserves more attention, and he has advanced our understanding in this regard.[95] I suggest that the theistic natural law interpretation developed in this book sheds new light on Hobbes's use of bodily health and disease metaphors because, like the individual human body, the proper functioning of the parts of the body politic has normative value by God's ordained power. If this is right, Hobbes's language is more than merely clever usage of the body metaphor.

Hobbes compares the various parts of the commonwealth to bodily parts: private and political systems resemble muscles; public ministers of general administration resemble "nerves and tendons that move the several limbs of a body natural"; public ministers in capacities of teaching and judicature "may fitly be compared to the organs of voice in a body natural"; ministers who execute the law are "answerable to that of the hands in a body natural." For its nourishment, the commonwealth needs "plenty of matter," which consists in commodities from land and sea; the circulation of money is as the blood or "sanguification of the commonwealth," for "natural blood is in like manner made of the fruits of the Earth; and circulating, nourisheth by the way, every member of the body of man"; colonies and plantations are "children" of the commonwealth.[96]

Accordingly, the principles of destruction and dissolution in the commonwealth are compared to diseases of the body that threaten natural death: unlawful systems are compared to "wens, biles, and apostems";[97] want of absolute power is like a "defectuous procreation";[98] seditious doctrines—including private judgment of good and evil, rights of conscience, pretense of inspiration, subjecting power to the civil laws, absolute property rights, and dividing the sovereign power—are so many diseases. When young men read Greek and Roman writers and are thereby encouraged to become democrats, the commonwealth becomes infected with tyrannophobia, which is like when a person gets bitten by a mad dog (the Greek and Roman writers) and gets hydrophobia. The doctrine of two cities and two jurisdictions, temporal and spiritual, leads to faction and civil war and is like the disease of epilepsy because it produces violent convulsions.[99] The doctrine of mixed government—in which the powers to levy money, to conduct and command, and to make laws are divided among three persons or assemblies respectively—is to divide the commonwealth into three:

> To what disease in the natural body of man I may exactly compare this irregularity of a commonwealth, I know not. But I have seen a man that had another man growing out of his side, with an head, arms, breast, and stomach, of his own; If he had had another man growing out of his other side, the comparison might then have been exact.[100]

Each of the diseases of the commonwealth is like a disease of the body in that it impedes the good of the whole. Just as the health of the bodily parts consists in their proper functioning for the life of the individual, so the health of the commonwealth consists in the members thinking and willing the unity of peace.

Notice that Hobbes is comfortable using the language of health and disease to discuss the condition of commonwealth. I argued in chapter 3 that Jean Hampton's version of the impotent thesis cannot make sense of the normative value of proper biological functioning, in Hobbes's terms. My interpretation of Hobbes's axiology (that the good of life is objective) is essential to making sense of a distinction between normally functioning and abnormal, between healthy or "right" desires and unhealthy or "wrong" desires. I have argued that, if reason were an impotent, calculating slave of the passions, we could not know *which* desires are "right" or "wrong," and that the death seeker is fully rational as long as he calculates correctly about means. Here we see how for Hobbes, just as the good of life is the criterion for what counts as a disease for an individual, so the common good of security provides the objective criterion for what sorts of political doctrines and opinions are diseases for the commonwealth. In the case of the individual and the commonwealth, that which is diseased is morally "wrong" because it conduces to the death or dissolution of the whole. Moreover, the "wrongness" or *evil* of such diseases parallels the evil of dysfunctional bodily organs, inasmuch as the proper functioning of the parts of the individual and the social body has a lawlike character.

We are now in a position to turn to part e of Hobbes's definition of commonwealth. Hobbes's thin notion of the common good, when combined with the notion of unlimited sovereignty for the sake of peace, entails a unitarist conception of a healthy commonwealth. In this section I have suggested that various social and institutional ills track those doctrines that Hobbes believes would destroy this unity. In this way Hobbes makes powerful use of his mimetic principle: those doctrines that cause civil war and the dissolution of commonwealth are like natural diseases that destroy the unity of an individual substance in its enjoyment of the good of life.

Hobbes's Unitarist Conception of Commonwealth

Taken together, parts d and e of Hobbes's definition are indicative of his absolutist notion of absolute sovereignty for the sake of peace. Hobbes's theory of commonwealth shows how the thin conception of the common good, in combination with an absolute right of the sovereign to the means to pursue that end, entails a unitarist conception of commonwealth. In this subsection I show how this constitutes a significant break from the Aristotelian-Thomistic notion of social pluralism.

Hobbes addresses the dignity of subpolitical societies or groups of persons through the prism of his thin doctrine of peace. Hence, the recognition of small groups and societies by the sovereign will turn on their harmlessness. As we saw, the end of sovereign office is the peace of security. Because of the urgency of this good, the sovereign is authorized to act as he deems necessary to secure it. Hobbes formulates this principle as "Whosoever has the right to the end has the right to the means."[101] Because the sovereign has the prerogative to act expediently for the "peace and defence of his subjects," it follows that the recognition of subpolitical group entities must be by permission of the sovereign inasmuch as he judges that they conduce to or do not hinder the security of the realm.[102] As Hobbes puts it, "The sovereign, in every commonwealth, is the absolute representative of all the subjects; and therefore no other can be representative of any part of them, but so far forth as he shall give leave."[103] Subpolitical societies—be they universities, labor unions, towns, churches, families, or others—can attain the legal recognition or the dignity of group personhood only by the permission of the sovereign.

True, the sovereign is bound to protect the "harmless liberty" of citizens, which includes the liberty to associate in the pursuit of goods relegated to the private realm. But all nongovernmental associations attain protection of the law only by the sovereign's *permission*—and, hence, it would not be false to say that this tends toward atomization inasmuch as persons in subpolitical groups lack the dignity of group personhood prior to the state's say-so. Inasmuch as this is the correct picture of Hobbes, he could be said to be a forefather of the "familiar individual-state-market grid" of social ontology that endures today.[104] In this conception, social reality is constituted by the following triad: atomized individuals, their transitory associations, and the state (which decides which transitory associations are permitted and which are not). This triad—which is characteristic of some strains of liberalism—is presaged when Hobbes labels persons in unrecognized subpolitical groups as diseases or worms infesting the body politic. It was on this score that the English pluralists—the early twentieth-century proponents of a sort of neo-Aristotelian social ontology—singled out Hobbes for special condemnation.[105]

From the Aristotelian perspective, the criticism was not without warrant. The Aristotelian-Thomistic position was that group personhood was a reality wherever a unity of order obtained.[106] Since subpolitical societies like families, churches, and other *communiones* are true societies and hence bear a dignity prior to the state's say-so, a state that fails to protect the dignity of subpolitical societies does so on the pain of injustice. Hence the common good as the unity of peace is a unity of unities of order—a *communitas communitatum*. Because there is a dignity intrinsic to any true society in its own common activity and ends, the ruler's charge over the political common good includes not only directing persons toward more perfect unity but also protecting the dignity of subpolitical unities because they enjoy intrinsic common goods and aims which are irreducible to self-preservation and which need not threaten the security of the realm.[107]

Consider Hobbes's treatment of the subpolitical society of the family, which is a society allowed to exist by the sovereign.[108] Here again we see Hobbes's break with the older tradition playing out in terms of his conception of the common good. Notably, in Aristotelian political science the family has a special place as a society that is a sort of cell of political society. For Hobbes, subpolitical societies like the family can and did exist in the state of nature as sovereignties "by acquisition."[109] Hobbes was even willing to call the family in the state of nature a "little city."[110] But small families or even unions of families in the state of nature are not sufficient to secure the chief human good of self-preservation. Again, while Hobbes thinks there is a natural inclination of the sexes to one another and to children—and, presumably, there is an intrinsic pleasurable good that attaches to such a union—Hobbes instrumentalizes the unity of the family to preservation. Whatever order and unity obtains in the family—including that between parent and child—is due principally to the end of preservation:

> For it [the child] ought to obey him by whom it is preserved, because preservation of life being the end, for which one man becomes subject to another, every man is supposed to promise obedience, to him, in whose power it is to save, or destroy him.[111]

Given Hobbes's conviction that life is the basic good, it only follows that the dignity of a society will be conditioned on its instrumental value to the end of preservation. It is true that Hobbes identifies the traditional family as a society allowed by the sovereign. But his principles appear to indicate that this permission is subject to change if the sovereign deems it necessary for security.

In contrast, the Thomistic vision of the common good as the unity of peace is a unity of unities of order. Because there is a dignity intrinsic to any true society in its own common activity and ends, the ruler's charge over the political common good includes not only directing persons toward more perfect unity but also protecting the dignity of subpolitical unities because the common goods they enjoy are real ones. The members of subpolitical societies enjoy a real solidarity in their order to one another *qua* members of that society. Accordingly, Aquinas's account of the goods objectively knowable by reason includes the (common) goods of marriage and childrearing, which are not reducible to mere preservation. It follows that, in the Thomistic picture, the protection of the family is necessary for the common good of society as a whole.

But consider the possibility that Hobbes's skepticism about diverse persons agreeing on any object of common life beyond security flows from the *size* of the commonwealth Hobbes believes is necessary to secure the peace. Recall how generation of a commonwealth requires a "great multitude" to agree on the end to guide their common life. For "it is not the joining together of a small number of men that gives them this security" because the commonwealth must be large enough to withstand external attack.[112] Inasmuch as the absolute representation of the sovereign is confined to the aim of security—the authorization of the sovereign is for the sake of this end—why shouldn't Hobbes allow for the possibility that, through the exercise of their "harmless liberty," smaller communities could arrive at (agree to a common life constituted by) richer notions of the common good? The *scope* of Hobbes's account of the common good as security need not go beyond the nation-state. Even in Hobbes's own terms, smaller communities need not be "worms" infesting the body politic because Hobbes explicitly connects the "excessive greatness of a town" with a threat to security, that is, its ability to furnish "a great army."[113] It certainly seems possible that there are social groups who enjoy real common goods, and therefore are bearers of dignity and rights, but who are unable to furnish "a great army," and therefore cannot be reasonably considered threats to security. If so, this would be a case in which Hobbes's conclusion is not warranted by his premises, a case of Hobbes trying to outrun his own feet.

A modern-day defender of Hobbes might retort and insist that the sovereign has power that he won't necessarily exercise or even that he is unlikely to exercise. And the modern Hobbesian might allow a whole array of social groups who by long-standing custom or law have been given freedom to act in the realm. But, the defender of Hobbes might insist, sovereignty consists precisely in the capacity to *decide the exception* when security demands it.[114] This retort is a serious one and deserves more careful consideration than can be given here. The next chapter's discussion of acts inconsistent with sovereignty offers at least some preliminary considerations that should be part of the discussion of this question.

So far we have analyzed the kinds of person and the fitness of matter ("the great multitude" of people) to incorporate into commonwealth and the covenantal act by which they so incorporate. Inasmuch as the natural is the reasonable, it is natural for the multitude to incorporate through the sovereign-making covenant for the sake of peace, understood as security. Covenanters authorize the sovereign to take all means necessary to secure the peace—and this entails Hobbes's unitarism. In doing so, they imitate God's own artifice plan as expressed in nature by God's power in the ordained mode. While Hobbes breaks with the Aristotelian-Thomistic tradition regarding his notion of the common good, we could readily imagine that they would come up with a similar social ontology if they had had the same thin axiology as Hobbes. Hobbes agrees with that tradition in that he believes the commonwealth constitutes a distinct kind of social entity. We can now elucidate the kind of person the commonwealth is: one truly representative artificial person.

One Truly Representative Artificial Person

In this section I argue that the person of the commonwealth should be understood as a truly representative artificial person. I argue, moreover, that this kind of group-person is essentially distinct from other associations due to its aim, the pursuit of the common good. We have been told that the society generated by Hobbesian construction is "nothing more than a person 'by fiction'" and that it is composed of a mere "aggregate of individuals."[115] But I contend that Hobbes is closer to the classical natural law notion of society as a true group-person or society that is neither a mere fiction nor a mere aggregate of its parts.[116] Whereas for Aristotle and Aquinas the commonwealth is a unity of order, for Hobbes the commonwealth is an artificial unity—but they are both real unities in pursuit of a truly common good. Hence, for Hobbes the commonwealth is a social reality that is essentially distinct from other forms of association. I suggest that this account can shed light on the controversy over the relationship between the person of the sovereign and the person of the commonwealth.

In chapter 17 of *Leviathan*, Hobbes describes the generation of the civil person or the person of the commonwealth in this way:

> The only way to erect such a common power as may be able to defend them from the invasion of foreigners and the injuries of one another, and thereby to secure them in such sort as that by their own industry, and by the fruits of the earth, they may nourish themselves and live contentedly, is to confer all their power and strength upon one man, or upon one assembly of men, that may reduce all their wills, by plurality of voices, unto one will, which is as much as to say, to appoint one man, or assembly of men, to bear their person, and every one to own and acknowledge himself to be author of whatsoever he that so beareth their person shall act, or cause to be acted, in those things which concern the common peace and safety, and therein to submit their wills, every one to his will, and their judgments, to his judgment. This is more than consent, or concord; it is a real unity of them all, in one and the same person, made by covenant of every man with every man, in such manner as if every man should say to every man *I authorize and give up my right of governing myself to this man, or to this assembly of men, on this condition, that thou give up thy right to him, and authorize all his actions in like manner.* This done, the multitude so united in one person is called a Commonwealth, in Latin Civitas. This is the generation of that great Leviathan, or rather (to speak more reverently)

of that *Mortal God*, to which we owe under the *Immortal God*, our peace and defence.[117]

Commenting on this passage, Quentin Skinner is intent upon clarifying what Hobbes is saying:

> This is not of course to say that the Person engendered out of the union of the multitude is a real or substantial one. Rather, it amounts, in Hobbes's words, to nothing more than a Person "by Fiction." As he emphasizes "it is the *Unity* of the Representer, not the *Unity* of the Represented, that maketh the Person *One*," and "*Unity*, cannot be otherwise understood in Multitude."[118]

Skinner thus makes the artificial person to have only fictional being. This fiction permits us to speak of a distinct person having one will, but the fictional person is composed of a "mere aggregate of individuals."[119] Skinner sharpens the fictional character of Hobbes's sovereign in an earlier piece: "To quote Hobbes again, the state has no capacity 'to doe any thing'; it is 'but a word, without substance, and cannot stand.'"[120]

Let us set aside the obvious difficulty of how such an ontologically impotent entity could keep men in awe and bind them in conscience. Upon close examination, one finds that Skinner misleadingly quotes the text. What Hobbes actually says is that "the commonwealth is no person, nor has capacity to do anything, *but by the representative*" (emphasis mine). And, in the second quote, "that a commonwealth *without sovereign power* is but a word without substance, and cannot stand" (emphasis mine). When these texts are quoted in context, nothing in them need suggest Skinner's imputation of ontological impotence to Hobbes's state. On the contrary, the claim that artificial personhood comes into being "by fiction" is in direct conflict with Hobbes's discussion of personhood in chapter 16. As we have seen, "by fiction" adds a specific difference to "artificial person" to signify artificial persons representing those (like bridges, madmen, and idols) that cannot self-authorize their representation in contrast with truly representative artificial persons. The commonwealth cannot be a person "by fiction" because it is truly representative.

Is it not clear that Hobbes marks off the truly representative character of the commonwealth in the quoted passage? Hobbes's sovereign-making formula begins with "*I authorize* . . ." But we saw earlier that the function of fictional personhood is to personate persons and things that cannot self-authorize. Therefore, by the very form of Hobbes's sovereign-making formula, the commonwealth is not a person by fiction.[121]

Hence Hobbes's statement that unity cannot be otherwise understood in multitude than in the unity of the representer does not mean that the unity of the multitude is a mere fiction. Here Hobbes is reinforcing two points. First, against various parliamentarian writers of the day, he wants to deny that the people retain corporation apart from their representation by the sovereign, because this would be a pretext for rebellion.[122] This is a key contrast between Hobbes's political theory and that of John Locke.[123] (We shall return to this point later.) Second, he is simply reinforcing the point that a concord of wills of numerically distinct natural persons does not dissolve the unity of each natural person.[124]

Would it follow, as Skinner suggests, that the union of the multitude for Hobbes is a "real or substantial one"? While Skinner's equation of "real" and "substantial" is not explained, he seems to be equating "real" with individual substances. It is true enough that we can safely say that for Hobbes the unity of the multitude is not a *substantial* unity. Indeed Hobbes never says that societies enjoy the unity individual substances enjoy. For Hobbes the individual substances constituting an artificial person make up the "matter" of that person.[125] Because its formal unity flows from authorization, it is an artificial or man-made—but real—unity. So, contrary to Skinner's suggestion, Hobbes does not think that because some entity does not enjoy the unity of an individual substance it is not real. Therefore, if it's true that Hobbes's artificial person is composed of a mere aggregate of individuals considered one person by a mere fiction, it is not for any of the reasons Skinner has given.

Hobbes himself never uses the phrase "mere aggregate of individuals." Strikingly, he reserves the label "aggregate" for the multitude prior to the sovereign-making covenant or after their sovereign has been dissolved. The point of Hobbes's claim that the commonwealth "is no person, nor has the capacity to do anything, but by the sovereign power" is to *contrast* the truly representative artificial person of the commonwealth with an aggregate. Hence, on Hobbes's terms, it is nonsense to speak of the people either as incorporated apart from the sovereign or as an aggregate once truly represented by the sovereign. Otherwise, Hobbes's closest concept to a "mere aggregate" is a concourse or a conflux.[126]

When discussing concourses, Hobbes gives the example of a marketplace. The example is telling. When we speak of a queue waiting to purchase bread at the marketplace we are indeed speaking of a single thing. But it's difficult to see how a queue could have any unity transcending the aggregate of its parts. What about the marketplace as a whole? Whatever unity it has seems to be nonintentional. Buyers, sellers, and goods flow in and out according to a mass of individual designs. The order that ensues seems to be more along the lines of what Friedrich Hayek calls catallaxy.[127] At any one moment, a marketplace enjoys only an aggregative unity because it is merely a grouping of buyers and sellers with overlapping private aims.

Hence Hobbes distinguishes the marketplace as "having no representative" because representation goes hand in hand with deliberate common action for a common aim.[128] Representation by an authorized sovereign marks off the commonwealth as a form of association essentially distinct from all others. The unity-in-plurality characteristic of commonwealth requires real representation, the criterion for which is the reduction of the wills of the multitude into a single will. (Hence, for Hobbes, for an assembly to be truly representative it must be governed by the norm of majority rule.) In the sovereign-making covenant, the covenanters authorize a man or an assembly to represent them. The man or the assembly now has "the *right* to *present* the person of them all (that is to say, to be their *representative*)."[129] We have already seen the rider that attaches to covenanters appointing one man or assembly of men to bear their person: "every one to own and acknowledge himself to be author of whatsoever he that so beareth their person shall act, or cause to be acted, *in those things which concern the common peace and safety*."[130] A commonwealth is distinct from aggregative associations because it reduces a plurality of wills to a single will for the common good of the group: it is a truly representative artificial person.

And whereas, like a conflux, entrance into and exit from the marketplace has the aspect of ephemerality, the authorization and common action characteristic of commonwealth has the aspect of permanence. In Hobbes's language, the feature of permanence is the "artificial eternity" of the artificial person.[131] Here one might think of the example of Abraham Lincoln's interpretation of the American constitutional order, where perpetuity is a distinguishing feature of American political society and, in Lincoln's view, of any healthy political order.[132] Hobbes agrees: the death of the sovereign does not entail the decapitation and hence the dissolution of the commonwealth.

The artificiality of the artificial person of the commonwealth lies not in its "fictional" status but in its construction by man. It is real in the way *automata* are real. Its life is an artificial life. Like an engine or a watch, the artificial person is in mechanical motion and hence has artificial life. The life of the artificial person is like that of the natural person in that it consists in continual vital motion. The artificial person dissolves (or "dies") apart from the sovereign—and this is because, as the "artificial soul," the sovereign is as a form that "gives life and motion to the whole body."[133] The way the human form constitutes matter into new natural persons in Hobbes's notion of human generation is analogous to the way the political form incorporates natural persons into a new social entity in Hobbes's civil science.[134] Hence the sovereign representative, once authorized, is the formal principle of the commonwealth, and the political form includes the right of succession.

Hobbes should be understood in continuity with the realistic tradition of political philosophy in its concern to identify regime types. However, he identifies only three—monarchy, aristocracy, and democracy—in contrast with the six of traditional Aristotelian theory. I suggest that, again, this is an outflow of his thin theory of the good. Because sovereignty obtains just through the commonwealth's provision of the common good of security, the order to the common good is built into Hobbes's threefold typology. Since to be represented in pursuit of the common good of security is to be in a commonwealth, it follows that only three types of commonwealth exist. So when Hobbes dismisses the existence of tyranny and oligarchy as the political forms of monarchy and aristocracy merely misliked, he is making a point that flows from his fundamental axiology and social ontology. Absent sovereignty, there is no commonwealth at all. (In the next chapter I discuss how, by his natural law doctrine, Hobbes circumscribes the set of actions that can be counted as *acts of sovereignty*.) Notably, Hobbes proceeds in an Aristotelian spirit to discuss the advantages and disadvantages of each political form and retains the classical idea of a best regime.[135] And, as Aquinas did in *De Regno*, Hobbes explicitly grounds the preeminence of monarchy on the basis of its imitation of the governance of the universe by *one* God.[136] The unity and dispatch of monarchy, unencumbered by constitutional limitations and forms, is best because it is best suited to procure the common good of security.

So form takes on a metaphysical importance in explaining the feature of permanence essential to the commonwealth. Since in each of the three types of government "the matter [is] mortal," the form identifies the city over time.[137] In other words, the city is named not according to its mere matter but according to its form, such that the city persists over time even when its material parts change—when sovereigns (and citizens) die or are born. Recalling that the city comes into being only with the institution of the sovereign—the artificial soul giving life and motion to the whole body—Hobbes can say that the city is identical over time inasmuch as the form giving motion to the whole perdures: "for such form as is the beginning of motion, then, as long as that motion remains, it will be the same *individual* thing as [for example] . . . the same city, whose acts proceed continually from the same institution, whether the men be the same or no."[138] Hobbes makes powerful polemical use of this point against the parliamentarians. That the English monarchy was already the erected truly representative person "is so manifest a truth" that Hobbes wonders how it could be missed. For "in a monarchy, he that had the sovereignty from a descent of 600 years, was alone called sovereign, had the title of Majesty from every one of his subjects, and was unquestionably taken by them for their king."[139]

Hobbes also builds his ecclesiology upon his theory of civil personhood, which he deploys polemically against Protestant dissenters and Roman Catholics. He defines the church as

> *a company of men professing Christian religion, united in the person of one sovereign, at whose command they ought to assemble, and without whose authority they ought not to assemble.*[140]

Hobbes wields this definition of the church to defend the authority of the king not only as the highest civil power but also as the highest religious authority or chief pastor of the realm. He could thus offer his doctrine as supportive of the Anglican settlement, which held the English sovereign to be head of the English church. The body politic, as it were, encompasses the body of Christ. Hobbes's theory of sovereign personhood is intended to stave off threats to civil peace from religious disagreement via a civil authoritarianism in matters of religion.

We should note that there is an ongoing discussion among commentators over how Hobbes's thinking on religion relates to liberalism. Alan Ryan distinguishes three positions: first, that the sovereign should exercise complete control over the thoughts of subjects in totalitarian fashion; second, that Hobbes was concerned mainly with *outward* uniformity in religious confession; and third, that Hobbes had a more positively liberal concern for liberty of conscience than is often recognized.[141] In my view, Hobbes seems pretty clearly to deny the first option. He contends that one of the doctrines of darkness is to extend the power of law "to the very thoughts, and consciences of men, by examination, and inquisition of what they hold, notwithstanding the conformity of their speech and actions." By this practice, "men are either punished for answering the truth of their thoughts, or constrained to answer an untruth for fear of punishment."[142] Hobbes interpreted his philosophical rival Descartes in this light. John Aubrey, in a marginal note in his papers, notes that Hobbes used to say that Descartes would have been the greatest geometer in the world if he hadn't professed belief in transubstantiation.[143] Hobbes asserted that this was actually contrary to Descartes's conscientious belief, implying that Descartes was merely publicly obeying French religious authority.[144] Does this comment suggest that the second position is incorrect? Hobbes said he could not "pardon" Descartes for his action—a striking claim given that his action conformed to religious authority.

In the same *Leviathan* passage already quoted, Hobbes countenances the sovereign power to regulate action. Thus he formulates the belief-action dichotomy that is a keystone of liberal constitutionalism. This dichotomy in Hobbes is perhaps most strikingly illustrated in his use of the story of Naaman to justify outward idolatry accompanied by inner freedom to reject idolatry. As initially developed in the context of American constitutional law, that dichotomy was used to justify a constricted view of religious freedom. In the first case in which the U.S. Supreme Court considered the free exercise clause of the Constitution, a free exercise claim by Mormons of the right to practice plural marriage, the Court held that Congress was "deprived of all legislative power over mere opinion, but was left free to reach actions which were in violation of social duties or subversive of good order."[145] This reasoning has a Hobbesian flavor: a premium is placed on public order, and private religious opinion is subordinated thereto when it is not considered "harmless." And yet the same dichotomy was enlisted by the Court several decades later when it incorporated the free exercise clause as a limitation on the states and arrived at a liberal outcome, providing a basis for broadening religious liberty.[146]

Clearly, Hobbes understood the power of religion as both a potential dissolvent and a potential social glue promoting the unity of commonwealth. I suggest that the belief-action dichotomy introduces at least a hairline fracture in the sacral edifice of Christian commonwealth that Hobbes built. By allowing subjects to exclude their sincere suprarational beliefs as actionable reasons when they conflict with the sovereign's laws, Hobbes effectively requires them to fall back on natural reasons to obey authority. In other words, where suprarational state doctrine and suprarational private opinion conflict, the common ground of the natural law remains. Such a principle is ripe to generate or foster a sociological soil of religious pluralism and the conditions for constitutional nonestablishment. Hobbes at one point muses about the possibility of independency and a civil order of a more robust religious liberty of conscience and religious pluralism, saying that it would be "perhaps the best."[147] In my view, we should be careful not to read too much into this passage.[148] But this passage, considered alongside Hobbes's suggestion that Descartes *should* have publicly acted upon sincerely held private beliefs contrary to those of public authority (and that such an action should have been accommodated?), is evidence in favor of the third position. Still, even if there are proto-liberal principles in Hobbes's discussion of conscience, his social ontology requires that polity be a social whole essentially distinct from other kinds of groupings—and the suggestion of this book has been that Hobbes would maintain that his distinctive natural law theory constitutes a public philosophy that is an essential principle of social unity.

So, then, Hobbes distinguishes the commonwealth from aggregates and concourses or confluxes according to a few identifiable features. First, the commonwealth is truly representative.[149] As such, it is characterized by common action for a common aim. This suggests that the common good characterizes the life of the person of the commonwealth rather than being a mere overlap of private aims or goods. Second, the real unity of a society has the aspect of permanence. This sets society apart from groups characterized by temporariness, such as business partnerships. In the concourse of a marketplace, the agents are pooling their private goods to increase private profits. Membership in the commonwealth entitles each member to enjoy what is common, namely, peace. Such are the features of Hobbesian artificial (made by natural persons) unity—the artificial man.

Notably, the Hobbesian artificial unity of natural persons is structurally similar to the Thomistic notion of the unity of order of natural persons. Aquinas, like Hobbes, was interested in the etymology of the word "persona": "The word person seems to be taken from those persons who represented men in comedies and tragedies."[150] Following Boethius, Aquinas states that the Greek word had originally signified the mask worn to represent some character on stage and now has come to signify those of great dignity. But since individual substances of a rational nature were dignified, they were properly called persons, whom Hobbes came to call "natural persons." With Aquinas, we can consider human beings in two ways: first as individual persons and second as members of a community.[151] Thomas calls the latter consideration a *collegium*. The *collegium* known as the political community is considered *quasi uno homo*—a social reality reckoned as one human being or person.[152] Indeed, any group of natural persons united in common action toward a goal can be considered as one agent. Aquinas gives the example of persons united in rowing a boat.[153] The individual persons *qua* members of the crew team enjoy a unity of action and participate in an entity irreducible to its singular parts. The example of the crew team indicates that when any number of natural persons come together for an enduring common purpose through common action, a society has come to be that, as in Hobbesian artificial unity, is a unity transcending a mere aggregation.

We have already seen that the difference between Hobbes and Aquinas lies in their doctrines of the good. Since for Hobbes the basic good is life, the only common good available is security. But Aquinas believed that there was a broader range of intrinsic common goods that were not merely instrumental to preservation: the unity of the *communiones* of families, religious believers, and other friendships. Accordingly, Thomas held that there is a range of societies that enjoy a dignity prior to the state's say-so and that the sovereign must care for inasmuch as he cares for the common good. The Thomistic commonwealth is a unity of unities of order because of the thick theory of the good. The Hobbesian commonwealth is a monolithic artificial unity because of the thin theory of the good.

It is apparent now how the common good account can help us make sense of the relationship between the person of the commonwealth and the person of the sovereign. While Hobbes says that the sovereign "representeth two persons"—"one natural and another politic"—for example, the monarch "hath the person not only of the commonwealth, but also of a man,"[154] it has been said that he "notoriously" does not always clearly distinguish between the person of the commonwealth and the person of the sovereign bearing it.[155] Hobbes does sometimes suggest that, inasmuch as the sovereign man (or group) truly represents the people, he is identical with the artificial person of the commonwealth.[156]

I believe that the best way to make sense of Hobbes is to make a distinction. When we are talking about a truly representative artificial person, we can, on Hobbesian grounds, make a logical distinction between the person of the people incorporated—the represented—and the person of the bearer *as bearer*—the representer. But this can be a logical distinction only because in reality there is one commonwealth ("one person"), that is, one people incorporated by and through the sovereign. As the frontispiece of *Leviathan* suggests, to speak of a truly representative artificial person or commonwealth without the sovereign is like speaking about a man with his head cut off. That would be to take away the power of the sovereign, which is "destructive of the very essence of government."[157] On the other hand, the sovereign-less people are a disunited multitude or aggregate. So whenever Hobbes seems to identify the person of the commonwealth with the sovereign representative (or the represented), it should be understood simply as synecdoche.

The sovereign can speak either as a natural person or as a truly representative artificial person. In the former way, the sovereign's words represent only himself. In the latter way, the words spoken by the sovereign represent those of the multitude who have authorized him. The words of the single commonwealth—a truly representative artificial person—are spoken by the sovereign. The words spoken as sovereign representative are those "acts" referred to in part b of the definition of commonwealth.

In conclusion, the one person referred to in the definition of "commonwealth" is not a person "by fiction" but a truly representative artificial person. We have seen the ways in which Hobbes is a transitional thinker. He holds onto traditional natural law doctrines such as relying on the purposiveness in created nature as the basis of his mimetic theory of constitutional design, emphasizing the need for force-and-fear law as a condition of social peace, and differentiating the distinct essence of political wholes as real unities characterized by pursuit of the common good. Meanwhile, he anticipates liberalism in various ways, such as by thinning out the common good knowable by unaided reason, positing a prototype for the state–individual–private association triad, requiring the protection of harmless liberty, and formulating the belief-action dichotomy. I have also argued that this account could help make some headway in the controversy over the relationship between the person of the commonwealth and the person of the sovereign. The person of the sovereign bears the persons of those he represents, and it is in this capacity that he speaks. In this capacity he speaks as a truly representative artificial person: he acts for the common good. The principal "acts" of the "one person" are the civil laws. In the next chapter I examine Hobbes's natural law account of civil law.

CHAPTER 6

Hobbes's Natural Law Account of Civil Law

In this chapter I complete my interpretation of Hobbes's natural law account of morality and the commonwealth and seek to defend a reading of Hobbes's account of civil law as properly a natural law account.[1] On the natural law account, for some ordinance to fully bind one with the force of civil law it must be both systemically and morally valid. Hobbes's account of civil law qualifies as a natural law account because for him a datum is systemically valid if the sovereign commands it and morally valid if it does not contravene natural law. If the command or judgment is morally invalid, it does not attain the status of civil law for the addressee. Nonaddressees who rightly reason can see commands in contravention of natural law as systemically valid but morally invalid. Morally invalid laws and judgments will tend to weaken actual allegiance and obedience to the sovereign.

If the argument of the foregoing chapters has been successful, we have solid grounds to take reason's fundamental grasp of the desirability of life and the undesirability of death to bind rational agents to pursue peaceful plans of life. For the theist—who is a rational actor, according to Hobbes—the judgment that life is to be preserved, and so, too, the means necessary thereto, binds with the force of law. Because the basic duty to preserve one's life is considered as prior, the catalogue of laws of nature, while always binding *in foro interno*, can fail to bind *in foro externo*. They can fail when the sufficient security condition fails. That is, the laws of nature can fail to bind *in foro externo* because there can fail to be an entity with sufficient power to sanction noncompliance with the laws of nature, in which case obedience *in foro externo* would make one prey to others and contravene the more basic rational necessity to pursue life. The sovereign-making covenant is enacted *for the sake* of peace—in contrast with war, in which the good of life is severely threatened—which is another way of saying that the sovereign is created in order to meet the sufficient security condition of the laws of nature obtaining *in foro externo* force. If this account is true, the moral validity of civil law must turn on whether its demands and permissions are congruent with one's basic duty to preserve one's life. The basic good of life, and the force with which it binds rational actors, amounts to a content-based criterion for the moral validity of civil law. Because right reason judges that this order of goodness is willed by God—who by his irresistible power rightly orders all things—and because this is an order governing man as a rational animal, it has the character of law prior to civil law. Commands of sovereigns must conform to the natural law to achieve the status of law. In other words, commands of sovereigns must be genuinely ordered to peace or the common good of security.

But how can such a claim be accorded with what Hobbes says about the civil law? When he discusses civil law in relation to natural law, he makes a number of remarks that suggest that the ultimate source of law is the will of the commonwealth or sovereign. The suggestion is apparent in Hobbes's definition of civil law:

> Civil law, *is to every subject, those rules, which the commonwealth hath commanded him, by word, writing, or other sufficient sign of the will, to make use of, for the distinction of right, and wrong; that is to say, of what is contrary, and what is not contrary to the rule.*[2]

Hobbes's theory of civil law has been taken to be an expression of legal positivism when legal positivism is understood principally to mean that the existence of a law depends on its pedigree, irrespective of its merits or content.[3] As indicated in the quoted passage, the necessary pedigree lies in *having been commanded*. This has appeared to some to be an early version of what latter-day positivist theory refers to as the "sources thesis." According to the sources thesis, the truth of the statement "Legally, Jones ought to Ø" or "It is the law that Jones ought to Ø" depends on "an appropriate social fact specifiable without resort to moral argument."[4] Hence, to know whether some action is legally demanded or permitted requires one to advert to a relevant social fact—in Hobbes's case the relevant social fact would consist in the will of the sovereign commander, as expressed in word, writing, or some other sufficient declaration of will. The sources thesis entails some version of the "separability thesis."[5] That is, since the legal status of any datum depends solely on its pedigree, its status as a law does not turn on its moral content because, like its pedigree, the content of the law is a matter of social fact.

In order to assess the positivist interpretation, we need a bit more clarity on the latter-day legal philosopher's distinction between systemic and moral validity, which, strictly speaking, is a distinction that it is anachronistic to attribute to Hobbes. But I suggest that the distinction is helpful in making sense of what Hobbes is trying to do. The detour will also help us to compare Hobbes to the positivist tradition of jurisprudence.

The Positivist Tradition

Legal positivists today would not largely defend Hobbes's (supposed) version of legal positivism. A consideration of the positivist tradition since John Austin, Hans Kelsen, Oliver Wendell Holmes, and H. L. A. Hart will illuminate the point. The detour will also yield the grounds for the latter-day distinction legal philosophers make between the "systemic validity" and "moral validity" of law—a distinction that I suggest can illuminate Hobbes's account of civil law.

Twentieth-century legal positivism has built on the work of Hart, who sought to salvage the core ideas of legal positivism from the tradition of Austin, Kelsen, and Holmes. Austin had claimed in unabashed terms that law in its essence is a command to perform or forbear from performing an act that is backed up by the threat of sanction for noncompliance—and that the study of law is, properly speaking, the study of human positive law.⁶ Austin took this to be the "key" to the science of jurisprudence and morals. Kelsen retained the centrality of source and sanction when formulating law as the "primary norm which stipulates the sanction" such that there is no law prohibiting (say) murder, but only a law directing officials to apply sanctions to those who commit murder.⁷ Holmes formulated the prediction theory of the law—that law is nothing more pretentious than what the courts will in fact do. Hart sought to defend the idea of law as a source-based matter of social fact but rejected Austin's, Kelsen's, and Holmes's theories as oversimplifications of our experience of law.

While Austin's theory arguably provided a good explanation of criminal law, Hart argued that it oversimplified things. Hart likened Austin's account to a scenario in which a gunman orders his victim to give up her purse and backs up the order with a threat of violence for noncompliance.⁸ Hart points out that the experience of giving up one's purse when ordered to do so and that of obeying the law when ordered to do so are very different—the former is done primarily from fear, while the latter may be done primarily from respect for authority.⁹ Moreover, the simple command account ultimately fails to explain the following: the *content of laws*, since some rules confer public and private powers (e.g., rules that condition the validity of wills on the presence of two witnesses don't fit the threats-backed-by-punishments paradigm because "nullity" is not a "breach" or "violation"); *the range of application of laws*, since, unlike the gunman, the legislator binds himself as well as others; and *the modes of origin of the laws*, since not all rules arise through the visible performative act of a legislative command but often arise through custom. Similarly, Kelsen's theory, by attempting to reduce the essence of law to a single form ("If anything of a kind X is done or omitted or happens, then apply sanction of a kind Y"), purchased simplicity at the price of distortion of the social functions legal rules perform.¹⁰ The laws function not merely to specify sanctions in the case of noncompliance but *to guide action*. The law provides reasons for action to citizens. Hence Holmes's understanding of the law from the "bad man's" perspective also fails to identify the essence of law. It fails to account for the perspective of the "puzzled man" or the "man who seeks to arrange his affairs." Both are willing to do what is required but need guidance. The predictive theory of law, moreover, mischaracterized legislative and judicial self-understanding: a legislator or judge doesn't see a rule as merely a prediction of his behavior but also as a reason for action. Thus Hart clears the way for his own view of the "essence of law"—the conjunction of primary and secondary rules.

Hart distinguished between rules as follows. There are primary rules that require persons to perform or abstain from certain actions, laws that create rights and obligations, and secondary rules parasitic on the first: provisions for persons to say and do certain things in order to produce, eliminate, or modify primary rules. The secondary rules make up the "rule of recognition" by which the validity of primary rules is adjudged—a rule that is, in turn, constituted by the social practices of officials, legislators, and judges in a legal system. Because the observable social practices or factual behavior of officials constituting the rule of recognition provide the ultimate criteria for valid laws, the rule of recognition is the beating heart of Hart's version of the sources thesis.[11] In short, the conjunction of primary and secondary rules becomes the essence of law—it is Hart's own vision of the "key to the science of jurisprudence."[12]

With this account in hand, the latter-day legal positivist can distinguish between a law's "systemic validity"—the fact that it has a proper legislative pedigree according to the rule of recognition—and a law's "direct" or "moral validity"—whether one should actually take the law to bind one in conscience.[13]

So while Hart rejects Austin's gunman account, Kelsen's *grundnorm* account, and Holmes's predictive account of law as oversimplified, he retains the core thesis of legal positivism, namely, that the existence and content of law are matters of social fact, or proper pedigree. Hart himself identified Hobbes as a member of the positivist pedigree faction in the history of legal philosophy.[14] But is it true that the existence and content of law are merely matters of pedigree, independently of its moral content, according to Hobbes?

Morally Valid Civil Law

Hobbes declares that law, in its proper acceptation, *binds*. Law, says Hobbes, "determineth and bindeth."[15] It is not that law merely claims to obligate but that, as indicated by Hobbes's definition of law in general, it is of the very nature of law to obligate. So Hobbes also says that "law in general is not counsel, but command; nor a command of any man to any man, but only of him whose command is addressed to one formerly obliged to obey him."[16] Hence, for something to *be* positive law is for it to *obligate*: it binds one, in conscience, to act or forbear. In Hobbes's lingo, it binds both *in foro interno* (in conscience) and *in foro externo* (putting it into outward act).

So since, by definition, the sovereign's command to his subjects is civil law, and since law of its very nature binds, it might appear that Hobbes is a legal positivist, believing that the existence and content of the law are known by reference to the sovereign's will, and the law binds. That would mean that any command of the sovereign would attain the status of civil law—and hence, bind one to act or forbear—regardless of its content. But the plot thickens when one considers that Hobbes also indicates that part of the reason law binds, properly speaking, is because it provides one with a sufficient reason for action:

> COMMANDING, which is that speech by which we signify to another our appetite or desire to have any thing done, or left undone, for reason contained in the will itself: for it is not properly said, *Sic volo, sic jubeo*, without that other clause, *Stet pro ratione voluntas*: and when the command is a sufficient reason to move us to the action, then is that command called a LAW.[17]

In this passage Hobbes seems to indicate that a command is properly called law only when it provides one with a sufficient reason for action. In other words, the fact of some edict's having been commanded is not sufficient for it to attain the status of civil law (which, of its very nature, binds in conscience).

As I have contended throughout this book, *the* basic good grasped by reason (or, we might say, the basic reason for action) in Hobbes's scheme is life or self-preservation.[18] Because God, who rightfully governs nature by his irresistible power, orders man toward life—as is evident in the order of our bodily parts, passions, and right reason—the duty to preserve one's life binds with the force of law for rational (reasonable) actors. It follows that any command that would require one to destroy one's life could not provide a sufficient reason for one to act. I suggest that this is how we ought to understand Hobbes's claim that there are certain actions that a man can never be bound by the sovereign's command to take: "not to defend [his] own body," "to kill, wound, or maim himself," "not to resist those that assault him," "to abstain from the use of food, air, medicine, or any other thing without which he cannot live," to accuse himself or self-incriminate without the assurance of pardon, or to serve as a soldier.[19]

Hobbes's catalogue of inalienable rights is explicable in terms of the basic duty to preserve one's life, because one always acts blamelessly when doing that which is necessary to perform one's duty. Sometimes this has been stated as the "ought implies can" principle. Disobeying a command not to defend or nourish oneself is always done with right, because such acts would likely cause one's death. But any command of the sovereign that attains the status of civil law is not disobeyed with right. It follows that the good of life is a content-based limitation that bounds the set of the sovereign's commands that attain the status of civil law. A command to perform or forbear from performing acts that would destroy one's life would lack moral validity for the addressee. In the older natural law tradition, such commands were called "perversions of law."

Aquinas deploys this locution, *perversitas legis*, when considering the nature of a tyrannical command and is willing to use phrases like "unjust law" and "corruption of law" for edicts that contravene natural law.[20] In locutions such as "unjust law," "corrupt law," and "perverse law," the adjectives "unjust," "corrupt," and "perverse" modify "law." Aquinas's way of speaking suggests that he would agree that some iniquitous enactment could have systemic validity. Attempts to summarize Aquinas's position by merely quoting the "unjust law is not a law" dictum, without this nuance, would be a parody. Aquinas can thus accept a partial truth in the legal positivist's sources and separability theses.[21] Any legislative enactment with systemic validity by that very fact has in some measure the character of law.[22] However, inasmuch as it contravenes natural law, it lacks moral validity and hence fails to be law in the focal sense of law—it will, in other words, lack the full character of law. The natural law theorist thus can accept the distinction between systemic and moral validity and still insist that mere systemic validity does not suffice to tell us whether some edict is the peripheral or focal case of law—i.e., whether it binds in conscience *as law*.

Admittedly, Hobbes himself does not use the locution "perversion of law." But the point is that, like Aquinas, Hobbes seems to recognize that commands of a sovereign can lack moral validity. Moreover, since both Aquinas and Hobbes hold that the natural law has legal force by God's will, the claim that civil law must be morally valid to have the binding character of law ultimately means that it must be congruent with God's will.

These initial reflections have moved too quickly, however, because we have so far abstracted from passages in which Hobbes obfuscates the distinction between moral and systemic validity. The success of our interpretation will require an account of these obfuscations. The distinction between systemic and moral validity in Hobbes is obscured for at least two reasons. The first reason is Hobbes's collapsing of a law's pedigree and its justice under the will of the sovereign, a collapse that he grounds in his theory of authorization. The second is his claim that the law of nature and the civil law are of "equal extent"—a claim that Kavka has aptly termed the "mutual containment thesis." Let us consider these two reasons for the obscurity.

Authorization, Mutual Containment, and the Sovereign Command

While Hobbes requires that law provide one with a sufficient reason for action—a claim that I have suggested introduces an inchoate distinction between systemic and moral validity in Hobbes's account of civil law—he obscures this distinction in his account of the justice of the sovereign's command.

The obscurity is evident if we look at Hobbes's answer to the following two questions that can be asked of any putative law: (1) *Is this enactment systemically valid?* and (2) *Is this enactment just?* Hobbes says that both questions can be answered by knowing the answer to just one question: (3) *Was the datum commanded by the sovereign?* Hence, Hobbes collapses the answers to questions 1 and 2 into the facticity of the sovereign's command. He does this because, in his view, the sovereign's command is always the source of positive law and is always just.

Hobbes offers a few different arguments as to why the sovereign's command is never "unjust." The arguments revolve around Hobbes's understanding of the sovereign-making covenant.[23] His principal ground in *Leviathan* is his theory of authorization in the sovereign-making covenant. In the covenantal formula a person says, "I authorize and give up my right of governing myself and authorize all the sovereign's actions."[24] Since a covenanter authorizes the sovereign to do whatever he (or it) will do to him as a subject, the sovereign cannot be accused of injustice.[25] It follows that the sovereign's command cannot be unjust— "no law can be unjust."[26] Since Hobbes suggests that the answer to questions 1 and 2 depends solely on the sovereign will, the distinction between systemic and moral validity is obscured—but it remains to be seen whether it is destroyed.

The second way that the distinction between moral and systemic validity is obscured is through Hobbes's "mutual containment thesis." Hobbes puts it this way: "The law of nature and the civil law contain each other, and are of equal extent."[27] This claim apparently has two parts. The first part, about the containment of the civil law in the natural law, seems straightforward. The laws of nature direct men to lay down their right to all things, erect a sovereign power, and perform the covenant they have made. The second part of the thesis is more difficult. How is the natural law contained in the civil law? Clearly, the civil law is supposed to enforce the dictates of reason with a power sufficient to sanction noncompliance. But does it mean something more than that? An available interpretation—and, apparently, an influential one—is that of S. A. Lloyd.[28] According to Lloyd, the mutual containment thesis is indicative of what she calls Hobbes's "self-effacing" natural law theory. The natural law itself directs agents to authorize an unassailable judge to determine what the law—including both civil and natural law—is. Such an interpretation of Hobbes as a "practical legal positivist," for Lloyd, means that there is no legitimate perspective from which to criticize the sovereign. In other words, an interpretation of the natural law is morally valid just in virtue of its having been interpreted by the sovereign.

In short, we have identified two different ways in which Hobbes obscures the distinction between systemic and moral validity: through the reduction of the justice of law to the sovereign's command by the theory of authorization and through the mutual containment thesis, which might just be Hobbes's way of saying that natural law itself requires the erection of a sovereign with absolute authority to judge the meaning of natural law.

The first obscurity is nothing new. Hobbes's earliest critics, including Robert Filmer, George Lawson, and Bishop Bramhall, pointed out the apparent contradiction between his sovereign-making formula and the right to resist the sovereign in self-defense.[29] The apparent contradiction is manifest in our foregoing considerations. By the sovereign-making act, a person says, "I authorize and give up my right of governing myself and authorize all the sovereign's actions."[30] From this formula, Hobbes infers that the sovereign can never do his subjects an injustice, since the subject authorized all his actions. But we also saw how Hobbes maintains that the right to preserve one's life is inalienable. Accordingly, as we have seen, Hobbes lists a number of acts that the sovereign can never bind a subject to perform that pertain to self-destruction.[31] And that which one cannot be bound by law to do is done with right, just as one cannot be taken to authorize an absolutely unlimited sovereign if that entails the transfer of an inalienable right.[32] So apparently the subject does and does not authorize an absolute sovereign; the subject does and does not act justly when he or she disobeys the sovereign's command to act (or forbear) in a way that would destroy one's life.

These obscurities may be instances in which Hobbes is simply irreconcilable with himself, as Bramhall alleged. Or they may be instances in which Hobbes was, in his own words, "a forgetful blockhead."[33] But there may be solutions available in Hobbes's own terms.

Hobbes's apparently contradictory theory of authorization and inalienable rights seems to obscure the distinction between the systemic and moral validity of law. But if it can be shown that the absolute justice of the sovereign's commands is compatible with an inalienable right to self-defense, then, upon that ground, the morally-systemically valid distinction will be vindicated. And, on that ground, our thesis that Hobbes's account of civil law is properly a natural law account can be vindicated. Regarding the mutual containment thesis, the challenge will be to show how this thesis is compatible with the claim that civil law can fail to be morally valid and how the thesis does not entail a practical legal positivism. Let us first see how Hobbes's theory of authorization and inalienable rights might be clarified.

INALIENABLE RIGHTS AND UNLIMITED SOVEREIGNTY

How can we reconcile Hobbes's claim that the sovereign-making covenant authorizes an unlimited sovereign with his claims that one always retains those inalienable rights necessary to preserve one's life? I argue that the sovereign acts unlimitedly *inasmuch as he is sovereign*. That is to say, when the sovereign acts as sovereign, his command is sufficient to make something into civil law. But that *inasmuch as* qualification turns out to import the content-based limitation we have suggested that natural law places on what can achieve the status of law for the addressee of a command.

When Hobbes is discussing those rights that are inalienable, he remarks that, when a person makes a covenant, he must always be understood to act under the aspect of the good: "The object is some *good to himself*."[34] But this claim is compatible with Hobbes's distinction between apparent and actual goods—and in this book I have argued at length that the basic object of any reasonable life plan for Hobbes is the good of life. Hobbes's axiology is best understood as a thin theory of the good objectively knowable by unaided reason—and this is the principal contrast with Aquinas's natural law account of the civil law, because Aquinas had a thicker account of the good. Hobbes appears to be saying that someone who enters into a covenant can be presumed to meet the minimum condition of practical reasonableness that they take the good of life as basic.[35] Hence, anyone who enters the sovereign-making covenant is presumed to take life as good. So Hobbes says in the same passage: "The motive and end for which this renouncing and transferring of right is introduced, is nothing else but the security of a man's person, in his life and in the means of so preserving life as not to be weary of it."[36] From these points Hobbes concludes that someone who performs a covenantal act should never be taken to forfeit the end for which the covenant was made:

And therefore if a man by words or other signs, seem to despoil himself of the end for which those signs were intended, he is not to be understood as if he meant it, or that it was his will.[37]

Earlier we saw that Hobbes's covenantal formula included a person's authorization of all the sovereign's acts. If we take Hobbes at his word, such an authorization cannot be a sign that would despoil the covenanter of the end for which he covenants, namely, the security of his person and the means to preserve his life. I suggest that the covenantal formula authorizes a person to command a set of ordinances, O_1, inasmuch as the person acts as sovereign. The set O_1 is distinct from the set of all possible ordinances, O_2. My claim is that, if and only if the command is of the set O_1 can it achieve the status of civil law for the addressee. How can a sovereign fail to act as a sovereign?

Hobbes clearly recognizes that a person or persons with sovereignty act in ways that cannot be considered actions taken *as sovereign*. The sovereign (whether a man or an assembly) bears "two persons"—his own natural person and the person of the commonwealth. Hence, the monarch "hath the person not only of the commonwealth, but also of a man."[38] When a sovereign acts "as a man" or in his "natural capacity," his acts are not understood as representative of his subjects. Hence, Hobbes distinguishes between public ministers who are empowered by the sovereign to administer the realm and servants of a monarch who serve him in his "natural capacity." When a sovereign orders his ministers, his act is essentially different from that taken when he orders his private servants. In the latter case, he does not act *as bearer* of the commonwealth and hence does not act with the authority of the sovereign. When the sovereign does not speak as the sovereign representative, his words do not attain the status of civil law.

Still, the example of a sovereign giving orders to servants, stewards, chamberlains, and the like does not get to the heart of the difficulty we are interested in. The controversy lies precisely in potential scenarios in which the sovereign, in his public capacity, commands one to perform acts destructive of one's life. I claim that such commands fail to achieve the status of civil law for the addressee of the command because when the commander so acts, he is not acting as sovereign.

Consider Hobbes's claim that when public ministers act in the name of the sovereign:

> Every subject is so far obliged to obedience, as the ordinances he shall make, and the commands he shall give, be in the king's name, and *not inconsistent with his sovereign power*.[39]

The passage indicates that there are potential ordinances that would be inconsistent with the sovereign power—ordinances that, if commanded, would not oblige subjects. But what is the criterion for inconsistency? There are, of course, a number of rights that inhere in the sovereign power.[40] But the office of the sovereign includes not only rights and powers needed to duly execute the office—it also includes the end for which those powers are ordained, that is, the end for which the office was created:

> The office of the sovereign (be it a monarch, or an assembly) consisteth in the end for which he was trusted with the sovereign power, namely, the procuration of the *safety of the people*, to which he is obliged by the law of nature, and to render an account thereof to God, the author of that law, and to none but him.[41]

Indeed, Hobbes indicated the telic nature of the sovereign power before either the covenantal formula or any of the essential rights of sovereignty:

> The final cause, end, or design of men (who naturally love liberty, and dominion over others) in the introduction of that restraint upon themselves in which we see them live in commonwealths is the foresight of their own preservation, and of a more contented life thereby; that is to say, of getting themselves out from that miserable condition of war, which is necessarily consequent (as hath been shown) to the natural passions of men, when there is no visible power to keep them in awe, and tie them by fear of punishment to the performance of their covenants and observation of those laws of nature set down in the fourteenth and fifteenth chapters.[42]

The criterion of inconsistency is nothing other than that for which the covenant was formed. Importantly, this statement of the end of the sovereign-making covenant comes in the same chapter in which Hobbes gives us the covenantal formula. I suggest that Hobbes does not include the *telos* in the actual formula because he has already stated it and, as before, we can presume that covenanters are practically reasonable. Just as any covenanter is presumed to be taking the good of life as basic, any person who participates in the authorization of the sovereign by the covenantal formula is presumed to be quitting the condition of war for the sake of security. That is, covenanters authorize the sovereign to secure the peace or, as we saw in the previous chapter, to procure the common good.

We have seen that Hobbes's view of peace, in contrast with the Thomistic natural law tradition, is thin: it aims somewhere between (1) the mere absence of civil strife and (2) the agreement of citizens on important matters. Hobbesian covenanters do not aim at a thicker notion of peace that is higher on the scale of the unity of peace. They do not aspire to (3) civic friendship or (4) complete harmony of persons' affections within and choices without. But they do aim at peace understood principally as security. The sovereign is thus bound by the covenantal aim. In Hobbes's words, "All the duties of rulers are contained in this one sentence, *the safety of the people is the supreme law.*"[43] Accordingly, "He, who being placed in authority, shall use his power otherwise than to the safety of the people, will act against the reasons of peace, that is to say, against the laws of nature."[44] It follows that the sovereign's authorization extends only to acts that secure and maintain peace understood in contrast to acts that destroy security. Therefore, by the terms of the sovereign-making covenant, a man or an assembly acts consistently with the sovereign power—acts as a sovereign—when he or it acts for the sake of peace.

In this reading, the sovereign's power remains absolute. But Hobbesian absolute sovereignty does not entail the authority to command any member O_2. Within Hobbes's notion of absolute sovereignty is built the limitation of what gets to count as an *act of sovereignty*—and acts of sovereignty are always acts for the security of subjects. So we must take exception to Paul DeHart's recent argument that Sophocles' Creon is the ideal Hobbesian sovereign in that a "ruler set up by the city must be obeyed in whatever he commands."[45] In my estimation, DeHart is entirely correct that a sheer ethical voluntarism is self-referentially incoherent since it is logically impossible to distinguish normative or binding acts of will from nonnormative or nonbinding acts of will on the basis of will alone. As DeHart explains, this is because, in the entire set of acts of will ($W_1, W_2, W_3 \ldots W_n$), no act of will, say, W_1, can be posited as normatively binding on the basis of will alone, since that would just be to posit another member of the set.[46] My disagreement with DeHart is in attributing this picture to Hobbes. In my reading, the set of acts that count as acts of sovereignty is cordoned by a standard external to that set considered as mere acts of will, namely, the common good of security.[47]

It should now be apparent how we can clarify Hobbes's account of absolute sovereignty to fit with the inalienable right to self-defense. When a sovereign orders one to perform acts destructive of one's life, the ordinance fails to be a binding command because the performance of such acts can never conduce to one's security. Such ordinances are *inconsistent with sovereignty*—call these IWS ordinances.

We can now assess the upshot of this account of sovereignty for Hobbes's understanding of civil law. If and when a sovereign dictates an IWS ordinance, it fails to have moral validity because the subject has not actually authorized it. The reason the subject has not authorized it is because covenanters are taken to be practically reasonable in that they take the good of life as basic and erect a sovereign for the sake of security. Commands to perform acts that would likely entail the destruction of one's life are just the sorts of ordinances that manifestly do not secure one's person. Since the sovereign is authorized only insofar as his acts secure one's person, it follows that such ordinances are not members of the set O_1—those ordinances that the sovereign is able to command *as sovereign*. In this light, consider the following passage:

> The obligation of subjects to the sovereign is understood to last as long, and no longer, than the power lasteth by which he is able to protect them. For the right men have by nature to protect themselves, when none else can protect them, can by no covenant be relinquished. The sovereignty is the soul of the commonwealth, which, once departed from the body, the members do no more receive their motion from it.[48]

This passage can easily be read to indicate the notion of sovereignty as the mere fact that a state has sufficient guns, police, and military forces. But in the foregoing interpretation, those members of the commonwealth who are addressees of a command in contravention to the basic precept of natural law to preserve one's life are addressees of commands inconsistent with sovereignty. Hence they are effectively not moved by the sovereign's command, as members of a body are not moved by the soul departed.

It is an interesting question as to the membership status in the commonwealth of the addressee of a morally invalid law. Is the addressee still a member of the commonwealth, retaining a right to resist the sovereign? Or is the addressee of an IWS ordinance thrown back into the state of nature, in which case his former sovereign is now a very powerful enemy? Those who defend the latter contend that, in commanding what I have called an IWS ordinance, the sovereign violates the covenant—and the very being of the commonwealth presupposes the covenant. So, commanding such an ordinance, the entity that was the commonwealth is no longer—at least for the addressee. At best it is an entity claiming to be a commonwealth. The strength of this solution is that it retains the absolutism of the commonwealth or state—as long as it qualifies as a state.[49] It also retains Hobbes's apparent commitment to forestalling all rebellion. Moreover, it takes seriously Hobbesian reckoning of the meaning of words. And the passage just quoted about the duration of obedience might be cited in its favor.

Still, those who defend the former solution maintain that the right to self-defense is properly a right of resistance against the state. In this reading, addressees of IWS ordinances remain members of the commonwealth but are justified in disobeying such commands. In favor of this solution is, chiefly, the fact that Hobbes refers to self-defense rights as liberties of subjects. So someone commanded to incriminate himself remains a member of the commonwealth—but has a right to disobey it. This may be taken to imply that addressees of IWS commands remain subjects.[50] The defender of this view could also enlist the previously cited passage about the duration of obedience in his favor.[51]

While I would prefer the former view, my argument is compatible with either solution. Under the first solution, an addressee of an IWS command rightly views it as not only morally invalid but systemically invalid as well, since the addressee would thereby no longer have a rule of recognition. Nonaddressees of the command, inasmuch as they rightly reason, will recognize the command as systemically valid but morally invalid. Under the second solution, both addressees and nonaddressees of an IWS command view it as morally invalid but recognize its systemic validity. If one remains a subject, one can recognize the systemic and moral validity of other laws of the sovereign.

What is the *status* of a morally invalid command, then? Is it a *law*? Given Hobbes's claim that it is of the nature of law to bind—*pace* latter-day positivists, Hobbes denies that law merely "claims" to bind—we must deny it the status of civil law for the addressee because such commands do not bind one to act. Civil laws, properly speaking, must proceed from acts of the sovereign as sovereign—and morally invalid commands do not proceed from the commander as sovereign. But, as we have suggested, this may be compatible with the addressee recognizing that some such edict has a measure of the character of law, inasmuch as it is systemically valid, if we take the addressee to still be a member of the commonwealth.

To sum up my solution to the obscurity of systemic and moral validity apparent in Hobbes's theory of authorization: persons covenant to authorize a sovereign for the sake of security. By its very nature, the covenantal act authorizes only those acts consistent with sovereignty—and I have argued that Hobbes builds into the notion of sovereignty not only the rights essential to execute its end but also the end itself for which the covenant was made. This is how Hobbes can have an absolute sovereignty that is compatible with inalienable rights to self-defense. Accordingly, this is how Hobbes can at once have an absolutist understanding of civil law while being able to retain content-based limitations on which ordinances can achieve the status of civil law (i.e., commands that of their nature bind in conscience). Indeed, this interpretation is supported by the so-called mutual containment thesis—the point of which is to secure the practical congruence between civil law and natural law. Let us now consider it in detail.

The Mutual Containment Thesis and the Sovereign Right of Judgment

A second way that Hobbes appears to obscure his properly natural law account of civil law is in his claim that the "law of nature, and the civil law, contain each other, and are of equal extent."[52] I have already suggested that this means at least that the sovereign is erected in order to provide the security condition for *in foro externo* validity of the laws of nature. The laws of nature will bind *in foro interno* only until a sovereign is erected to sanction noncompliance; if they bound *in foro externo* prior to the sovereign-making covenant, they would make one prey to others, contrary to the more basic rational necessity to preserve one's life. I shall argue that the mutual containment thesis actually supports my interpretation that there are content-based limitations on what can be effected into civil law, that is, that moral validity is a necessary condition for commands and judgments to bind subjects.

I alluded earlier to a possible interpretation that could present a challenge to my argument that Hobbes's account of civil law is, properly speaking, a theistic natural law account. I have in mind the recent work of Lloyd, who has argued that, while the laws of nature have a normative status prior to civil law, natural law is "self-effacing" and Hobbes is a practical legal positivist. This interpretation, Lloyd claims, is the key to understanding the mutual containment thesis. Notably, Lloyd's positivist interpretation of Hobbes is different from the standard positivist interpretations. The standard interpretations tend to trade on one of the secularist theses regarding God's nonessential role in Hobbes's legal philosophy: the historical, concealment, and practical severability theses. Lloyd explicitly avers that her interpretation is compatible with theistic interpretations of the laws of nature as really laws. I shall argue, on the basis of Hobbes's theories of equity and right judgment, that Hobbes is not a practical legal positivist. If successful, my argument will show how a theistic natural law reading of Hobbes is incompatible with a positivist reading of his theory of civil law.

Lloyd reads Hobbes's state of nature as a state of affairs in which there obtains "universal, unbridled private judgment" about what the natural law requires.[53] Because such a state of affairs devolves into war, we would want others to submit to a political authority, and so we ought to as well—this is an outworking of what Hobbes calls the "easy sum" of the laws of nature. Lloyd calls it the "summary formulation" (SF) of the laws of nature, and she reformulates it as the reciprocity theorem (RT)—*to do what one condemns in another is contrary to reason*—which we discussed in chapter 2.[54] But SF (or RT) requires each person to give up his private right of judgment over what the natural law requires. In other words, the most basic requirement of SF is for contractors to set up an objective supreme judge or arbiter—and for Lloyd this is the essential feature of the sovereign. This means that the sovereign is the authoritative interpreter of all disputes, and hence "it may legitimately settle disputes as to *what the law—including natural law—is*."[55] Thus Lloyd concludes that Hobbesian natural law is self-effacing because the natural law itself commits us to regard the sovereign's judgment in all disputes as decisive—even in disputes over what the natural law requires—and so no one can pretend to disobey sovereign positive law on the basis that it conflicts with the natural law. And it is in this way that the civil law contains the natural law; hence Lloyd's contention that her interpretation is the meaning of the mutual containment thesis.

From these grounds Lloyd infers that "there is no legitimate position or perspective from which we can criticize or resist the sovereign's decisions."[56] The sovereign's judgment is "like that of the Supreme Court": it is authoritative even if or when it is "cosmically incorrect."[57] The laws of nature "direct us to subordinate our judgment to that of the sovereign, even when his judgment is erroneous," because otherwise we would be reasserting a right of private judgment against SF, which would risk civil war and a return to the state of anarchy.[58] Whereas my foregoing argument suggested that the natural law provides a content-based criterion for what counts as acts of sovereignty, Lloyd claims that the natural law directs agents to completely subordinate private judgment to an unlimited sovereign judge—even when it is "cosmically" incorrect, which in Hobbes's terms would mean nothing other than the contravention of God's will manifest in natural law.

I maintain that such an interpretation fails to correctly understand both Hobbes's theory of equity as a moral check on the sovereign and the real import of the mutual containment thesis. Let us consider Hobbes's notion of equity.

We saw earlier how Hobbes maintained, regarding his theory of authorization, that nothing the sovereign can do is "unjust." My reconstruction of Hobbes suggested that this claim should be understood of the sovereign insofar as it acts as sovereign. That is, inasmuch as the sovereign acts according to its purpose. In this way, a sovereign that commands one to contravene the basic rational necessity to preserve one's life would not be acting *as sovereign*, so technically, "justice" is not implicated because the addressee exercises his right to self-defense outside the confines of covenant. While Hobbes won't admit that the sovereign can do an injustice, he does say that the sovereign "may commit iniquity."[59]

According to Hobbes, the "general rule of equity" is both "the law of reason" and "the law of God."[60] Equity consists in dealing equally when judging between man and man or in the "equal distribution to each man of that which in reason belongeth to him" and is properly the act of a judge or arbitrator.[61] As such, the natural law of equity is derived from fundamental human equality, since disputes between fundamentally equal men merit impartial judgment. The law is grounded in a deeper principle that Hobbes calls the "easy sum" of the laws of nature: "doing to others as we would be done to" or, in its negative formulation, "Do not that to another which thou wouldest not he should do unto thee."[62] Hence the judge who "performs his trust" deals equitably between persons; the judge who deals inequitably is "partial in judgment" and is a practitioner of "acception of persons."[63]

Hence Hobbes recognizes the possibility that the sovereign judge can fail to act according to the precept of equity. As Noel Malcolm puts it, Hobbes's notion of equity "shows that morality remains an objective standard, by which the laws or actions of the sovereign can be judged."[64] Such judgments can take the form of violation of the basic right to self-defense. Judgments of that kind are parallel to IWS commands. Yet the class of judgments properly called iniquitous broadens what counts as acts inconsistent with sovereignty. All iniquitous judgments are, properly speaking, inconsistent with sovereignty. Accordingly, all iniquitous judgments are morally invalid on the ground of the independent criterion of equity.

Hobbes's condemnation of the iniquitous judgments of his day is suggestive of their moral invalidity. One example is his criticism of a judgment set down by Sir Edward Coke that an innocent man accused of a felony who flees for fear of corrupt or partial judges and is afterward brought to trial and proved innocent shall, notwithstanding his innocence, forfeit his goods and property.[65] Hobbes rejects Coke's justification of the presumption of law that the one who flees is guilty as iniquitous. Such would be to deprive an innocent man of his due, in violation of the eleventh law of nature of equity, which requires judges to render "equal distribution to each man of that which in reason belongeth to him."[66] The natural law of equity requires that an innocent man not be deprived of his goods and property.[67] To this law of nature "there can be no exception at all."[68] As long as such a precedent stands by the sovereign's will or tacit permission, the law is systemically valid (and in some cases that is enough to garner merely prudential obedience; we consider the point further later). But the upshot of Hobbes's criticism is that it is morally invalid.

One immediately notices that, in criticizing the common law of his day, Hobbes himself does not practice the sort of absolute subordination of judgment that Lloyd claims Hobbesian natural law demands. Nor can we say that Hobbes's criticism is of Coke and not of the sovereign, since Hobbes maintains that common law has the force of civil law by the sovereign's tacit will. But let us set that point aside. The natural law of equity is supposed to be a principle binding the judge, and thus the judge can fail to judge equitably. Lloyd maintains that when judges fail, Hobbesian natural law unfailingly binds us to obey their judgments, because resorting to the right of private judgment would risk a return to anarchy.

But consider Hobbes's remark in his discussion of the natural law of equity that the acts of an inequitable judge are the "cause of war."[69] As Lloyd correctly points out, the sovereign is the supreme judge. It follows from Hobbes's remark that the sovereign will can fail to be equitable when he fails to perform its trust—and when he fails to judge equitably, he causes war. Because inequitable judgments are always bellicose, they are always inconsistent with sovereignty, since the very purpose of the sovereign office and power is the peace of security.

Why does the failure to judge equitably cause war? Hobbes answers that the inequitable judge "doth what in him lies to deter men from the use of judges and arbitrators."[70] It is fairly obvious why the deterrence of men from the use of judges brings on a state of war. Erecting a sovereign judge entails giving up the right to be the judge in one's own case. This means that one gives up the right of private judgment over good and evil. So to deter men from the use of judges and arbitrators is to encourage men to rely on the right of private judgment. But the widespread practice of the right of private judgment would inaugurate war. Hobbes is here indicating a point discussed in chapter 1: man's first disobedience to the rule of law was man's disobedience to God in Eden by usurping the right of private judgment over good and evil. Now, as a potential condition of actual fallen persons, the state of nature is a *reductio* of the practice of the right of private judgment on a massive scale.

Yet Lloyd's claim that the laws of nature direct subjects to completely subordinate our judgment to the sovereign judge on the pain of the subjects' causing war (or initiating a chain of causes leading to war)—even when his judgments are "cosmically" iniquitous—ignores Hobbes's point that it is *the sovereign* who causes war when he judges iniquitously. The sovereign itself causes a state of war by deterring agents from the use of judges. How is that?

The sovereign's iniquitous judgment need not initiate *actual* fighting or battle for it to cause war, according to Hobbes. War consists not in actual fighting but "in the known disposition thereto during all the time there is no assurance to the contrary."[71] Suppose there is a case in which the sovereign judges iniquitously and Smith discerns that he has been unreasonably harmed. Suppose further that Smith is a reasonable fellow and acts according to RT: he does not do that which he condemns in another. (These suppositions are warranted—when Smith becomes a subject, he does not become a new *kind* of thing; he is still a rational animal. Hence, he has not lost his reasoning powers in erecting a sovereign judge.[72]) Smith is now doubtful that he will get a fair shake from appealing to the sovereign judge. But Smith is not the only one. Insofar as iniquitous judgments of the sovereign are publicly known, others are deterred from the use of judges, too—and Smith knows that. He knows that his neighbor, Jones, is not assured of getting a fair shake from the sovereign judge. Hence Smith knows that Jones is deterred from appeal to the sovereign judge and encouraged to assume a right of private judgment—and he wouldn't blame him if he did. After all, Smith was the victim of the iniquitous judgment, and he wouldn't blame his neighbor if his neighbor judged that his person, family, and goods were no longer safe from iniquity in the sovereign's court. If we accept the RT as a valid formulation of the easy sum, if Smith is deterred from appeal to the sovereign judge (and accordingly assumes a right of private judgment), he acts reasonably, since he does not condemn that in Jones. This story shows, *pace* Lloyd, how the easy sum or its formulation in RT does not direct unfailing subordination of judgment to the sovereign.

Given the sovereign's iniquity and his neighbor's knowledge of it, Jones is reasonable to judge that the security of his person, family, property, and so on are in jeopardy not only from the sovereign but also from his neighbors. Hobbes explicitly warns that corrupt judgments will lead to this chaotic state of affairs. While this statement comes in the context of explaining what sovereigns should cause to be taught to subjects, Hobbes is actually teaching about the duty of the sovereign in his capacity as judge, and he may even be suggesting that subjects should remain vigilant to detect corruption in the sovereign's courts:

> For which purpose also it is necessary [subjects] be showed the evil consequences of false judgment by corruption either of judges or witnesses, whereby the distinction of propriety is taken away and justice becomes of no effect; all which things are intimated in the sixth, seventh, eighth, and ninth commandments.[73]

It follows that if the sovereign judges iniquitously at t_1, the sovereign has initiated a time series $(t_1, t_2, t_3 \ldots)$ in which men lack the assurance of peace; iniquitous judgment inaugurates a condition of war until such time as peace is reassured.

Since the sovereign's iniquitous judgment causes war, the absolute subordination of private judgment to the sovereign judge does not seem to be the meaning of the mutual containment thesis. I suggest that the true import lies in Hobbes's indication that commands and judgments fail to have moral validity because they incite war, and I further suggest that this is illuminated in Hobbes's *in foro interno–in foro externo* distinction. Hobbes writes:

> The laws of nature oblige *in foro interno*, that is to say, they bind to a desire they should take place; but *in foro externo*, that is, to

the putting them in act, not always. For he that should be modest and tractable, and perform all he promises, in such time and place where no man else should do so, should but make himself a prey to others, and procure his own certain ruin, contrary to the ground of all laws of nature, which tend to nature's preservation. And again, he that having sufficient security that others shall observe the same laws towards him, observes them not himself, seeketh not peace, but war, and consequently the destruction of his nature by violence.... The laws of nature are immutable and eternal; for injustice, ingratitude, arrogance, pride, iniquity, acception of persons, and the rest, can never be made lawful. For it can never be that war shall preserve life, and peace destroy it.[74]

The *in foro interno–in foro externo* distinction is supposed to make sense of how Hobbes's catalogue of natural laws can be immutably and eternally binding in a nonabsurd way, that is, in a way that would not conduce to one's own self-destruction, which is contrary to the very ground of all the laws of nature in Hobbes's scheme. The catalogue of natural laws does not always bind *in foro externo* in the state of nature—not because these laws aren't really laws by God's prior legislation but because of the risk of getting double-crossed. The situations Hobbes has in mind in which performance of a contract would lead to one's own destruction are those contracts and covenants formed in a condition in which there is not a common power to keep everyone in awe, that is, where there is no immediate palpable threat of sanction for breach of the natural law. This is the condition of war.

But when the sovereign judges iniquitously, he causes war. Hobbes seems to mean that, when the sovereign commands or judges contrary to basic equity, he has initiated a state of affairs in which men and women would be justified in judging that there is no longer "sufficient security" to observe the laws of nature *in foro externo*. We have already seen why. When the sovereign publicly judges iniquitously, he deters reasonable persons from appeal to him as judge. This has the potential to initiate a chain of causes in which reasonable persons will be deterred from adverting to the common judge and will be encouraged to assert a right of private judgment as a surer means to secure their persons, families, and goods. The state of war, as distinct from a state of peace, may be either a *disposition toward* or an *actual* assertion of the right of private judgment on a massive scale. Either way, such a condition is not a peaceful one. The nonpeaceful condition is one in which, by definition, sufficient security fails to obtain for the laws of nature to bind *in foro externo*. But the *in foro externo* "putting into place" of the laws of nature does consist in obeying (at least a major part of) the civil law, since it contains the natural law. Therefore, the warlike condition is one in which the civil laws do not bind one *in foro externo*.

It follows that the sovereign's own iniquitous judgment fails to attain the status of binding civil law because in the very act of commanding in this way, the sovereign brings on a state in which there will be a tendency to the widespread assertion of private judgment and fisticuffs. In that case, one would not be assured of the *in foro externo* compliance of others—and the only precept that would be binding both *in foro interno* and *in foro externo* would be the basic rational necessity to preserve one's life. This is another way of saying that for something to become civil law it must be congruent with natural law, which is ultimately congruent with God's ordained will.

Let us sum up our discussion of authorization and the mutual containment thesis. I have argued that Hobbes should be interpreted as having a properly natural law account of civil law. This means that an assessment of the legal status of some edict or ordinance cannot rest simply on its source or pedigree, independent of (or separable from) its moral content. For something to bind with the force of civil law it must give the addressee a sufficient reason to act—it must be both systemically and morally valid. Hobbes's theory of authorization and the mutual containment thesis have been taken to collapse systemic and moral validity under the sovereign will. This is in a sense true, but only inasmuch as the sovereign acts as a sovereign—and that "inasmuch as" imports the ends of the sovereign-making covenant, life and security, as validating conditions for which possible ordinances can count as civil law. Moreover, the natural law of equity limits the sorts of judgments that can count as properly sovereign acts and bind addressees.

In this light we can start to see more clearly how Hobbes could maintain that civil law and natural law are necessarily congruent, just as he can maintain a normatively charged notion of sovereignty for the sake of security. Natural law requires us to secure our persons. Hence, it requires us to erect a sovereign powerful enough to protect us. If and when the sovereign acts violently toward those who authorized him to secure the peace, the sovereign fails to bind addressees with the force of civil law. Hobbes has effectively ensured the practical congruence of natural law and civil law by declaring that for an ordinance to attain the full status of civil law (it binds the addressee *as law*), it must be systemically and morally valid. This account is compatible with an absolutist conception of the sovereign's lawmaking and adjudicative authority because morally invalid commands and judgments fail to be consistent with sovereignty.

Conclusion

Before readers even crack the spine of Hobbes's *Leviathan*, they have a portent of the doctrines that lie therein. As the frontispiece vividly portrays, Hobbes constructs an absolutist and unitarist theory of sovereignty out of a mass of individual wills that make up the body politic. There is an imposing crowned figure, brandishing sword and crozier, with a body made up of citizens. In the midst of the English Civil War—a time of misery, tragedy, and woe, if there ever was one—Hobbes's message seemed to be that in order to secure the peace, the sovereign must have the kind of power over the body politic that individuals have over their bodily members: a despotic power to command motion proper to their capacities. Above the imposing man, there is an inscription quoted from the Book of Job: *Non est potestas Super Terram quae comparetur* (the antecedent being the great beast Leviathan), which the Authorized Version translates "Upon the earth there is not his [its] like."

One of Hobbes's most intelligent critics was Bishop Bramhall, who was something of an English Thomist inasmuch as he defended a full-throated medieval version of Christian Aristotelianism. For Bramhall, Hobbes's theory was entirely novel, positing myriad doctrines couched within the language of natural law that had theretofore been thought unconscionable in the natural law tradition. Hobbes's principles, Bramhall believed, destroyed the very foundations of healthful commonwealth:

> His Principles are not only destructive to all Religion, but to all Societies; extinguishing the Relation between Prince and Subject, Parent and Child, Master and Servant, Husband and Wife: and abound with palpable contradictions.[1]

Thus Bramhall thought that the biblical quotation on the frontispiece was fitting: indeed, the world had never seen such a doctrine before. Thomas Hobbes's natural law theory was so novel (and for Bramhall, so pernicious) as to be without comparison.

For nearly four centuries since the publication of *Leviathan*, traditional natural law theorists—not to mention many other interpreters who are unsympathetic to the classical natural law tradition—have tended to agree with Bramhall that Hobbes jettisons the core theses of classical natural law. As I have presented it, classical natural law philosophy is distinctive in its approach to moral and political theory for a number of core theses. As a metaphilosophy, it is an approach that rests moral and political doctrines on the belief that there is a rationally knowable order in human nature that is one aspect of the larger order in nature as a whole, which provides the basis for intelligible statements about value and duty. The core theses of natural law theory are that practical reason grasps goods that provide intelligible, not merely instrumental reasons for action and that the practical necessities requisite to pursuit of these goods have a legal character. So stated, the structural foundations of Hobbes's moral and political thought are not as radically novel as Bramhall suggests.

Hobbes holds forth a natural law theory in which reason can grasp basic reason(s) for action and is perceptive. What is novel about Hobbes's natural law theory is its thin theory of the good. On this basis, Hobbes spins out a number of precepts and virtues that substantially overlap with the traditional morality defended in the tradition. His natural law doctrine is also buoyed by an Ockhamist-sounding voluntarism and nominalism. Still, Hobbes maintained, somewhat in the spirit of Aquinas, that there was a stability of the moral order that rested on God's ordained power. Moreover, Hobbes's resemblance nominalism wields Ockham's razor not to reconceive knowledge as a purely constructed world of mental fictions but in an attempt to reorient reason to the real, within the limits of what Hobbes was convicted that human reason could actually accomplish. On the basis of the thin theory of the good, Hobbes formulates a social ontology in which the common good of security marks off the commonwealth as the absolute representative and sets the end of the sovereign, which includes equitable law. The sovereign cannot make iniquitous laws or judgments without rupturing the bonds of commonwealth. While the thin theory of the good entails a rupture with Thomistic social pluralism and narrows the set of possible commands that would fail to bind in conscience, we can readily imagine that Aquinas would have deduced a similar set of doctrines if he had held a thin theory of the good.

How, then, should Hobbes be understood in the natural law tradition? In his magisterial account of the natural law tradition in political thought, Paul Sigmund concludes as follows:

> The continuities between the medieval theories and those of Hooker, Suarez, and Grotius are such that the real break in the history of natural law comes only with Hobbes. Although he used the traditional terminology, Hobbes redefined its content in such a way that his theory can only be associated with natural law if its egoistic and hedonistic elements are ignored or deemphasized.[2]

Sigmund adds that Hobbesian moral and political theory can be considered a "natural law" theory only because he derives moral principles from the truth about human nature—that the desire for self-preservation is a "psychological constant"—not because of the role of God in his thought. In a similar spirit, Johann Sommerville judges that Hobbes's theory can be classified as a "natural law theory" only if the scholar's "taste" would admit an egoistic and hedonsitic moral philosophy, effectively emptied of moral content, into the pantheon of natural law.[3] These judgments about Hobbes's place in the history of political thought effectively concur with John Finnis's judgment of the place of Hobbes in the history of moral and legal philosophy noted in the introduction.

If the argument of this book is correct, these interpretations, which are standard among most classical natural law theorists, stand in need of correction. Hobbesian reason is not a mere calculating slave of the passion for self-preservation, and this passion is not a psychological constant. Desire may or may not line up with the basic reason for action, bodily life and health. God's creation of nature, including human nature, sources the good of life and the dictates of right reason in a divine pedigree such that they have the force of law. It is proper to classify Hobbes's moral theory as a natural law theory on the basis of these two principles: (1) practical reason grasps basic reason(s) for action and (2) the practical necessities that correspond to the human good have a legal character—regardless of any particular scholar's "taste."

Hobbes retains the classical *sub ratione boni* thesis but has a transformative axiology. The thin theory of the good as bodily life and preservation colors his doctrine with a more individualistic flavor. But the virtues, held out as requirements for happiness, shape the desires to restrain the passions for immediate gain, for the sake of the common good of peace, which is one's good in the manner of participation. In this way another's good and obedience to law can be desirable for the virtuous person. So it is not right to say that he was an egoist if that is defined to mean that all human beings necessarily never act to benefit others or from a sense of justice.[4] Moreover, the "hedonistic element" of Hobbes's axiology—presumably referring to his identification of the good *propter se* with the pleasing—must be understood in conjunction with his understanding of how virtue habituates agents to feel as they ought. They ought not to take pleasure in acts and objects incompatible with subsisting as a desiring self. The difference from Aquinas's notion of *bonum honestum* is that the basic noninstrumental reason for acting is the good of life. Hobbes's empirical experience of vicious, fissiparous disagreement between human beings about what constitutes temporal beatitude led him to doubt that reason unaided could apprehend goods beyond preservation as objectively desirable. This is indeed a real break with the older tradition. Thus Hobbes reconstructs the common good as a thin conception of peace. Yet he retains the common good as the distinguishing principle of political social reality and the fixed end of the sovereign, which the sovereign is bound by the natural law to respect. The laws of nature, the ways of peace, circumscribe what can properly be called an act of sovereignty. Hobbes's break from the natural law tradition is not in inaugurating a doctrine of legal positivism. Even mortal gods are bound by eternal laws.

Such, at any rate, has been the argument of this book: that Hobbes's break from the tradition lies in his thin theory of the good and its concomitant wide conception of felicity pluralism. This doctrine, when taken in conjunction with Hobbes's doctrines of natural liberty and equality, the consent condition for legal obligation, the limited scope of government to the common good of security, the need to effectuate the laws of nature through legislation into civil law, and the natural law *obligation* binding the sovereign to secure the citizens' harmless liberty (including, possibly, hinting toward religious liberty of conscience), entails that Hobbes has a version of what Christopher Wolfe has called *natural law liberalism*. That is, Hobbes holds forth several of the core principles of liberalism—felicity pluralism, natural liberty and equality, consent, limited scope of government, rule of law, concern for civil liberty—while grounding them in natural law.[5]

I must immediately clarify what I am *not* saying by calling Hobbes a natural law liberal, a claim that can be elucidated by how it compares and contrasts with natural law liberalism in the American political tradition. As explained in chapter 5, this is not a claim that Hobbes was a constitutionalist, which liberalism has come to see as an essential means to securing liberty. Hobbes's rejection of constitutional means does not entail a rejection or lack of concern for liberal purposes (as essential aspects of the common good). Still, for Hobbes the duty to protect civil liberty is subordinate to the good of security because there are no civil liberties for dead citizens. Arguably, even constitutional republics ultimately betray their acceptance of this principle. One need only think of Lincoln's suspension of habeas corpus. Or consider *West Virginia v. Barnette*, the famous Supreme Court case that struck down the flag salute requirement for school children as a violation of their civil liberty. Justice Jackson's opinion in that case is usually remembered for its stirring civil libertarian language rejecting mere shadows of freedom. Yet, in a less quoted and remembered sentence, Jackson admitted that the state could curtail liberty "to prevent grave and immediate danger to interests which the State may lawfully protect."[6] From Hobbes's perspective, which is always cognizant of the urgency of security, the institutional fracture of sovereignty embodied in constitutionalism is an imprudent means of government because when the sovereign needs to act outside constitutional limits, citizens will see it as unjust and as grounds for rebellion and civil war. Moreover, while Hobbes believes that democracy is a legitimate kind of regime, he favors monarchy. But he believes that this is consistent with liberalism's concern for freedom since he denies that there is actually more liberty in democracy than in monarchy. My point here is not to defend these claims but simply to point out that Hobbes's favored regime structure is one aspect of his particular version of natural law liberalism. Having clarified this, I want to conclude by suggesting how Hobbes can be understood within the tradition of natural law liberalism.

Natural law liberalism has a familiar pedigree in the American political tradition. Jefferson and his co-signers of the Declaration of Independence appealed to the "Laws of Nature and Nature's God" and a number of inalienable rights as the moral foundation of just government. Both Federalists and Anti-Federalists appealed to natural law and natural rights in the constitutional debates. Natural law and natural rights provided a common framework for the debates over slavery in the antebellum period. So also with the early women's rights movement. At the 1848 Seneca Falls Convention, Elizabeth Cady Stanton and her collaborators appealed to natural law and natural rights as the basis of women's equality. The rhetoric of natural law and natural rights continued to frame debate in the postbellum Gilded Age and Progressive Era debates over property rights and the concentration of wealth, and into the familiar constitutional debates of the twentieth century.

The most famous twentieth-century expression of natural law liberalism began to be penned on a mild Saturday in April 1963 in Alabama. The object of the "Letter from a Birmingham Jail" was to defend civil disobedience of Alabama's segregationist laws to Southern white moderate pastors. Moreover, in it Martin Luther King Jr. sought to justify his actions to the public at large by appealing to principles he contended were available to unaided reason. King appealed to a criterion of right antecedent to positive law, what he called the "moral law or the law of God." King called upon the natural law tradition and specifically Thomas Aquinas to contend that segregation statutes failed to accord with the natural moral law and thus failed to bind as law: King wrote, "Any law that uplifts human personality is just. Any law that degrades human personality is unjust. All segregation statutes are unjust because segregation distorts the soul and damages the personality."[7] Echoing

Aquinas, King argued that an unjust law is "no law at all" because it fails to accord with the natural law.

King thus grounded a liberal doctrine of civil rights in higher law. If the argument of this book has been successful and Hobbesian mortal gods are bound by eternal laws, including the law of equity, there are good grounds to believe that Hobbes would agree with the civil rights movement's critique of *Plessy v. Ferguson* and its legacy of Jim Crow. Hobbesian equity requires that the sovereign judge arbitrate disputes without arbitrarily discriminating to treat similarly situated people equally. *Plessy* was a ruling that permitted states to require disparate treatment of persons on the basis of skin color alone, and therefore it failed to accord with the law of equity. But would Hobbes have countenanced civil disobedience? Isn't his theory of sovereignty supposed to rule out such a possibility? When Hobbes discusses how the title of his work was taken out of the Book of Job, he explains that, like the biblical beast, the commonwealth is "mortal and subject to decay, as all other earthly creatures are," and that there is one in heaven "that he should stand in fear of, and whose laws he ought to obey."[8] The reason that the sovereign ought to fear breaking the natural moral law of God is not only that he must render an account of it to God, the exclusive judge, on the final day of judgment, but also that he thereby sows the seeds of his own destruction.[9] If the argument of the previous chapter was sound, the sovereign itself can generate a state of affairs in which people are not assured of getting a fair shake before the sovereign's court when it judges iniquitously. In such a condition, people are inclined to reclaim the right of private judgment, one of the fatal diseases of commonwealth. Such a state of affairs is just the condition in which civil law fails to obtain, a state of nature. In that condition, there are strong Hobbesian grounds to resist the entity claiming to be one's sovereign, because one acts with right.

To justify resistance to inequity, King appealed to a "higher law," which he took to be grounded in truths about human nature, the world in which we find ourselves, and God's causal relation to the world, in the tradition of realistic political philosophy. My argument has been that Hobbes has a place in that tradition, albeit a peculiar one. While Rawls suspected that Hobbes was the first political liberal, the verdict of my argument has been that Hobbesian natural law liberalism stands in stark contrast to John Rawls's political liberalism. For Rawls, liberalism should be theorized as political, not metaphysical—and this is thought to be necessary for justice as fairness to obtain a critical mass of adherents in a condition of social pluralism. Coupled with Rawls's theory is an austere doctrine of public reason that restricts appeals that can be legitimately made to comprehensive doctrines when arguing in the public square about matters of justice and the common good. It is well known that Rawls has endured the criticism that his doctrine seems to rule out the kind of argument that Martin Luther King engaged in, and indeed the kind of public argument countenanced by the natural law tradition, of which Hobbes is a part.

Hobbes would thus reject the Rawlsian approach to civil philosophy, not least because it borrows on the cheap. In the spirit of eighteenth-century reactionary conservatism, it acquires liberal doctrines by appealing to a culture and history in which liberalism won out, through the very kinds of foundationalist arguments that early modern liberals made. Rawls would likely reply that this is a good thing, since the operation of free institutions has led to democratic peoples' obtaining an overlapping consensus. Hobbes would view this reply as naïve at best. As his historical writings indicate, he believes that there is no guarantee that sociological conditions will be favorable to ordered liberty. There is no necessary progress of history or any historical finality that can be attached to any particular sociological condition. The politically salient things that remain permanent include the condition of human nature, the dictates of reason, and God's causal relation to the world. As long as human nature is what it is, violence in the name of God and religion will remain a perennial problem that, in Hobbes's view, demands a natural law philosophy with the capacity to engage in substantive argument with rival worldviews. It is not enough to say that, with respect to "mad comprehensive doctrines," the problem is "to contain them so that they do not undermine the unity and justice of society."[10] For how are they to be contained? Will it not require engagement at the level of fundamental worldviews, the deepest wellsprings of action?

Rawlsian public reason rules out this public function of political philosophy. The problem of mad comprehensive doctrines, particularly those that hold that violence is justified when done in the name of God, is a more than marginal existential threat to liberalism. Hobbesian political philosophy is doubtful that the resources of Rawlsian public reason are robust enough to meet the challenge. An essential function of Hobbesian political philosophy is a willingness to engage in substantive theoretical, metaphysical, and theological argument. Somewhat in the spirit of the role of the *Summa Ratio* in Augustinian and Thomistic philosophy, Hobbes's doctrine of God's rational word plays an essential role in the Hobbesian conception of public reason, which has the capacity to engage with worldviews that claim God sanctions violence in his name. God does not command what is contrary to reason, and one of the fundamental dictates of reason is to will peace.

Hobbes would thus doubt that liberalism is improved by political liberalism's explicit refusal to claim that it is *true*.[11] Hobbes's whole conception of political philosophy is animated by the optimism that, by right reason, any person can affirm the truth of the natural law, the "true and only moral philosophy." The truth of Hobbes's natural law theory rests not on proto-Humean doctrines of the fact-value dichotomy, the autonomy of civil science, reason's enslavement to the passions, or skepticism about natural theology; nor does it rest on the rejection of the common good, the fictionalization of society, or the subversion of natural law principles into the positive command of the sovereign. Rather, the truth of Hobbesian natural law stands or falls upon whether Hobbes is warranted in modifying the broadly scholastic notion of natural law to embrace a thin theory of the good. Natural law theory holds that reason can grasp basic reasons for action and that the dictates of reason are divinely pedigreed by God's ordained power. Hobbesian natural law lops off such goods as family life and childrearing, knowledge, friendship, aesthetic experience, and so on, *qua* objective, which correspond to the higher inclinations in Aquinas's metaphysical stratification of human nature. *So understood*, it is unique *super terram*.

Thus is this book brought to an end, and it is not unfitting to appropriate Hobbes's own final words in his greatest work of political philosophy. This book has endeavored "without partiality, without application, and without other design" to "set before men's eyes" the truth about Hobbes's moral and political theory, which rests on the "condition of human nature and the laws divine (both natural and positive)," which "require an inviolable observation."[12]

NOTES

Introduction

1. Edwin Curley, "Reflections on Hobbes: Recent Work on His Moral and Political Philosophy," *Journal of Philosophical Research* 15 (1989–90): 169–226.

2. Gregory Kavka, *Hobbesian Moral and Political Theory* (Princeton, NJ: Princeton University Press, 1986), 3.

3. John Rawls, *Justice as Fairness: A Restatement* (Cambridge, MA: Belknap Press, 2001), 1.

4. Thomas Hobbes, *Leviathan with Selected Variants from the Latin Edition of 1688*, ed. Edwin Curley (Indianapolis: Hackett, 1994), 15.40, 100. Citations to *Leviathan* (hereinafter *L*) are to chapter, paragraph, and page number in this edition unless otherwise noted. It should be noted that Curley's edition modernizes Hobbes's spelling, capitalization, and punctuation. Interested readers can consult the page numbers in the Head edition of 1651, as referenced by Curley in brackets on the left-hand pages of his edition. I prefer this edition for its general accessibility in one volume, but interested scholars should consult the Clarendon edition of *Leviathan* edited by Noel Malcolm for a definitive critical edition of the English and Latin texts side by side. In this volume, all italics in quotations from Hobbes's works are his own unless otherwise noted.

5. See generally Samuel Mintz, *The Hunting of Leviathan* (Cambridge: Cambridge University Press, 1962).

6. At the outset it should be noted that my use of the terminology of "thick" and "thin" does not necessarily align with the way these terms are used by political scientists in different contexts of study. Cf. Benjamin Gregg, "Comparative Perspectives on Social Integration in Pluralistic Societies: Thick Norms versus Thin," *Comparative Sociology* 11 (2012): 629–48, and the rest of that special-topics issue; Michael Walzer, *Thick and Thin: Moral Argument at Home and Abroad* (Notre Dame, IN: University of Notre Dame Press, 1994). I thank Pete Mohanty for drawing my attention to this point.

7. John Finnis, "Natural Law: The Classical Tradition," *The Oxford Handbook of Jurisprudence and Philosophy of Law*, ed. Jules Coleman and Scott J. Shapiro (Oxford: Oxford University Press, 2002), 1–2.

8. Finnis, *Aquinas* (Oxford: Oxford University Press, 1998), 81.

9. Finnis, "Natural Law Theory and Limited Government?," in *Natural Law, Liberalism, and Morality* (Oxford: Clarendon Press, 1996), ed. Robert P. George, 4. Notably, Finnis has sought to present the goods and moral norms of classical natural law theory while accepting the fact/value dichotomy—that is, Finnis is concerned not to infer an "ought" from "is." He has been criticized by more traditional natural law theorists for this move. See Russell Hittinger, *A Critique of New Natural Law Theory* (Notre Dame, IN: University of Notre Dame Press, 1987); Henry Veatch, "Natural Law and the 'Is'–'Ought' Question," *Catholic Lawyer* 26 (1981): 251–65; Ralph McInerny, *Ethica Thomistica: The Moral Philosophy of Thomas Aquinas* (Washington, DC: Catholic University Press, 1982); Anthony Lisska, *Aquinas's Theory of Natural Law: An Analytic Reconstruction* (Oxford: Oxford University Press, 1998); J. Budziszewski, *Written on the Heart: The Case for Natural Law* (Downers Grove, IL: IVP Academic, 1997). Cf. Mark Murphy, *Natural Law and Practical Rationality* (Cambridge: Cambridge University Press, 2001).

10. Christopher Wolfe, *Natural Law Liberalism* (Cambridge: Cambridge University Press, 2006), 174.

11. A good can be "basic" in a genus of objects and activities, and one can intelligibly cite that good as one's reason for action when asked "Why did you do that?" It can be *an* endpoint without being an endpoint *full stop*, for the good can be considered in relation to higher and lower goods and to goodness itself. For example, when asked why I just played a game of baseball with my son, I could intelligibly answer, "Because play is good," without needing to add more to answer the question. The good of play is basic in that sense. But this need not imply that the good of play is equally important to, say, that of contemplation, study, and knowledge—or that a life plan subordinating the good of knowledge to the good of play is a rational one.

12. For criticisms of the new natural law theory's axiology and action theory, see Daniel McInerny, "Hierarchy and Direction for Choice," available online at the Maritain Center, maritain.nd.edu; Matthew O'Brien and Robert Koons, "Objects of Intention: A Hylomorphic Critique of the New Natural Law Theory," *American Catholic Philosophical Quarterly* 86, no. 4 (Fall 2012): 655–703; for a reply to the latter, see Christopher Tollefsen, "Response to Robert Koons and Matthew O'Brien's 'Objects of Intention: A Hylomorphic Critique of the New Natural Law Theory,'" *American Catholic Philosophical Quarterly* 87, no. 4 (Fall 2013): 751–78. For a range of traditionalist criticisms,

see the following issue, which is dedicated to this matter: *National Catholic Bioethics Quarterly* 13, no. 1 (Spring 2013). Such criticisms have led some scholars to seek other ways of recovering and reviving classical natural law theory. For an argument that a classical conception of natural law theory can be recovered and reconciled with natural rights, see S. Adam Seagrave, *The Foundations of Natural Morality: On the Compatibility of Natural Law and Natural Rights* (Chicago: University of Chicago Press, 2014).

13. Finnis, *Aquinas*, 128, 308. Here Finnis seems to walk back his earlier claim that natural law is only "analogically law"—a claim that clearly breaks with Aquinas's doctrine (*Natural Law and Natural Rights*, 280).

14. It is said that natural law "maximally has the character of law" (*lex naturalis maxime habet rationem legis*). This is the premise of an objection that Aquinas does not deny (*Summa Theologiae* I-II, 90, 4, obj. 1). Citations to Aquinas's *Summa Theologiae* (hereinafter *ST*) are to part, question, article. English translations are generally from the Dominican Fathers edition (Allen, TX: Christian Classics, 1981). The focal case of law for Aquinas is, of course, the eternal law. Yet, since natural law is not diverse from the eternal law but is rather a mode of the eternal law's promulgation, Aquinas could affirm the premise, properly understood. For discussions of the legal character of natural law in Aquinas's thought, see Russell Hittinger, *The First Grace* (Wilmington, DE: ISI Books, 2007); Stephen Brock, "The Legal Character of Natural Law According to Thomas Aquinas," Ph.D. dissertation, University of Toronto, 1988.

15. *ST* I-II, 95.3.

16. Here I follow the orthodox reading of Hume. However, it is notable that Thomas Merrill has developed a heterodox interpretation of Humean practical reasoning and the famous slave of the passions passage contra interpretations of Hume as an emotivist. See Thomas Merrill, "Hume contra Humean Practical Reason: Philosophy as Our Choice and Guide," PDF in author's possession; forthcoming in *The Modern Turn*, ed. Michael Rohlf (Washington, DC: Catholic University of America Press).

17. As Finnis puts it, Hobbes treats "our practical reasoning as all in the service of sub-rational passions such as fear of death, and desire to surpass others—motivations of the very kind identified by the classical tradition as in need of direction by our reason's grasp of more ultimate and better ends, of true and intrinsic goods, of really intelligent reasons for action. Hobbes proclaims his contempt for the classical search for ultimate ends or intrinsic reasons for action. Accordingly there can be for him no question of finding the source of obligation and law in the kind of necessity which we identify when we notice that some specific means is *required* by and for the sake of some end which it would be unreasonable not to judge desirable

and pursuit-worthy" (Finnis, "Natural Law," 5). See also Robert P. George, *Making Men Moral: Civil Liberties and Public Morality* (Oxford: Clarendon Press, 1993), 12, n. 12.

18. See Samuel Mintz, *The Hunting of Leviathan* (Cambridge: Cambridge University Press, 1962), 45; Quentin Skinner, "Hobbes's 'Leviathan,'" *Historical Journal* 7, no. 2 (1964): 332. For a recent summary of the reactions of Hobbes's contemporaries to Hobbes's theological views, as well as Hobbes's replies in the Latin *Leviathan*, see Noel Malcolm's discussion in Thomas Hobbes, *Leviathan Volume 1: Editorial Introduction*, ed. Noel Malcolm (Oxford: Clarendon Press, 2012), 148–58.

19. See Leo Strauss, *The Political Philosophy of Hobbes*, trans. Elsa M. Sinclair (Chicago: University of Chicago Press, 1952); Edwin Curley "'I Durst Not Write So Boldly,' or How to Read Hobbes' Theological-Political Treatise," in *Hobbes e Spinoza: Scienza e Politica*, ed. Daniela Bostrenghi (Naples: Bibliopolis, 1992).

20. See Gregory S. Kavka, *Hobbesian Moral and Political Theory* (Princeton, NJ: Princeton University Press, 1986), 362.

21. *L*, 15.18, 99; 26.40, 186. On the psychological diversity of Hobbesian persons, see S. A. Lloyd, *Morality in the Philosophy of Thomas Hobbes: Cases in the Law of Nature* (Cambridge: Cambridge University Press, 2009), 56–94.

22. Lloyd, *Morality in the Philosophy of Thomas Hobbes*, 200.

23. Hobbes, *De Cive: The Latin Version*, ed. Howard Warrender (Oxford: Oxford University Press, 1983), dedicatory epistle, 75. Tuck and Silverthorne translate the passage as follows: "Thus I obtained two certain postulates of human nature, one, the postulate of human greed, by which each man insists upon his own private use of common property; the other, the postulate of natural reason, by which each man strives to avoid violent death as the supreme evil in nature" (*On the Citizen*, ed. and trans. Richard Tuck and Michael Silverthorne [Cambridge: Cambridge University Press, 1998], 6). The translation of William Molesworth runs thus: "Having therefore thus arrived at two maximes of humane Nature, the one arising from the concupiscible part, which desires to appropriate to it selfe the use of those things in which all others have a joynt interest, the other proceeding from the rationall, which teaches every man to fly a contre-naturall Dissolution, as the greatest mischiefe that can arrive to Nature" (Molesworth, "Philosophical Rudiments Concerning Government and Society," epistle dedicatory in *The English Works of Thomas Hobbes of Malmesbury* [hereinafter *EW*], 11 vols., ed. William Molesworth (individual volumes published 1839–45 in London, some by John Bohn, some by Longman, Brown, Green, and Longmans), vol. II, viii.

24. I take up this interpretation in detail in chapter 1.

25. Bernard Gert has developed a powerful argument along these lines for a *complex* view of Hobbesian reason that is more than a merely reckoning or computing power. The power of Hobbesian practical reason includes the power to set its own goals. See Bernard Gert, "Hobbes on Reason," *Pacific Philosophical Quarterly* 82 (2001): 243–57; Bernard Gert, *Hobbes: Prince of Peace* (Cambridge: Polity Press, 2010) 73. For an argument that reason is a *counselor* to the passions, see Adrian Blau, "Reason, Deliberation, and the Passions," in *The Oxford Handbook of Hobbes*, ed. A. P. Martinich and Kinch Hoekstra (Oxford: Oxford University Press, 2013).

26. Hobbes, *De Homine* (hereinafter *DH*), 11.6, in *Opera philosophica quae latine scripsit omnia: In unum corpus nunc primum collecta studio et labore* (hereinafter *OL*), ed. Molesworth (London: John Bohn, 1839–1845), vol. II, 98.

27. On this point I agree with Mark Murphy. See Murphy, "Was Hobbes a Legal Positivist?," *Ethics* 105 (4): 846–73. However, I differ from Murphy in that I defend Hobbes's theory of the good as "reason-dependent" (to use Joseph Raz's phrase), and I hold that Hobbes understands the laws of nature to be truly laws, a point that Murphy says Hobbes does not explain.

28. Adrian Blau, "Reason, Deliberation, and the Passions."

29. It is an open question precisely how and to what extent Hobbes's more voluntarist notion of God's command breaks from Aquinas's more intellectualist notion.

30. G. E. M. Anscombe, "Modern Moral Philosophy," *Philosophy* 33, no. 124 (January 1958): 5.

31. A. E. Taylor, "The Ethical Doctrine of Hobbes," *Philosophy* 13, no. 52 (October 1938): 406–24; Howard Warrender, *The Political Philosophy of Hobbes* (Oxford: Clarendon Press, 1957); F. C. Hood, *The Divine Politics of Thomas Hobbes* (Oxford: Clarendon Press, 1964).

32. Brian Barry, "Warrender and His Critics," *Philosophy* 43, no. 164 (April 1968), 117–37.

33. Edwin Curley, "Reflections on Hobbes: Recent Work on His Moral and Political Philosophy," *Journal of Philosophical Research* 15 (1989–90): 190.

34. Of course Hobbes sets forth a number of nonstandard interpretations of the creeds. See generally A. P. Martinich, *The Two Gods of Leviathan: Thomas Hobbes on Religion and Politics* (Cambridge: Cambridge University Press, 1992).

35. Curley himself later admitted that Martinich's work was "arguably the best available book of its kind." See A. P. Martinich, "Calvin and Hobbes, or, Hobbes as an Orthodox Christian," *Journal of the History of Philosophy* 34, no. 2 (April 1996): 257.

36. A. P. Martinich, *The Two Gods of Leviathan*, 18–30; *A Hobbes Dictionary* (Hoboken, NJ: Wiley, 1995), 36.

37. Gottfried Leibniz to Hobbes from Mainz (July 1670), Letter 189 in *The Correspondence of Thomas Hobbes*, vol. II, ed. Noel Malcolm (Cambridge: Cambridge University Press, 1994), 717.

38. A. P. Martinich, "On the Proper Interpretation of Hobbes's Philosophy," *Journal of the History of Philosophy* 34, no. 2 (April 1996): 273–83. For Martinich's argument that his interpretation is true to various canons of interpretation, including conservatism, frugality, palpability, generality, consistency, completeness, connectedness, and defensibility, see Martinich, "Interpretation and Hobbes's Political Philosophy," *Pacific Philosophical Quarterly* 82 (2001): 309–31.

39. Martinich, "Interpreting the Religion of Thomas Hobbes: An Exchange," *Journal of the History of Ideas* 70, no. 1 (January 2009): 143–63.

40. Cf. Martinich, *The Two Gods of Leviathan*, 31.

41. *EW* IV, 365.

42. Martinich, "Thomas Hobbes's Interregnum Place of Worship," *Notes and Queries* 54, no. 4 (December 2007), 433–36.

43. Jeffrey Collins's rival interpretation of this evidence misses this point (Collins, "Interpreting Hobbes in Competing Contexts," *Journal of the History of Ideas* 70, no. 1 [January 2009]: 170).

44. Martinich, *The Two Gods of Leviathan*, 16. Such an assumption, as even Martinich admits, need not deny that Hobbes sometimes writes ironically.

45. While I agree with Martinich that God plays an essential role in Hobbes's natural law theory, my interpretation differs in a number of ways, as we shall see.

46. *L*, 46.14, 458.

47. *EW* I, x.

48. Ibid.

49. Ibid.

50. *ST* I 1.8, ad. 2.

51. *EW* I, x.

52. Ibid.

53. *L*, 46.18, 460.

54. Ibid.

55. *EW* IV, 271.

56. *EW* V, 63–64; see Luther's *Rationis Latominianae confutatio* of 1521 in *D. Martin Luthers Werke*, vol. VIII (Weimar: Herman Buhlau, 1889), 127. English translation from the American edition, ed. Jaroslav Pelikan (St. Louis: Concordia, 1955–86), vol. XXXII.

57. *L*, 4.13, 19.

58. We know that Hobbes had read late scholastics like Suarez and Bellarmine, and he suggests that he had read Duns Scotus. He would have known Aquinas's writing through these authors, who cite him as a doctor and often quote him directly. Furthermore, there is evidence that his knowledge of Aquinas was not entirely derivative. We are in the realm of conjecture, since, as James Jay Hamilton recounts, "There is direct evidence of only a few of the books Hobbes read." But Hamilton's research has revealed that Hobbes had access to both Aquinas's *Summa Theologiae* and his *Summa Contra Gentiles* at the library of the Cavendishes at Hardwick Hall. Indeed, the manuscript that lists Aquinas's work among the books available from 1630 until 1660 is a catalogue written in Hobbes's own hand. As Hamilton explains, "Hobbes catalogued the Hardwick Library using a distinctive system of shelf marks of his own devising. He seems to have served the Cavendishes as librarian, among other things." See James Jay Hamilton, "Hobbes's Study and the Hardwick Library," *Journal of the History of Philosophy* 16, no. 4 (1978): 445, 449, 446.

59. See Aurel Kolnai, "The Sovereignty of the Object: Notes on Truth and Intellectual Humility," in *Ethics, Value, and Reality: Selected Papers of Aurel Kolnai* (London: University of London Athlone Press, 1977), 23–43.

60. Josef Pieper, *In Defense of Philosophy* (San Francisco: Ignatius Press, 1992), 11–12.

61. J. G. A. Pocock, "Machiavelli, Harrington, and English Political Ideologies in the Eighteenth Century," *William and Mary Quarterly* 22, no. 4 (October 1965): 549–83.

62. See Leo Strauss, "What Is Political Philosophy?," in *An Introduction to Political Philosophy: Ten Essays by Leo Strauss* (Detroit: Wayne State University Press, 1989), ed. Hilail Gildin (Detroit: Wayne State University Press, 1989).

63. See also Garrett Ward Sheldon's definition of political theory in the *Encyclopedia of Political Thought* (New York: Facts on File, 2001), 235.

64. Strauss's *Natural Right and History* (Chicago: University of Chicago Press, 1953) is exemplary of this approach. As will become apparent, while I mostly share Strauss's understanding of political philosophy and his comparative-conversational approach to reading Western political philosophy, I don't accept his exclusionary definition of political theology (or his understanding of the relationships of philosophy to theology), nor do I share his intention to uncover the esoteric meaning of texts. For other examples of the conversational approach with narrow and broad subject matters, respectively, see, e.g., Garrett Ward Sheldon, *The Political Philosophy of Thomas Jefferson* (Baltimore: Johns Hopkins University Press, 1991), which also notes Pocock's

distinction, and Jeffrey Abramson, *Minerva's Owl: The Tradition of Western Political Thought* (Cambridge, MA: Harvard University Press, 2009).

Chapter 1. The Foundations of Hobbes's Natural Law Philosophy

1. *EW* II, iii.

2. See, e.g., Leslie Stephen, *Hobbes* (London: Macmillan, 1904); J. W. N. Watkins, *Hobbes's System of Ideas* (London: Hutchinson, 1965); M. M. Goldsmith, *Hobbes's Science of Politics* (New York: Columbia University Press, 1966).

3. John Wild, *Introduction to Realistic Philosophy* (New York: Harper and Row, 1948), 6.

4. Paul Sigmund, *Natural Law in Political Thought* (Lanham, MD: Winthrop, 1971), viii.

5. Robert P. George, *In Defence of Natural Law* (Oxford: Clarendon Press, 1999), 85.

6. Ibid. Still, it must be noted that George maintains that this concession is consistent with denying that one can infer moral truths from metaphysical anthropology. This claim seems more questionable from the perspective of the older tradition or realistic philosophy. Notably, George himself deploys the concepts of act, potency, and teleology in the course of making a number of moral arguments; each of those notions can be seen as aspects of metaphysical anthropology. See George and Patrick Lee, *Body-Self Dualism in Contemporary Ethics and Politics* (Cambridge: Cambridge University Press, 2008), 176–217.

7. See *L*, 5.3.2 and 5.4.

8. Yves Simon, *The Tradition of Natural Law: A Philosopher's Reflections* (New York: Fordham University Press, 1992), 129.

9. *De Corpore*, 6.10, in *EW* I, 77.

10. Ibid., 8.1, *in EW* I, 102.

11. For a discussion of Hobbes's theory of space and its anti-Aristotelian character, see Cees Leijenhorst, *The Mechanisation of Aristotelianism* (Leiden: Brill, 2001), 102–9.

12. *De Corpore*, 8.10, in *EW* I, 109. Hobbes uses the term "privation" interchangeably with "relinquishing." See *De Corpore*, 15.1, in *EW* I, 203.

13. Hobbes had sought out Galileo's writings as they arrived in England and encouraged their translation into English. On his third tour of the continent, in 1636, he would meet Galileo, who was under house arrest for publishing the very work Hobbes had recently sought out in England, namely the *Dialogue Concerning Two Chief World Systems*. See Letter 10 in *The Correspondence of Thomas Hobbes*, vol. I, ed. Noel Malcolm (Oxford: Oxford University Press),

19–20. For a discussion of this trip, see Martinich, *Hobbes: A Biography* (Cambridge: Cambridge University Press, 1999), 89–92.

14. *De Corpore*, 15.1, in *EW* I, 205.

15. *L*, 1.4, 6.

16. *De Corpore*, 15.2, in *EW* I, 206.

17. Cf. *EW* I, 448.

18. *L*, 1.4, 6.

19. *EW* IV, 3.

20. *EW* VII, 133; Letters 19 and 21 in *The Correspondence of Thomas Hobbes*, 34, 38. Hobbes's explanation is that the resin retains the same kind of motion as the tree it was derived from, but diminished, thus causing the appearance of a little tree by a little motion.

21. *EW* IV, 5.

22. *L*, 4.13, 19; 5.16, 25.

23. For defenses of a correspondence view, see F. S. McNeilly, *The Anatomy of Leviathan* (London: Macmillan, 1968), 47–51, and Jean Hampton, *Hobbes and the Social Contract Tradition* (Cambridge: Cambridge University Press, 1986), 42–51. For a defense of the conventionalist view, see Stephen J. Finn, *Thomas Hobbes and the Politics of Natural Philosophy* (New York: Continuum, 2004), 134–44.

24. Cf. *L*, 4.22, 21.

25. Contrary to the suggestion of McNeilly in *The Anatomy of Leviathan*, 50–51.

26. *L*, 2.2–3, 8.

27. In one of his letters Hobbes expresses his opinion that we remember the faces of people better the more time we have spent looking at their faces. See Letter 12 in *The Correspondence of Thomas Hobbes*, vol. I.

28. *EW* I, 16.

29. Ibid.

30. *De Homine* (hereinafter *DH*), 10.2, 39. References to *DH* in English are to chapter, paragraph, and page number of Bernard Gert's translation in *Man and Citizen* (Indianapolis: Hackett, 1991).

31. *DH*, 10.2, 39, emphasis added.

32. *EW* IV, 394.

33. Philip Pettit, *Made with Words* (Princeton, NJ: Princeton University Press, 2008), 31.

34. *L*, 4.6, 17.

35. Although we should note well that Hobbes says *nothing in the world* is universal. He does not say anything about what status, if any, universals have in the mind of God.

36. Michael J. Loux, *Metaphysics: A Contemporary Introduction* (Abingdon, UK: Routledge, 1998), 20.

37. My discussion is indebted to Robert Koons and Timothy H. Pickavance, *The Atlas of Reality: A Comprehensive Guide to Metaphysics* (West Sussex, UK: Wiley Blackwell, 2016).

38. For Hobbes's own consideration of the quality of hardness, see *De Corpore*, 8.2, in *EW* I, 103.

39. *L*, 4.7, 17.

40. *EW* I, 19–20. Still, extensionality problems remain for the resemblance nominalist, such as the difficulty of co-extensive properties. A standard example is the property of having a heart, which is co-extensive with the property of having a kidney (see, e.g., Helen Beebee, Nick Effingham, and Philip Goff, *Metaphysics: The Key Concepts* [Abingdon, UK: Routledge, 2011], 223). The resemblance nominalist says that things with hearts resemble other things with hearts, and then they explain the property of having a heart in terms of that resemblance. But all such things also resemble each other in terms of having a kidney. How can the resemblance nominalist distinguish between the properties of having a heart and having a kidney? We cannot reply that we can distinguish between resemblances with respect to having a heart and having a kidney because these properties are the very things that need to be explained.

41. See generally Robert C. Koons and Timothy Pickavance, *The Atlas of Reality: A Comprehensive Guide to Metaphysics* (Hoboken, NJ: Wiley, 2017), 125–69.

42. *De Corpore*, 6.2, in *EW* I, 67.

43. *EW* IV, 2.

44. Cf. *L*, 4.8 17. I leave open the possibility that by "similitude," Hobbes means "exactly similar," given Hobbes's general presentation of the language of passages that indicate the universality of correct reasoning.

45. Yves Simon, *The Tradition of Natural Law: A Philosopher's Reflections*, ed. Vukan Kuic (New York: Fordham University Press, 1999), 8. See also Peter J. Stanlis, *Edmund Burke and the Natural Law* (Piscataway, NJ: Transaction, 2003), 17.

46. *De Corpore*, 1.7, in *EW* I, 8.

47. Simon, *The Tradition of Natural Law*, 7.

48. William of Ockham, *Ordinatio*, dist. 2, q. IV, in *Opera Philosophica et Theologica*, ed. Stephanus Brown and Gedeon Gál (New York: Saint Bonaventure, 1970), vol. II, 116.

49. *EW* VII, 3.

50. *EW* IV, 310. See also *EW* I, 446.

51. *L*, 17.13, 109.

52. *EW* I, 10.

53. For Hobbes this is not to deny that God is material but only that God's materiality is not the sort that is finite, generable, or comprehensible. Hobbes says that God is "a most pure, and most simple corporeal spirit," and by "spirit" Hobbes means a "thin, fluid, transparent, invisible body" (*EW* IV, 306, 309).

54. See Hobbes, *Thomas White's De Mundo Examined*, trans. Harold Whitmore Jones (London: Bradford University Press, 1976), 26.1–7, 304–8, where Hobbes argues that demonstrations of God's existence are unphilosophical and contrary to the Christian religion. But, as A. P. Martinich points out, Hobbes's point is against *a priori* demonstrations, whereas proofs of the existence of things require empirical premises (Martinich, *The Two Gods of Leviathan*, 348). Moreover, Hobbes seems to be primarily concerned with demonstrations of the existence of the Christian God and how these would undermine the gratuity of faith (26.5).

55. *EW* I, 412. Notably, Hobbes says, we cannot prove by natural reason that the first mover is itself immoveable. This is a puzzle, because if God is in motion, then either God was moved by another or God is excepted from the principle that nothing is moved by itself. Hobbes says that to conjecture about God's movability is to pry into God's nature in a way that is unknowable to us and known only to God. Therefore, this question must be resolved by God's lieutenants.

56. *L*, 34.4, 263.

57. Hobbes and Aquinas agree that man cannot know God's essence. However, Aquinas thinks reason can go much further than Hobbes thinks in apophatic and analogical reasoning to affirm what God *is not*.

58. *L*, 3.12, 15.

59. *L*, 12. Cf. John Calvin, *Institutes of Christian Religion*, trans. Henry Beveridge (Edinburgh: Calvin Translation Society, 1846), book I, chap. 4.

60. *EW* V, 436.

61. Robert Arp, "The *Quinque Viae* of Thomas Hobbes," *History of Philosophy Quarterly* 16, no. 4 (1999): 367–94.

62. Thomas Hobbes, "Objection V, On the Third Meditation: Of God," in René Descartes, *Meditations on First Philosophy with Selections from the Objections and Replies*, trans. Michael Moriarty (Oxford: Oxford University Press, 2008), 112.

63. *L*, 12.6, 64.

64. *Thomas White's Du Mundo Examined*, trans. Harold Whitmore Jones (Bradford, West Yorkshire: Bradford University Press, 1976), 318.

65. *EW* IV, 308.

66. *De Corpore*, 6.19, in *EW* I, 115.

67. *EW* IV, 309–10.

68. Edwin Curley, "Calvin and Hobbes, or Hobbes as an Orthodox Christian," *Journal of the History of Philosophy* 34 (1996): 257–71. Martinich replies to this in the same issue in "On the Proper Interpretation of Hobbes's Philosophy," 273–83. Curley is given the final word, also in this issue, in "Reply to Professor Martinich," 285–87.

69. George Wright, "Curley and Martinich in Dubious Battle," *Journal of the History of Philosophy* 40 (2002): 461–76.

70. Patricia Springborg, "Calvin and Hobbes: A Reply to Curley, Martinich, and Wright," *Philosophical Readings* 4.1 (2012): 3–17.

71. Springborg, "Calvin and Hobbes," 6.

72. *EW* IV, 348.

73. *EW* IV, 300–302; Springborg, "Calvin and Hobbes," 9–10.

74. *EW* IV, 302.

75. Ibid.

76. For Springborg's argument that Hobbesian Trinitarian doctrine is subversive and the ensuing debate with Martinich, see Springborg, "Calvin and Hobbes," 12–17; A. P. Martinich, "On Thomas Hobbes's English Calvinism: Necessity, Omnipotence, and Goodness," *Philosophical Readings* 4.1, 18–28; Springborg, "Reply to Martinich on Hobbes's English Calvinism," *Philosophical Readings* 4.1, 84–94; Martinich, "Epicureanism and Calvinism in Hobbes's Philosophy: Consequences of Interpretation," *Philosophical Readings* 4.3 (2012): 3–15.

77. *EW* IV, 349.

78. Ibid.

79. *EW* IV, 308

80. *EW* IV, 310.

81. Cees Leijenhorst, "Hobbes's Corporeal Deity," in *New Critical Perspectives on Hobbes's Leviathan upon the 350th Anniversary of Its Publication*, ed. Luc Foisneau and George Wright (Milan, Franco Agnelli, 2005), 73–95. I note that, while Leijenhorst has helpful things to say about the relationship between reason and faith in Hobbes, my account differs from his, as is apparent in the text. See also his discussion of the relationship between Hobbes's views in the *De Motu* and *Elements of Law* in his later works.

82. Spinoza presented *Deus seu Natura* (God or Nature) as the infinite, indivisible, and eternal substance of the universe (Spinoza, *Ethics* [1677], part IV, preface).

83. Edwin Curley argues that the interpretation of God as a part of the universe still entails atheism, since Hobbes denied in *Anti-White* that a part of

a whole could be infinite (Curley, "'I Durst Not Write So Boldly,' or How to Read Hobbes' Theological-Political Treatise," in *Hobbes e Spinoza*, ed. Emilia Giancotti [Naples: Bibliopolis]). Curley doubts whether this is actually true, since the set of even numbers is an infinite part of the set of integers. Says Curley, "But was this clear to Hobbes? . . . Even if we give up the assumption that every part of every whole is finite, isn't there something uncomfortable about representing God as one material object among others?" Leijenhorst replies to Curley by pointing out that Hobbes affirms a principle of mereology, that part-whole terminology cannot be meaningfully applied to infinite entities (Leijenhorst, "Hobbes's Corporeal Deity," 87, quoting *De Corpore*, 7.12). But I don't think Leijenhorst's reply works because it doesn't make sense of Hobbes's part-whole application to God in his answer to Bishop Bramhall in *EW* IV. To Curley I would say that he does not consider the sense of part-whole that I outline in the text. Moreover, I would reply that, if my interpretation actually entails a change on Hobbes's part from his very early *Anti-White* position, that presents no special problem on Curley's own terms, since Curley holds that Hobbes alters his views on matters over time. If Hobbes sincerely wanted to wed materialism and theism throughout his career, it is certainly possible that he evolved his thinking as he saw fit to achieve that goal. In other words, the *tenacity* (the degree to which a person is unwilling to give up a belief) of Hobbes's beliefs in materialism and theism was stronger than the tenacity of his belief in the mereological principle stated in *Anti-White*. For a discussion of tenacity as a property of beliefs, see A. P. Martinich, "Interpretation and Hobbes's Political Philosophy," *Pacific Philosophical Quarterly* 82 (2001): 309–31.

84. *EW* I, 412.
85. *EW* II, 214.
86. *ST* I, 3.8.
87. Cf. Mark Murphy, "Deviant Uses of 'Obligation' in Hobbes's '*Leviathan*,'" *History of Philosophy Quarterly* 11, no. 3 (1994): 281–94.
88. *EW* IV, 276.
89. Cf. *EW* V, 366.
90. *EW* II, 215–16.
91. *L*, 17.13, 109.
92. *EW* V, 15.
93. *L*, 18.19, 117.
94. Ibid.
95. *EW* II, 216.
96. *DH*, 14.1, 71.
97. Hobbes seems to recognize that Bramhall has an honest desire to honor God even in the course of his "canting": "They are unseemly words to

be said of God: I will not say, blasphemous and atheistical, which are the attributes he gives to my opinions, because I do not think them spoken out of an evil mind, but out of error" (*EW* V, 342).

98. See, e.g., *L*, 31.15–16, 239.

99. *L*, 31.14, 239.

100. *ST* I, 4.1, ad. 3.

101. Cf. *L*, 31.13 and 31.8, 237, 239: The worship we give to God "proceeds from our duty, and is directed according to our capacity, by those rules of honour," and honoring "consisteth in the inward thought, and opinion of the power, and goodness of another: and therefore to honour God, is to think as highly of his power and goodness, as is possible."

102. *L*, 10.2, 50.

103. *ST* I, 2.3.

104. *EW* II, 214.

105. *L*, introduction, 1, 3.

106. *EW* VII, 176.

107. *EW* V, 14.

108. *OL*, II, 6. Compare Locke's argument against Filmer's paternal ownership thesis by natural right: parents don't *own* their children as property because *they did not make them*; God did (*First Treatise*, §51–53). For an argument that Locke's argument here is not only sincere but absolutely essential to his critique of Filmer and securing natural liberty and equality, the entire basis of his political philosophy, see Kody W. Cooper and Justin Dyer, "Thomas Jefferson, Nature's God, and the Theological Foundations of Natural-Rights Republicanism," *Politics and Religion*, 2017, 1–27, doi:10.1017/S1755048317000104.

109. See Strauss, *The Political Philosophy of Hobbes*, 123, n. 3. For an argument against Strauss regarding fifth-way language, see K. C. Brown, "Hobbes's Grounds for Belief in a Deity," *Philosophy*, 37, no. 142 (1962): 336–44.

110. *L*, 6.1, 27.

111. Arp, "The *Quinque Viae* of Thomas Hobbes," 381.

112. See Leon Harold Craig, *The Platonian Leviathan* (Toronto: University of Toronto Press, 2010), 112. However, tellingly, Craig gives no attention to the Thomistic tradition of Christian Aristotelianism. And Craig's rehashed arguments for the concealment thesis appear blind to Hobbes's version of the five ways and their implications (36–44).

113. *EW* IV, 303.

114. Ibid.

115. The example is mine, based on what Hobbes says. See *De Corpore*, 11.7, in *EW* I, 136.

116. *De Corpore*, 11.7, in *EW* I, 137.

117. This is not to say that, in Hobbes's terms, Socrates was a person from the moment his motion began. Hobbes avers a version of what some latter-day scholars have called a performance conception of personhood, i.e., that a being is a person only if the being functions in a particular way. For Hobbes this is the performance of "words or actions" (*L*, 16.1, 101). For further discussion, see chap. 5.

118. For one such recent treatment, see Samantha Frost, *Lessons from a Materialist Thinker: Hobbesian Reflections on Ethics and Politics* (Stanford, CA: Stanford University Press, 2008), 15–35.

119. Peter van Inwagen, *Material Beings* (Ithaca, NY: Cornell University Press, 1990), 87.

120. For a contemporary defense of hylomorphism, see David Oderberg, *Real Essentialism* (New York: Routledge, 2007).

121. *EW* IV, 32.

122. *L*, 4.13, 19.

123. *L*, 5.5, 24.

124. Cf. *EW* IV, 309.

Chapter 2. Hobbesian Moral and Civil Science: Rereading the Doctrine of Severability

1. I thank *Hobbes Studies* for permission to reproduce in modified form "Reason and Desire after the Fall of Man: A Rereading of Hobbes's Two Postulates of Human Nature," *Hobbes Studies* 26, no. 2 (2013): 107–29.

2. Lloyd, *Morality in the Philosophy of Thomas Hobbes*, 375.

3. Ibid., 376.

4. John Gray, "Can We Agree to Disagree?," *New York Times Book Review*, May 16, 1993; Rosamond Rhodes, "Reading Rawls and Hearing Hobbes," *Philosophical Forum* 33, no. 4 (Winter 2002): 393–412. Rhodes also cites Gray's work.

5. Lloyd, *Morality in the Philosophy of Thomas Hobbes*, 376.

6. Ibid. (emphasis in original).

7. *L*, "The Introduction," 9, 48.

8. Kavka, *Hobbesian Moral and Political Theory*, 11.

9. *L*, "The Introduction," 3, 4.

10. *DH*, 11.10, 50. David Johnston cogently argues that Hobbes came to prioritize literary form and rhetorical persuasion to mathematical demonstrative rigor, and he corrects claims that there was a hard break between Hobbes's humanist period, culminating in the translation of Thucydides, and his scientific later years. Therefore, it is incorrect to say that Hobbes came to doubt history as a source of political knowledge (David Johnston, *The Rhetoric of Leviathan* [Princeton, NJ: Princeton University Press, 1986], 4–25).

11. Lloyd, *Morality in the Philosophy of Thomas Hobbes*, 391.
12. *L*, "The Introduction," 1, 3.
13. Ibid.
14. *EW* III, 383. Cf. *ST* I, 2, proemium.
15. *EW* III, 92.
16. *L*, 17.13, 109.
17. The Latin *Leviathan* was published in 1688.
18. *OL* IX, in *Leviathan with Selected Variants*, 50 (translated by Curley).
19. For a careful discussion of the so-called Lubienski-Tricaud hypothesis, that the Latin *Leviathan* has an essential priority over the English, and some strong arguments against it, see Malcolm, *Leviathan Volume 1: Editorial Introduction*, 168–75. As Malcolm shows, the rejection of that hypothesis accounts for the evidence of, on the one hand, abridgment, omission, and occasional hasty translation of the English into Latin and, on the other, important substantial additions.
20. Hobbes, *Philosophical Rudiments*, preface to the reader, *EW* II, xx.
21. *EW* I, 72.
22. *EW* I, 73.
23. *EW* I, 74.
24. Ibid.
25. *EW* I, ix.
26. *EW* II, xiv–xv (emphasis mine).
27. *EW* II, xiv (emphasis mine).
28. *EW* II, 108–9.
29. *L*, 13.11–12, 77–78.
30. Laurie M. Johnson, *Thucydides, Hobbes, and the Interpretation of Realism* (DeKalb: Northern Illinois University Press, 1993), 4–27.
31. Cf. *L*, 13.7, 13.12. The claims about how men act in a condition of peace *intra* civil society are in tension with Hobbes's definition of war not as in the time of actual fighting but in the time in which "the will to battle is sufficiently well known" or during the time when there is a "known disposition thereto" (*L*, 13.8, 76).
32. *De Cive*, in *EW* II, xvii.
33. *De Cive*, in *EW* II, xv.
34. Hobbes, *On the Citizen*, 4.
35. Thus Hobbes is a "term empiricist," because terms denote bodies in the world that have operated on the senses. And universal terms denote several similar bodies: "One universal name is imposed on many things for their similitude in some quality or other accident" (*L*, 4.7, 17). This seems to sit uneasily with the "propositional rationalist" side of Hobbes, his view of "science" as

definitional-geometrical definitions and their consequences, which Hobbes sometimes suggests is *a priori* (as opposed to "opinion," which is belief formed on the basis of other modes of discourse). See A. P. Martinich's discussion of possible contradictions in *Hobbes* (New York: Routledge, 2005). See also Noel Malcolm, *Aspects of Hobbes* (Oxford University Press, 2003), 178–80.

36. *L*, "The Introduction," 3, 4.

37. Ibid., 4, 5.

38. See Tom Sorell, *Hobbes* (Abingdon, UK: Routledge and Kegan Paul, 1986).

39. *L*, "The Introduction," 3, 4.

40. Edward Earl of Clarendon, *A Brief View and Survey of the Dangerous and Pernicious Errors to Church and State, In Mr. Hobbes's Book, Entitled Leviathan* (Oxon, UK: Printed at the *Theatre*, 1676), 11.

41. *L*, 13.1, 74.

42. *EW* II, 8; *L*, 13.3, 75.

43. *L*, 25.11, 169.

44. *L*, 12.13–16, 67.

45. *L*, 13.3, 75.

46. Hobbes, *Behemoth, or the Long Parliament*, in *EW* VI, 280–81.

47. *De Cive*, 3.12; *L*, 15.20, 96; *EW* IV, 10 (*Elements of Law, Natural and Politic*, 16.11).

48. See Kavka, *Hobbesian Moral and Political Theory*.

49. *L*, 26.40, 186.

50. In a sense the end of commonwealth (barring a world state) is always "particular" in its less-than-universal membership. But the end of commonwealth, the common good of peace, is universal in the sense that it is always the end of anything that counts as a "commonwealth."

51. Johnston, *The Rhetoric of Leviathan*.

52. Hobbes, *On the Citizen*, 6; *EW* II, vii.

53. Leo Strauss, *The Political Philosophy of Hobbes*, trans. Elsa M. Sinclair (Chicago: University of Chicago Press, 1952), chap. 2.

54. Strauss, *The Political Philosophy of Hobbes*, ix. I focus here primarily on Strauss's interpretation of the two postulates in *The Political Philosophy of Hobbes*. I have not found evidence that Strauss fundamentally altered his understanding of the two postulates in his later work, but I leave it as an open question as to how Strauss's other views on Hobbes evolved in his late work. For a discussion, see Thomas G. West, "The Primacy of the Good in Hobbes's Political Philosophy: A Reconsideration of the Straussian View," paper presented at the annual meeting of the American Political Science Association, September 2005, revised September 2005–11 (PDF in my

possession). For clear statements of Strauss's intellectual development and his mature political thought on the whole, see, respectively, Daniel Tanguay, *Leo Strauss: An Intellectual Biography*, trans. Christopher Nadon (New Haven, CT: Yale University Press, 2007), and Thomas Pangle, *Leo Strauss: An Introduction to His Thought and Intellectual Legacy* (Baltimore: Johns Hopkins University Press, 2006). For a helpful discussion of Strauss's work on Hobbes within the context of his larger project, see Devin Stauffer, "Reopening the Quarrel between the Ancients and the Moderns: Leo Strauss's Critique of Hobbes's 'New Political Science,'" *American Political Science Review* 101, no. 2 (May 2007): 223–33.

55. Strauss, *The Political Philosophy of Hobbes*, x, 29. In his letter to Hans-Georg Gadamer and Gerhard Krüger, in which Strauss describes the theses of his book, Strauss puts the point this way: "In order to assess Hobbes's significance, it is essential to figure out what is for him the decisive *outlook* [*Gesinnung*]." See Strauss, *Hobbes's Critique of Religion and Related Writings*, trans. and ed. Gabriel Bartlett and Svetozar Minkov (Chicago: University of Chicago Press, 2011), 160.

56. See *De Corpore*, I.6.6–7, in *EW* I, 72–3; *De Cive*, preface to the reader, ed. and trans. Richard Tuck and Michael Silverthorne (Cambridge: Cambridge University Press, 1998), 13 (subsequent references to *De Cive* are to this edition; otherwise references to *De Cive* are to the version in *EW* II); *Leviathan*, 2. Cf. Strauss, *The Political Philosophy of Hobbes*, 6–7.

57. Strauss, *The Political Philosophy of Hobbes*, 9.

58. *EW* VII, 73.

59. Strauss, *The Political Philosophy of Hobbes*, 11.

60. Ibid.

61. Ibid., 18.

62. Ibid., 19.

63. Ibid.

64. Ibid., 15. Cf. Strauss, *Natural Right and History*, 201.

65. Strauss, *The Political Philosophy of Hobbes*, 150.

66. Ibid., 27. Similar statements in later works include, from *Natural Right and History*, "Natural law must be deduced from the most powerful of all the passions . . . the fear of violent death at the hands of others" (180), and "Vice for all practical purposes becomes identical with pride or vanity" (188); from *What Is Political Philosophy?* (Glencoe, IL: Free Press, 1959), "Fear and glory are both equally natural, yet fear is the natural root of justice and glory is the natural root of injustice" (192); and from *An Introduction to Political Philosophy*, "Hobbes conceives of man in terms of a fundamental polarity of evil pride and salutary fear of violent death" (83).

67. See also Strauss, *Hobbes's Critique of Religion and Related Writings*, 160.

68. Strauss, *The Political Philosophy of Hobbes*, 12.

69. Ibid., 13.

70. Ibid., 3.

71. Ibid., 14.

72. *De Cive*, preface, 11.

73. As Daniel Tanguay points out, "In the course of his works Strauss asserts Hobbes' atheism with increasing clarity, by the end holding him to be a 'blasphemer.'" See *Strauss: An Intellectual Biography*, 109–10. Still, it should be noted that it is disputed among interpreters of Strauss whether Strauss really did evolve on this point. I thank Devin Stauffer for pointing this out to me.

74. Strauss, *The Political Philosophy of Hobbes*, 75.

75. Strauss, "What Is Political Philosophy?," 189–90.

76. Strauss, *The Political Philosophy of Hobbes*, 28; *An Introduction to Political Philosophy*, 83; *Natural Right and History*, 184.

77. The full sentence is as follows: "The other is when, imagining anything whatsoever, we seek all the possible effects that can by it be produced; that is to say, we imagine what we can do with it, when we have it" (*L*, 3.5, 13). Absolute dominion is obviously something that is included in the set of "anything whatsoever."

78. *L*, 3.5, 13.

79. *L*, 12.1, 63.

80. *L*, 11.24, 62.

81. *De Corpore*, I.1.2 in *EW* I, 3.

82. *L*, 6.7, 28.

83. *L*, 11.24, 62. The passage could be accurately reworded thus: It is the desire for a distant future apparent good (and/or corresponding aversion from a distant apparent evil) that disposes men to inquire into causes.

84. It also suggests that man's peculiar foresight comes with reason— and Hobbes counts "foresight of the time to come" as a feature that distinguishes human from animal nature (*L*, 12.4, 63).

85. One might reply: Why can't the situation be like that of the bird whose wings take time to grow? Just because birds can't fly from birth, so the argument goes, no one would deny that their capacity for flight is innate. This argument fails because the capacity for flight in a bird is disanalogous to the capacity in man to engage in evil acts. The former is a power of the bird that is oriented toward its flourishing and, when properly functioning, is constitutive of its flourishing. The latter is not a power ordered toward the flourishing of the person but the capacity of the person to misuse his or her powers to indulge

appetites outside the bounds of reason. In other words, the bird is properly functioning, it is living a "happy" bird life, when its power of flight becomes an active potentiality. But evil acts are not the products of properly functioning powers; rather they are products of the dysfunction of reason and appetite. The corollary of dysfunctional powers is that the evil person is not flourishing. For Hobbes, evil acts are unreasonable (as I go on to outline) and hence entail a malfunction of reason and/or appetite. A dysfunctional person is one whose appetites are unruly, untamed by practical reason and the virtues.

86. *EW* VII, 73.
87. *L*, 12.4, 63.
88. *De Cive*, "Preface to the Reader," 11.
89. This is compatible with the idea that the dominion-seeker's cupidity is caught up in and transformed by reason to become "infinite" or to transcend mere immediate external sensory stimuli.
90. *De Cive*, "Preface to the Reader," 11.
91. *L*, 13.4, 75 (emphasis mine).
92. Cf. *De Cive*, 1.4; *Elements of Law: Natural and Politic*, 14.3.
93. *L*, 6.39, 31.
94. Ibid.
95. This does not deny that the confident man in the state of nature has a deeper desire for absolute dominion.
96. *De Cive*, "Preface to the Reader," 11; cf. *Elementorum Philospohiae Sectio Tertia De Cive*, prefatio ad lectores, in *OL* II, 147.
97. *L*, 26.12, 177.
98. *L*, 13.10, 77.
99. *De Cive*, "Preface to the Reader, 11.
100. Ibid.
101. Strauss, *The Political Philosophy of Hobbes*, 24; *Natural Right and History*, 180–82.
102. Cf. *L*, 13.10 and 13.13, 77–78. Some would take these passages to reject the view of the *De Cive* passage. But I believe that nothing in these passages denies the existence of evil persons in the state of nature. When Hobbes refers to justice and injustice here, he is referring to the technical definition of justice created by *positive* law—he is not denying the existence of prior standards of natural law and equity, and therefore countenances the possibility of their breach.
103. *L*, 15.36, 99.
104. *L*, 27.4, 191; 27.13, 194. Hobbes seems to contradict himself when he speaks of vainglory in this passage differently than he did before.
105. Bernard Gert, "Hobbes on Reason," and *Hobbes: Prince of Peace* (Cambridge: Polity, 2010). *De Homine*, 11.6, in *OL* II, 98.

106. *De Cive*, 1.7, 27.
107. Ibid.
108. *L*, 14.1, 79.
109. *De Cive*, 1.4.
110. *L*, 32.2, 245–46.
111. *L*, 31.4, 235; 32.9, 249.
112. Helen Thornton, *State of Nature or Eden: Thomas Hobbes and His Contemporaries on the Natural Condition of Human Beings* (Rochester, NY: University of Rochester Press, 2005).
113. Romans 7:23.
114. *ST* I-II, 90.1.
115. *ST* I-II, 91.2; *Quaestiones Disputate de Veritate*, 17.3.
116. *L*, 26.12, 177 (marginal note).
117. *ST* I-II, 92.2.
118. *ST* I-II, 91.2, ad. 3.
119. *L*, 31.2, 234.
120. Cf. *EW* V, 105.
121. *ST* I-II, 91.6.
122. *ST* I, 95.1.
123. *ST* I, 91.6.
124. Aristotle, *Politics*, trans. Peter L. Simpson (Chapel Hill: University of North Carolina Press: 1997), 1254b2–4.
125. *ST* I, 81.3, ad. 2.
126. But might it be objected on the basis of Genesis 3:6 that it was Eve's imagination of the taste of the forbidden fruit and, hence, animal passion that inclined her to sin against God's decree? Not according to St. Thomas. The deception of Eve and her subsequent eating of the fruit followed upon a first act of disobedience that was an interior act of pride, of inordinate self-love. It was a sheer turning of the will away from God to self. As Augustine put it: "The woman could not have believed the words of the serpent, had she not already acquiesced in the love of her own power, and in a presumption of self-conceit" (*ST* I 94.4).
127. *ST* I-II, 30.3; II-II, 24.8, obj. 2; I-II, 95.1, ad. 2; cf. I-II, 40.1.
128. *L*, 35.3, 272.
129. *L*, 38.15, 310.
130. Yet the picture is not incompatible with his presentations of the state of nature. Rather it provides the explanation of why man's condition can degenerate into a state of nature. It is not surprising that readers of Hobbes have missed this point, given the widespread propensity to read parts I and II of *Leviathan* while ignoring parts III and IV.
131. *L*, 38.2, 301.

132. *L*, 43.3, 398.

133. *L*, 38.15, 310.

134. *L*, 13.10, 77, n. 7.

135. Compare Thornton's discussion of scriptural commentators on Genesis 4 in *State of Nature or Eden*, 86–97.

136. While Hobbes at times suggests that the state of nature is merely a mental consideration (*De Cive*, 8.1), he also emphasizes its threefold obtainment in reality: savage patriarchal rule, international relations, and civil war (*L*, 13.11–12, 77–78).

137. Aristotle, *Politics*, 1253a28; Aquinas, *Sententia Libri Politicorum*, lib. I, n. 31, 27. Cf. *ST* I-II, 2.6, ad. 2; I-II, 95.1; I-II, 96.2.

138. For one contemporary use of the latter metaphor in moral psychology, see Jonathan Chaidt, *The Righteous Mind: Why Good People Are Divided by Politics and Religion* (New York: Vintage, 2013).

139. *L*, 15.40, 100.

140. Lloyd, *Morality in the Philosophy of Thomas Hobbes*, 394 (emphasis in original).

141. *L*, 20.17, 134.

142. *ST* I-II, 76.3, ad. 3.

143. *ST* I-II, 89.6. For Hobbes's distinction of sins according to gravity, see *Leviathan*, 350.

144. *De Cive*, "Preface to the Reader," 11.

145. Romans 3:23.

146. 1 John 1:8.

147. Rousseau believed that evil inclinations arose contingently in history through the development of agriculture and metallurgy and such institutions as private property.

148. *L*, 38.15, 310.

149. *L*, 43.3, 398.

150. See Eric Voegelin, *The New Science of Politics: An Introduction* (Chicago: University of Chicago Press, 1987).

151. Stephen B. Smith, *Modernity and Its Discontents* (New Haven, CT: Yale University Press, 2016), 70. Smith suggests that Hobbes was a Christian, albeit one who was a "sect of one" (85).

152. See Thucydides' famous account of the Corcyrean civil war in *History of the Peloponnesian War*, 3.81–84 (*EW* VIII, 346–53).

153. It is not in our scope to speculate about Thucydides' theology—although, notably, Hobbes denies that Thucydides was an atheist: "For in philosophy, he was the scholar (as also was Pericles and Socrates) of Anaxagoras; whose opinions being of a strain above the apprehension of the vulgar,

procured him the estimation of an atheist: which name they bestowed upon all men that thought not as they did of their ridiculous religion, and in the end cost him his life.... For though he were none, yet it is not improbable, but by the light of natural reason he might see enough in the religion of these heathen, to make him think it vain and superstitious; which was enough to make him an atheist in the opinion of the people.... In his writings our author appeareth to be, on the one side not superstitious, on the other side not an atheist" (*EW* VIII, xiv–xv). Paul Rahe, an advocate of the concealment thesis, takes Hobbes's wording of this passage as indicative of Hobbes's own skepticism (*Against Throne and Altar* [Cambridge: Cambridge University Press, 2008], 282). This is a baffling interpretation. The natural and straightforward interpretation is that Hobbes sees himself in Thucydides as a fellow rationalist theist who is critical of superstition in religion.

154. Lloyd, *Morality in the Philosophy of Thomas Hobbes*, 405–6.

155. Lloyd does not explain this distinction, but if it implies that the dutiful religious are somehow not willing their eternal happiness (because that would be egoistic), Lloyd appears to be applying a Kantian framework to explain something for which Hobbes himself does not offer a Kantian explanation.

156. *De Cive*, 14.19 and n. 2.

157. *EW* IV, 294.

158. A Hobbesian pluralism could include, minimally, all those of Abrahamic faith. Orthodox Jews, Muslims, and Christians all affirm this basic foundation within their comprehensive faith tradition. (Notably, these three groups would also converge in their vision of the historical fall of man.)

Chapter 3. Hobbes and the Good of Life

1. *L*, 15.18, 99; 26.40, 186.

2. Taylor and Warrender never mention Aquinas, and Gert's sole mention of Aquinas is negligible. Martinich reads Hobbes in light of Aquinas and provides some insights into the similarities between their theories of law. But he misreads the role of command in Aquinas's natural law theory and misses the interesting structural similarities in their accounts of practical reason.

3. Michael Zuckert, "Do Natural Rights Derive from Natural Law?," *Harvard Journal of Law and Public Policy* 20 (1998): 720–21.

4. *ST* I-II, 94.2.

5. *Summa Contra Gentiles* III, 3.7, 4.5 (citation is to book, chapter, and paragraph number).

6. That is, the *person*, by the power of the appetite, desires under the aspect of the good.

7. *ST* I, 82.1.

8. *EW* IV, 83.
9. *EW* II, 8.
10. Quoted in Denis J. M. Bradley, *Aquinas on the Twofold Human Good: Reason and Happiness in Aquinas's Moral Science* (Washington, DC: Catholic University Press, 1997), 281.
11. *DH*, 11.5, 48.
12. Ibid.
13. *DH*, 11.6, 48.
14. Ibid.
15. *ST* I-II, 94.2.
16. Ibid.
17. See Stephen L. Brock, "Natural Inclination and the Intelligibility of Good in Thomistic Natural Law," *Vera Lex* 6, nos. 1–2 (2005): 57–78.
18. *ST* I-II, 94.2, ad. 2.
19. *L*, 30.12, 224.
20. *L*, 6.8, 29.
21. See David Boonin-Vail, *Hobbes and the Science of Moral Virtue* (Cambridge: Cambridge University Press, 1994). This thread of Hobbes scholarship is picked up and defended by Peter Berkowitz. See *Virtue and the Making of Modern Liberalism* (Princeton, NJ: Princeton University Press, 1999). For a critique of Berkowitz, see Robert C. Miner, "Is Hobbes a Theorist of the Virtues?," *International Philosophical Quarterly* 41, no. 3, issue 163 (September 2001): 269–84.
22. *EW* I, 349.
23. Ibid.
24. *DH*, 13.3, 64–65.
25. *DH*, 11.3.
26. For a discussion, see Russell Hittinger, "Natural Law and Virtue: Theories at Cross Purpose," in *Natural Law Theory: Contemporary Essays*, ed. Robert P. George (New York: Oxford University Press, 1992).
27. Cf. *L*, 11.2, 58.
28. *DH*, 11.15.
29. *L*, 15.40, 100.
30. Luther, *Von anbeten des Sacraments des heyligen leychnams Christi* [1523], quoted in Brad S. Gregory, *The Unintended Reformation: How a Religious Revolution Secularized Society* (Cambridge, MA: Belknap Press, 2012), 88.
31. William Chillingworth, *The Religion of Protestants: A Safe Way to Salvation* (Oxford: Leonard Lichfield, 1638), 375, emphasis in original. On Hobbes and the Great Tew circle, which he would have visited at least occasionally between 1634 and 1640, see Martinich, *Hobbes: A Biography*, 102–13.

32. Gregory, *The Unintended Reformation*, 91.
33. Ibid., 74.
34. See Macpherson, *The Political Theory of Possessive Individualism*, reprint (Oxford University Press, 2011).
35. *L*, 15.40, 100.
36. *L*, 8.14, 41.
37. *L*, 19.3, 119. Hobbes's early readers challenged him on this reading of English history. See, e.g., George Lawson, *An Examination of the Political Part of Mr. Hobbs His Leviathan* (London, 1657), 39–40.
38. *L*, 11.21, 61.
39. *EW* VI, 167.
40. *L*, 31.41, 243–44; *L*, 30.14, 225. In the Latin *Leviathan*, the nod to custom is explicit when Hobbes remarks that he hopes that one day the doctrine of *Leviathan* will be "made more tolerable by custom." See Curley's note 15 to *L*, 31.41, 244.
41. *L*, 11.1, 57.
42. *L*, 11.6, 59.
43. *L*, 15.6, 92.
44. *DH*, 11.15, emphasis mine.
45. *ST* I-II, 2.8.
46. *EW* IV, 32.
47. Mark Hanin, "Thomas Hobbes's Theory of Conscience," *History of Political Thought* 31, no. 1 (Spring 2012).
48. For a discussion, see Douglas C. Langston, *Conscience and Other Virtues: From Bonaventure to MacIntyre* (State College: Pennsylvania State University, 2001).
49. Cf. Michael G. Baylor, *Action and Person: Conscience in Late Scholasticism and the Young Luther* (Leiden: E. J. Brill, 1977), 75ff.
50. See Baylor, *Action and Person*, 173–209.
51. Ibid., 209.
52. Calvin, *Institutes of the Christian Religion*, book IV, chap. 20.16.
53. Stephen J. Grabill, *Rediscovering the Natural Law in Reformed Theological Ethics* (Grand Rapids, MI: Wm. B. Eerdmans, 2006), 95–96.
54. *L*, 15.35, 99.
55. *EW* II, 51.
56. See A. E. Taylor, "The Ethical Doctrine of Hobbes," *Philosophy* 13 (1938): 422, and the discussion in chapter 4.
57. *EW* II, 152.
58. *L*, 29.7, 212.

59. I agree with Lloyd that the good for Hobbes is not simply synonymous with "desired by the agent" (*Morality in the Philosophy of Thomas Hobbes*, 83).

60. Martinich misreads Aquinas on this point (*The Two Gods of Leviathan*, 133). Cf. *ST* I-II, 90.4, ad. 1; 93.5; *De Veritate* 17.3 All of Aquinas's works are available at www.corpusthomisticum.org/iopera.html. Hobbes and Aquinas differ on the theological knowledge requisite to know the natural law *as law*. For more on this, see chapter 4.

61. *L*, 6.7, 28–29.

62. David Gauthier, "Thomas Hobbes: Moral Theorist," *Journal of Philosophy* 76, no. 10 (1979): 548.

63. See also Hampton, *Hobbes and the Social Contract Tradition*, and Kavka, *Hobbesian Moral and Political Theory*. For recent discussions, see Stephen Darwall, "The Right and the Good in Hobbes's Moral Philosophy" (unpublished manuscript), and S. A. Lloyd, *Morality in the Philosophy of Thomas Hobbes*, 78ff.

64. *L*, 6.7, 28–29.

65. Peter Geach, "Good and Evil," reprinted in *Theories of Ethics*, ed. Phillipa Foot (New York: Oxford University Press, 1976), 64–73. Lloyd makes a similar argument. See *Morality in the Philosophy of Thomas Hobbes*, 83.

66. See Constance M. Lewellen and Steve Seid, *Ant Farm: 1968–1978* (Berkeley: University of California Press, 2004).

67. Lloyd, *Morality in the Philosophy of Thomas Hobbes*, 83.

68. Stephen Darwall argues against subjectivist interpretations of Hobbes. See Darwall, "Normativity and Projection in Hobbes," *Philosophical Review* 109, no. 3 (2000): 313–47. However, if my argument is correct, Darwall's "projectivist" solution mistakenly reads Hume back into Hobbes.

69. *L*, 6.2, 28.

70. *L*, 6.4, 28.

71. *L*, 6.6, 28.

72. Hence, this claim would be compatible with an empirical observation that most or all people have this desire and/or that it is the strongest desire most or all people have.

73. Cf. Michael Oakeshott, "The Moral Life in the Writings of Thomas Hobbes," in *Hobbes on Civil Association* (Berkeley: University of California Press, 1975), 90.

74. *L*, 8.16, 41.

75. *L*, 8.2–3, 38.

76. *L*, 13.12, 78.

77. *L*, review and conclusion (R&C.7), 491. See also *EW* VI, 133–4, where Hobbes argues that killing another by mere misfortune (as when a man

picking apples in his apple tree accidentally falls on a passerby below) is not a felony because it was not intentional.

78. *L*, R&C.1, 489.
79. Ibid.
80. *L*, R&C.4, 489.
81. *L*, 18.20, 118.
82. *L*, 8.17, 41.
83. *L*, 8.23, 42–3.
84. Bernard Gert, "Introduction," in *Man and Citizen*, 29; Gert, *Hobbes: Prince of Peace*, 70.
85. *EW* II, 209.
86. See Charles Watson, Matthew Kirkcaldie, and George Paxinos Watson, *The Brain: An Introduction to Functional Neuroanatomy* (Burlington, MA: Elsevier, 2010), 123–24.
87. See Elaine Setiawan, Robert O. Pihl, Alain Dagher, et al., "Differential Striatal Dopamine Responses Following Oral Alcohol in Individuals at Varying Risk for Dependence," *Alcoholism: Clinical & Experimental Research* 38, no. 1 (2014): 126–34. For a layman's summary, see "Alcoholism: Effects on the Brain's Dopamine System," *McGill University News* (August 2013), available online at http://www.mcgill.ca/channels/news/alcoholism-effects-brains-dopamine-system-229843, accessed November 1, 2014.
88. See generally Norman Dodge, *The Brain That Changes Itself*, revised edition (Melbourne: Scribe, 2010).
89. *EW* II, 209. For my argument that this should be understood in light of Hobbes's doctrine of irresistible power, see chapter 4.
90. ASAM, "Definition of Addiction," available online at http://www.asam.org/for-the-public/definition-of-addiction, accessed November 1, 2014, emphasis in original.
91. *L*, 15.34, 99.
92. Hampton, *Hobbes and the Social Contract Tradition*, 40. Cf. her discussion of "basic" and "motivated" desires in "Hobbes and Ethical Naturalism," *Philosophical Perspectives* 6 (1992): 340–43. Her interpretation of "real" versus "apparent" good is not sufficient to prove his subjectivism. On the contrary, the key passage that distinguishes real from apparent is immediately followed by a flat assertion that life is the *bonum maximum*, which provides the most basic reason for action.
93. It is a testament to Hampton's intellectual honesty and seriousness that she herself seems to recognize the force of my criticism in a later article when she remarks that "health and madness are shot through with norms: to judge someone as sick or well, sane or mad, is to judge him using an ideal as

one's yardstick" ("Hobbes and Ethical Naturalism," 345). Indeed, and the yardstick for Hobbes is whether a desire conforms to reason's goal of preserving life. I differ from Hampton in her later position in that I don't think Hobbes intended a proto-Humean understanding of practical reason and "illicitly" smuggled a normative standard into his ethics, since in my interpretation the order of the bodily parts and functions toward the good of life has normative force grounded in God's having artificed man.

94. Jean Hampton, "Hobbes and Ethical Naturalism," *Philosophical Perspectives* 6 (1992): 339.

95. *L*, 15.40, 100.

96. Ibid.

97. On this point I agree with David Boonin-Vail. See his *Hobbes and the Science of Moral Virtue* (Cambridge: Cambridge University Press, 1994), 181–82.

98. Hampton, "Hobbes and Ethical Naturalism," 350.

99. Hobbes tells us that state of nature is an "inference, made from the passions," and that "reason suggesteth convenient articles of peace." But it isn't as simple as passions = war and reason = peace. A wide range of passions can cooperate with reason to incline man toward peace. Hobbes likes to mention the passions of fear of death and the desire for commodious living as two of the chief passions that cooperate with reason in inclining man to peace. However, it is a mistake to claim these passages as evidence that reason is a mere instrument by which to obtain these desire-set goals. The negative passions of fear of death and wounds as well as the positive desire for ease or commodious living are parasitic on the reason's fundamental grasp of the notion that life is good and death is to be avoided. This is why such passions do not make someone "mad." Some passions have a note of madness in and of themselves, such as vainglory. Other passions' order toward sanity turns on their compatibility with the goods of life and the security of peace. For example, the desire for knowledge and love of the arts are normally good because pursuit of these goods requires peace (*L*, 11.4, 58; 13.10, 77; 13.14, 78).

100. Lloyd advances these against Gert's interpretation of the good of life as a rationally required end. Hence they are effectively objections against my reading, which agrees with Gert on this point.

101. Lloyd, *Morality in the Philosophy of Thomas Hobbes*, 189.

102. Johan Olsthoorn, "The Non-Preservationist Foundations of Hobbes's Moral Philosophy," *Hobbes Studies* 27 (2014): 148–70.

103. *L*, 15.8, 92.

104. *L*, 32.1, 245.

105. *L*, 32.2, 245–46.
106. *L*, 38.3, 302–3; 42.11, 338.
107. *L*, 6.58, 34.
108. *EW* IV, 271.
109. *L*, 45.22, 446. See 2 Kings 5.
110. *L*, 45.27, 448.
111. *EW* II, 318.
112. *EW* III, 364, 386, 553, 590–602. For a discussion of this article as the *unum necessarium* for salvation in Hobbes's thought, see Michael P. Krom, *The Limits of Reason in Hobbes's Commonwealth* (London: Continuum, 2011), 148–53.
113. *L*, 12.20, 69.
114. *EW* VI, 281.
115. *EW* II, 318.
116. *EW* IV, 378.
117. *L*, 6.39, 31, emphasis mine.
118. Ibid.
119. *L*, 38.4, 304.
120. *EW* IV, 303.
121. *L*, R&C.5, 490.
122. *L*, 15.6, 92.
123. *L*, 39.4, 315–16.
124. Chapter 42 of *Leviathan*, "Of Power Ecclesiastical," is actually the longest chapter in the book. In it Hobbes engages in an extended discourse and critique with a great Roman Catholic Jesuit apologist and contemporary of Hobbes's, Saint Robert Bellarmine.
125. For more discussion of this Hobbesian doctrine, see chapter 5.
126. *DH*, 11.6, 49.
127. *EW* VI, 88.
128. *L*, 18.20, 117–18.
129. *L*, 26.16, 179.

Chapter 4. The Legal Character of the Laws of Nature

1. Hobbes, *Elements of Law Natural and Politic*, 15.1, in *EW* IV, 87.
2. Ibid., 17.12, in *EW* IV, 109.
3. *EW* II, 16.
4. *EW* II, 166.
5. *DC*, 15.1, 15.3, in *EW* II, 204, 205.
6. *L*, 14.3, 79.

7. See, e.g., Kavka, *Hobbesian Moral and Political Theory*, 343.

8. Here I do not use "usufruct" in its technical sense in civil law. I suggest it as a term to capture the sense of Hobbes's definition of the twelfth law of nature.

9. *L*, 14.1, 79, emphasis mine. For an interpretation that natural right is prior to and conditions law, see Strauss, *Natural Right and History*, 181–82.

10. *L*, 14.3, 79.

11. *L*, 18.8, 113; 30.1–3, 219–20.

12. Thomas Tenison, *The Creed of Mr. Hobbes Examined in a Feigned Conference between Him and a Student in Divinity* (London, 1670), 147, 127.

13. Samuel Parker, *A Discourse of Ecclesiastical Politie* (London, 1671), 120.

14. J. Shafte, *The Great Law of Nature, or, Self-Preservation Examined, Asserted and Vindicated from Mr. Hobbes His Abuses in a Small Discourse, Part Moral, Part Political and Part Religious* (London, 1673), 4.

15. Ibid., 10.

16. Clarendon, *A Brief View*, 36.

17. Robert Filmer, *Observations on Mr. Hobbs's Laviathan*, http://quod.lib.umich.edu/e/eebo/A41307.0001.001/1:17?rgn=div1;view=fulltext.

18. Lawson, *An Examination of the Political Part of Mr. Hobbs His Leviathan*, 2–3; 70–72.

19. *EW* IV, 286.

20. Samuel Pufendorf, *The Law of Nature and Nations*, trans J. Barrow (London, 1749), III.3.16, 136.

21. Martinich discusses Tenison, Shafte, and Parker. Martinich, "Law and Self-Preservation in *Leviathan*: On Misunderstanding Hobbes's Philosophy 1650–1700," in *The Persistence of the Sacred in Modern Thought*, ed. Chris L. Firestone and Nathan A. Jacobs (Notre Dame, IN: University of Notre Dame Press, 2012), 38–65.

22. *L*, 15.36, 99.

23. *L*, 26.6, 174.

24. *L*, 14.18–14.26, 84–86.

25. For a discussion of the point, see Matthew B. O'Brien, "Practical Necessity: A Study in Ethics, Law, and Human Action," Ph.D. dissertation, University of Texas at Austin, 2011.

26. *EW* II, 206, 209.

27. *L*, 15.41, 100.

28. For one recent example, see, e.g., Perez Zagorin, *Hobbes and the Law of Nature* (Princeton, NJ: Princeton University Press, 2009), 51.

29. Martinich, *Hobbes: A Biography*, 84.

30. *L*, 31.3, 235. Hence, the oft-repeated claim that Hobbes does not secure the legal character of the laws of nature prior to biblical positive law—God's "prophetic word"—must be rejected (cf. Hood, *The Divine Politics of Thomas Hobbes*, viii, 4).

31. Lloyd, *Morality in the Philosophy of Thomas Hobbes*, 184.

32. J. P. Sommerville, *Thomas Hobbes's Political Ideas in Historical Context* (New York: St. Martin's Press, 1992), 79.

33. *EW* V, 116.

34. *EW* II, 209.

35. William J. Courtenay, *Capacity and Volition: A History of the Distinction of Absolute and Ordained Power* (Bergamo: P. Lubrina, 1990).

36. Augustine, *De Natura et Gratia*, 8. English translation available online at http://www.newadvent.org/fathers/1503.htm, accessed December 1, 2016.

37. Francis Oakley, "Jacobean Political Theology: The Absolute and Ordinary Powers of the King," *Journal of the History of Ideas* 29, no. 3 (1968): 334.

38. Aquinas cites Matthew 26:53, where Jesus asks rhetorically if his listeners think he cannot call upon legions of angels. But since he did not, God can do what he does not.

39. Aquinas argues that this is compatible with such necessities as are intrinsic to his nature (knowing and loving himself) and with necessities of supposition, necessities that follow upon acts of God's free will (*Summa Contra Gentiles*, I.80, 83).

40. See *ST* I.25.5; *De Potentia Dei*, I.5; *Summa Contra Gentiles* I.84.

41. As Michael Gillespie correctly points out, the condemnations focused on Averroistic Aristotelianism (Gillespie, *Theological Origins of Modernity* [Chicago: University of Chicago Press, 2008]), 21.

42. Francis Oakley, "The Theology of Nominalism" *Harvard Theological Review* 56, no. 1 (1963): 61.

43. Quoted in ibid., 60.

44. Oakley, "Absolute and Ordained Power of God in Sixteenth and Seventeenth Century Theology," *Journal of the History of Ideas* 59, no. 3 (1998): 447; Oakley, "Omnipotence and Promise: The Legacy of the Scholastic Distinction of Powers," Etienne Gilson Series 12 (Toronto: Pontifical Institute for Medieval Studies, 2002), 9.

45. See also William Courtenay, "Nominalism and Late Medieval Religion," in *The Pursuit of Holiness in Late Medieval and Renaissance Religion*, ed. Charles Trinkaus and Heiko A. Oberman (Leiden: Brill, 1974), 39.

46. John Duns Scotus, *Ordinatio* I, dist. 44, in *Opera Omnia*, ed. A. Sépinski (The Holy See: Vatican, 1963), vol. VI, 363–69, translated in Allan B. Wolter, *Duns Scotus on the Will and Morality* (Washington, DC:

Catholic University Press, 1986), 254–55, and quoted in Courtenay, *Capacity and Volition*, 101.

47. William of Ockham, *Quodlibeta septem* VI.1, *Opera Theologica* vol. IX, 585–86, translated in Ockham, *Quodlibetal Questions*, vol. II, trans. Alfred J. Freddoso (New Haven, CT: Yale University Press), 491–92.

48. On this point, Oakley came to change his mind to essentially agree with Courtenay. See Oakley, "Locke, Natural Law, and God: Again," in *Politics and Eternity: Studies in the History of Medieval and Early Modern Political Thought* (Leiden: E. J. Brill, 1999), 233, n. 50.

49. Armand Maurer, *A History of Philosophy: Medieval Philosophy* (New York: Random House, 1962), 287.

50. See, e.g., John Kilcullen, "Natural Law and Will in Ockham," in J. Kilcullen and J. Scott, *A Translation of William of Ockham's Work of Ninety Days* (Lewiston, NY: Edwin Mellen Press, 2001), vol. II, 851–82; A. S. McGrade, "Natural Law and Moral Omnipotence," in *The Cambridge Companion to Ockham*, ed. Paul Vincent Spade (Cambridge: Cambridge University Press, 1999), 273–302.

51. Gerald Postema, "Law as Command: The Model of Command in Modern Jurisprudence," *Philosophical Issues* 11 (2001): 470–501.

52. William of Ockham, *Reportatio*, II sent., q. 15, in *Opera Theologica*, ed. Gidean Gál and Rega Wood (St. Bonaventure, NY: St. Bonaventure University, 1981), vol. V, 352.

53. Ockham, I *Dialogus* 6.100; III *Dialogus* II, book II, chap. 15, both in William of Ockham, *Dialogus*, ed. John Kilcullen, John Scott, George Knysh, et al., produced under the auspices of the Medieval Texts Editorial Committee of the British Academy. Draft critical edition available online at http://www.britac.ac.uk/pubs/dialogus/, accessed June 20, 2017. See also III *Dialogus* II, chap. 6, translated in *Letter to the Friars Minor and Other Writings*, ed. A. S. McGrade and John Kilcullen (Cambridge: Cambridge University Press, 1995).

54. Ockham, III *Dialogus* II, book III, chap. 6.

55. The second mode of natural law is the natural equity that characterized prelapsarian man's common ownership of common things; the third is constituted of precepts proper to the postlapsarian condition and therefore *ex suppositione*. For example, the precept requiring the return of money or things deposited is based on the supposition of the existence of private property, a state of affairs that obtains after the fall of man. Ockham's theory seems tailored to his controversy with Pope John XXIII over poverty and property in the mendicant orders.

56. Ockham, *Ordinatio*, dist. 41, q. 1, in *Opera Philosophica et Theologica*, ed. Girardus I. Etzkorn and Franciscus E. Kelley (New York: St. Bonaventure, 1979), vol. IV, 610.

57. On this point I disagree with Marilyn McCord Adams, who claims that the divine precepts derive their authority from the dictates of right reason. See Adams, "The Structure of Ockham's Moral Theory," *Franciscan Studies* 46 (1): 1–35 (1986): 24.

58. Ockham, *Quodlibet* II.14, in *Opera Philosophica et Theologica*, ed. Joseph C. Wey (New York: St. Bonaventure, 1980), vol. IX, 176–78.

59. Ockham, *Quodlibeta septem* II.8, in *Opera Philosophica et Theologica*, vol. IX, 146. Cf. Freddoso's note in his translation: *Quodlibetal Questions*, vol. 1, 124, n. 124.

60. *Quodlibet septem* I.16, in *Opera Philosophica et Theologica*, vol. IX, 87.

61. J. Kilcullen, "Natural Law and Will in Ockham," 871; reprinted in J. Kilcullen and J. Scott, *A Translation of William of Ockham's Work of Ninety Days* (Lewiston, NY: Edwin Mellen Press, 2001), vol. II, 851–82.

62. *Reportatio*, in IV sent., q. 16, in *Opera Philosophica et Theologica*, vol. 7, 352.

63. Francisco Suárez, *Tractatus*, book II.15.5, in *Selections from Three Works* (Oxford: Clarendon Press, 1944), vol. II, 288. Hence, for Suárez, God cannot fail to prohibit intrinsically evil acts: *Tractatus*, II.6.23, in *Selections*, vol. II, 206.

64. Ockham, *Ordinatio*, dist. 2, q. IV, in *Opera Theologica* II, 116. Gillespie notes this but does not discuss it in light of the absolute-ordained distinction.

65. Ockham, *Opera Theologica*, vol. VI, 335–37. For a discussion, see Marilyn McCord Adams, *William Ockham*, vol. I (Notre Dame, IN: University of Notre Dame Press, 1987), 117–20.

66. For the theological story, see Oakley, "The Absolute and Ordained Power of God in Sixteenth- and Seventeenth-Century Theology," *Journal of the History of Ideas* 59, no. 3 (1998): 437–61.

67. *Luther's Works*, ed. Jaroslav Pelikan (St. Louis: Concordia, 1955–86), vol. III, 274–90, cited in Oakley, "The Absolute and Ordained Power of God in Sixteenth- and Seventeenth-Century Theology," 456.

68. See also *On the Bondage of the Will*, sec. 94, in *Luther's Works*, vol. XXXIII.

69. See Calvin, *Institutes of Christian Religion*, book III, 23.2, 761.

70. Ibid., I.17.2, 182.

71. See Oakley, "The Absolute and Ordained Power of God and King in the Sixteenth and Seventeenth Centuries: Philosophy, Science, Politics, and Law," *Journal of the History of Ideas* 59, no. 4 (1998): 669–90.

72. Suárez, *Tractatus de legibus ac deo legislatore*, book II, chap. 2.4–6.

73. *L*, 26.6, 174.

74. *L*, 21.4, 137.

75. *L*, 37.6, 295.
76. *EW* V, 13.
77. *EW* V, 103.
78. *EW* V, 13.
79. *EW* V, 14.
80. Hobbes, *Historia Ecclesiastica*, ed. and trans. Patricia Springborg, Patricia Stablein, and Paul Wilson (Paris: Honoré Champion Éditeur, 2008), 307.
81. Hobbes, *Thomas White's Du Mundo Examined*, 391. George Wright argues that Hobbes's position is evident in his 1688 appendix to *Leviathan*. See Wright, "1688 Appendix to Leviathan," *Interpretation* 18 (1991): 411, n. 219.
82. *L*, 37.5, 294.
83. *L*, 37.7, 296, emphasis removed.
84. *EW* I, xiii.
85. Ibid.
86. *L*, 44.11, 416.
87. *EW* VII, 3.
88. *L*, 37.3, 294.
89. Hobbes, *Historia Ecclesiastica*, lines 684–85, 383. Hobbes continues to cite several of the actions of Christ as examples of miracles.
90. For example, the analogy of absolute and ordained is implicit when Hobbes argues that the sovereign can bind the commonwealth to positive law while retaining the freedom to abolish burdensome laws and legislate anew.
91. Exceptions include Oakley, "The Absolute and Ordained Power of God and King in the Sixteenth and Seventeenth Centuries," 675–76, and George Wright, "1688 Appendix to Leviathan," 347, n. 78.
92. *EW* II, 208.
93. *EW* VII, 133.
94. *L*, 36.15, 288.
95. EW II, 209.
96. *L*, 35.3, 272.
97. *L*, 31.5, 235. In this passage Hobbes is using "creation" with the connotation of freely conferring a gift in contrast with "creation" in the sense of ordering by sovereign right. At any rate, God's right to bind does not *depend* on granting benefits, which is compatible with saying that God's ordained power in fact orders us toward our good.
98. *EW* II, 209.
99. Even angels, presumably much more powerful beings than men, are metaphysically dependent and hence can neither create nor annihilate. See *L*, 37.9, 297.

100. *EW* II, 209.

101. *EW* VII, 73; cf. chapter 2.9.

102. *L*, 29.16, 217.

103. *EW* II, 216; III, 318; cf. IV, 286.

104. *L*, 31.8, 237.

105. Voegelin, *The New Science of Politics*.

106. On this point, see Michael Krom, *The Limits of Reason in Hobbes's Commonwealth* (London: Continuum, 2011).

107. I believe that Hobbes's solution to the problem of evil, the theory of affliction, and the theory of annihilation for the damned should be read in this light.

108. *EW* IV, 32.

109. For Hugo Grotius's view, see *The Rights of War and Peace*, ed. Richard Tuck (Indianapolis: Liberty Fund, 2005), prolegomena, para. 11. Samuel von Pufendorf rebukes Grotius, taking the side of Suárez, in *The Law of Nature and Nations*, trans J. Barrow (London, 1749), III.3.16, 139.

110. Suárez, *Tractatus de legibus ac deo legislatore*, II.6.3–4.

111. Ibid., II.6.24.

112. For a discussion of how Suárez's doctrine on this point breaks from Aquinas's, see Russell Hittinger, *The First Grace* (Wilmington, DE: Intercollegiate Studies Institute, 2007), 52–57.

113. *ST* I-II, 90.4, ad. 1.

114. *L*, 31.1, 234.

115. I have come to change my mind on this point from previous work.

116. A. E. Taylor, "The Ethical Doctrine of Hobbes," *Philosophy* 13 (1938): 422.

117. *L*, 31.3, 235.

118. Bramhall argues that Hobbes's inconsistency and irreconcilability with himself are manifest in that his catalogue of laws of nature does not make any mention of religion or bear "the least relation in the world to God." Hence, Bramhall alleges, "This great clerk forgetteth the God of nature, and the main and principal laws of nature, which contain a man's duty to his God, and the principal end of his creation" (*EW* IV, 284). Hobbes replies:

> After I had ended the discourse he mentions of the laws of nature, I thought it fittest in the last place, once for all, to say that they were the laws of God, then when they were delivered in the word of God; but before, being not known by men for any thing but their own natural reason, they were but theorems, tending to peace, and those uncertain, as being but conclusions of particular men, and therefore not properly laws. (*EW* IV, 284–85)

David Gauthier has taken this passage to weigh conclusively against the theistic interpretation of Hobbes's natural law theory (Gauthier, "Hobbes: The Laws of Nature," *Pacific Philosophical Quarterly* 82, nos. 3–4 [September 2001]: 284, n. 6). But that interpretation seems rather too quickly formed, given the good reasons we have for supposing Hobbes's theological sincerity. The first point that leaps out of the controversy is this: Hobbes was inconsistent with himself in the very act of defending his consistency. Bramhall quoted from chapter 31 of *Leviathan*, where Hobbes points out that natural reason judges God to exist and assigns duties for honoring God. In Hobbes's reply, as Gauthier notes, he appears to contrast man's natural reason with the "word of God." But, in the same chapter Bramhall quotes from, Hobbes had said that "God's word" is threefold: rational, sensible, and prophetic—and that "right reason" corresponds to the rational word of God.

Why didn't Hobbes cite this passage as evidence of his consistency? Hobbes's answer to Bramhall indicates that Hobbes was thinking not about God's rational word but about his "prophetic word." Hobbes goes on to say: "Besides, I had formerly in my book *De Cive*, cap. iv, proved them severally, one by one, out of the Scriptures, which his Lordship had read and knew." But God's prophetic word seems irrelevant to the bishop's allegation that Hobbes had forgotten the God of nature.

One possible explanation of the passage is that it is further evidence of the insincerity of Hobbes's natural theology since he says that the laws of nature as known by natural reason are not really laws. But such an interpretation would not make much sense out of Hobbes's controversy with Bramhall as a whole. The entire concern of Hobbes's answer for the first several pages is to defend himself from Bramhall's charge of atheism. It is, of course, a real possibility that Hobbes's concern with publishing a response to Bramhall stemmed from his fear of persecution by Parliament. But if Hobbes were intent on proving his consistent theism—specifically, on defending his claims in chapter 31 that we can know by natural reason that God exists and is due honor—then, surely it would have been a better strategy for Hobbes to recall the passages in the same chapter in which he asserted that the laws of nature corresponded to the rational word of God. Alas, he did not. But Hobbes's failure to have recourse to his own argument hardly seems "conclusive" evidence that Hobbes disbelieved that God's existence is known by unaided reason or that God's rational word made the laws of nature lawful. It need only prove that, in this instance at least, either Bramhall was right that Hobbes was inconsistent or Hobbes was right in his claim that he was sometimes a "forgetful blockhead" (*EW* IV, 287). Alternatively, Hobbes may have been speaking about the *civil* legal character of the laws of nature.

119. *ST* I-II, 71.6, obj. 5 and ad. 5.
120. Kavka, *Hobbesian Moral and Political Theory*, 362.
121. *L*, 4.12, 19.
122. See Murray Campbell, A. Joseph Hoane Jr., and Feng-hsiung Hsu, "Deep Blue," *Artificial Intelligence* 134 (2002): 58.
123. Notably, Kasparov accused IBM of cheating in game 2.
124. Campbell, Hoane, and Hsu, "Deep Blue," 62.
125. McNeilly, *The Anatomy of Leviathan*, 91.
126. Ibid., 184.
127. John Deigh, "Reason and Ethics in Hobbes's *Leviathan*," *Journal of the History of Philosophy* 34, no. 1 (1996): 43
128. Ibid., 50.
129. Ibid., 39–40. Bernard Gert makes a similar point against Gauthier. See Gert, "Hobbes on Reason," *Pacific Philosophical Quarterly* 82 (2001): 246.
130. Deigh, "Reason and Ethics in Hobbes's *Leviathan*," 59–60.
131. Kavka, *Hobbesian Moral and Political Theory*, 8–9.
132. *ST* I-II, 94.2.
133. *L*, 4.12, 19.
134. *L*, 27.2, 190.
135. *EW* I, 7.
136. Lloyd, *Morality in the Philosophy of Thomas Hobbes*, 104. See also, Gert, *Hobbes: Prince of Peace*, 70, 82.
137. Some secularist interpreters seem willing to bite this bullet. See, e.g., Gauthier, "Hobbes: The Law of Nature," 263.
138. *EW* II, 206.
139. Cf., e.g., *EW* II, 110.
140. Sigmund, *Natural Law in Political Thought*, 56.
141. Suárez, *Tractatus*, III.2.4, in *Selections*, 375.
142. The relevant passage is *ST* I-II, 90.3. Aquinas remarks that the authority to make law resides either in the whole people or in a representative of the people. However, as John P. Hittinger has shown, this does not require that the representative consult the people through referendums or elections or that he derive his power by some act of transmission; it requires only that the representative act for the good of the whole people. See Hittinger, *Liberty, Wisdom, and Grace: Thomism and Democratic Political Theory* (Lanham, MD: Lexington Books, 2002), 4.
143. *EW* V, 180.
144. *L*, 15.4, 90.
145. Ibid.

146. *EW* IV, 33–34.

147. Cf. Aristotle's discussion of accidental causality in *Metaphysics*, 1025a15–30.

148. *L*, 15.5, 91.

149. *L*, 15.5, 92.

150. *L*, 15.4, 90.

151. For a discussion, see Pietro Bembo, *History of Venice*, vol. II, ed. and trans. Robert W. Ulery Jr. (Cambridge, MA: Harvard University Press, 2008), 135–37.

152. Harvey Mansfield, *Machiavelli's Virtue* (Chicago: University of Chicago Press, 1996), 7.

153. *L*, 15.7, 92.

154. William Shakespeare, *Richard III*, act 5, scene 6, in *The Oxford Shakespeare: The Complete Works*, 2nd ed., ed. Stanley Wells et al. (Oxford: Clarendon Press, 2005), 220.

155. *EW* VI, 157.

156. *Henry IV*, part 2, act 3, scene 1, in *The Oxford Shakespeare*, 551.

157. Hobbes, of course, is aware that dominion is sometimes *acquired* and that the vanquished can render the new order just by covenanting with one another to authorize the usurper as a new sovereign. But even in cases of conquest, there is the question of the equity or iniquity of the ruler, as well as the prince's previous actions of justice or injustice in the technical sense, knowledge of which can make a difference to the stability of the new order.

158. Ernest Fortin, "New Rights Theory and Natural Law," *Review of Politics* 44, no. 4 (October 1982): 590–612, quote on 611.

159. See, e.g., Thomas Pangle, "A Critique of Hobbes's Critique of Biblical and Natural Religion in *Leviathan*," *Jewish Political Studies Review* 4, no. 2 (1992): 50.

160. See Aristotle, *Metaphysics*, 1027a29–1027b16; Aquinas, *Sententia libri metaphysicae*, lectio 3.

161. *EW* II, 199.

162. Kinch Hoekstra, "Hobbes and the Foole," *Political Theory* 25, no. 5 (1997): 620–54.

163. *L*, introduction, 3, 4.

164. *L*, 15.6, 92.

165. Cf. Hobbes, *Historia Ecclesiastica*, 737–38, 389.

166. *EW* IV, 294.

167. Hobbes also believes through the testimony of revelation and faith that God will finally punish atheists as enemies (*EW* II, 199).

Chapter 5. The Essence of Leviathan: The Person of the Commonwealth and the Common Good

1. These laws have the status of rational necessity for nontheists who otherwise reason rightly, but they are not, properly speaking, *laws*. The *force* of the fundamental law of nature and the second law of nature is then only recommendatory for nontheists.

2. *L*, 17.13, 109.

3. David Runciman, "What Kind of Person Is Hobbes's State? A Reply to Skinner," *Journal of Political Philosophy* 8, no. 2 (2000): 274.

4. Here I confine myself to *Leviathan*. It is true that Hobbes offers differing definitions of a person in *De Homine* and the Latin *Leviathan*, both later works. But I do not see any discernible development of the definition of personhood over and above Hobbes's supple account in *Leviathan*. If anything, Runciman seems right that "later accounts . . . are less complete, and do not improve on [the earlier account]." See Runciman, "What Kind of Person Is Hobbes's State?," 278.

5. *L*, 16.1, 101.

6. Here I use "fictitiously representative" as shorthand for "representing the words or actions of another man or of any other thing to whom they are attributed by fiction" and "truly representative" as shorthand for "representing the words or actions of another man or of any other thing to whom they are attributed truly."

7. *L*, 16.8, 102.

8. For the use of "fiction" to mean "counterfeit," see the *Oxford English Dictionary*, 2nd ed., 1989, "fiction, n." For the use of "counterfeit" in the false representation of persons, see *Oxford English Dictionary*, "counterfeit, adj. and n."

9. Thomas Tenison, *The Creed of Mr. Hobbes Examined*.

10. *L*, 16.8, 102. Hence, feigned persons turn out to be simply natural persons, albeit natural persons dissembling.

11. *L*, 16.9, 102.

12. If correct, David Copp's rejection of the *Leviathan* definition of personhood is unwarranted. Copp springs for Hobbes's definition of the person in *De Homine* because the inclusion of "whether truly or by fiction" would include stage actors as artificial persons, a usage that would "blur an important distinction." See Copp, "Hobbes on Artificial Persons and Collective Actions," *Philosophical Review* 89 (1980): 579–606, 583, n. 6.

13. To Copp it appears that Hobbes includes truly representative artificial persons under the heading "fictional" in *Leviathan*, and he struggles with this

("Hobbes on Artificial Persons and Collective Actions," 584 and n. 9). Hanna Pitkin offers a much more penetrating analysis of Hobbes's definition of personhood and the meaning of representation by fiction. See Pitkin, "Hobbes's Concept of Representation," *American Political Science Review* 58, no. 2 (June 1964): 328–40. However, even Pitkin at times equates fictional with artificial: "In Hobbes's terminology the fiction or artifice about an artificial person is that the actions he is performing are not (considered) his own but those of someone else" (329).

14. Cf. Skinner's decidedly elaborate interpretation in "Hobbes and the Purely Artificial Person of the State," *Journal of Political Philosophy* 7, no. 1 (1999): 1–29.

15. Fortin, "New Rights Theory and the Natural Law," 602.

16. *L*, 17.6, 108.

17. *DC*, 5.5.

18. Pettit, *Made with Words*, 97.

19. *L*, 17, 108–9. For a criticism of Hobbes's argument from the perspective of Darwinian biological science, see Larry Arnhart, *Darwinian Natural Right: The Biological Ethics of Human Nature* (Albany: State University of New York Press, 1998), 58–64.

20. Aristotle, *Politics*, 1253a7; Aquinas, *De Regno*, chap. 1, para. 7.

21. *Politics*, 1253a7–a18.

22. *L*, 17.1, 106.

23. See chapter 2.

24. *L*, 17.2, 106.

25. *L*, 13.4, 75.

26. *ST* I-II, 95.1.

27. Roy J. Deferrari has, for *aptitudo*, "suitability, fitness, inclination, proneness towards" (Deferrari, *A Lexicon of St. Thomas Aquinas Based on the Summa Theologica and Selected Passages of His Other Works* [Fitzwilliam, NH: Loreto], vol. A, 78).

28. *ST* I, 93.4: "Man possesses a natural aptitude for understanding and loving God (*homo habet aptitudinem naturalem ad intelligendum et amandum Deum*)."

29. *ST* I-II, 95.1.

30. *EW* VI, 4: "I agree with Sir Edward Coke, who upon that text farther says, that reason is the soul of the law; and upon section 138, *nihil, quod est contra rationem, est licitum*; that is to say, nothing is law that is against reason; and that reason is the life of the law.... It is also a dictate of the law of reason, that statute laws are a necessary means of the safety and well-being of man in the present world, and are to be obeyed by all subjects, as the law of reason ought

to be obeyed, both by King and subjects, because it is the law of God." *ST* I-II, 93.3: "Human law has the nature of law in so far as it partakes of right reason; and it is clear that, in this respect, it is derived from the eternal law."

31. *ST* I-II, 95.1.

32. *ST* II-II, 132.1; *ST* II-II, 36; *ST* II-II, 34.3; *ST* II-II, 110.1; *ST* II-II, 111.1. Obstinacy and discord are the daughters of vainglory. See Aquinas, *De Malo* q. 9, art. 3.

33. "*Ad societatem ergo homo aptus, non natura sed disciplina factus est.*"

34. *ST* I-II, 2.6, ad. 2.

35. A. P. Martinich, *Philosophical Writing: An Introduction*, 3rd ed. (Hoboken, NJ: Blackwell, 2005), 62.

36. *DC*, I.13.

37. *ST* I-II, 95.1, ad. 1.

38. Given Aquinas's view that law is necessary to secure a peaceful state of affairs, Aquinas would have agreed that a lawless condition is potentially one in which the passion of fear would obtain on a mass scale, since fear is a shunning movement of the sensitive appetite when one apprehends some object to be a future evil, difficult and hard to resist. Presumably a condition in which we could not discern those who are evilly disposed from the good would be one that would strike fear into us. What would Aquinas make of Hobbes's argument that, even if the good outnumber the evil, our inability to distinguish between them requires us to suspect, guard against, and anticipate others? It is difficult to say, because Aquinas considers this question in the context of a normal case, i.e., one in which persons are under positive law, living in peace. Aquinas points out that if judgment of suspicion is to be lawful, it must not be formed on slight indications, it must not affirm with certainty that another is evil, and it must not condemn the other on mere suspicion. The former two are in the realm of mere opinion and are still considered injurious to various degrees. The rightness of such a judgment must follow upon "evident indications of a person's wickedness" (*ST* II-II, 60.4). I think that for Aquinas this principle would hold even in abnormal conditions of anarchy. So Aquinas would not countenance the rightness of Jones in a lawless condition and without evident indication, asserting as true of any particular person A that "A is evil" and fearing A on that basis. But I think Aquinas's anthropology permits him also to say this: Jones is able to judge of the set of all persons in a state-of-nature condition, S1 [= A, B, C, . . .], that "possibly any particular member of S1 is evil" (call this judgment J1). I take Hobbes's Fear and Ignorance Principle to be similar to J1 in that neither entails asserting with certainty the evil of all individuals or of any particular person with a slight indication of their evil or none. (This seems necessary for Hobbes, given his optimism that this condition can be exited through covenant, which

presupposes some minimal threshold of trust to even get off the ground.) What J1 does seem to require is acting prudently, for the sake of the good. For Aquinas this good would include Jones's preservation and the protection of Jones's family. The virtue of prudence includes elements that would contribute to judgments of how Jones ought to act or order his external affairs, for the preservation of his life and lives of his family, as if J1 were true: memory, understanding, docility, shrewdness, reason, foresight, circumspection, and caution (*ST* II-II, 49). Inasmuch as Jones's (virtuous) end in such a condition would include protection of his self and his family, it would seem to require taking certain defensive measures. However, I am dubious that Aquinas would endorse Hobbes's claim that prudence requires us to *subjugate* others (suggestive of Hobbes's best-offense-is-a-good-defense principle) because of Aquinas's thicker account of the good and an according denial of any possible individual right to all things.

39. *EW* IV, 2.
40. *L*, 14.3, 79.
41. *L*, 17.13, 109.
42. *L*, 14.4, 80.
43. *L*, 14.5, 80.
44. *L*, 17.13, 109.
45. *L*, 17.1, 106.
46. *L*, 17.13, 109.
47. Ibid., emphasis mine.
48. *L*, 30.1, 219.
49. *DH*, 11.4, in *Man and Citizen*, 47.
50. Aquinas, *De Regno* (trans. Gerald B. Phelan), chap. 3, para. 17, available online at http://dhspriory.org/thomas/DeRegno.htm, accessed June 21, 2017.
51. Aquinas, *Sententia libri Ethicorum*, lib. 3, lectio 8, available online at www.corpusthomisticum.org, accessed June 21, 2017.
52. Here I follow Michael Pakaluk, "Is the Common Good Limited and Instrumental?," *Review of Metaphysics* 55, no. 1 (September 2001): 57–94.
53. As the physical trainer's science of fitness employs the absolutely best regimen of dieting and exercising as an ideal standard of excellence to adapt to the bodily health of his patients according to their fitness, equipment, and circumstances, so Aristotle's rational political science employs the best regime as its standard of excellence for assessing the health of the body politic (Aristotle, *Politics*, ed. Peter L. Simpson [Chapel Hill: University of North Carolina Press, 1997], 1288b10–b35).
54. But, as I read Aquinas, *complete* harmony between persons is nothing other than perfect *tranquillitas ordinis*, which is impossible to achieve in

this world because such unity of persons can be had only in the vision of God, the extrinsic common good of the whole universe. Because such an end exceeds man's natural powers in and of themselves, a person or society can be ordered to such an end in its acts and operations only with the help of grace. But Aquinas thinks there is a certain integrity in human nature, and so we can speak of a (proximate) extrinsic common good of a society available to man unaided by grace, and this will look something like the ideal of Aristotelian *eudaimonia* somewhere between (iii) and (iv). Hence we can draw a comparison within the order of nature.

55. Cf. *DC*, 1.2.

56. John Rawls, *Lectures on the History of Political Philosophy*, ed. Samuel Freeman (Cambridge, MA: Belknap Press, 2008), 84.

57. Cf. also *L*, 19.4, 120.

58. For a discussion of Hobbes's theory of taxation and various other principles of the Hobbesian common good, with an eye toward contemporary issues, see *Hobbes Today: Insights for the 21st Century*, ed. S. A. Lloyd (Cambridge: Cambridge University Press, 2012).

59. *EW* VI, 154.

60. *EW* II, 179.

61. *L*, 29.3, 211.

62. J. Judd Owen, "The Tolerant Leviathan," *Polity* 37, no. 1 (2005): 137.

63. Ibid., 139.

64. On the primacy of the common good in Aquinas, see Charles de Koninck, *On the Primacy of the Common Good: Against the Personalists and the Principle of the New Order*, trans. Sean Collins, reproduced *in Aquinas Review* 4 (1997).

65. *L*, 15.40, 100, emphasis mine.

66. *DH*, 11.6.

67. *DH*, 11.5; *L*, 6.8, 29.

68. Aquinas divides the good into the *honestum*, *utile*, and *delectibile* and identifies the *honestum* as that which is intrinsically good or per se desired (*ST* I.5.6). The *bonum honestum* is in itself a perfective or fulfilling activity to which pleasure is a fitting accompaniment. It is not *necessarily* pleasurable, but it will be for a virtuous person, whose emotions are attuned to right reason. We already saw that Hobbes famously rejects a *summum bonum*. But he always qualifies his rejection: "*as is spoken of in the books of moral philosophers*" (*L*, 11.1) or "*in the present life*" (*DH*, 11.15). It is at least possible that Hobbes is rejecting only the possibility of final beatitude in this life—and if so, Hobbes and Aquinas are on the same page in that respect (*ST* I-II.3.8).

69. *L*, 6.8, 29; 15.22, 97.

70. *L*, 15.40, 100.
71. *L*, 30.1, 219.
72. See, e.g., Pierre Manent, *An Intellectual History of Liberalism* (Princeton, NJ: Princeton University Press, 1996).
73. *L*, 17.12, 109.
74. Aquinas, *Politics*, 1253a30. Cf. Aquinas, *ST* I-II, proemium.
75. Aquinas, *Commentary on the Politics*, proemium.
76. *L*, introduction, 2, 4.
77. *L*, 17.1, 106.
78. Raia Prokhovnik, "Hobbes's Artifice as Social Construction," *Hobbes Studies* 18 (2005): 74.
79. *L*, introduction, 1, 3.
80. Ibid.
81. *L*, introduction, 1, 3–4.
82. Aquinas, *Physics*, 2.2, 194a22–27; Thomas Aquinas, *Sententia libri Politicorum*, proemium.
83. Cf. Aquinas, *In Lib. Phys.*, 2 lect. 4, no. 170.
84. Cf. Aquinas's "fifth way," *ST* I, 2.3.
85. *L*, 11.25, 62.
86. *EW* V, 14.
87. Alvin Plantinga, *Warrant and Proper Function* (Oxford: Oxford University Press, 1993), 21.
88. Ibid., 21.
89. See, e.g., Larry Arnhart, *Darwinian Natural Right* (Albany: State University Press of New York, 1998).
90. Plantinga, *Warrant and Proper Function*, 21.
91. *L*, 29.1, 210.
92. The principle that art imitates nature does not imply that the political artist must be a metaphysician. It need mean only that humans' practical reasoning is informed by often messy, unorganized apprehension of natural things common to all persons. And if nature appears as something ordered or at least minimally ordered, nature has an informing relation to civil science inasmuch as it orders toward ends, the chief of which for Hobbes is self-preservation. You can also know what you would think and feel if a massive worst-case scenario like the state of nature ensued and, by *nosce teipsum*, read what others would think and feel, too—and that condition appears to us as something in which reasonable persons pursue the good of life.
93. Cf. Aristotle, *Politics*, 1252a20–24. The watch analogy reinforces the point that the resolutive-compositive method can be applied to bodies both natural and man-made (and, hence, can drive the theorems and conclusions of two

real sciences). As the resolution of the watch reveals springs and wheels as its basic parts in motion and contact performing operations integral to the whole, so the method reveals that the members of the commonwealth are natural persons and groupings thereof moving and functioning as the integral parts of the political body while retaining the freedom of their own operations where the law permits.

94. Cf. Annabel Brett, "'The Matter, Forme, and Power of the Commonwealth': Thomas Hobbes and Late Renaissance Commentary on Aristotle's Politics," *Hobbes Studies* 23 (2010): 25.

95. Krom, *The Limits of Reason in Hobbes's Commonwealth*, 48–61.

96. *L*, 23.3, 23.9–10, 156, 158; 24, 159–65.

97. *L*, 22.34, 155.

98. *L*, 29.2, 210.

99. *L*, 22.34, 155, and, generally, *L*, 29.

100. *L*, 29.17, 217. Hobbes goes on to identify a few more diseases that are "not so great; which neverthelesse are not unfit to be observed" (*L*, 29.18, 217).

101. *L*, 18.8, 113.

102. Ibid.

103. *L*, 22.5, 146.

104. Mary Ann Glendon, *Rights Talk: The Impoverishment of Political Discourse* (New York: Free Press, 1991), 143.

105. See, e.g., J. N. Figgis, "The Great Leviathan," and H. J. Laski, "The Personality of Associations" and "The Pluralist State," all reprinted in *The Pluralist Theory of the State*, ed. Paul Q. Hirst (London: Routledge, 1989), 121, 179, 184. See also F. W. Maitland, "Moral Personality and Legal Personality," reprinted in David Nicholls, *The Pluralist State*, 2nd ed. (London: Macmillan, 1994), 175. Nicholls traces the influence of the work of Otto von Gierke on the English Pluralists (43–48). See also generally David Runciman, *Pluralism and the Personality of the State* (Cambridge: Cambridge University Press, 1997). Gierke's work sought to home in on Hobbes's novelties vis-à-vis older scholastic theories of group personality. See his *Natural Law and the Theory of Society: 1500 to 1800*, with a lecture on the ideas of natural law and humanity by Ernst Troeltsch, translated and with an introduction by Ernest Barker (Clark, NJ: Lawbook Exchange, 2010).

106. Aquinas, *Metaphysics*, 1075a13–16; *Sententia libri metaphysicae*, lectio 12, nn. 2629–2637; *Sententia in libros Ethicorum*, lectio 1, n. 5. For a discussion, see Russell Hittinger, "The Coherence of the Four Principles of Catholic Social Doctrine: An Interpretation," in *Pursuing the Common Good: How Solidarity and Subsidiarity Can Work Together*, Proceedings of the 14th Plenary Session of the Pontifical Academy of the Social Sciences, May 2–8, 2008 (Vatican City: Pontifical Academy of Social Sciences), 75–123.

107. As I read Aristotle and Thomas, these doctrines are present in their writings but in seminal form. For a discussion of how the principles take shape in Aquinas's defense of the mendicant orders, see Hittinger, *The First Grace*, 293–312; Kenneth L. Grasso, "The Rights of Monads or of Intrinsically Social Beings? Social Ontology and Rights Talk," *Ave Maria Law Review* 3 (2005): 233–58.

108. *L*, 22.26, 152–53.

109. Sovereignty of parent(s) over their children is through "natural force," i.e., "being able to destroy them if they refuse." *L*, 17.15, 109–10.

110. *DC*, 15, n. 4; cf. the discussion of "small families" in *L*, 17.2, 107.

111. *L*, 20.5, 130.

112. *L*, 17.3, 107. Cf. *L*, 25.16, 172: "And as for very little commonwealths, be they popular or monarchical, there is no human wisdom can uphold them longer than the jealousy lasteth of their potent neighbours."

113. *L*, 29.21, 218.

114. Carl Schmitt famously argued that this was the chief feature of sovereignty. See *Political Theology: Four Chapters on the Concept of Sovereignty*, trans. George Schwab (Chicago: University of Chicago Press, 2005).

115. See Quentin Skinner, *Hobbes and Republican Liberty* (Cambridge: Cambridge University Press, 2008), 188–89; cf. Sheldon Wolin's claim that in Hobbes's commonwealth each person "remains a discrete individual and each retains his identify in an absolute way" (*Politics and Vision: Continuity and Innovation in Western Political Thought*, exp. ed., [Princeton, NJ: Princeton University Press, 2004], 238). Cf. Quentin Skinner, "Hobbes and the Purely Artificial Person of the State," *Journal of Political Philosophy* 7 (1999): 1–29; David Runciman, "What Kind of Person Is Hobbes's State? A Reply to Skinner," *Journal of Political Philosophy* 8 (2000): 268–78. While Skinner had argued in the article cited earlier that the civil person is in the special category of a "purely artificial person," he later suggested that he had been convinced by Runciman that Hobbes's state is a person "by fiction." See his "Hobbes on Representation," *European Journal of Philosophy* 13, no. 2 (2005): 183, n. 139.

116. For an excellent account of Aristotelian-Thomistic social ontology to which I am indebted, see Russell Hittinger, "The Coherence of the Four Principles of Catholic Social Doctrine." See also Finnis, *Aquinas*, 23–29.

117. *L*, 17.13, 109.

118. Skinner, *Hobbes and Republican Liberty*, 188.

119. Ibid., 189.

120. Skinner, "Hobbes and the Purely Artificial Person of the State," 2.

121. It is also noteworthy that when Hobbes gives examples of what he means by a "FICTION of the mind," he mentions a golden mountain and castles

in the air but not the commonwealth. See Hobbes, *Human Nature and De Corpore Politico* (Oxford: Oxford University Press, 1994), 3.4, 28.

122. Hobbes, *Human Nature and De Corpore Politico*, 21.11.

123. See John Locke, *Second Treatise of Civil Government*, §89, §211.

124. Cf. *De Corpore* 11.2, in EW I, 133.

125. *L*, introduction, 2, 4.

126. *L*, 22.4, 146.

127. Friedrich Hayek, *Law Legislation and Liberty*, vol. II: *The Mirage of Social Justice* (Chicago: University of Chicago Press, 1976), 108–9.

128. *L*, 22.4, 146; *DC*, 5.4.

129. *L*, 18.1, 110.

130. *L*, 17.13, 109, emphasis mine.

131. *L*, 19.14, 124.

132. In Lincoln's words: "I hold that in contemplation of universal law and of the Constitution the Union of these States is perpetual. Perpetuity is implied, if not expressed, in the fundamental law of all national governments. It is safe to assert that no government proper ever had a provision in its organic law for its own termination. Continue to execute all the express provisions of our National Constitution, and the Union will endure forever, it being impossible to destroy it except by some action not provided for in the instrument itself." See his "First Inaugural Address—Final Text," in *Collected Works of Abraham Lincoln*, ed. Roy P. Basler (New Brunswick, NJ: Rutgers University Press, 1953), vol. 4, 264–65.

133. *L*, introduction, 1, 3.

134. In the older Aristotelian ontology, substantial forms radically constituted prime matter to bring into being an individual substance of some natural kind. Aristotle describes the identity of the regime over time using an analogy to matter-form composite in natural substances (the focal case) and human artifacts. The people are as matter and the regime as the form, as the notes are as the matter to the form of the musical mode (*Politics*, 1276b8–9). The change of regime is analogous to substantial change in natural substances (*Politics*, 1303a1). Hobbes famously and vociferously rejects Aristotelian substantial forms as "jargon" that frights men "from obeying the laws of their country, with empty names, as men fright birds from the corn with an empty doublet, a hat, and a crooked stick" (*L*, 46.18, 460). In Hobbes's ontology substance is identical to body and the form that constitutes body in generation and destruction is an accident, which Hobbes innovatively identifies with essence (*De Corpore*, in *EW* I, 116–17). The upshot is that in Hobbes's thought accidental form becomes the functional equivalent of substantial form. As we saw in chapter 1, Hobbes wants to maintain a kind of matter-form distinction that

can account for personal identity over time and provide the basis for a thinned-out teleology.

135. Hobbes notes, however, that his doctrine of monarchy as the best regime is only "probably stated" (*EW* II, xxii).

136. *EW* II, 129.

137. *L*, 19.14, 124.

138. *De Corpore*, 11.7, in *EW* I, 138.

139. *L*, 19.3, 119.

140. *L*, 39.4, 315–16.

141. Alan Ryan, *The Making of Modern Liberalism* (Princeton, NJ: Princeton University Press, 2012), 206. For a recent discussion, see Richard Tuck, "Hobbes, Conscience, and Christianity," in *The Oxford Handbook to Hobbes*, ed. A. P. Martinich and Kinch Hoekstra (Oxford: Oxford University Press, 2016), chap. 21.

142. *L*, 46.37, 466.

143. John Aubrey Papers, MS Aubr. 9, folio 8, Bodleian Library, Oxford, UK.

144. For Arnauld's objection that Descartes's teachings undermined the doctrine of transubstantiation, and Descartes' replies, see "Fourth Objections and Replies," in René Descartes, *Meditations on First Philosophy with Selections from the Objections and Replies*, trans. Michael Moriarty (Oxford: Oxford University Press, 2008).

145. *Reynolds v. United States*, 98 U.S. 145 (1878).

146. *Cantwell v. Connecticut*, 310 U.S. 296 (1940).

147. "And so we are reduced to the independency of the primitive Christians, to follow Paul, or Cephas, or Apollos, every man as he liketh best. Which, if it be without contention, and without measuring the Doctrine of Christ by our affection to the person of his minister (the fault which the apostle reprehended in the Corinthians), is perhaps the best. First, because there ought to be no power over the consciences of men but of the Word itself, working faith in every one, not always according to the purpose of them that plant and water, but of God himself, that giveth the increase. And secondly, because it is unreasonable (in them who teach there is such danger in every little error) to require of a man endued with reason of his own, to follow the reason of any other man, or of the most voices of many other men (which is little better than to venture his salvation at cross and pile)" (*L*, 42.20, 482).

148. Even here, anticipating Locke after him, the text suggests that Hobbes is imagining toleration of only *some* rival *Christian* sects—excluding, at least, Catholics (the following paragraph, a précis of Hobbes's doctrinal

anti-Catholicism, compares the papacy with the kingdom of fairies). Cf. John Locke, *Letter on Toleration* (Indianapolis: Hackett, 1983).

149. Hobbes apparently believes this holds even for commonwealths that arise "by acquisition," i.e., "where the sovereign power is acquired by force." This is so because even in these kinds of commonwealth, the conquered "do authorize all the actions of that man, or assembly, that hath their lives and liberty in his power" (*L*, 20.1, 127). One might wonder whether this kind of authorization is not really freely entered into or whether it is entered into from fear. Hobbes's reply is that fear and liberty are consistent—one freely throws his goods overboard when his ship is sinking because he is free to refuse to do so (and free to perish, if he will) (*L*, 21.3, 136).

150. *ST* I.29.3, obj. 2; cf. *L*, 16.3, 101.

151. Aquinas, *De Malo*, q. IV, art. 1.

152. See also *ST* I-II, 90.3 for Aquinas's use of the term *personam publicam* for the representer of the multitude.

153. Aquinas, *Summa Contra Gentiles*, II.30.12.

154. *L*, 23.2, 156.

155. Brett, "'The Matter, Forme, and Power of the Commonwealth.'"

156. See, e.g., *L*, 26.10, 175.

157. *L*, 21.17, 143.

Chapter 6. Hobbes's Natural Law Account of Civil Law

1. Thanks to the *British Journal of American Legal Studies* for permission to reproduce in modified form my article "Commanding Consistently with Sovereignty: Thomas Hobbes's Natural Law Theory of Morality and Civil Law," *British Journal of American Legal Studies* 3 (2014): 165–96.

2. *L*, 26.3, 273.

3. For interpretations of Hobbes as a legal positivist, see J. W. N. Watkins, *Hobbes's System of Ideas*, 2nd ed. (London: Gower, 1973), 114; Gregory S. Kavka, *Hobbesian Moral and Political Theory* (Princeton, NJ.: Princeton University Press, 1986), 248–50; Jean Hampton, *Hobbes and the Social Contract Tradition* (Cambridge: Cambridge University Press, 1986), 107– 10; Norberto Bobbio, *Thomas Hobbes and the Natural Law Tradition*, trans. Daniela Gobetti (Chicago: University of Chicago Press, 1993), 147–48; M. M. Goldsmith, "Hobbes on Law," in *The Cambridge Companion to Hobbes*, ed. Tom Sorell (Cambridge: Cambridge University Press, 1996), 275ff; John Gardner, "Legal Positivism: 5½ Myths," *American Journal of Jurisprudence* 46 (2001): 200. For a recent assessment, see Zagorin, *Hobbes and the Law of Nature*, 2–3, 49–54. For a critique of positivist readings of Hobbes, see Mark Murphy,

"Was Hobbes a Legal Positivist?," *Ethics* 105, no. 4 (1995): 846–73, and David Dyzenhaus, "Hobbes and the Legitimacy of Law," *Law and Philosophy* 20, no. 5 (September 2001): 461–98.

4. Joseph Raz, *The Authority of Law*, 2nd ed. (Oxford: Oxford University Press, 2009), 65.

5. Sometimes this is formulated as "There is no necessary connection between law and morality" and alongside the sources thesis constitutes the "core commitments of positivism" (Jules L. Coleman and Brian Leiter, "Legal Positivism," in *A Companion to Philosophy of Law and Legal Theory*, ed. Dennis Patterson [Hoboken, NJ: Blackwell, 1996], 241). But compare John Gardner's claim that the "no necessary connection thesis" is one of the myths of legal positivism: "This thesis is absurd and no legal philosopher of note has ever endorsed it as it stands." According to Gardner, contrary to impressions, Hart did not really endorse this thesis (Gardner, "Legal Positivism," 223; cf. H. L. A. Hart's 1958 essay "Positivism and the Separation of Law and Morals," in *Essays in Jurisprudence and Philosophy* [Oxford: Clarendon Press, 1983]).

6. John Austin, *The Province of Jurisprudence Determined* (London: John Murray, 1832), 6.

7. Hans Kelsen, *General Theory of Law and State*, trans. Anders Wedberg (Clark, NJ: Lawbook Exchange, 2007), 63; H. L. A. Hart, *The Concept of Law*, 2nd ed. (Oxford: Oxford University Press, 1997), 35–36.

8. Hart, *The Concept of Law*, 6.

9. Ibid., 20.

10. Ibid., 36–40.

11. Ibid., 101.

12. Austin, *The Province of Jurisprudence Determined*, 6.

13. See Raz, *The Authority of Law*, 149–53. Cf. Hart, *The Concept of Law*, 103: "For the word 'valid' is most frequently, though not always, used, in just such internal statements, applying to a particular rule of a legal system, an unstated but accepted rule of recognition. To say that a given rule is valid is to recognize it as passing all the tests provided by the rule of recognition and so as a rule of the system. We can indeed simply say that the statement that particular rule is valid means that it satisfies all the criteria provided by the rule of recognition." According to Leslie Green, "No legal positivist argues that the systemic validity of law establishes its moral validity." "Legal Positivism," *Stanford Encyclopedia of Philosophy*, http://plato.stanford.edu/entries/legal-positivism/#Bib, accessed February 20, 2012.

14. Hart, *The Concept of Law*, 187–95

15. *L*, 14.3, 79.

16. *L*, 26.2, 173.

17. *EW* IV, 74–75.

18. Deploying Razian terminology to explain Hobbes's view, Susanne Sreedhar refers to the basic good of self-preservation as a "non-excludable first-order reason for action" (*Hobbes on Resistance* [Cambridge: Cambridge University Press, 2010], 108–31). While I would not go as far as Sreedhar in deploying Raz's sophisticated account of law to Hobbes, I do think Sreedhar's discussion illuminates what Hobbes was trying to do—and my interpretation is in many ways compatible with her account.

19. *L*, 21.11–13, 141–42.

20. *ST* I-II, 92.1, ad. 4; cf. *ST* I-II, 93.3, ad. 2, where Aquinas uses the locution *lex iniqua*; *ST* I-II, 95.2, where he uses the locution *legis corruptio*; *ST* I-II, 94.6, ad. 3, where legislation against the natural law is called *statuta*. Roy J. Deferrari has, for *statutum*, "statute, law, decision, determination" (Deferrari, *A Lexicon of St. Thomas Aquinas* [Baltimore: John D. Lucas, 1949], 1051).

21. For discussions, see John Finnis, "The Truth of Legal Positivism," in *The Autonomy of Law*, ed. Robert P. George (Oxford: Oxford University Press, 1999), 195–214; "Natural Law: The Classical Tradition," in *The Oxford Handbook of Jurisprudence and Philosophy of Law*, 8–15; Robert P. George, "Natural Law," in *The Oxford Handbook of Law and Politics*, ed. Gregory A. Caldeira, R. Daniel Kelemen, and Keith E. Whittington, 409–11.

22. Aquinas also notes that even unjust laws derive from the eternal law (and hence, have something of the character of law) because they are framed by those in power, and all power is derived from God, according to Romans 13:1 (*ST* I-II, 93.3, ad. 2).

23. One example of such an argument is based on Hobbes's technical definition of justice as nonviolation of covenant. Because the sovereign is not party to the sovereign-making covenant—subjects covenant *between themselves* to grant their rights to a sovereign—the sovereign is not party to the covenant and so cannot be accused of injustice.

24. *L*, 17.13, 109.

25. *L*, 18.6, 112–13. Hereafter, any time the pronoun "he" or "his" is used for a sovereign, "or it/its" is understood.

26. *L*, 30.20, 229.

27. *L*, 26.8, 174.

28. See, e.g., Zagorin, *Hobbes and the Law of Nature*, 54.

29. See *Leviathan Parts I and II, Revised Edition*, ed. A. P. Martinich and Brian Battiste (Peterborough, Ontario: Broadview Press, 2010), appendixes A, B, and D.

30. Martinich correctly points out that this formula as it stands is self-contradictory. See *The Two Gods of Leviathan*, 167–69.

31. *L*, 21.11–13, 141–42.

32. "There be some rights which no man can be understood by any words or other signs to have abandoned or transferred. As, first, a man cannot lay down the right of resisting them that assault him by force, to take away his life, because he cannot be understood to aim thereby at any good to himself . . . the same may be said of wounds, and chains, and imprisonment" (*L*, 14.8, 82).

33. *EW* IV, 287.

34. *L*, 14.8, 82, emphasis mine.

35. The presumption seems warranted, since those who do not take it as basic will typically be the sorts of people who cannot or will not enter the covenant.

36. *L*, 14.8, 82.

37. Ibid.

38. *L*, 23.2, 156.

39. *L*, 22.3, 156, emphasis mine.

40. See generally *L*, 17.

41. *L*, 30.1, 219.

42. *L*, 17.1, 106.

43. *EW* II, 166.

44. *EW* II, 167.

45. Paul R. DeHart, "Leviathan Leashed: The Incoherence of Absolute Sovereign Power," *Critical Review: A Journal of Politics and Society* 25, no. 1 (2013): 1–37.

46. See also DeHart, "Covenantal Realism: The Self-Referential Incoherency of Conventional Social Contract Theory and the Necessity of Consent," *Perspectives on Political Science* 41 (2012): 165–77.

47. This parallels the right of nature's telic order toward the basic good of life.

48. *L*, 21.21, 144.

49. See Peter J. Steinberger, "Hobbesian Resistance," *American Journal of Political Science* 46, no. 4 (October 2002): 856–65. See also S. A. Lloyd, *Ideals as Interests in Hobbes's "Leviathan": The Power of Mind over Matter* (Cambridge: Cambridge University Press, 1992), 75.

50. Hence, in this interpretation the notion of a rebel subject is not oxymoronic. See Sreedhar, *Hobbes on Resistance*, 156–57.

51. Notably, Bramhall cited the earlier passage as evidence that *Leviathan* was a *rebel's catechism*. For an argument that subjects retain a right not only to self-defense but also to rebellion, see generally Sreedhar, *Hobbes on Resistance*.

52. For an interesting account of the mutual containment thesis, which seems compatible in many ways with my own account, see Timothy Fuller, "Compatibilities on the Idea of Law in Thomas Aquinas and Thomas Hobbes," *Hobbes Studies* 3 (1990): 112–34.

53. S. A. Lloyd, "Hobbes's Self-Effacing Natural Law Theory," *Pacific Philosophical Quarterly* 82 (2001): 305, n. 20.

54. RT = If one judges another's doing of an action to be without right, and yet does that action oneself, one acts contrary to reason. That is, to do what one condemns in another is contrary to reason (Lloyd, *Morality in the Philosophy of Thomas Hobbes*, 219–20).

55. Lloyd, "Hobbes's Self-Effacing Natural Law Theory," 295. Cf. Lloyd, *Morality in the Philosophy of Thomas Hobbes*, 280.

56. Lloyd, "Hobbes's Self-Effacing Natural Law Theory," 295.

57. Lloyd, *Morality in the Philosophy of Thomas Hobbes*, 342.

58. Ibid.

59. *L*, 18.6, 113.

60. *EW* VI, 21–22.

61. *L*, 15.24, 97.

62. *L*, 15.35, 99; 42.11, 339.

63. *L*, 15.24, 97.

64. Noel Malcolm, *Aspects of Hobbes* (Oxford: Oxford University Press, 2002), 437. While Malcolm helpfully illuminates the sovereign's office to promote the good of the people, my argument suggests that Malcolm is incorrect that the sovereign is "jurally entitled to treat them just as he would his enemies" if we take "civil law" to be a jural term (446).

65. *L*, 26.24, 181–82; cf. Hobbes, *A Dialogue between a Philosopher & a Student of the Common Laws of England*, in *EW* VI, 137–38, and Coke, *The First Part of the Institutes of the Laws of England*, 8th ed. (London: 1670), §709.

66. *L*, 15.24, 97.

67. *EW* VI, 21–2.

68. *EW* VI, 137.

69. *L*, 15.23, 97.

70. Ibid.

71. *L*, 13.8, 76.

72. Timothy Fuller makes a similar point. See Fuller, "Compatibilities on the Idea of Law in Thomas Aquinas and Thomas Hobbes," *Hobbes Studies* 3, no. 1 (1990): 114–15.

73. *L*, 30.12, 224, emphasis mine.

74. *L*, 15.36, 99.

Conclusion

1. Bramhall, *The Catching of Leviathan or the Great Whale*, in *The Works of John Bramhall*, vol. 4 (Oxford: John Henry Parker, 1844), 547.

2. Sigmund, *Natural Law in Political Thought*, 204–5.

3. Sommerville, *Thomas Hobbes's Political Ideas in Historical Context*, 79.

4. See also Bernard Gert's introduction to *On Man and the Citizen*.

5. Wolfe identifies five similar principles as the core principles of liberalism. Wolfe, *Natural Law Liberalism*, 144–45.

6. 319 U.S. 624 at 639.

7. Martin Luther King Jr., "Letter from a Birmingham Jail," in *Why We Can't Wait*, reissue edition (Boston: Beacon Press, 2010).

8. *L*, 28.27, 210.

9. *L*, 44.27, 426–27.

10. Rawls, *Political Liberalism* (New York: Columbia University Press, 2005), xvii.

11. Ibid., 150–54.

12. *L*, R&C 17, 497.

INDEX

Note: Several concepts in the text occur often—including "appetite," "cause," "commonwealth," "desire," "evil," "God," "good," "judgment," "knowledge," "law," "motion," "nature," "natural law," "passion," "peace," "person," "power," "reason," "science" "sovereign"—and are indexed only in connection with the major themes of the book.

Abel, 86
Abraham, 154
Adam and Eve, 28, 85–89
addiction, 121–22
Agathocles, 174
Anabaptist, 105–7
anarchy, 157, 249, 251, 307n.38
anger, 59, 76, 78–79
Anglican Church, 11, 35, 107, 130–31, 226
Anscombe, Elizabeth 9, 21
appetite, 50, 59, 63–67, 72–74, 78, 80, 83–84, 87–88, 96–97, 100, 103, 106, 108, 112–15, 156–57, 192, 236, 285n.85, 289n.6, 307n.38. *See also* desire; passion(s)
arbitration, 135
Aristotle, 90, 189–90, 208–9, 211, 304n.147, 308n.53, 310n.93, 312n.107, 313n.134
  and the good, 97, 104, 182–83, 201–2, 220
  Hobbes's criticism of, 12–14, 107–8, 123–24, 176

  and the passions, 85–87
  and virtue, 101–2, 193
Arp, Robert, 35, 48
atheism or atheist, 7, 9, 11, 38–40, 43, 81, 93, 134, 138, 170, 177–78, 278n.83, 279n.97, 285.n73, 288n.153, 301n.118, 304n.167
Aubrey, John, 226, 314n.143
Augustine of Hippo or Augustinian, 35, 82, 86–87, 89, 145, 158, 194, 265, 287n.126
Austin, John, 233–35
authority, 5–6, 61–62, 87, 106–7, 128–30, 159, 169, 187, 203–4, 225–27, 240–45
aversion, 59, 65, 68, 80, 96, 106, 113, 119. *See also* passion(s)
axiology, 4, 96–97, 100, 103, 112. *See also* good(s)

Bacon, Francis, 152, 155
Balaam's donkey, 155
Barry, Brian, 9
Baylor, Michael, 110

321

322 *Index*

Behemoth, or the Long Parliament, 106, 124, 158, 173, 186
Bible, 12–14, 40, 44, 82, 89, 96, 104–5, 107, 129–31, 143, 145, 301n.118
  as foundational to Hobbes's political theory, 82–93, 126–30
  as God's prophetic word, 81–82, 154
Blau, Adrian, 8, 271n.25
Boethius, 228
Boonin-Vail, David, 101–2, 294n.97
Borgia, Cesare, 173–74
Bork, Robert, 66
Boyle, Joseph, 4, 21, 152
Boyle, Robert, 152
Bramhall, John, 10, 12–14, 48, 107, 138, 278n.83, 279n.97, 301n.118, 318n.51
  criticism of Hobbes, 2, 8, 37–43, 240, 257–58
Brock, Stephen, 99
Budziszewski, J., 21

Cain, 86
Calvin, John, and Calvinism, 9, 35, 82, 104, 110, 112, 152
Campbell, Murray, 164
Campion, Edmund, 128
Catholic or Catholicism, 127–31, 178, 225, 295n.124, 314n.148
cause or causation, 14, 23–25, 36–37, 45, 60, 209–10
  accidental, 172, 176–77
  final, 50–51, 210
  formal, 48–51
  and God's ordained power, 157–58, 176
Charles I, 105, 175, 178

Chillingworth, William, 105
Christianity or Christian, 10, 12, 13, 35, 37, 40, 43, 70–71, 74–75, 81–82, 84, 86, 89–93, 105, 108, 145–46, 153–55, 166, 169, 225, 227, 257
church-state relations, 10–11, 35, 107, 130–31, 225–26
civil law, 3, 16, 79, 187, 263
  defined, 232
  and equity, 249–55
  Hobbes on, 81, 144, 182, 230–33, 235–41, 245–56
  See also positive law
civil science, 44, 118, 310n.92
  Hobbes's theory of, 20–23, 50–51, 53–59, 67, 69–70, 91–92, 210–15, 224, 265
civil war, 10, 61–62, 88–91, 106, 111, 158, 186, 192–93, 214–15, 249, 257, 262, 288n.136
Clarendon, Earl of (Edward Hyde), 65, 137
clemency, 135
Coke, Sir Edward, 106, 251, 306n.30
command, 46, 75, 85, 126–27, 159, 182, 205, 225
  of the sovereign and law, 231–56
  See also God, as commander
common good, 3, 5–6, 16–17, 67, 69, 104, 107, 117, 125, 148, 179, 197, 259–61, 264–65
  Aristotelian-Thomistic theory of, 201–2, 217–18, 228–30, 308n.54
  as distinguishing principle of commonwealth, 219–25, 228, 259–61, 283n.50
  as the goal of the sovereign command and civil law, 232, 244–45

Hobbes's theory of the, 181–84, 188–90, 198–210, 215, 217–19
commonwealth, 16, 23, 54, 57, 258–59
   and the body metaphor, 213–15
   creation of, 199, 207–13
   defined, 57, 182
   Hobbes's common good account of, 198–207
   membership in, 245–47
   and the sovereign, 182, 199–200, 213, 216, 220, 223, 229–30
   as a truly representative artificial person, 188, 213, 219–30
   types of, 224–25
conatus, 25, 65, 96
conscience, 96, 171, 214, 221, 226–27, 235–36, 259, 261. *See also* natural law, and conscience
consent, 113, 134, 169–70, 176, 190, 200, 220, 261
Constitution, U.S., 204–5, 224–27, 261–62, 313n.132
contract or contractor, 61, 141–42, 169, 199, 249, 254. *See also* covenant
contumely, 135
Courtenay, William, 144, 146–47
covenant, 57, 93, 108, 130, 135, 141–42, 173, 178, 181–84, 186–88, 190, 194, 197–201, 207–23, 239–50, 254–255, 304n.157, 307n.38, 317n.23, 318n.35
Cromwell, Oliver, 175, 178
cupidity, 8, 76–82, 86, 89, 98, 191–96, 286n.89
Curley, Edwin, 1, 9, 37, 42, 86, 278n.83

d'Ailly, Pierre, 159
Darwall, Stephen, 292n.68
death, fear of. *See* fear
Decameron Physiologicum, 72
De Cive, 8, 19, 23, 27, 43, 46, 58–63, 74, 75, 79, 98, 133–34, 144, 184, 189, 196, 203, 286n.102, 301n.118
De Corpore, 19, 36, 58–59, 101
De Corpore Politico. *See The Elements of Law, Natural and Politic*
Deep Blue, 163–64
definitions, 27, 51, 164–68
DeHart, Paul, 244–45
De Homine, 45, 100–103, 108, 305n.4, 305n.12
Deigh, John, 164–68
deism, 43
democracy, 261–65
Descartes, René, 36, 49, 55, 152, 226–27, 314n.144
desire
   for dominion, 75–78
   for honor, 69
   predominant, 7, 69, 170
   in relation to reason, 6–8, 70, 73–81, 85–87, 91, 95–98, 101–4, 112–18, 120, 122–25, 215, 260
   —in the Augustinian tradition, 86
   —as understood by Aristotle and Aquinas, 85, 87
   for self-preservation, 6–7
   universal, 6–8, 69, 77
   See also appetite; human nature, Hobbes's theory of, and the two postulates of; passion(s)
dignity, 45–46, 80, 84, 118, 209, 213, 216–19, 228–29

324 *Index*

diplomatic immunity, 84, 135
disease
   of the body, 121–23, 156, 172,
      311n.100
   of the commonwealth, 213–16, 263
drunkenness, 100, 102, 119–20, 172
Dukakis, Michael, 66
duty, 78, 80, 92, 117–18, 133, 141,
      258, 280n.101, 301n.118
   of self-preservation, 134, 136, 138,
      144, 178, 189, 232, 236–37
   of the sovereign, 203, 253, 261

ecclesiology, 91, 130–31, 225
Eden, 85, 87–88, 191, 252
education, 5, 65–66, 68, 106, 112,
      192, 206
Edward II, 174
Edward III, 174–75
Edward VI, 105
The Elements of Law, Natural and
   Politic, 133, 278n.81
Elizabeth I, 105
endeavor, 87, 111, 115, 157, 168
England, 1, 10, 35, 105, 152, 174–75,
      186, 274n.13
English Civil War, 88–89, 106–7,
      111, 158, 186, 257
envy, 59, 61, 86, 87, 190, 192, 193
Epiphany Rising, 175
episcopacy, 11
equality, 137, 169, 250, 261, 262,
      280n.108
equity, 135, 203, 248–51, 254–55,
      263, 286n.102, 298n.55,
      304n.157
evil, 71, 74–81, 85–91, 98–99, 120,
      122, 215
   of death, 71, 86, 103, 109–12, 122

faith, 11–2, 82, 85–86, 90, 104,
      127–28, 174, 194, 277n.54,
      289n.158, 304n.167
   and reason, 21, 43, 53, 92, 107,
      126, 130, 143, 167, 278n.81,
      314n.147
fall of man, 75, 84–89, 289n.158,
      298n.55
family, 81, 110, 217–18, 253, 265,
      307n.38
fear, 8, 10–11, 59–68, 72–79, 125,
      157, 175–77, 189, 192–96, 226,
      234, 263
The Federalist, 204, 262
felicity, 100, 108, 112, 117, 130,
      177–78, 206–7, 261. *See also*
      happiness
Filmer, Robert, 137–38, 240,
      280n.108
Finnis, John, 4–6, 21, 259, 268n.9,
      269n.13, 269n.17
Fisher, John, 128
Foole, the, 134, 157, 170–78
Fortin, Ernest, 176, 189
fortuna, 171–2
Fuller, Timothy, 11, 319n.52,
      319n.72

Galileo, 25, 274n.13
Gassendi, Pierre, 152
Gauthier, David, 113, 124, 301n.118
Geach, Peter, 114
geometry or geometrical reasoning,
      163–67
George, Robert P., 21, 274n.6
Gerson, Jean, 159
Gert, Bernard, 80, 98, 118–20,
      271n.25, 289n.2, 294n.100,
      303n.129

Gillespie, Michael, 297n.41
Glaucon, 170
God
  Aquinas's conception of, 5–6, 12–13, 35–36, 46–47, 56, 83–84, 145, 161–62, 308n.54
  as commander, 6, 8–9, 79–80, 84, 112, 131, 133–34, 142–44, 148–50, 153–54, 155, 159–63, 265
  as creator, 22–23, 51, 55–58, 71, 75, 208, 210–13, 260
  Hobbes's materialist conception of, 37–44, 277n.53
  Ockham's conception of. *See* William of Ockham
  and the origin of language, 28, 156
  power of, 33–34, 102–3, 142
  —absolute and ordained, 144–62, 176, 178–79, 210, 212–3, 219, 258, 265
  as practically severable from Hobbes's political theory, 7, 102, 120, 163, 165
  —critique of, 121, 163–9
  proofs for the existence of, 34–37, 44–47
  quidditative knowledge of, 44, 161, 166
  the rational word of, 126, 142–43, 156–57
  —as known, 143–44, 159–62, 168–69
  role of in Hobbes's natural law theory, 3–11, 79–81, 142–44, 153–62, 168–69
  Scotus's conception of. *See* Scotus, John Duns
  See also Bible

good(s)
  actual versus apparent, 116, 131, 192, 206, 241, 285n.83
  Aquinas on, 4–6, 97–100, 309n.68
  basic, 3–6, 8, 15, 21, 51, 95–99
  different kinds of according to Hobbes, 100, 103–4
  historical-cultural sources of disagreement about, 104–7
  of life, 5, 8, 15–16, 50–51, 69–70, 80, 95–100, 102–3, 108–9, 115–16, 122–23, 125–32, 136–41
  practical reason's grasp of, 8, 97, 109–11, 115–18
  relation of appetite to, 50, 64–69, 96–101, 103, 115
  subjectivity of the, 112–115
  thin theory of the, 3, 8, 95–100, 109, 184, 208, 224, 229
  virtue and, 100–102
  See also common good
Grabill, Stephen, 110
grace, 75, 85, 90, 108, 127, 130, 144–45, 147, 154, 193–94, 308n.54
gratitude, 135, 157, 161, 254
Gray, John, 54
Gregory, Brad, 105–6
Gregory of Rimini, 159
Grisez, Germain, 4, 21
Grotius, Hugo, 159, 259, 301n.109

Hampton, Jean, 122–25, 215, 293nn.92–93
Hanin, Mark, 109
happiness, 5–6, 73, 85, 102–4, 107–9, 112, 167–68, 177, 189, 205–7, 260, 289n.155. *See also* felicity
Hart, HLA, 233–35, 316n.5, 316n.13
hedonism, 259–60

Henry V, 175
Henry VI, 175
Henry VIII, 105
Historia Ecclesiastica, 154
history, 55, 90, 145–46, 152, 154, 173–75, 235, 259, 264
    of political thought, 6, 169, 189, 259
Hittinger, John, 303n.142
Hittinger, Russell, 21
Hoane, Joe, 164
Hoekstra, Kinch, 177
Holmes, Oliver Wendell, 233–35
Hood, F. C., 9
hope, 59, 63–67, 157. *See also* passion(s)
Hsu, Feng-hsiung, 164
human nature, 3–8
    Hobbes's theory of, 48–50, 54–57, 60–71
    —as foundational to Hobbes's civil science, 19–22, 51, 58–64, 67–71, 90–93
    —as shaped by education and custom, 64, 66, 106, 206
    —and the two postulates of, 50–51, 63–64, 70–75, 80–83, 89–90, 95, 98, 191, 193, 196
Hume, David, or Humean, 6, 8, 21–22, 96, 265, 269n.16, 292n.68, 293n.93

imagination or imagining, 24, 27, 44, 47, 59, 62, 73, 75–78, 85, 118, 129, 155, 185, 187, 285n.77
impartiality, 135, 250
impotent thesis, 6–8, 73, 96–97, 106, 113, 116–18, 122–23, 215. *See also* desire, in relation to reason

inclinations, 156, 190, 217, 288n.147, 290n.17, 306n.27
    Aquinas's theory of, 99–102, 148, 192, 265
Independent or Independency, 11, 70, 89, 107, 178
introspection, 53–54, 58, 62–64, 69, 90, 92, 139, 167. *See also* passion(s), introspection upon
Isaac, 154

Jackson, Robert H., 261
James I, 105
Jefferson, Thomas, 262
Job, 176, 257, 263
John XXIII, Pope, 298n.55
Johnson, Laurie, 61
Johnston, David, 70, 281n.10
judgment, 3, 66, 70, 80–81, 98, 104, 116–17
    private, 88–89, 104–5,
justice, 13, 29, 55, 60, 81, 84, 93, 126, 135, 152, 169–73, 176–77, 199, 203, 217, 238–40, 250, 253, 260, 264, 286n.102, 304n.157, 317n.23

Kant, Immanuel, 21–22, 142
Kasparov, Garry, 164
Kavka, Gregory, 1, 54, 58, 69, 124, 163, 167, 238
Kelsen, Hans, 233–35
Kennedy, Anthony, 66
Kilcullen, J., 150
Kilwardby, Robert, 146
King, Martin Luther, Jr., 262, 264
knowledge, 16–17, 19–20
    as beginning in the senses, 24–26
    of causes, 23–24, 34, 76

of external reality, 27–32
of God. *See* God, proofs for existence of; God, quidditative knowledge of
of human nature, 50–51, 60–71
moral, 99, 168. *See also* natural law
as representation, 26
Krom, Michael, 213

language, 17, 27–28, 45–47, 50, 148, 161, 190, 209, 213–14, 224
  Hobbes's theory of, 27–28, 166, 211
law. *See* civil law; natural law; positive law
laws of nature. *See also* natural law
  list of, 135–36
Lawson, George, 138, 240
legal positivism, 232–35, 316n.5, 316n.5
  interpretations of Hobbes as, 241, 248–49, 260
Leijenhorst, Cees, 42, 278n.81, 278n.83
lex indicans, 151, 159–160
lex praecepiens, 160
liberalism, 16, 207, 216, 230, 261–262, 320n.5
  Rawlsian version of, 54–55, 92–93, 263–65
  and religious tolerance, 226–28
liberty, 80–81, 135–37, 153, 157, 169, 198–99
  harmless, 112, 198, 203–7, 216, 218, 230, 261
  religious, 225–28
life. *See* good, of life
Lincoln, Abraham, 205, 224, 261, 313n.132

Lisska, Anthony, 21
Lloyd, S. A., 7, 68, 87–88, 92–93, 114
  on Hobbesian civil science, 53–58
  on Hobbes's natural law theory, 239, 248–53
  on transcendent interests, 125–29
Locke, John, 1, 104, 205, 222, 280, 314n.148
Lombard, Peter, 145
Luther, Martin, or Lutheran, 13, 82, 104, 105, 110, 112, 152

Machiavelli, 171–74
MacIntyre, Alasdair, 21, 104
Macpherson, C. B., 106
Madison, James, 204
madness, 118–22
Magnus, Albertus, 145
Malcolm, Noel, 250, 282n.19, 319n.64
Mansfield, Harvey, 174
Maritain, Jacques, 21, 99
Martinich, A. P., 9–11, 37, 133, 138, 142–44, 168, 195, 272n.38, 277n.54, 289n.2, 292n.60, 318n.30
martyr or martyrdom, 127–28
materialism, 14, 24–25, 43, 47, 49–51, 54, 92, 278n.83
Maurer, Armand, 148
McInerny, Ralph, 21
McNeilly, F. S., 164–65, 168
Melancthon, Philip, 13, 104
Merrill, Thomas, 269n.16
Mersenne, Marin, 152
mimesis or mimetic, 155, 183–84, 208, 210–13, 230
miracles, 143, 155, 300n.89
modernity, 18

modesty, 135
monarchy, 1, 224–25, 262
money, 214, 298n.55
Montefeltre, Guidobaldo de, 173
More, Thomas, 128
Mormons, 227
Mortimer, Roger, 174
motion, 14, 24–27, 32, 35–37, 45–50, 58–60, 65, 72, 96, 100–104, 108–9, 111, 115–16, 121, 127, 156, 204, 206, 210, 213, 224–25, 245, 257
Murphy, Mark, 11, 21, 271n.27

natural law
　Aquinas's theory of, 4–6, 99–100, 102, 109–10, 148, 160–62
　and conscience, 109–12, 141, 143, 160–61
　and the debate over "new" vs. "old", 4, 268nn.9, 12
　Hobbes's theory of
　—cataloged, 135–36
　—and the definition of the law of nature, 133–34, 138
　—and the duty of self-preservation, 134, 136–44, 178
　—and equity, 249–55
　—and the fundamental law of nature, 198
　—as legislated by God, 142–44, 153–62, 168–69
　—as an objective theory of the good, 96–104, 112–18
　—in relation to positive law, 235–47
　—and the second law of nature, 198–99
　—standard interpretations of, 6–8
　—as theorems of prudence, 162
　—as a thin theory of the good, 3, 96–101
　and liberalism, 16, 261–65
　Ockham's theory of, 149–51. See also William of Ockham
　promulgation of. See God, the rational word of, as known
　Suárez's theory of, 159–60. See also Suárez, Francisco
　three foci of, 23
　two requirements of theories of, 3–5
　and virtue, 101–2
nature, 22–24, 28, 46, 48, 55, 93. See also human nature; natural law
Nicene Creed, 9, 39, 145
nominalism, 28–33, 39, 51, 66, 146, 151, 165, 258–59

Oakeshott, Michael, 116
Oakley, Francis, 11, 144–46, 152
Oberman, Heiko, 146
obligation, 9, 15, 21, 92–93, 120, 134, 141–44, 148–51, 157, 169, 199, 235, 245, 261, 269
Olsthoorn, Johan, 127
opinion, 55, 65–68, 80, 105, 118, 128, 215, 227
Owen, J. Judd, 205

Pakaluk, Michael, 201
pantheism, 42
Parker, Samuel, 136
passion(s), 8, 68–69, 73, 75, 79–80, 87
　introspection upon, 3, 62–67
　as rooted in appetite and opinion, 65–67

vehemency of, 118–22, 125
    See also appetite; desire
peace, 2, 12, 15–16, 67, 79–81, 89, 112, 125, 129, 135, 157–58, 160, 168, 181–83, 190–207, 215–30, 251–56
person, 184–88
    artificial, 184–88, 219–30
    of the commonwealth. *See* commonwealth, as a truly representative artificial person
    fictional, 185–88, 220–24, 230
    feigned, 184–88
    natural, 185–86, 188
Peter, Hugh, 89
Pettit, Philip, 29, 190
Pieper, Josef, 16
Plantinga, Alvin, 212
Plato or Platonic, 12, 29, 33, 42, 48, 55, 87, 90, 120, 151, 170
pleasure, 73–74, 77, 101–2, 121, 172, 192, 260, 309n.68
Plessy v. Ferguson, 263
pluralism, 93, 112, 117, 177, 184, 207, 215–19
pluralists, English, 216
Pocock, J. G. A., 17
political theory, 16–18
positive law, 5–6, 62, 68, 81, 86–87, 90, 158, 191, 196, 233–35, 249, 262
    Aquinas on, 84, 192–194, 237–38
    Hobbes on. *See* civil law
positivism. *See* legal positivism
power, 46, 72–78, 80–81, 103. *See also* God, power of; human nature, Hobbes's theory of, and the two postulates of; sovereign or sovereignty

Presbyterianism, 11, 70, 107, 131, 178
pride, 61, 73, 75, 81, 88–89, 92, 135, 191
property, 203, 214, 251, 262, 270n.23, 280n.108, 288n.147, 298n.55
Protestant or Protestant Reformation, 37, 40, 44, 105–7, 131, 152, 154, 225
psychological diversity, 7–8, 68–69
Pufendorf, Samuel, 138
punishment, 61, 83–88, 135, 138, 172, 192–94, 203, 206, 226, 234
Puritanism, 131

Rawls, John, 1, 22, 53–55, 60, 92–93, 202, 263–67
Reagan, Ronald, 66
realistic philosophy, 15, 20–22
reason, 51, 55–56, 58, 64–71, 73, 75–82, 104, 106, 108–12, 115–20, 157, 172, 191–92, 236
    as calculative or computational, 96–97, 134, 163–68
    in pre- and postlapsarian man, 83–89
    public, 158, 264–65
    as ratiocination, 59, 76, 90, 126
    See also desire, in relation to reason; good, practical reason's grasp of; human nature, Hobbes's theory of, and the two postulates of
rebellion, 89, 204–5, 222, 246, 262
reciprocity, 112, 135, 249, 252–53
recusal, 135
Rhodes, Rosamond, 54
right of nature, 80, 136–37, 188, 318n.47

rights, 54, 60, 126, 135, 175, 189, 199, 203, 214, 219, 235, 237, 240–41, 243, 246–47, 262–63, 317n.23
Rousseau, Jean Jacques, 90, 288n.147
Runciman, David, 184
Ryan, Alan, 226

scholasticism, 110, 112, 134, 145–46, 152–53
  Hobbes's criticism of and relationship to, 11–15, 43–44, 46, 82, 155, 265, 273n.58
science, 15–16, 19–20, 25, 28, 44, 49, 72, 107, 121–22, 163–67, 211. *See also* civil science
Scotus, John Duns, 110, 144, 146–48, 150, 152–53, 155, 158, 162
scripture. *See* Bible
self-preservation. *See* good, of life
Seneca Falls Convention (1848), 262
sense or sensation. *See* knowledge, as beginning in the senses
Shafte, J., 137
Shakespeare, William, 163, 175, 187
Sigmund, Paul, 20–21, 259
Simon, Yves, 21, 23, 32–33
sin, 79, 83, 85–89, 93, 111, 162, 172, 176, 192
Skinner, Quentin, 188, 221–22
sociability, 135
Socrates, 33, 49–50, 151, 170, 281n.117, 288n.153
Sommerville, Johann, 144, 259
Sophocles, 244
Sorell, Tom, 64
sovereign or sovereignty, 34, 45, 87–88, 182–84, 219
  and the authority to bind through law, 238–56
  as bearer of the commonwealth, 229–30, 242
  as head of the church, 35, 90, 107, 130–31, 225–26
  office of the, 199–207
  as soul of the commonwealth, 213, 224
Spinoza, Benedict de, 42, 278n.82
Springborg, Patricia, 37–39, 43
Stanton, Elizabeth Cady, 262
state, 60, 107, 185, 204, 210, 213, 216–17, 221, 227, 246, 261. *See also* commonwealth
state of nature, 60–61, 66, 73–75, 93, 287n.130, 288n.136
  as condition void of positive law, 62, 77–79, 195, 217
  conflict in, 67–70, 173, 286n.95, 294n.99
  laws of nature in, 71, 79, 81, 248, 252, 263, 286n.102, 310n.92
  as a postlapsarian condition, 82, 85–89
Strauss, Leo, 17, 47, 53, 273n.64
  on Hobbes's two postulates of human nature, 71–75
  —critique of, 75–82
Suárez, Francisco, 150, 152–53, 159–62, 169, 259, 273n.58
suicide, 68, 125, 128–29, 131–32
synderesis, 109–12, 141. *See also* natural law, and conscience

Taylor, A. E., 9, 111, 144, 161, 289n.2
teleology, 47–48, 50, 102, 274n.6, 285n.84, 313n.134. *See also* cause or causation, final
Temper, Etienne, 146

temperance, 101–2, 122, 134, 136, 172
theism, 9, 15, 37, 43, 51, 74, 81, 177, 278n.83, 301n.118. *See also* God
Thornton, Helen, 82
Thucydides, 91, 281n.10, 288n.153
toleration, 227–28, 314n.148
truth, 4, 15–17, 19–20, 27–28, 56–59, 62–64, 66, 91–92, 99, 107, 111, 117–18, 159, 164–65, 226, 265
tyranny, 224

unity, 29, 33, 183
   aggregative, 184, 189, 220–23
   artificial, 202, 209, 220–25, 228–29
   of God, 158
   of order, 201, 217, 220, 228
   social, 201–2, 205, 227–28
   substantial, 221–22

vainglory, 75–78, 129, 193, 294n.99
van Inwagen, Peter, 49–50
Veatch, Henry, 21
ventral tegmental area, 120
Voegelin, Eric, 158

virtue(s), 77, 101–4, 117, 122, 124, 157, 167, 171–74, 192, 205–6, 260
war, 78, 80–81, 86–89, 106, 129–30, 172–73, 189–91, 232
   as caused by the sovereign, 248–55
   See also civil war
Warrender, Howard, 9, 144, 289n.2
West Virginia v. Barnette, 261
White, Thomas, 34, 154
Wild, John, 20–21
William of Ockham, 33, 110, 146–52, 155, 158–62, 169, 258–59, 298n.55
wisdom, 21, 103
   defined, 19
   of God, 13, 145, 149–50. *See also* God
Wolfe, Christopher, 261
words, 13, 19, 27–32, 164, 166–68, 185–88, 230, 246
Wright, George, 37

Zuckert, Michael, 96
Zwingli, Ulrich, 104–5

Kody Cooper is assistant professor of political science and public service at the University of Tennessee, Chattanooga.

www.ingramcontent.com/pod-product-compliance
Lightning Source LLC
Chambersburg PA
CBHW071016240426
43661CB00073B/2330